# Writing the Lives of the English Poor, 1750s–1830s

# States, People, and the History of Social Change

Series editors Rosalind Crone and Heather Shore

The States, People, and the History of Social Change series brings together cutting-edge books written by academic historians on criminal justice, welfare, education, health, and other areas of social change and social policy. The ways in which states, governments, and local communities have responded to "social problems" can be seen across many different temporal and geographical contexts. From the early modern period to contemporary times, states have attempted to shape the lives of their inhabitants in important ways. Books in this series explore how groups and individuals have negotiated the use of state power and policy to regulate, change, control, or improve peoples' lives and the consequences of these processes. The series welcomes international scholars whose research explores social policy (and its earlier equivalents) as well as other responses to social need, in historical perspective.

# Writing the Lives

## *of the*

# English Poor,

## 1750s–1830s

STEVEN KING

McGILL-QUEEN'S UNIVERSITY PRESS

Montreal & Kingston · London · Chicago

© McGill-Queen's University Press 2019

ISBN 978-0-7735-5648-5 (cloth)
ISBN 978-0-7735-5649-2 (paper)
ISBN 978-0-7735-5650-8 (ePDF)
ISBN 978-0-7735-5651-5 (ePUB)

Legal deposit first quarter 2019
Bibliothèque nationale du Québec

Printed in Canada on acid-free paper that is 100% ancient forest free
(100% post-consumer recycled), processed chlorine free

Funded by the Financé par le
Government gouvernement
of Canada du Canada | Canada

Canada Council Conseil des arts
for the Arts du Canada

We acknowledge the support of the Canada Council for the Arts,
which last year invested $153 million to bring the arts to Canadians
throughout the country.

Nous remercions le Conseil des arts du Canada de son soutien. L'an
dernier, le Conseil a investi 153 millions de dollars pour mettre de
l'art dans la vie des Canadiennes et des Canadiens de tout le pays.

**Library and Archives Canada Cataloguing in Publication**

King, Steven, 1966–, author
Writing the lives of the English poor, 1750s–1830s / Steven King.

(States, people, and the history of social change ; 1)
Includes bibliographical references and index.
Issued in print and electronic formats.
ISBN 978-0-7735-5648-5 (cloth).–ISBN 978-0-7735-5649-2 (paper).
–ISBN 978-0-7735-5650-8 (ePDF).–ISBN 978-0-7735-5651-5 (ePUB)

1. Poor–England–Correspondence. 2. Poor–England–History–
18th century. 3. Poor–England–History–19th century. 4. Public
welfare–England–History–18th century. 5. Public welfare–
England–History–19th century. 6. Great Britain–Social policy.
7. England–Social conditions–18th century. 8. England–Social
conditions–19th century. I. Title.

HC260.P6K56 2019     361.6'5094109033     C2018-905402-6
                                          C2018-905403-4

For Maria, Ian, Astra, Tarun, and Jared

# Contents

### PART THREE

## *Rhetorical Structures*

### PART FOUR

## *Self and Meaning*

# Tables and Figures

## TABLES

## FIGURES

# *Preface*

This book started with the discovery in the archives at Leeds of a set of
pauper letters for the area around Calverley in West Yorkshire on 17
December 1989. My doctorate, then in its very early stages, involved
undertaking a family reconstitution for Calverley-cum-Farsley and surrounding villages and subsequently linking it to other sources related to
the everyday lives of ordinary people. Until that December, my efforts
to understand the experiences of the poor and the place of the poor law
in their demographic and socio-economic life-cycle had concentrated on
the overseers' accounts. I had taken this record of payments made to the
poor on a daily and weekly basis as a firm record of who got what and
thus of the place of the poor law in everyday life in that locality. The letters of William Spacey turned this comfortable train of thinking on its
head. He was not locally resident at the time he wrote, although he had
been before and would be afterward. His letters were of the oral writing
style that characterises *Writing the Lives of the English Poor*, with little
punctuation, random capitalisation, and the poorest of spelling, overlaid
with a strong thread of local dialect. They were fascinating as material
objects and for what they revealed about a seam of popular literacy that
I had been led by the historiographical literature to believe did not exist.
But they were important too for other conceptual reasons. Over a series
of letters, Spacey made claims on his settlement parish that included payment of arrears of rent, cash allowances, and a demand that the parish

supply a midwife for the birth of his eighth child. His letters were polite but firm, and they occasioned several replies from local overseers, both positive and negative. The essence of this process was that poor relief was negotiated, sometimes between the claimant and the overseer and sometimes through the intervention of someone writing on Spacey's behalf. In this process, he did not get all that he requested, which clearly suggests that what was recorded in the overseers' accounts represents the end of a process of relief, with the actual amount and form of relief given potentially bearing no relation at all to what was asked for. Here, however, was a further puzzle because, although I knew that Spacey had gained relief given that his letters acknowledging such survived, there was no record of him in what were seemingly highly comprehensive overseers' accounts. It took me many months to work out that all relief given to the poor of the town in which Spacey lived was bundled together and given as a lump sum to a local grocer who dispensed relief when business took him to that place. The payment was to him, not the thirteen or so claimants who lived in the same community as Spacey. Further research brought the discovery of sections of the Calverley vestry book, which showed very clearly that the same negotiation process was at the heart of the relief eventually recorded in the overseers' accounts for the proximately resident settled poor. And a further chance discovery of a payment ledger for a grocer in Leeds who was tasked with paying allowances to those settled in Leeds but resident in the Calverley area added more complexity. None of the poor named in that ledger, although variously observable in the reconstitution, appeared in the overseer's accounts for Calverley, such that a parallel system of poor relief for the nonsettled poor was actually in process.

The logic of these discoveries had important implications for my doctorate. Subsequently, my work on the Old Poor Law began to reveal many hundreds more collections of letters that mirrored or exceeded those identified for Essex by Thomas Sokoll. A careful consideration of vestry minutes (where letters of this sort were read out or otherwise recorded) and overseers' accounts (where the costs of receiving and responding to letters were recorded) showed clearly that letters were sent in large numbers to every parish in England and Wales, and indeed in

Scotland. The fact that large collections of letters written by the poor, advocates, overseers, and other officials survive in places such as Kirkby Lonsdale or Hulme, I understood, was simply an accident of preservation. All parish archives would once have looked, at least in terms of the volume of letters, like these. Some confirmation of that fact was had when I found that an overseer in the town of Thrapston in Northamptonshire had at some point disposed of individual letters but copied all of them into letter books, which then survived in the town's archive precisely because they were books. In this sense, and given the sometimes contemporaneous survival of vestry books for hundreds of parishes, it became plausible and essential in my view to write about the "process" of poor relief rather than simply about the outcomes that have underpinned almost all of the historiography of the Old Poor Law. A grant from the Wellcome Trust and two grants from the Arts and Humanities Research Council, along with the efforts of many paid and unpaid research assistants, volunteers, and friends, generated a substantial set of letters by or about the poor, allowing me with confidence to reconstruct the tripartite epistolary world of the parish: claimant, advocate, and official.

This book, then, is the product of research started in 1989 and shared with and by many others. At its heart is a dual proposition: for both the proximately resident poor and those who wrote from other places, garnering poor relief was a process, and at the heart of this process was the act of negotiation. Without an understanding of these two issues, I suggest, perspectives drawn from end-of-process overseers' accounts give a very lopsided picture of the character, meaning, and role of the Old Poor Law. To put it crudely, two entries of 5 shillings side by side in an overseer's account do not mean, and were not meant to mean, the same thing. It matters for our understanding of both the meaning of relief and the role of the Old Poor Law what those two people had originally asked for, how and whether they had negotiated, and how parochial officials had received those acts of negotiation. Giving an allowance willingly to a blind woman of 102 years of age was different from giving an allowance of the same amount to a charlatan whom officials wished to heaven that they could get rid of.

Against this backdrop, *Writing the Lives of the English Poor* presents five central contentions. First, officials, claimants, and advocates shared a common pot of language – a common linguistic register, as it were – with which they framed the negotiation process, whether the poor were inside or outside the parish. They spoke (and wrote) in a common currency. Second, claimants and officials understood and accepted that the stories told by and to them would have an element of fiction. In part, this aspect of the letters reflects the organic nature of the claims of individual poor people, but there was also a wider process at work in the sense that uncovering "truth" was for officials likely to be a costly and time-consuming business. The poor marshalled their histories and sought narrative consistency rather than absolute truth. Officials punished narrative inconsistency rather than partial truth and acts of fiction. Third, officials expected, and were expected by the poor and their advocates, to engage actively in the process of negotiation and epistolary communication. A failure to reply to letters or to negotiate in good faith allowed claimants and their advocates to extend their case and solidify their position on the relief lists. Fourth, although officials, advocates, and the poor shared a common pot of language, what mattered for the negotiation process was the way that this language was confected in rhetorical terms to press levers of deservingness. I reconstruct this rhetorical infrastructure – which might for instance include dignity, suffering, character, and gender – and develop a new model for classifying and analysing pauper letters and other correspondence in the tripartite epistolary world of the parish. Finally, the poor and their advocates used their letters and personal vestry appearances to construct a distinctive "pauper self." Most of those who wrote or appeared before the vestry had experienced long periods of their lives as independent economic actors. Many would go on to regain this status. Writers thus sought to construct themselves as "ordinary" and their temporary dependence as "extraordinary" and in some senses inevitable given the precarious nature of the lives of ordinary people.

Collectively, these arguments add up to a different sort of Old Poor Law from what we see in much of the historiographical literature, one with agency and negotiation at its core and one in which the power and rules of the state were essentially malleable at the local level. The complete and universal inability of parish officers to get the charlatan poor off of relief lists and to keep them off, which is played out in deep colour across the letter collections, tells us something important about the essential character and role of the Old Poor Law. Two allowances of the same amount side by side in the overseers' accounts really are not the same, and those end-of-process accounts really cannot locate the sentiment and meaning of poor relief, especially during the last few decades of the Old Poor Law during its so-called crisis phase. I construct, then, a more positive Old Poor Law process in which, contrary to much ingrained historiographical perspective, the poor did not lose their legitimacy in the eyes of ratepayers after the 1790s. For a council estate boy, the sense that the rules of the state were not, and were not meant to be, fixed and immovable but negotiated and negotiable is heartening.

# Acknowledgments

This book employs material collected since 1989, but its central data were assembled under a grant from the Arts and Humanities Research Council and the Deutsche Forschungsgemeinschaft, jointly held with Professor Andreas Gestrich of the German Historical Institute (GHI), London, under grant reference number AH/I500561/1. I am grateful to colleagues at the GHI for their work designing the database, online edition tools, and transcription guidance. Peter Jones was the senior research officer on the project, and as well as overseeing data input and quality control, he located and transcribed many collections himself. The full transcription of the Kirkby Lonsdale letters was in particular a monumental task, and I am grateful to him for his work and always insightful intellectual agenda. Ben Harvey undertook a doctorate as part of the grant and also collected and transcribed material that forms part of the narrative corpus. His research concentrated on Wales and the Welsh borders, and I have consciously avoided any intensive discussion of these areas in what follows.

Numerous other researchers have collected and transcribed material. Jane Rowling, Richard Gilbert, Steven Taylor, Carol Beardmore, Margaret Hanly, Geoff Hooker, Alison Stringer, Alan Weaver, Catherine Robertson, and Maria Longhurst all did significant work, and I am grateful to them. Colleagues across our profession were extremely generous with material and guidance, and I am particularly grateful to Thomas Sokoll and Alannah Tomkins for input on my projects that has spanned the decades. More recently, Paul Carter at the National Archives has sharpened my view of pauper letters, encouraging me to step beyond 1834 and to plan a more ambitious narrative project for the post-1834 period. Andreas Gestrich was a companion on the current sojourn, and without his intellectual input and practical sense of the material, this book would be much the poorer.

The words of "my" poor writers, sometimes hilarious but often dripping with despair, will be consigned to an archive so that others from across the world may reuse them. Elizabeth would, I think, argue that I never get close enough to the characters emerging from the archive – that I should have compassion, empathy, and a joyous regard for the colour of their stories. Here, I may have crossed to the dark side. If you think that I have not, then my book of poetry, *On the Poor* (2018), may also suit your tastes.

# PART ONE

## *Starting Points*

# I

## *Welfare, Power, and Agency*

### CONSTRUCTING WELFARE

Established between 1597 and 1601, the Old Poor Law created a framework for the relief of the "impotent" (later "deserving") poor. Ecclesiastical parishes were tasked with raising an annual tax – the poor rate –
on local property to generate the necessary resources for this obligation.
A new parish office, the overseer of the poor, was created and subject to
annual election, and this person was to be responsible for receiving
claims to welfare and the dispensation of cash or other forms of support.
Those paying the local poor rate were given collective oversight of the
nature and scale of spending, exercised through the vestry, although by
the eighteenth century this role, if fulfilled at all, was beginning to pass
to a smaller, elected group of such ratepayers, who formed the select
vestry. Where poor applicants thought that their cases had been treated
unfairly, they had the right to appeal directly to the magistrates either at
the Quarter Sessions or (later) individually. An obvious flaw in the initial
legislation – rational applicants would apply for welfare to the places
they perceived as having most resources – took more than sixty years to
rectify. The resulting settlement acts established that poor people could
apply for welfare only in the place where they were settled, as well as
establishing the strict terms under which a settlement in one place rather
than another might be deemed to exist. Such rules might work well for

stable populations, but in the increasingly mobile society of the eighteenth and nineteenth centuries, parishes either fought at law over their relative settlement liabilities or developed a system of reciprocal payments – the out-parish system – which allowed those without settlement to remain in the communities where they fell into need.

It took almost a century for the Old Poor Law to become firmly embedded as a truly national welfare framework for England and Wales.[1] Even then, it remained an essentially discretionary system. The range of people to be encompassed by terms like "impotent" or "deserving" was never clearly defined, and no tariff or schedule of benefits was linked to these categories. Although the poor had a right to apply for welfare in or at their place of settlement, the parish and its officers had no legal duty to accede to such requests.[2] The costs of poor relief increased significantly over time. Indeed, many historians have seen a crisis of confidence in the Old Poor Law from the 1790s as bills spiralled upward and the poor became an object of suspicion and mistrust. Yet at no point did the poor acquire a right to relief or the central state seek to assert direct control. This remained an essentially local system in which the looseness and ambiguity of the law created an absolute necessity for negotiation.

The past two decades have witnessed considerable advances in our understanding of the character, role, and practices of this Old Poor Law. The discretion written into the very fabric of the institution yielded variable spending and welfare outcomes in different communities and over time.[3] Historians have been unable to agree on the nature of this spatial and typological variation. Was the jurisdiction of the Old Poor Law composed of a series of welfare republics that were held loosely together by a national legal framework and that granted only magistrates the right to prevent the exercise of unbridled power by local officials?[4] Were its outcomes at the community level the essential product of relative wealth versus the situational causes of poverty? Or can we trace long-term regional differences in parochial attitudes toward, and thus in the form and level of spending on, the poor?[5] The recent work of John Langton, linking variability of poor law practice in Oxfordshire to underlying soil types and topography, complicates this picture still further, speaking directly of wider attempts to understand how and why state and elite

4

power manifested itself at the regional and local levels.[6] The fact of variation in policies and outcomes is, however, incontrovertible. In turn, as Joanna Innes ably shows, the palette of national legislative initiatives on and around the Old Poor Law was always, and was always meant to be, catching up with innovations and changes in local practice.[7] It is perhaps this essential flexibility that explains why the Old Poor Law survived so long against the backdrop of persistent criticism of it from the later eighteenth century onward.[8]

A developing picture of fluidity of practice even within a single national legislative framework has informed wider reconsideration of the uniqueness of the Old Poor Law on the European stage. This leitmotif of earlier work[9] has given way to a sense that European welfare regimes shared common pressures, ideologies, processes, definitions, and decision-making apparatuses, with regions and communities traversing a spectrum of consequent policy over time.[10] Particularly important for this study, it is clear that the question of what communities should do with the migrant poor became increasingly insistent across both Catholic and Protestant Europe as the eighteenth century progressed. The highly mobile British population identified by Colin Pooley and Jean Turnbull was replicated on the Continent, with the added complications of mass movements occasioned by war, religious persecution, and the progressive failure of traditional upland economies.[11] European communities responded with gradations of citizenship and associated welfare benefits, complex structures of inclusion and exclusion, and the development of sophisticated reckoning and money-transmission mechanisms.[12] The documentation attached to these policies – official correspondence, on the one hand, and the appeals and petitions of paupers or their advocates, on the other – survives in huge volume in many European states and has begun to drive an ambitious reconstruction of the experiences of, and attitudes toward, the poor.[13]

As part of this process, the complexity of the balancing act between the extent of communal resources, the willingness of a relatively small component of local populations to tax themselves (in the case of the Old Poor Law) or to be taxed, and accumulating demands on such resources has been thrown into sharp relief. For England and Wales, the middling sorts who came to be central to poor law administration in the later stages of the Old Poor Law were anything but a unified group at the collective or parochial level.[14] The vestry or the office of the overseer represented not simply a forum to consider and dispense welfare but also one in which authority could be asserted, identity created, and networks built. Yet collective meetings yielded constant potential for friction. Disputes over rates, the building of workhouses, and farming the poor[15] regularly pitted ratepayers against each other.[16] More widely, members of the parochial elite often appealed to or threatened other men of similar standing in their own parish or more distant places when confronted by requests from individual paupers to intercede in the relief process.[17] Magistrates likewise intervened against their neighbours when faced with individual petitions.[18] Ratepayers simply held very different, often entrenched, beliefs on their individual and collective philanthropic duty, the nature and force of custom, their role as men and fathers, and the humanitarian or Christian imperative that had always driven the relationship between parish residents, migrants, and those with resources.[19]

Whatever the attitudes of individual ratepayers and the relative force of contrasting beliefs represented in the ever-changing composition of the vestry, below such men – and for much of the Old Poor Law's duration given the relatively late acceleration in the formation of select vestries, in substitution of these men[20] – stood the overseers, who were responsible for the implementation of policy. Although increasing numbers of these overseers, some of whom were women, were paid and of long office, few were as efficient or clinical in the enforcement of national rules and local convention as officials in the London parish of St Martin in the Fields.[21] Rather, overseer practice in most places comprised a complex amalgam of action, inaction, overreaction, and negotiation.[22] It is for this reason that parishes were usually spectacularly unsuccessful in reviewing the stock of relief recipients, throwing them off the relief lists, reducing their allowances, and keeping them "off the parish." The personality of the overseer mattered.[23] In this sense, it is surprisingly difficult to trace a single, coherent, and chronologically stable "parochial policy" toward the poor.

*builds on the recent work focusing on sub-groups*

What *is* clear, however, is that this rich patchwork of practice, sentiment, and fractured power fed into the consciousness of the poor and their experience of the poor law. Indeed, one of the most formidable recent developments in welfare historiography has been the tendency to dissect the lumpen mass of the poor and to concentrate on the detailed histories of definable subgroups such as the aged, widows, the sick, and the unemployed or underemployed. Research on these groups has generated striking conclusions. There is evidence, for instance, that the generosity and meaning of the parish "pension" for older people changed significantly between the early and later eighteenth century.[24] The range and depth of healthcare provided or funded by the Old Poor Law increased decisively between the 1790s and 1830s, such that a rapidly increasing proportion of ratepayer resources was devoted to the sick poor from the 1820s onward.[25] When faced with sickness, however caused, parochial officers had to balance the prospect of substantial expenditure in the present against elongated and expanding commitments in the event that the sick person got sicker or died, and they usually erred on the side of granting relief. By contrast, welfare historians such as Samantha Williams and Thomas Sokoll have questioned the existence, longevity, and stability of parochial allowance systems that related relief to family size.[26] More widely, it seems clear that although the Old Poor Law granted no legal rights to receive relief, certain groups of the life-cycle poor managed to both achieve and maintain de facto rights to welfare or at least a favourable hearing of their cases.[27]

Later chapters consider the rhetorical and strategic approach to negotiation used by some of these definable subgroups of the poor. Meanwhile, it should be noted that recent writers have added important nuance and detail to these general perspectives. Samantha Shave, for instance, has suggested that the "mesmerising levels of flexibility" in welfare practice are partly to be explained and understood through a renewed focus on the process of policy formation and execution. The reach of legislative initiatives such as Gilbert's Act or Sturges Bourne's Act, she argues, was greater than welfare historians have allowed and was reflective of the fact that "policy making and policy implementation are a continuous process"

susceptible to the influence of all parties in the relief bargain.[28] Peter King
has noted that summary courts were the forum in which parishes simultaneously worked out their attitudes toward the financial costs of relief
and sought to "patrol the many problematic borders of the poor law system."[29] Painstaking work by Henry French linking overseers' accounts
and a family reconstitution for Terling in Essex suggests that in the early
nineteenth century the percentage of distributed parochial welfare resources shifted strongly away from "traditional" welfare recipients and
toward unemployed men.[30] These important perspectives add to a sense,
outlined above, that the discretionary Old Poor Law comprised a richly
coloured, and probably relatively unstable, patchwork of parochial practice across England and Wales.[31] It is necessarily the case, then, that poor
law resources had an uncertain and often unpredictable place in the
makeshift economies of the dependent and marginal poor. As Richard
Wall recounts, the poor law allowances of Corfe Castle in Dorset provided 14 per cent of the household resources of women (but 39 per cent
for widows) and just 5 per cent for men. In the household budgets employed by Sarah Horrell and Jane Humphries, the importance of poor
relief was fleeting for families involved in manufacturing but more fundamental to households where the major focus of work was agriculture
or casual trades.[32] Poor relief of all sorts was never meant to be more
than a supplement to family care, charity, and the resources garnered
through casual work. Yet the variable yardsticks by which entitlements
were judged and by which the scale of allowances was calculated must
have affected the way that those sinking into poverty conceived of the
poor law and the way that ratepayers, or those who represented them,
understood the cases they saw.

If the burgeoning micro-detail of local practice has advanced our understanding of the role and character of the Old Poor Law, the experiences of the poor, and the local and regional composition of allowance
forms, it has also caused welfare historians to lose focus. Almost all studies of Old Poor Law practice rest upon sources – overseers' accounts,
parliamentary returns, and magistrates' books and orders – that touch
upon the *end* of the process by which allowances were considered, decided, accepted, given, and recorded. The problems with them as end-

of-process sources are well known, even if regularly underplayed. Overseers' accounts always include income and spending that are not strictly (or at all) related to the poor.[33] Studies that do not control for this can significantly overstate both spending and free resources. Nor was the cost of the Old Poor Law always (or for some places usually) covered by rates raised. Debt-financed spending required increasing later interest payments, which reduced subsequent resources for the poor. Above all, overseers' accounts – and thus any aggregate analysis that flows from them – were subject to innumerable recording deficiencies. A significant minority of overseers could not correctly add up numbers, but the recording problems go much further than that.[34] When the Northamptonshire shoemaking town of Kettering determined in the 1790s that any individual member of the vestry was allowed to make payments to paupers in great need and without a formal case being made at a scheduled meeting, it provided the ideal mechanism for missing and inaccurate payments to the poor.[35] The town was not alone in this practice, and even a cursory look at overseers' correspondence books shows them dispensing cash on the move, losing slips of paper and letters in which allowances were detailed, failing to transfer entries to the formal accounts from other more transient records, and acting without reference to past practice.[36] The sick posed a particular problem for recording practices because overseers often had to visit the homes of the sick, with all that this task meant for risks of disease, something hardly conducive to good accounting. These deficiencies can lead the unwary into an unwarranted and misleading reliance on the accuracy of the final accounts.

Moreover, if we step back further and look at the *whole* process by which relief was determined, a rather bigger interpretive issue emerges. The relatively few studies of vestry books as opposed to overseers' accounts show that officials received appeals for new or augmented allowances and for the maintenance of current relief from both inside and outside their parish. They also received periodic orders from magistrates, the unsolicited return of parishioners from host communities, and the casual claims of vagrants and other travellers passing through the parish. Except in the most intensely urbanised parishes, where officials often lost control of the relief process, these claims were *not* simply met. They might be investigated with more (or sometimes rather less) vigour, weighed against custom and past practice, set against current resources, negotiated, followed up by claimants or their advocates, modified, or turned down well before they made it to the end-of-process overseers' accounts.[37] Select vestry minutes, as I have suggested, lay bare some of this story,[38] but where these bodies did not exist, the task of sifting and accepting or rejecting fell to the overseer and for this reason has usually been regarded as invisible. How officials handled the process of relief is, however, vital for our understanding of the character, role, and experience of the poor law. If the process was short, comprehensive, consensual, and uncontested, resulting in relatively small numbers of claims being rejected or modified, we can have sustained confidence in parochial accounts, and the essential meaning of individual payments is easy to grasp. By contrast, a long, conflictive, contested, or exclusionary process could mean that there is little relationship between the numbers of poor who applied, what they asked for, when they first applied, the nature of the poverty they represented, and the people and allowances that appear in the final accounts. Ultimately, there is no way of knowing for most places which sort of poor law we are looking at.[39] Even if that could be known, it is the details of the negotiation process, rather than its outcome, and the meaning of the allowance, rather than simply its recording, that are important for understanding the character and role of the Old Poor Law and pauper experiences of it. This study is thus about the nature of the negotiation of relief, not about relief outcomes per se.

The need for this approach is emphasised by an additional development in the welfare literature that allows us to step even further back to survey the process of poor relief. Starting with James Stephen Taylor and continuing through the work of Pamela Sharpe, Tim Hitchcock, and Thomas Sokoll, we have gained a much clearer appreciation of the scale and value of collections of pauper letters. From its earliest legal incarnation, the Old Poor Law had struggled with what to do about three sorts of migrant: vagrants and the wandering poor, economic migrants in search of work, and families moving for a variety of reasons. Early attempts at punishment and expulsion having failed, the settlement laws (noted above) and the issuing of certificates by settlement parishes, which were in effect a promise to pay if the migrant fell into poverty, seem to have had a controlling effect for over a century.[40] From the 1780s onward, this precarious balancing act became impossible. An increasing scale of migration, the concentration of more migrants in urban areas, improved mechanisms for money and intelligence transmission, and rapid increases in the legal and other costs associated with enforcement of the settlement laws all undermined parish practice. Above all, increasing assertiveness by the poor respecting their claims – namely that they should be allowed to remain in their host communities and in the economic and social networks that this situation involved rather than automatically being removed – is readily apparent. It is against this backdrop that we see the development, albeit patchy at first, of the so called "out-parish" system, an extra-legal mechanism whereby overseers agreed between themselves to meet the costs of paupers living outside their settlement communities with allowances paid through the host community either via third parties or directly to the pauper concerned.[41] Both the host and settlement parishes appear to have benefited from this emerging relationship, the latter invariably paying lower allowances than they might have had to pay if the pauper had been at "home" and the former avoiding the legal, administrative, and personal costs of removal or other actions.[42]

In turn, this way of dealing with the migrant poor was largely based upon epistolary communication. The status of the resulting letters as material objects, rhetorical and strategic vehicles, negotiating devices, and evidence of the words and feelings of the poor themselves is revisited throughout this study. For now, even the most cursory reading of them clearly establishes the question of who got what relief recorded in overseers' accounts as a negotiated process. Poor people knew the stipulations of the Old Poor Law, contested and disputed refusals to engage in negotiation, wrote in sustained fashion to develop their case and shape the support attached to it, and pulled every lever they could to gain and maintain relief.[43] Of course, these were largely people out of their place of settlement at the time they needed aid, but the in-parish poor were equally likely to contest and negotiate their relief. The *process* of poor relief, then, provides the framework within which we must understand

*Focus on the process of relief*

the role and character of the Old Poor Law and the meaning of the welfare it provided. This study takes us on a detailed journey of that process and explores the particular question of how claimants might exercise agency in a system that notionally afforded them none.

## AGENCY AND NEGOTIATION

The literature on early modern England suggests that the balancing act between the rights and duties of ratepayers, recipients, officials, and those who controlled other aspects of the makeshift economy, such as endowed charities, left little room for the agency of the poor.[44] Henry French and Jonathan Barry, for instance, state that the poor had to continually work to "establish their honesty, or their social and moral autonomy" and that there was an inherent bias on the part of parish officials against "claims of truthfulness and honesty" by the poor.[45] Steve Hindle has argued persuasively that dependence in this period came to be associated with a loss of dignity and with submission to a relationship in which ongoing entitlement was closely linked to obedience to moral codes, the rhetorical and behavioural norms of deference and gratitude, and subjection to the will of the donor.[46] Although the poor (but rarely the dependent poor) might have been called upon to give evidence in manorial, church, and criminal court cases, we must acknowledge "the degrees of translation and structuring to which [their voices] were subjected in the process of their production" in the written records of these venues.[47] Perhaps unsurprisingly, then, some early modern historians have suggested that we struggle to hear the genuine voices of the poor themselves.[48] Indeed, Alexandra Shepard argues that the voices of the poor are "muffled, audible only in relation to (and deeply shaped by) the highly strategic negotiations of formal poor relief."[49] Yet even in the early modern period, symbolic acts of resistance or agency – such as occupying the church porch – can be uncovered, albeit operating within the confines of the referential structure of the elites' understandings of their Christian or paternalistic duties.[50] Sometimes, these early modern acts were more substantial, provocative, and purposeful, as for instance

---

when the poor applied to Quarter Sessions alongside or in substitute for their engagement with parishes.[51]

The situation from the later eighteenth century onward is more ambiguous. The poor appreciated that multiple overlapping and competing versions of national and local law left large and growing areas of ambiguity over eligibility for relief.[52] Moreover, as we will see in chapter 3, when transport and the transmission of written communication improved from the 1780s onward, poor people engaged in multiple opportunities to press their case in person or by letter. They understood and engaged with the essential economics of the local poor law, knew when meetings were taking place, and participated in the wider development of literate culture to garner independent support for their cases from neighbours, friends, employers, clergy, and even gentlemen. Very few writers took up their right of appeal to magistrates, preferring instead to engage local officials again, again, and again with their cases, whether in person or in writing. They understood, as argued in subsequent chapters, the borderlands in which they could actively seek to shape relief and the "fragile process of containment" that these borderlands offered.[53] Officials in their turn appear to have been relatively powerless in the face of resistance or active disobedience. Robert Sharp of South Cave was shocked when an applicant whose case had been turned down by the vestry threw a stone at him, but there is no evidence that the person was prosecuted or admonished.[54] At the other end of the country, the Sussex memorialist Thomas Geering noted that the Old Poor Law overseer "had been the best abused man in the parish" and that "various and sometimes grave, were the charges [i.e., rumours] brought against him."[55] Rumours were also spread when the poor died in institutions and cases had to be explored in the confines of the coronial courts. These examples of resistance and agency stand alongside the undoubted cases of brutality, neglect, incompetence, and contempt that were a leitmotif of early perceptions of the character of the poor law and its officers.[56]

The fact of agency and negotiation, on the one hand, and the tolerance of officials, on the other, are perhaps not surprising given the task facing parishes by the later eighteenth century. If one could reconstruct a typical community for, say, the 1790s, its dependent, episodically dependent, and marginally poor populations would comprise a very complex typological spectrum, varying in composition according to local transport infrastructure, landownership, urbanity, economic complexion, and conditions such as the scale and direction of prior migration. Table 1.1 sets out the key characteristics of this typological spectrum. Crudely, we can see that officials, particularly in larger settlements, had to worry about the known and unknown, or at least unrecorded, poor and to deal with endlessly complicated settlement and liability issues. They did so in a context where statute law was ambiguous and case law multiple, such that the scope for error was wide.[57]

This abstract compositional spectrum is brought to life by the overseer of Bolney in Sussex.[58] He audited his store of settlement certificates in 1763, deciding to trace what had happened to each of the named individuals and families. Of these sixty-three certificates, sixteen related to people who had moved on or died. A further three people had gained settlement, and a fourth woman had married a parishioner. This tally left forty-three cases of people still resident on the basis of certificates from other places, and since most related to individuals and "wife and family," it is necessarily the case that a substantial proportion of this rural parish's estimated population of 450 were not settled there. If we add to this picture the flow of people in and out under removal orders, several of which were contested, the complexity of the overseer's task in this fluid population is clear.[59] The out-parish poor simply added to this complexity.

More widely, the cross-section of communities encompassed by my corpus of surviving overseers' correspondence indicates that officials ended up in a constant stream of negotiations – with each other, with advocates of various stripes, and with the poor themselves, either face-to-face or via letters – arising out of the increasingly complex composition of the poor and marginal populations. The poor who had previously crowded the entrances to churches or elite gatherings were by the later eighteenth century clamouring at the doors and writing desks of the overseers themselves. In these circumstances, it was inevitable that, inter alia, people who were not entitled to relief got it, claims were missed or took

Table 1.1
*Composition of the poor population of a typical community*

| |
|---|
| The settled poor in their place who might apply to overseers or vestry members in person or, for larger places or when sick, either by writing or through advocates and substitutes. |
| The settled poor out of their place and paid for by their settlement parish while still resident in a host community. These arrangements and payments might or might not be recorded in vestry minutes or overseers' accounts. |
| The settled poor of other places paid for directly by the settlement parish to the overseer of the host community under a settlement certificate. |
| The settled poor of other places paid for directly by the settlement parish |to the overseer of the host community but without a settlement certificate. |
| The settled poor of other places paid for by the settlement parish in alternative ways, which rarely made it into the overseers' accounts. |
| The poor in the process of being removed from or to a place. |
| Travellers and others of uncertain settlement, many of whom claimed or experienced sickness. |
| Poor people of uncertain settlement, notably maiden settlements,* bastards, and so on. |
| Poor people of all sorts who were paid relief by order of magistrates. The tolerated poor, who were relieved by host parishes even though settlement lay elsewhere. |

* On this matter, see Sharpe, "Parish Women."

longer to address than they should have done, claims would be dismissed, claimants would be given less than what was requested or given a modified form of welfare, and allowances might be limited by time or circumstance or be freighted with onerous conditions. Overseers' accounts give little sense of this *process* of poor relief. Yet it matters for our understanding of the nature and role of the Old Poor Law and the wider experiences of being poor, including whether claimants could actively shape the allowances they were given, whether what they asked for and thought they should get gained traction with officials, and whether limitations on relief were ultimately enforceable in the face of pauper contestation. When people dropped off a relief register but had not obviously died, it matters whether and how they had tried to stay on the list, not least because the poor learned from each other's approach to the negotiation of welfare. It matters even more in this sense whether they got back on the welfare list and managed to stay there. In practice, two relief entries of the same amount side by side in the overseers' accounts but relating to different paupers should not be regarded as somehow "the same." How claimants navigated a discretionary welfare system – the language and rhetoric they used, the yardsticks of deservingness they employed, the tropes they inscribed in their negotiations, and the way their appeals were received and acted or not acted upon – is also important for answering other and much bigger questions. Is it true that the poor saw their legitimacy in the eyes of ratepayers and wider elite culture drain away beginning in the later eighteenth century? How malleable was the state apparatus in this massive area of government spending and action supposed to be? How did the poor identify as individuals, on the one hand, and as a class or group, on the other? How did elite groups and ratepayers construct themselves and their humanitarian, Christian, and philanthropic duties in the last decades of the Old Poor Law? And does the failure of contemporaries to understand the poor law as a process help to explain the rapid retreat and subsequent transformation of the later New Poor Law?

## SOURCES AND SCAFFOLDS

These broad questions are threaded throughout subsequent chapters. Exploring them requires a significant national dataset, for which we turn to the writing of the poor and the surrounding scaffold of overseers' correspondence, letters of epistolary advocates, bills and certificates, and vestry minutes or other parochial data. Historians have not by and large held positive views of the penetration and functionality of popular literacy, and even in the early nineteenth century, literate and oral cultures con-

1.1  A well-written letter. LIRO 13/2/102.

tinued to overlap and reinforce each other in very complex ways.[60] Reading skills, which were invariably taught before writing in the circumscribed schooling available to the poor, persisted longer than writing, but more generally literacy was something that could be lost over the life-cycle or through lack of practice.[61] The "democratisation of writing" was a feature of the later nineteenth century for European states, and most scholars who have studied autobiographies and diaries by ordinary people consider it no accident that these modes of writing increased rapidly in number at this date.[62] Chapters 2 and 5 treat the question of literacy at greater length. Undeniably, the poor *did* write. Their letters to officials, advocates, magistrates, landlords, and kin crossed a material spectrum. This range included controlled, well-structured, and beautifully written letters (figure 1.1), highly "oral" narratives lacking punctuation, structure, and form (figure 1.2), and desperate one- or two-line notes (figure 1.3). Such letters differ from the formal petitions to overseers, magistrates,

1.2 An example of "oral" writing. LIRO 13/2/79.

To Mr Munday Overseer

in the Parish of Caistor

County of Lincon

to your chad of sutterdown one gine
for those but I could not Attend
it Whas dew to give it up and
my full dependence is on my
Wifes Working for us all

if you pleas to send me fos
pounds to quet my Wife over her
Infeinment till she is Abel to goto
Work Agane I think Wee Cane doo
And if not send me thard as
that Is posable dont delo for I must
own Is posable dont delo for I must
other Somever or stove I am gilson
direct for Mr James gilson
No 18 saint Johns Qur in the parish
of saint Johns into London Middlesex
or in the Gounty of Middlesex

1.3 A desperate short note. LIRO 13/2/67.

and landlords that have been studied by Jonathan Healey or Rab Houston and that are also representative of much communication upward on the Continent.[63] In other work, Peter Jones and I have traced the "journey" from petition to letter in England, Wales, and Scotland, a matter considered in greater depth in chapter 2.[64]

Against this backdrop, it is clear that the heyday of the pauper letter and its associated epistolary scaffolding dated from the 1780s. Such letter writing gathered pace in the 1810s and continued, albeit directed to the central authorities, for the entire period of the New Poor Law.[65] The reasons for this sort of chronology are not hard to find. Growing migration, urbanisation, and industrial and agrarian change created a group of people who needed to communicate with parochial officials when poverty threatened, continued, or intensified. Table 1.1 and the succeeding discussion have suggested the size of this group and the complexity of the negotiation over welfare that inevitably followed, a theme to which chapter 2 returns when considering the representativeness of letters. The poor did not write without purpose. Craig Muldrew and I have argued that from the 1780s onward a significant increase in the availability of small

change, as well as the development of more reliable and sophisticated re-
source-transmission mechanisms such as the post, networks of carriers
and tradespeople, and bills of exchange, meant that money could follow
letters quickly and easily.[66] The development of reliable postal services
was as important for the communicative world of the poor as it was for
the middling sorts, whose medical and material existence was increasingly
shaped by epistolary culture.[67] Of course, such postal services were by
no means cheap before the advent of prepaid stamps. In 1884 Thomas
Geering noted of the early nineteenth century that "Eightpence, prepaid,
was the postage to London. Then, among working people, there was very
little gossipy letter-writing, and few of this present generation can appre-
ciate the advantage of the postal change and accommodation [i.e., the
penny post] in contrast with the old system."[68] Against this observation,
we must set the balancing perspective of furious letters from overseers to
individuals admonishing them for writing so frequently and, because one
paid to receive a letter, at such a great cost to the parish coffers. Chapter
3 takes up these issues in more depth.

When we locate the epistolary practices of the poor in the context of
the much wider rise of epistolary and literate culture from the later eighteenth century onward, this surge in letter writing is unsurprising. Martyn Lyons reminds us that it took confidence, encouragement, and energy
for "ordinary" people to write in a sustained fashion.[69] Moreover, it required a stock of language and rhetorical modalities, and it demanded
practice in marshalling and rehearsing a coherent story. Certainly, by the
early nineteenth century, the dependent and marginal poor had begun
to accumulate extensive experience of such marshalling through witness
statements, standing before magistrates rehearsing their lives for settlement examinations, and recounting their sickness histories to doctors or
hospital staff. By the 1820s a widespread culture of petitioning Parliament must have fed into how the poor understood their right to be heard
and also into how they ought to frame their stories.[70] The rise of newspaper culture, the exponential increase in the publishing of literature on
a spectrum from balladry to sermons and novels, and the rapid development of official and semi-official correspondence, such as overseers
letters, guidance manuals and letters, prescriptions, and magistrate or-

ders, from which language and phrases could simply be lifted, provided a stock of references for poor writers.[71]

Chapter 5 returns to some of these themes. For now, it is important to re-emphasise that the poor wrote in large numbers. In common with other studies of epistolary collections, whether emigrant letters or appeals to Soviet administrations,[72] it is impossible to know how many letters were originally sent. Collections of such documents might be weeded, rationalised, or (particularly where they were moved around) lost. In the case of letters from the poor, relatively few were bound into volumes, which might have increased the likelihood of survival. Even where they survive as individual documents or collections, their accession into record offices often seems to have attracted the most casual labelling, with the term "voucher" being the most common hiding place. Such letters can be found gathered in defined collections, pasted into overseers' accounts or vestry books, hidden in settlement examinations, or even preserved as uncatalogued bundles in parochial or family and estate archives. Some remain in the parish chests that originally held them. What is clear, however, is that many more letters were sent and received than have survived. Almost all vestry minutes record the receipt and reading of letters from claimants, other parochial officials, and advocates, and we thus have a record of them and their concerns even if the narrative itself has gone. Similarly, overseers who received letters or sent them incurred postage costs that had to be recorded in the annual accounts along with the costs of paper, ink, sealing wax, and the candles to write by. Self-referential letters from officials, paupers, and others also evidence the sending or receipt of correspondence even if it has not survived. These are universal issues for all studies that use epistolary collections, and at least for our purposes, there is no reason at all to believe that the survival of pauper letters is anything other than random.

This study, then, is based upon a very large corpus of writing by, for, or about the poor. Unlike Thomas Sokoll's classic edition of pauper letters for Essex, my sample includes overseer and advocate correspondence alongside letters written by or for the poor themselves.[73] For the purposes of this book, it is not sensible or desirable to separate these elements of the epistolary world of the parish, a point developed over subsequent chapters. The core of the corpus was identified and collected under the auspices of a grant from the Arts and Humanities Research Council and the Deutsche Forschungsgemeinschaft. A team transcribed most surviving manuscript collections of pauper narratives and surrounding advocate and overseer correspondence for every county in England, Wales, and Scotland.[74] This material was augmented by transcriptions of letters and vestry minutes that I had made for earlier research projects and by previously published editions, the latter with a particular focus on Essex, Wiltshire, Shropshire, and Staffordshire. We did not seek to recheck the transcriptions of these editions, which are listed in the bibliography and included in figure 1.4. The corpus was augmented with the texts of letters that no longer survive but were read out, summarised, or transcribed in vestry minutes and other parochial sources. Our transcription policy involved the creation of a main text comprised of the contents of the letter itself and a circumtext encompassing other writing on the letter, including draft answers from officials, attestations enclosed with the letter, and material on the outside of the envelope or folding, such as postmarks. Following a standard set of templates, we retained all original spelling, punctuation (or more usually the lack of it), superscript and subscript, contractions, crossing-out, insertions, underlining, and line breaks. For emphasis, italics were added to some of the letters discussed here. Illegible words were signified with placeholders and then double or triple checked by other members of the team. Those that remained at the end of this process were signified with the square-bracketed direction "illegibile," as were words or segments of the text obscured by sealing, tearing, or other contemporaneous or later damage. In some cases, the type of damage was inserted in square brackets rather than "illegible." Within the circumtext, we also retained original spelling and punctuation, even if – as for instance with addresses – later letters from or about the same person suggested a more familiar and standardised spelling. This approach, we felt, took us more closely to the genuine voice, sentiment, and intent of the letter writers.[75]

In total, the English and Welsh corpus comprises 25,652 items by, for, or about the poor, including overseers' correspondence. The underlying

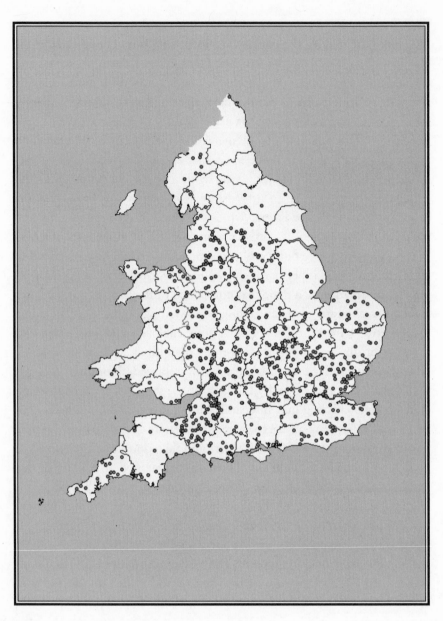

1.4 The spatial distribution of receiving communities.

community collections vary radically in size from one or two examples to more than 1,000 items for Kirkby Lonsdale in Westmorland. The ten biggest community samples – Kirkby Lonsdale, Sandal Magna, Hulme, Rothersthorpe, Lewes, Totnes, Peterborough, Colchester, Bury St Edmunds, and Lutterworth – boast a collective 5,311 items. These sorts of disparity clearly reflect survival rates rather than the volume of letters originally existing. Some letters went a considerable distance, including for instance correspondence between Carlisle and Cornwall, but a striking and insistent feature of the data is that a significant minority were exchanged between communities that were in relatively easy walking distance. This remains the case even if we control for claims that writers were too sick to attend the settlement parish in person, suggesting indirectly the ingrained nature of epistolary negotiation under the poor law in its so-called crisis period.

Figure 1.4 visits the spatial distribution of the 559 *receiving* communities. The sample includes a wide spatial coverage within and between English and Welsh counties. Eleven of these receiving communities got letters from or about their poor in Kidderminster in Worcestershire, and eight received correspondence from Wisbech in Cambridgeshire, even though they were not generally proximate to either place. Significant numbers of letters were also sent from places like Gosport in Hampshire and Whitehaven in Cumberland. Relatively few letters have been *retained* in the parochial archives of London, something also observed in the London Lives project.[76] This observation extends to the fastest-growing industrial and warehousing towns of the midlands and north, although not necessarily their suburbs. It is perhaps also important to note that 172 out of the 559 receiving communities were simultaneously among the "sending" communities, testimony to the existence of a deep and sustained network of correspondence in the early nineteenth century even if the individual parish archives have now disappeared.

As we might expect given that urban areas grew primarily through in-migration prior to the onset of natural growth in the 1830s,[77] the majority of letters were *sent* from definably urban areas and received by rural or smaller urban communities, county towns, and proto-industrial areas.[78] The number of sending communities was high, and their socio-economic range was wide. Excluding the 740 letters that either had no identifiable place of sending or, more usually, could not be reliably identified in a modern mapping package, the corpus encompasses around 1,500 sending communities. More precision is impossible given deep uncertainty over whether a named hamlet near, for instance, Manchester was part of the town or a distinct settlement at the date concerned. This is a particular problem for northern proto-industrial hamlets and Welsh hill communities, some of which have now been absorbed into larger areas or simply disappeared. Collectively, London parishes constitute the single biggest sending "community." The 1,147 letters sent from the metropolis equates to 4.4 per cent of the corpus. Although this is below London's share of the national population, it may not be that far out of line with its share of the dependent poor by the early nineteenth century. More widely, sending communities encompassed every major market, county, and industrial town in England, with especially significant letter sets – often spanning several recipient communities – relating to Leeds, Sheffield, Bath, Hull, Manchester, Winchester, Preston, and Mansfield. In addition, letters were sent from most of the major seaside towns and ports, the Channel Islands, the Isle of Wight, and the Isle of Man. Although there are many potential problems with pauper letters, a theme considered in chapter 2, a bias toward any particular community type is not one of them.

The surviving collections encompass the narratives of three broad types of writer, although determining the exact boundaries between them and the number of distinct individuals involved is complicated by undated and unsigned letters, instances where people seem to change the spelling of their names even as their handwriting remains the same, and issues of authorship or ownership of letters explored in chapter 2. The first group was comprised of those who wrote either a single or small number of letters, usually related to a single issue or event. These people account for the majority of distinct poor *writers*, at around 64 per cent. A second group, by contrast, wrote in sustained fashion, with regular correspondence accumulating into the thirties and forties of narratives, alongside official and advocate correspondence. This group constitutes the bedrock of the collection of *letters*, at roughly 60 per cent. A third group wrote on a more episodic basis, often shifting into more regular correspondence as individuals entered old age or what they thought might be a final illness.[79] Those writing in sustained fashion have a core place in this study. Yet this material cannot be considered in isolation. The project has also involved the identification and transcription of a sample of vestry books and other parochial sources, where possible overlapping with the pauper letter collections at the community level. These sources can throw additional light on how the claims of the poor and their advocates were received and acted upon, but they also provide a mechanism for understanding whether the settled poor living in their home parishes shared the same concerns, sentiments, and negotiation expectations as those living farther afield. The wider question of what those who wrote asked for is taken up in chapter 4.

The chronological distribution of the corpus is uneven, an observation that applies to all three elements of the epistolary world of the parish: official correspondence, the letters of poor writers, and advocate texts. As figure 1.5 shows, the earliest parish collection, that of Oxford St Martin, begins in the 1750s. Yet the chronological heart of the material is from the 1790s, likely due in part to changes in settlement law in 1795 that made quick and easy removal more difficult. There is also a particularly steep rise in the number of letters written in the later 1810s and the 1820s. The unevenness would persist even if we assumed that a significant number of the 1,416 undated letters in the corpus were written before, say, 1816. This late "surge" lends itself to many readings and explanations: a renewed parochial interest in enforcing settlement legislation in the aftermath of the Napoleonic Wars of 1803–15 and the recession of the 1820s might have driven an upsurge of writing by people keen to remain in host communities; better and cheaper postal services may have led to more people trying their luck with a letter; migration surges in the later eighteenth and early nineteenth centuries might have resulted in many older people being out of their place when they fell into need by the 1820s; an increasing number of professional overseers and select vestries might have been determined to roll back lax administrative practice; poverty might simply have been increasing; or the Old Poor

Law may have been an early tool in the development of the nineteenth-century information state. These are more than academic questions in the sense that the particular reasons for chronological concentration could have influenced the content and strategy of letters and the particular composition of the communities from which they were sent. Yet we can also take such concerns too far. Where there is evidence that a particular collection is complete – as for instance in Rothersthorpe – the steep upward shift in the number of letters available seen in figure 1.5 is much more muted, suggesting that issues of retention, rather than systemic influences on the out-parish relief system, are also in play.

The majority of all letters, some 68 per cent, were sent by or for men, but this concentration probably reflects the fact that they applied on behalf of other household members rather than arising out of differential literacy rates or need. Indeed, the three most prolific writers in the collection were women. There are no systematic chronological trends in the presence or absence of letters written by or for women, and women were no more or less likely to write from or to particular types of community. Children are clearly underrepresented as authors in their own right – a function of limited schooling and the fact that application was usually made for them[80] – as are lunatics or those with mental impairments. By contrast, the aged are overrepresented in most parish collections given the likely proportion of the poor over sixty. This is a consistent feature of the corpus across all potential chronological constellations of the data, and the "surge" in available letters from the mid-1810s onward, insofar as it is "real," is not due to an increasing preponderance of aged writers. The aged were simultaneously those most likely to fall into need, those most likely to want to stay in their host community, the sort of people least likely to be wanted at "home" by settlement parishes, and those seemingly most able to garner advocate support for the cases they made. In short, the observed concentration and continuity are not unexpected.

Scottish and Welsh writers are well represented in the collections of English parishes, but few English people wrote back to settlement parishes from Scotland or Wales, a clear indication of the direction of migration flows. Although it is difficult to estimate what proportion of immigrant writers one ought to expect, at least before the start of naturalisation doc-

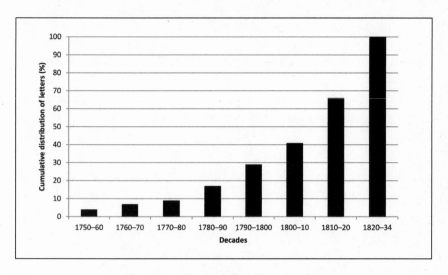

1.5 The chronological distribution of letters.

umentation explored so well by Laura Tabili,[81] the collection contains
letters by and for American and European immigrants as well as black
seafarers and ex-slaves.[82] Clearly, then, this remarkable collection of "ordinary writing," life writing, or ego documents is different by many degrees from anything previously assembled in Britain or Europe, with the
exception of the London Lives project. Looking at the corpus collectively
and employing emblematic case studies, it is possible to reconstruct the
*process* of poor relief, the meaning of allowances granted, and the nature
and quality of pauper agency. We can also address a wider suite of questions about the manifestation and malleability of state power, the history
of ordinary literacy, and the character of social relations in the 16,000 or
so parishes of the early nineteenth century.

This remains a study largely of England, rather than of all the home
nations, for two core reasons. First, although we have collected material
for every Scottish county, the remarkable, and remarkably large, collection of narratives and pauper petitions for Glasgow in the Mitchell Library
has been only lightly sampled. Doing more would require a nationwide
effort. Second, the Scottish welfare system up to (and beyond) 1845 was
distinctive in intent, financing, and outcomes. Peter Jones and I have argued that by the later nineteenth century Scottish paupers had adopted
the same rhetorical, linguistic, and expectational platforms as their English

counterparts, but prior to this time the singularity of Scotland is compelling.[83] Wales, by contrast, was subject to the same legislative imperatives as England, but even then Ben Harvey has identified sufficient distinctiveness to require a study of the nation in its own right. For this reason, Welsh material is used lightly here and only for the broadest comparative context. The study also has temporal restrictions, with a clear and deliberate focus on the period between the 1750s and 1830s. This approach is in part driven by the chronological focus of the dataset, discussed above, but the wider rationale is to concentrate on the period when the absolute costs of poor relief began to spiral upward and when historians have conventionally seen a crisis of the Old Poor Law system.[84] It is precisely these laboratory conditions that allow us to test the power and resilience of pauper agency and the robustness of the local state.

## LOOKING FORWARD

Developing the themes outlined above, chapter 2 asks how historians should conceptualise the corpus of letters, specifically how we should understand their structure and form, whether we can rely on their contents, and whether the perspective on agency and negotiation that they seem to embody can be applied to a wider group of the locally resident settled poor. Thereafter, the study is divided into three further substantive parts.

Part 2, comprising chapters 3 to 6, deals with acts of navigation and reception. Chapter 3 asks how the poor themselves navigated the act of letter writing, exploring where they found their paper, pens, and ink, how they conveyed and received letters, and what the materiality of writing can tell us about agency, negotiation, and the process of poor relief. Chapter 4 investigates the reception of letters and analogous appearances before the vestry. This chapter ultimately considers the outcomes of the process of poor relief, but its central concern is how officials and vestrymen saw and constructed their relationships with claimants and how this might have affected the ways that poor people approached them and the parishes that they represented. Chapter 5 is framed by the deceptively simple question of where poor people found a stock of words to write.

It shows that they appropriated words from other texts and other writers but that ultimately the officials who received letters and the poor who wrote them shared a common linguistic inheritance and canvas through which they could conduct the accepted performance of negotiation. They spoke, in other words, the same language. Chapter 6 focuses on the stories told by the poor, showing that they were not, and were not meant to be, comprehensive and complete. With the shared linguistic register highlighted in chapter 5 went an acceptance of the concept of negotiation and the tolerance of a certain degree of fiction in correspondence.

Part 3, comprising chapters 7 to 11, deals with the interrelated questions of how the poor rhetoricised the stories they had assembled and used the linguistic register they shared with officials and advocates. Chapter 7 provides a broad overview of the rhetorical spectrum, arguing that we can detect key regularities – which I label anchoring rhetoric – that were played out across most letter types and life-cycle stages. It also identifies a set of extending rhetoric that came into play more selectively. Chapters 8 through 11 explore the detail of this anchoring and extending rhetoric, visiting themes such as dignity, character, gender, struggle, custom, law, and life-cycle conditions.

Part 4, comprising chapters 12 and 13, returns to some of the larger questions outlined in this chapter. How did the poor define and understand themselves, and how were they in turn understood? Did they lose legitimacy during the crisis period of the Old Poor Law? How was the process of poor relief negotiated, and with what effect? Was the agency of the poor as fragile and illusory as some have claimed? How malleable were the rules of the state in their local manifestation, and how malleable were they meant to be? And how does a focus on the voices and agency of the poor, and on their connectedness in the epistolary world of the parish, shape our reading of the character, role, and meaning of poor relief and the poor law?

# 2

## Points of Navigation

### OVERVIEW

On 13 February 1826, Frances Soundy, living in Battersea Fields in London, addressed herself to the "Honerable Gentellmen the Curchwardins & Oversears of the Parrish of Pangborn" in Berkshire. This was the seventh letter in a trail of correspondence *written* by the same person but variously signed by Soundy, her husband, their children, and even neighbours. The unfortunate overseers of this place were eventually to receive a total of thirty-eight letters. Frances would "bag pardon" for writing,

but I do not no wot corse to take in this our distress. Throw surporting our son his wife and child gentillmen I would not have trobelled you a gain could I by any meanes have avoided it but throw my husband illness at Christmas and keep in of them as inthralled us so much in debt that I can not assist them any longer my son now would I exspet git in to work in a week or 2 if he ad deasent things to put on but he can not put a foot out doors for he have not a shoe to his feet and he must apeer tidy be fore the gentillman and it do not lay in my power to git him any of my salf indeede Gentillmen could I by any meanes assist them any longer I would as I no that if he ad any a parrell he would soune be in work gentillman if you have any doubt that I haved serliseted you in behalf of my son and deept wot you have been so kind to sand thay have now lived with me 11 weeks if you think proper to ourthories any one to inquire you will find gentellmen that I have not mencioned one half of the distress that we have brote to throw surporteing of them for I keeps it as much as I can in my hone brest Gentillman I humbley intreet you that you will assist them in a trifell to git him sum close as the Gentillmen will be exspect I meet next tusday or wansday to sattell wan thay shall sat on and he can not attend unless you stand his frand in regard to my salf I leave that to you gentillmen if you will by assist them on the turms that I requested in my letter dated 2 feb 1826 so that I can git him into work as he may be able to maintain thar salves and I will repay it a gain if required of by you.[1]

Her letter finished with Soundy adopting the guise of embodied belonging – "*your* distressed Perrishoner" – before closing with the supplicatory phrase "in duty bound your Perrishoners will ever Pray" for the gentlemen ratepayers of the parish.[2]

This idiosyncratic letter can truly be appreciated and understood only when read aloud.[3] It raises important questions. Should we believe Soundy's multilayered tale of woe, stretching from accrued debt and unemployment created by lack of clothing through to a veiled assertion that she had not told the gentleman one half of her sad story? Was Frances really the author of this extraordinary letter, or was it another member of her family or even a neighbour? If she was not the author but had perhaps dictated the narrative, ought this to shape the way we read and understand the experiences, rhetoric, and feeling embodied in it? What do the form and conduct of the letter tell us about literacy, on the one hand, and claimant perceptions of agency, on the other? How did it fit with others in the series and what similarities and differences are there with other writers? Did those who approached the overseer directly rather than writing exhibit the same range of concerns and use the same reference points when they made their case in person? And how might Soundy's letter have been received? Did the overseers respond quickly, as she hoped, creating a two-way dialogue that could form the basis of ongoing negotiation, or did they hesitate, delay, or simply file the letter and hope not to receive another? The answers to these questions reach to the very heart of the utility of the letters of the poor as a source and the depth and reach of agency as an experience. They also speak to the way that we as historians should navigate the corpus. Thus the next section turns to the trustworthiness and representativeness of letters as a source. I suggest that most letters were "owned" by those who purported to sign them and that they can be seen to embody the essential voice of the poor in the process of poor relief. The chapter then moves on to the structural form of letters, emphasising in particular their dissimilarity from petitionary or patronage styles. Existing models for classifying letter sets are found wanting, not least because they tend to meld issues of structure and intent with rhetorical and strategic content. They also, incorrectly, disengage pauper letters from overseers' correspondence and the appeals of epistolary advocates that make up the rest of the epistolary world of the parish. The chapter develops a new typological framework focused on form and the place of letters in the framework of negotiation. Broadly, the intent of the chapter is to provide a navigation map for the complex corpus that I draw upon in the rest of the study.

## MATTERS OF AUTHORSHIP, HONESTY, AND REPRESENTATIVENESS

The utility of pauper (and other)[4] letters is intricately entwined with questions of authorship – of who actually formed the ideas embodied in a letter and wrote what appears on the page.[5] As chapter 1 observed, historians of literacy in England have generally been sceptical of the penetration of reading and writing to the working classes prior to the 1860s. David Vincent concludes both that the arrival of a letter for most people was a "rare event" and that it would take a major crisis "to engage directly or by proxy" in letter writing.[6] Against this backdrop, it is easy to assume that the authors of these letters were scribes, educated neighbours, or family members or, as Keith Snell has argued, that letters were the product of collective endeavour.[7] The corpus certainly has examples where an "author" sits firmly in the shadows: parents writing for children, children writing for parents, midwives writing for female patients, husbands writing for wives or vice versa, and employers writing for employees. Overseers, landlords, neighbours, or creditors both wrote on behalf of claimants or their families *and* authored letters signed by them.[8] Moreover, teachers, clergymen, military men, and others were enjoined to write letters that were then simply signed by the poor person.[9] It is through this process of accumulating help, words, and voices that we end up with letter series like that from Sarah Hughes, living at various addresses in London but settled in Pangbourne. Her letter of 9 May 1828 noted,

> I take the liberty of Riting these few lines to you hoping to find you in good health as I am at Present and likewise to in form you that the 8 Weeks is up on Sunday the 11th inst and I should be much ablaiged to you if you to send the money that is due to me [under a prior agreement to grant her a weekly allowance]. Sarey Haughes.[10]

This was one of nineteen letters from Hughes, and although all had the same signature, the letters were variously written in six different hands. Some writers actively acknowledged authorial help, as for instance did Hannah Billingshurst of Merrow in Surrey, who agreed to have local rector Arthur Onsolow explain in a reply to the overseer that she had asked Onslow to help "answer your letter to her."[11]

Yet Frances Soundy and most other serial letter writers in the corpus do not exhibit such obvious signs of support, suggesting that concerns about authorship might be overstated. There is little evidence of the existence of a class of full-time scribes to match those in France and elsewhere who might write letters to officials for a fee.[12] Almost none of the letters in the corpus exhibit the sorts of formality, grammatical structure, and use of stock phrases that tend to be generated in scribal relationships.[13] This finding is perhaps unsurprising given the informal nature of the appeal mechanisms under the discretionary Old Poor Law when compared to those that had to be used by the poor in Prussia, France, or Italian states.[14] Nor, as seen from the style and structure of writing in Soundy's letter, is there any evidence that the poor or those who wrote for them were simply working to or copying from letter-writing manuals of the sort that we know to have circulated in eighteenth- and nineteenth-century England.[15] Her irregular style is toward the more extreme end of a typological spectrum, but even David Clarke's letter from Norwich to Peterborough in February 1801, which more clearly locates the archetypal tone and style of the corpus, falls into the category of what Thomas Sokoll characterises as "oral writing."[16] Clarke was

> sorry the distress of the times forces me to implore your immediate assistance I need not point out the dearness of articles of life flattering myself I write to gentlemen well aquainted with every circumstance of the kind and whome I trust are Gentlemen Ridy to redress your porre parishoners real distresses haveing laboured under depravity of site for several years and my wife under a very bad state of health ... In this Distrest situation I am force contrary to my wishes to ask your relief being quite unable to get through life I have no family that can come charge to you but hour selves but the frequent whant of work and the state of health we now labour under forcess your perishoners than to address you.[17]

Whatever the stylistic features, there is also surprisingly little evidence of collective writing, an issue to which I return in chapter 3 when looking at the materiality of letters.

By contrast, there *is* considerable evidence to support the view of Sokoll and others that letters *were* largely written by the people who claimed to send them. A cross-corpus analysis of handwriting in letters versus that employed in addressing the envelope or the outside folds of a letter sealed in other ways reveals few obvious discrepancies. This finding suggests that the people who wrote the narratives usually addressed them as well. In circumstances where scribal or group support for writing was likely to be disengaged from the sending of the resulting narrative, the coincidence of handwriting is significant.[18] Moreover, within series of letters purportedly from the same person, variation in handwriting over time tends to be minimal or at least situational. These series can be both large and long. Sophia and Jacob Curchin wrote forty-nine times from Wisbech in Cambridgeshire to Thrapston in Northamptonshire between 1812 and 1828, and William Lloyd wrote thirty-seven times from Hulme in Lancashire to Llanasa in North Wales between 1808 and 1817.[19] It is implausible that the poor would have found the same person to write for them over these periods and on such a sustained basis. Moreover, letters, even those in shorter series, also tended to be self-referential, calling the attention of officials to previous correspondence, promises made, and prior personal visits at the settlement parish. Thus James Tomblin wrote in October 1833, "My circumstances are well known to many of the inhabitants of Peterborough." Further, "I applied to the overseers personally a few weeks ago and went away under the hope that something would be done for me as I was not positively refused but promised that my case should be considered and an answer sent. I have received no answer – and to come again to Peterborough involves a loss of time and some expense."[20] It seems improbable that Tomblin was not the author of the narratives that were sent in his name. For other writers, we can be rather clearer about this matter because they went out of their way to emphasise that overseers were reading their genuine authorial voice. Hence Joseph Smallwood wrote an undated letter from Chichester in Sussex to say that the overseers of his host parish required further written authority to continue paying his allowance. The officials "said they would write to the Genteelmen for me, I told them I could write my-self."[21]

Yet we might also follow Maarten van Ginderachter and ask whether locating the exact authorial voice(s) really matters for the way that we should understand and read the letters of ordinary people.[22] When Thomas Pask of Lincoln wrote to the overseer of the hamlet of Croft, both in Lincolnshire, on 17 November 1799, he did so in his own voice:

I have this day been *applied to and desired* by Ann Brown the wife of William Brown whose settlement is in your Parish *to inform you*, that on account of her Husband having volunteered into the 5th Regiment, the Militia Money formerly paid to herself and one child, is taken from her, consequently is now distressed for want of that to support them, *I am therefore desired by her* to sollicit the favor of your attention to this request, that as there will be half a years Rent of her House due at Martinmas next, amounting to £1 4s 0d & not being able to pay it herself, that you will have the Goodness to pay the Rent for her when due by sending it to me or to her, otherwise her Goods will be seized and Sold, and *she will then be obliged to come to your Parish*, otherwise will not trouble you for any thing more, but endeavor to support herself & Child.[23]

There can be no doubt at all that, as the italicised phrases show, Ann Brown was present as or when the letter was written, and it is inconceivable that it was not read to her. Indeed, advocates often note that incoming or outgoing mail had been read to the person concerned.[24] That the letter itself contains threats and phrasing common to innumerable other narratives – notably for instance the threat that she would have to return home and thus cost the settlement parish more – suggests that she may have had an active role in dictating what was written. And of course Brown herself may have been literate but have simply chosen to have her case represented by an epistolary advocate to enhance its weight and reach.[25] Just because this letter is mediated by the handwriting of someone else does not, therefore, compromise the act of agency, the rhetoric of communication and negotiation, or the truth and force of the case presented. We might draw the same conclusions where letters were a collective endeavour in which a neighbour or friend wrote down a composite of sentences drawn from a group of people rather than a single individual.[26]

These considerations feed into a second important concern over the letters of poor people: their honesty and authenticity.[27] Ever present are the possibilities that those at a distance might embellish their stories, omit detail, or simply lie, both because they could and because their letters simultaneously represented and embodied a vehicle for conveying information, claims making, strategic representation or silence, and attempting to influence the scale and duration of relief as opposed to simple eligibility.[28] Indeed, some historians, as we saw in chapter 1, have contended that the very status of the poor made their testimony and claims less believable, such that their letters would inevitably have been viewed with suspicion.[29] It is certainly possible to detect in the corpus inveterate charlatans like Jacob and Sophia Curchin. Living in Wisbech in Cambridgeshire but settled in Thrapston in Northamptonshire, the couple lied about their financial situation, rent arrears, being distrained for debt, and individual and familial illness. Piecing together their narratives reveals that Sophia Curchin was ostensibly pregnant in the 1820s and 1830s more often than is biologically possible, even allowing for miscarriages.[30] Their lies prompted a letter in June 1824 to the overseer of Wisbech stating, "I beg to observe that he [Jacob Curchin] is a very troublesome and imposing man, and therefore shall be obliged by your being guarded against his crafty insinuations."[31]

Sometimes, lies and deception might even take the form of forgeries of official documents. Thomas Martain, for instance, was exposed by the overseers of East Grinstead for forging a settlement certificate from the parish of Hucking, both in Sussex, and signing the names of the churchwarden and overseer.[32] For some people, no detective work at all was needed because their neighbours, work colleagues, or officials in their residence parish informed on them. John Deaking, the overseer of Leicester, wrote to his counterpart in Market Harborough in Leicestershire on 25 February 1823 to contradict the story of Widow Stringer. He wished to inform Market Harborough that "no such Person has ever applied ... for relief" and that "the rest of her tale is a fabrication ... and I take pleasure in exposing her, this is one of many impositions I have exposed of Paupers endeavouring to impose on Parishes to which they belong."[33] Similarly, Thomas Derwin wrote from Leicester to the overseers of Oxendon in Leicestershire to "Inform you of the conduct of a man named James Harmstead & his wife," whom he claimed were "living in Drunkenness, Riot and Debauchery" while receiving a parochial allowance. Worse, their house was a meeting point for "men of Bad character at all hours of the Night, and at present they have 5 Lewd women in the house."[34] In chapter 9, I return to the question of how parishes ultimately dealt with the "unworthy" poor of this sort.

Meanwhile, it should be noted that in response either to their own experiences of individuals or to these sorts of tip-off, there are also examples of officials doubting the stories of those who wrote to them.[35] The overseer of Epworth in Lincolnshire was very direct in his instructions to Elizabeth Field. A letter from Joseph Cheetham, the overseer of Selby in Yorkshire, on 22 September 1794 noted that Field "still continues verry Poorly and not able to Do anything at all." Cheetham asked that Epworth grant her a regular weekly allowance and assured the overseer that "Her Brother and Sister will Endeavour to Support Her while please God She gets Better and then She will go to Place as soon as ever She is able." A note appended to the bottom of the letter said, "P.S. as you *wished her* to get the Letter Signed by the Churchwardens or Overseers of the Poor I expect she will do so."[36]

Although entertaining, however, these stories are also relatively unusual. The letters of the poor were public documents. They might be read out and read by others as or when they were originally written. They were certainly read out and circulated upon receipt, as we will see in chapter 4. It is inconceivable, as anonymous and signed "information" letters show, that the stories of individuals and their relief did not seep into the domain of various publics and that deception went unnoticed.[37] Thomas Sokoll has suggested that Essex writers generally told the truth because they could easily be inspected by their home parish or because officials could ask others, such as visiting tradesmen and fellow overseers, to drop in on them.[38] Overseers might also write to claimants and others seeking information on the condition of individuals and families. The sources are replete with spot-checks of this sort. Taking advantage of unexpected opportunities for inspection – changes in demands from writers, the ending of relief that was limited by time or circumstance, and wider reviews of allowances – officials accumulated information about new and existing welfare recipients. Such checks were not numerically overwhelming, but they were frequent enough to have discouraged outright deception or outrageous embellishment. Thus, writing to his counterpart in Sawston in Cambridgeshire on 3 March 1835 to authorise an increase in the regular allowance of Widow Naylor during the time of her sickness, the overseer of Oundle in Northamptonshire added a caveat:

We consider that as spring is coming on some part of her family *may or ought* to be able to earn Something towards their support. *She told us* that she thought she could get employ for some of the Boys directly she got to Sawston At any rate our vestry will not allow more. In yr next letter I shall feel obliged by your sending me the ages & names of her Children that we may judge the best to be done with them and also if any of them have any employ or earn anything.[39]

This institutional memory of Naylor's promise, clearly made in person because no letter survives in an otherwise comprehensive archive, is important and suggests that the parish always meant to check up in this case.

Such examples can be reproduced many hundreds of times, but the key point is that when inspections did take place or when information was elicited and sent, few writers were found to be lying. Indeed, and as the overseer of Wellingborough in Northamptonshire found in the 1790s, inspection usually revealed that paupers had understated the severity of their case.[40] The frequent claim in letters – seen so clearly in the Frances Soundy narrative opening this chapter – that the writer had told officials only a fragment of their suffering seems to ring true. I take up this matter in chapter 8. For now, it is important to note that surprisingly few writers were removed from relief lists for lying or embellishing, as opposed to ideological reasons that applied to all recipients. Equally, there are just a handful of documented incidences of allowances being reduced because of undisclosed circumstances. These observations should perhaps not be surprising given that letters were often just one element of the patchwork of contact between paupers and officials. They might be preceded or succeeded by personal visits to the parish, supplemented by letters to kin or other friends, or interspersed with letters or testimony from epistolary advocates, such that the ability to sustain a lie was challenging. In this context, writers and advocates frequently went out of their way to establish the veracity of what they said. Apart from ubiquitous claims shared by both the in- and out-parish poor to be telling the truth, strategic mechanisms included promises not to claim relief for longer than was needed, statements that the aim of the applicant was not to become a long-term burden but to return to independence, attestations of character and situation by themselves or others, claims that their dire situation was well known in the neighbourhood, and actively inviting inspection. I return to many of these strategic and rhetorical themes in later chapters.

The poor also, of course, followed unconventional paths to simultaneously establish the veracity of their stories and convey the depth of their need. Thus Thomas Laister wrote to Epworth from Whitworth in Lancashire on 25 March 1794 to say that "I Expect that I shall come short of Money," and he asked officials in his settlement parish to send him whatever funds they thought appropriate. Clearly in Lancashire to wait upon the nationally famous "Whitworth doctors," Laister added a postscript to his short and direct letter: "Please do not fail sending as the Docter can not give any acount how Long I shall have to stop here and I will give you a strict acount of every peney I lay out and if I should spare any when I return I will Diliver it up to you Evry farthing, …"[41] Laister meant to go on with his postscript but broke off and dispatched it mid-sentence. Nonetheless, the intent – to indicate his honesty with a faithful promise to spend as little and to repay as much as possible – is clear. Also in Lancashire, William Brown's letter to Hulme on 30 January 1824 noted that he had suffered for a long time and was now in desperate need. His state had "appeared in the News," and "Mr Pond will put My Story likewise into a Small Book."[42] Advocates, too, adopted subtle means to establish the accuracy of what they wrote, as for instance in the case of Mr Shearsmith, who wrote from Brighton to Worthing, both in Sussex, on 19 April 1834 after having been asked to comment on the case of George Butcher. Finding him in a desperate state, Shearsmith wrote that "I have sent this by his wife, that you might be assured relief is requisite," confirming once more the subtle interplay of personal and epistolary appeal.[43] In short, following Sokoll, I understand the corpus of letters that underpin this volume as broadly truthful.

Whether they are also representative – of the letters that were sent but do not survive and of the rhetoric, strategy, and experiences of those who

made their case in person – is more difficult to know.[44] A consideration
of instances where letters that do not survive as physical objects were
read out at vestry meetings or noted in minutes suggests no differences
in structure, intent, rhetoric, or content from the surviving corpus. In
some of these cases, letters were brought physically by the poor people
concerned, who thus made out their case simultaneously in writing and
orally, as we have already seen above. Cornelius Stovin, the overseer of
Hirst in Lincolnshire, for instance, seems to have expected people to
convey their letters *and* his directly to their home parishes.[45] Yet perhaps
the clearest evidence that surviving letters are representative of the wider
epistolary world from which they are drawn is provided by the parish
of Thrapston. Here, the overseer disposed of inward items of parochial
correspondence but copied the text of the discarded narratives, as well
as a selection of his own replies, into bound copy letter books. Although
these copies lack the random use of capitalisation likely to have been in
the originals, in all other respects they appear to be faithful copies of the
content, structure, and spelling. That there is no difference at all in the
characteristics of these letters versus those in the wider corpus does much
to confirm representativeness.[46]

Nonetheless, there are good reasons to think that the tactics adopted
by those who negotiated with their settlement parishes on paper might
differ from the tactics of those who could approach the overseer in person. When they did apply, the visual signifiers of need, despair, and hopelessness implicit in face-to-face encounters were missing from their
letters, and the matching responses of paternalistic humanism or Christian duty also went unrecorded. Moreover, it might be that claimants
writing from a distance, often to parishes where they had not been seen
for a while, would have to spend more time conveying their trustworthiness and deservingness than would someone applying in person, who
could be viewed easily by ratepayers and officials. And it could be argued
that analysing letters foregrounds the experiences, strategy, and rhetoric
of the "noisy poor" and those with the freedom to write. The representativeness of the letters of the poor in these terms depends in part upon
how many people were "out of their place" and thus potentially tied

into the out-parish relief system that largely generated such letters. Of course, no national perspective can be drawn, but table 1.1 suggests that this is a much more complex question than it at first seems. A village or inner-city parish could host *and* simultaneously be responsible for large numbers of people "out of place," or they might have none. In eighteenth-century Stratford-on-Avon, at least 25 per cent of all households were comprised of residents without settlement, and a large number of Stratford residents had migrated outwards, creating potential parochial liabilities (and thus letters) elsewhere.[47] For the North Riding of Yorkshire, the figures are even more compelling. Between 50 and 100 per cent of all pensioners notionally recorded in the overseers' accounts of some parishes were actually either nonresidents or physically present but the responsibility of parishes elsewhere.[48] Thus, although settlement and removal activity could be profound, the singular lesson for the parishes underpinning this study is that the out-parish relief system ensured that only a minority of those who could have been removed actually were.[49] Indeed, for some places, it is possible to argue that those who *remained* in their settlement parish were unrepresentative.[50]

It is also important when considering the representativeness of letter writers and the letters they wrote to remember that not all of those who applied for relief while resident in their settlement community did so in person. Some people in large or topographically difficult parishes, where it might take several hours to get to the seat of local power and back, wrote to officials. Such letters were carried by friends, relatives, neighbours, or work colleagues, and vestry minutes suggest that these people might also turn up to simply convey (and thus mediate) stories of need in their own voice. This was particularly true when applicants styled themselves as too old or sick to make even the shortest journey, a common enough claim among poor letter writers as well. A surprising number of the in-parish poor *both* appeared before the vestry or overseer *and* wrote letters, either contiguously or sequentially. The vestry minutes of Oundle, for instance, make a subtle distinction between the in-parish poor who "applied" for relief – that is, wrote notes, only a handful of which survive – and those who "attended" to make their case in person.[51] It seems unlikely that their rhetorical and strategic approaches would have been very different in either forum or different from those of the out-parish poor. There is thus a considerable risk of overemphasising the discreteness of oral and literate cultures.[52]

A simple dichotomy between the in- and out-parish poor is also misleading, offering the illusion of the in-parish poor as somehow a homogeneous group. In practice, whether individuals made their case at the vestry, overseer's office, or home, or simply accosted ratepayers in the street, might shape the language and strategy they employed as well as their capacities for negotiation. There is ample evidence that officials received, considered, and decided on cases while on the move and that visiting people in their own homes to negotiate relief was not uncommon. Indeed, vestries often directed such visits. Where recommendations and case histories were taken back to vestries by overseers after these encounters, the voices of officialdom melded with and mediated the voices of the poor and their advocates, much as happened in the out-parish system when overseers wrote about the poor from host communities. More widely, an analysis of extant vestry minutes suggests that when we control for the impossible, such as the fact that in-parish paupers could not threaten to come "home," those who made their cases to the vestry in different ways used the same strategic and rhetorical vehicles and exercised the same agency – on a spectrum from dogged perseverance to threats of calling in magistrates – as did those who wrote letters. The minuting process stripped people of their distinctive voices but not of their strategies and agency. This symmetry between the poor in different residential and settlement situations is perhaps not unexpected given the complex patterns of belonging signalled by table 1.1. There are also other reasons to expect more similarity than difference. Both the in- and out-parish poor faced two shared conundrums that ought to have shaped their claims-making strategy in similar ways: how to navigate entitlement in a system where there were few fixed rules and how to approach the different stages of the process of obtaining relief, including the decision to ask for help, making a case, appeals to higher authorities when unsuccessful, and the decision to accept relief. As I discuss further in chapter 11, this situation was particularly true of the aged, whose letters *and* appearances before the vestry share the basic rhetoric that a progressively decrepit old age equated to an absolute obligation for the parish to provide regular support.[53]

Thus, although the letters of the poor require careful use and judicious linkage to other forms of evidence, it seems clear that they can be yoked to the key questions outlined in chapter 1. Even if some historians are uncomfortable with the view that such letters provide us with an – or perhaps *the* – authentic voice of the poor, we can have confidence that they represent and embody a set of rhetorical and strategic models and approaches to agency that were recognisable across the spectrum of poor writers and by a range of recipients. Nonetheless, as historians, we still need to navigate the corpus. In particular, we need to understand the basic form of the pauper letter, the ways that we might seek to impose conceptual order on the data, and the place of individual letters or letter sets within a wider epistolary network focused on the parish. It is to these themes that the rest of the chapter turns.

## FORM AND CLASSIFICATION

The letters coalesce, as we have already seen, into the broad category of "oral writing," or alternatively epistolary literacy and skeletal communicative competence. Against this backdrop, as chapter 1 began to discuss, handwriting might be tight, fluent, and characterised by appropriate capitalisation and punctuation. Most handwriting, however, was of open form, contained misspelling on a spectrum from minor to unintelligible, lacked any semblance of punctuation, and used random capitalisation. Where series of letters survive for ostensibly the same person, we can see that writing was highly situational. Handwriting deteriorated with old age, sickness, and haste, and indeed some writers offered apology either for their inexperience in writing or for the particularly poor state of an individual letter. Such, for instance, was the case with John Hennis, who wrote to the parish of St Clements Dane in London on 4 March 1814 to ask for the return of his granddaughter from the parish workhouse. In a postscript, he added, "Sir I am very poorly for some days back I fear you cannot read this Scrawl."[54]

Whereas the style of the letters was irregular, their form, at least in the broadest sense, was often both regular and familiar. Surveying the whole corpus of English and Welsh material, it is clear that the majority opened and closed in highly structured and formulaic fashion.[55] In just one collection, from the cathedral town of Peterborough in central England, openings include: "Sir, I hope no offense for takeing the liberty of writeing to you"; "Sir I take the liberty to aquaint you"; "Gentlemen I am sorry the distress of the times forces me to implore your immediate assistance"; "Gentlemen, With much concern I again trouble you to beg"; and "I hope it will not be considered an intrusion to state."[56] Closing usually involved different permutations of "Your humble servant," followed by a signature, mark, or directions of address. The apologetic opening tone adopted by most of those writing for the first time is consistent with the discretionary nature of welfare under the Old Poor Law and also – particularly through closing phases such as "humble servant" – with wider Georgian and Hanoverian notions of respect, respectability, and patronage.[57] This formulaic approach is not confined to poor people. Epistolary advocates, professional men and women, and even officials themselves used similarly structured openings and closings during this period. For the poor, such structural and linguistic form reveals something of the heritage of the pauper letter in petitions to rich families or magistrates.[58]

Yet the letters of the poor are *not*, as chapter 1 began to argue, petitions. We see variety in the openings and closings of letters that reflected individual character, regional norms, and the situation of the writer. As Clare Brant reminds us, most writers had to think about the balance "of plain writing against polite writing; plain might offend, polite might be ignored."[59] William Dunkley wrote from Wisbech in Cambridgeshire to Peterborough on 11 April 1806, the second in a series of eight narratives. He closed his letter, much as one would expect from the petitionary or patronage traditions, with "sincere thanks for all past Favours and is greately oblige to you for the same." By contrast, his opening was much more direct and challenged the overseer: "Sir, I hope you will be as good as your word in regard of what you told my wife when she was over."[60] Other writers dropped any semblance of supplicatory greeting. John Horseford, writing from Boston in Lincolnshire to Peterborough on 20 October 1833, simply asked, "Gentlemen Overseers Will you be so kind as to send the Rent as the landlord as called for it and my wife is verey hill so I cold not rite before."[61] Richard Coates was downright terse when he wrote from Brighton in Sussex to Guildford in Surrey on 31 March 1826. Demanding his allowance, Coates would "thank you not to delay sending of two [quarters' allowance] Has I want it for my Landlord."[62]

Moreover, at the level of the individual letter, whatever the outline structure of greeting or sign-off, we see little of the structural regularity – apology, background, case, remedy – that might be expected of a petition. In fact, the poor knew the difference between the two forms of appeal. Elizabeth Wady wrote from Saville Row in London to her settlement parish of Worthing on 20 February 1835 with a classic petition. It opened with an apology – "I humble trust you will have the humanity and condescension to pardon this application to your benevolence" – and went on to make a case for her to receive arrears of welfare payments. She noted that a "kind friend" had "most humanely wrote a petition for me," which she now sent to her home parish.[63] Yet formal petitions of this sort truly stand out in the corpus for their rarity. Rather, writers variously quoted the law, threatened to come home, to exercise violence, or to revert to magistrates, called on officials to act as a friend, begged, cajoled, made sarcastic comments, apologised, and appropriated the voices of others in their support. Their individual letters exhibit little by way of developmental structure and share much with the letters that might have been exchanged between family members. Indeed, some parochial collections include letters to relatives, often written in the most breathless of tones, alongside those sent to officials.

Moving from individual narratives to *sets of letters* by the same person reveals the clearest distinction between petitionary-patronage traditions and these letters. Here, we invariably *do* see development of form, particularly where engaging and lengthy letters at the start and middle of an exchange are followed by the breathless and increasingly short note-like narratives of a correspondence that was closed by the death of the writer. We also see development of rhetoric and strategy.[64] Although these matters are taken up in later chapters, examples might include promises to become independent of the parish succeeded by narratives of decay or endogenous circumstances that prevented independence, as well as the appropriation of the voices of prior epistolary advocates by the later letters of a set of correspondence. The corpus thus poses complex interpretational problems. Notwithstanding their clear central purpose – to obtain, maintain, or extend relief payments in a discretionary system of welfare where every payment had an opportunity cost in higher local taxes for communities – one letter was *not* just like another in form, structure, purpose, or rhetoric.[65]

Unsurprisingly, historians have struggled to impose organisational and conceptual structure on community and, much more rarely, county collections. Thomas Sokoll argues that we must read the texts of the poor as "familiar letters" rooted in concepts of dynamic exchange and the construction of personal relationships.[66] This conceptual structure is not, however, unproblematic since familiarity in epistolary terms implies a hierarchical parity between writer and receiver.[67] Moreover, as Leonie Hannan reminds us, letters were often fluid in terms of form, mode, or genre and might be simultaneously communicative and performative. Although she was concerned with early modern female letter writers, these conclusions are clearly portable to the corpus of pauper, advocate, and overseer letters.[68] Clare Brant's understanding of "personal" letters as texts that "articulate in miniature the concerns of a wider society" or grouping might have more traction in this context.[69] Even here, however, the ostensibly unequal relationship between writer and recipient and the consequently strong performative and rhetorical colour of the letters of poor writers complicate simple classificatory structures. Andreas Würgler suggests an alternative approach, arguing that so-called "ordinary writing" might be classified as petitions, gravamina – that is, collective writing seeking relief from a load or burden – and supplications. The latter, which might encompass requests, demands, and complaints written by people anywhere in the local social structure, were narratives that recognised the discretionary power of the recipient.[70] This concept gets closer to the form and function of a pauper letter, but it still fails to do justice to the variety of writing and tonal qualities that we find in the letters used here.

Three core features of the corpus over and above its scale suggest that a new approach to organisational and conceptual structure is needed. The first is its sheer diversity. I juxtapose letters from as far north as the Scottish border towns to Lostwithiel in Cornwall and from coastal Wales to coastal Kent, with all of the consequences of such a distribution for highly localised dialect, traditions of writing and petitioning, and expectations of writers by officials.[71] Some letters are written in the Welsh language, whereas others are unintelligible in any language. The corpus brings together letters from the meanest beggar through to former ratepayers and parish officers. It melds letters written from London, and all that this context might imply for a more developed frame of rhetoric,[72] with letters from remote rural parishes that were little more than a random collection of houses. Flat conceptual labels such as the familiar letter or the supplication letter cannot do justice to this diversity. A second problem is that although the letters of the poor *are* intelligible as a genre, their content, intent, rhetoric, and structure can be truly understood only when they are set against other sorts of letter – overseers' correspondence, letters of epistolary advocates, notes from professionals, and letters between kin – that form part of the epistolary world in which writers were enmeshed. They are in part contingent documents. Existing conceptual and organisational models do not, arguably, have the flexibility to deal with this multigenre synthesis. In turn, a third and related issue is that these models attempt to do too much, confronting simultaneously matters of letter type, function, strategy, and rhetoric on the assumption that there is an inevitable relationship between these variables.

Table 2.1 offers a different conceptual approach. Encompassing the whole corpus of material from overseers' correspondence through to the letters of poor writers, it outlines classificatory structures based primarily upon their *type*, *function*, and *characteristics and tone*, with variables such as content, style, strategy, and the place of letters in the process of negotiating relief being subsidiary to these primary drivers. These variables are explored at greater length in chapter 7. For now, the letter types can be exemplified by dissecting the collections for West Sussex. *Instigatory letters* were written at the start of each discrete

Table 2.1
*Letter types and their function, characteristics, and tone*

| Type | Function | Characteristics and tone |
| --- | --- | --- |
| Instigatory | To start a story or to start it again after a break | More lengthy than other letter types, broad regularity of structure, consistent tone, and use of logos |
| Renewing | To extend the duration or intensity of relief | Block structure, submissive tone, and promises of return to independence |
| Extending | To change the type of relief | Assumed institutional memory, confidence, description of exogeny, shorter length, and core performative element |
| Testamentary | To state one's condition at any point in a relief history | Cases that speak for themselves, logos, implied right, respectful tone, and variable length |
| Desperate note | To convey a hopeless position at any point in a relief history | Owned by the poor, short on words, pathos, and supplicatory tone |
| Ending | To make a final statement (although it was not always such) | Often lengthy, reflective, pathos, assumed institutional memory, confidence, gloom, and a concern for those left behind |
| Interspersing | To follow up the writer's own correspondence or letters of advocates and officials at any point after an instigatory letter | Often lengthy, assumed rights and duties, confident tone, intermixing of pathos and logos, and fluid situational structure |

application for relief and might be sent by officials, advocates, or the poor themselves. Occasionally petitionary in tone, they usually opened much as Maria Longhurst did when she wrote from Brighton on 13 May 1802: "I am Sorrey to be under the Necistey of Troubling you but it is illness that as Drove me to it I have been ill for some time past but I am unable to Eren a Moral of Bread."[73] They were on average longer than other letter forms, something that is true across the spatial dimensions of the corpus. Instigatory letters might assume some residual institutional memory of prior claims or prior histories in and with parishes, but most followed a regular structural form of apology, justification, elaboration, desired outcome, close, and direction. *Renewing letters* were those that attempted to extend the duration or increase the intensity of relief already granted. When written by the poor, they invariably opened with apology and progressed to combine three blocks: account and recount, statements of exogenous conditions, and the "ask," which might encompass specific sums and allowances in kind or simply take the form of a request for a trifle or whatever the overseer thought best. Although their tone was essentially submissive, at the more robust end of the spectrum, they might include threats to come home or to use the law. One such instance is the letter of Joseph Smallwood, encountered earlier in this chapter, who wrote from Chichester on 15 November 1838 to seek a renewal of a prior allowance of 3 shillings per week:

> sorry that I am under the necessity of writing you for some assistance this winter as Bread is so dear and haveing a large family, and but little employment to be had during this season, I have twelve Children and Eight of them at home, the youngest 15 months old, two of the eight and myself have no employment, six of them not being the age to work, I hope and trust you will be so kind as to take my case into consideration as it is impossible for me to remain here without some assistance, if you would be kind enough to allow 3 shillings per week during this winter I should be very thankful, I have done the best I could to keep from the Parish as I know how hard it is to pay Poors Rates, I can asure you we have not had but one bit of meate to eat since last Harvest, be so kind as to have the

goodness to write me an answer to this as soon as Possible you can make it convenient, as the Majestrates said I had better write to the Overseers of Broadwater myself and if you thought proper not to relieve me I must be return'd by this Parish and sent home, which hope and trust will not be the case, I must once more beg of you to allow me a weekly allowance during this winter.[74]

Officials and advocates wrote similar renewing letters, and those from advocates in particular shared much of this base structure, often augmented by assurances that the writer would endeavour to contain the costs of any renewal or that the duration of the requested relief might be limited by death or full recovery. *Extending letters* are a subgenre of this form. Because they involved an attempt to move from one type of allowance to another – for instance, from ad hoc or otherwise constrained relief to the provision of encompassing and indefinite pensions – these letters had a distinctive tone. Although occasionally framed in terms of apology, most narratives of this sort tried to portray the decline into long-term dependence as inevitable and the requested parochial response as somehow natural. Writers rarely adopted the submissive tone and tropes that we see in renewing letters, having in their own minds nothing for which to apologise. Shorter than either institgatory or renewing letters, these narratives were framed by an assumed institutional memory of the case, and most were comprised of three distinct blocks: reminder of the original case; account of deterioration, which was often not associated with exogenous conditions, as in renewing letters; and the case for extension.[75] The majority of writers did not make an "ask," preferring to leave the need for a generous reaction as a liminal and unspoken ending. Advocates who wrote on behalf of the poor, and sometimes even officials, followed exactly the same structural and tonal path as poor writers themselves. In this sense, extending letters have a strong performative element compared to other letter types and irrespective of who the actual authors were.

*Testamentary letters* might be written and sent by the poor, overseers, or advocates at any point in the relief process, and they form a distinct and distinctive subgenre of letters. Their central function was to provide a statement of the condition or experience of a claimant, and writers invariably adopted the tonal qualities that we would usually associate with the provision of evidence as fact in a legal or depositionary context. Such letters did not, in the way that we see for renewing or extending narratives, seek to build a case, and thus in structural terms they tended to be relatively "simple," opening and closing with "standard" forms of address and then comprising a single core text that the author often assumed should speak for itself in terms of the appropriate reaction of officials. Mary Colderwood wrote such a letter from Brocklehurst in Hertfordshire to Peterborough on 6 December 1833. Opening with apologies for writing, she noted,

> I am in great distress, having four of my children still at home. My eldest daughter has been obliged to leave her place in consequence of being suddenly seized with villent fits, four persons cannot hold her during their continuance. One of my little boys has also met with an accident from the kick of a horse. *My troubles are indeed very great* and I *trust* you will have compassion on me.[76]

It is clear that Colderwood presumed the parish would recognise, without further elaboration, the necessity of supporting a woman burdened with four children, one of whom was subject to epilepsy.

At the opposite end of the spectrum, the *desperate note* forms a subgenre of the testamentary letter. It, too, might be sent at any point in the relief process, but it was particularly likely to be written at the end of a period of inadequate relief or nonresponse by officials and was particularly likely to be written by the poor rather than by others involved in the epistolary world of the parish. We know from vestry minutes that the desperate note had its equivalence in oral encounters as attendees drew attention to their hopeless position.[77] These notes were sometimes written onto cropped pages and always conveyed cropped text. Unlike their testamentary counterparts, they offered little evidence of the causation of the situation and instead focused in the bleakest and quickest terms on the immediacy of the position. One such instance is the letter of Jane Vinall written to Great Bookham in Surrey on 2 January 1834 to say, "I shall be greatly obliged to you to send my money as I am in great need of it, and my legs are so bad I cant get about much."[78] The *ending letter* is of a different genre compared to the desperate note. Written in anticipation of a final encounter with death or ruin, these letters involved reflective self-construction. Circumstances particular to the individual or family were entwined with universal conditions, notably old age, to inject a gloomy tone into the correspondence. These texts, akin in structure and intent to the resignation letters of modern politicians, meld together self-satisfaction, hope for those left behind, justification, and residual obligation in order to solicit from the recipient a reply that combined acknowledgment, support for the future, and obligation.

Finally, most letter series by or about individuals contain some form of *interspersing* correspondence. Where these letters were written by officials or advocates, they might combine three essential structural elements: reportage and reflection on the claimant, the relief history, or the nature of the epistolary conversation; a request to act or admonishment for not acting; and personal opinion on the case and/or the poor person. These sorts of letter were the most common form of the interspersing genre. Poor people, however, might also write such letters to add their voice to a letter set otherwise dominated by a case made through officials or advocates, as a deliberate follow-up to a letter sent by an advocate, or when acting as an advocate for husbands, wives, and children. These letters were structurally fluid, but they all embodied some combination of a recount, as in so-and-so has written to you; a call to action, as in you have not acted and should have done or you have agreed to act; a right to be heard; a summative statement, as in my condition has or has not changed since the last letter; and a threat of further action. Often written toward the tail end of a correspondence set, such letters could in a tonal sense be the most hostile in the corpus. In practice, of course, a set of letters related to or written by an individual might encompass some or all of the structural and intentional forms outlined here. Through their own endeavours or by appropriating the voices and influence of others, claimants had to continually restate, reimagine, and re-evidence their claims to be heard and considered deserving in a discretionary system. A single convincing claim was, for some writers, enough. We see a single letter and associated poor law dependence, and then the individual disappears forever. At certain life-cycle stages, during sickness, or as trades declined and died, however, a case had to be made and remade. Tone, structure, strategy, image, and story had to be right in the sense of being calibrated to the evidence presented, the intended recipient, and the history recounted. This was a skill, one we see powerfully played out in subsequent chapters, where multiple letter writers are frequently at the core of my analysis, and particularly in chapter 12, where I turn to the question of the creation of the pauper self.

## CONCLUSION

Martyn Lyons has argued that the English labouring poor were probably much more literate than has often been supposed or measured.[79] That their letters exist in large numbers and that many more were sent than have survived suggest that this is *definitely* the case. Writing by the poor was often highly "oral," and the grammatical structure of their letters is, to say the least, challenging, but the same might also be said of the official correspondence and the narratives of epistolary advocates that also form part of the corpus. Although there are many potential reasons to doubt the ownership of the authorial voice, the honesty of the letters received, and their representativeness, these doubts can be substantially overplayed. Indeed, this chapter has argued that most letters were written by the people who signed them and that a combination of surveillance mechanisms and the basic rules of epistolary exchange ensured that the information conveyed was broadly accurate and honest.

For historians, however, navigating this corpus is by no means easy. The letters of the poor are complex documents that entangle the reporting of fact, embellishment, appropriation of the voices of others, rhetorical flourishes, half-truths, a strong emotional backbone, and acts and structures of negotiation and performance. They must also be understood and read holistically, as part of a wider set of epistolary conversations at the parochial level. In form and rhetoric, these letters do not fit easily into broad existing genres, and it has been necessary to develop a new scheme of classification, one that dissociates rhetoric from form and intent but is fluid enough to encompass the whole epistolary conversation related to individual claimants. Rhetoric and strategy are the domain of part 3 of this study. This chapter has provided a better sense of the nature and dynamics of the corpus and a crude map of how historians might navigate it. Poor relief in this sense was undoubtedly a process rather than an act, one that demands new analysis if we are to understand the nature and role of the Old Poor Law and the real experiences of the poor who were enmeshed within it.

In turn, a core part of understanding those experiences is to return to some basic questions about the interface between claimants and their parishes. Where did the poor find the materials to write? What time could they devote to the act of writing? How did they convey letters and with what symbolism? How realistic was poor writers' hope that their letters would be received, read, and acted upon? Were they, in other words, part of a process of co-respondence, and can we trace what officials thought about the letters they received?[80] Where did the poor find the words that appeared on paper, and how did their linguistic register develop over time? Did poor writers, their advocates, and officials share a common linguistic register and an understanding of the grounds on which relief eligibility could be contested? Were the out-parish poor part of the same two-way conversation that in-parish paupers might have experienced when they turned up at the vestry or met the overseer in the street or his parlour? These themes are taken up in the four chapters of part 2, which collectively construct the process of poor relief as highly contested. Just as letters became a "subterranean mode of power" for the middling sorts of the eighteenth and early nineteenth centuries,[81] the process of writing and sending letters and having them received and considered by a "home" parish gave a new – and, as part 2 argues, a mutually agreed – agency to the poor at a time when the Old Poor Law is usually thought to have been in crisis mode.

# PART TWO

# *Contexts and Yardsticks*

# 3

## *Mundane Articles*

### OVERVIEW

The discretionary Old Poor Law was, for the actual and prospective poor, a complex system without any universal road map. They entered the negotiating space provided and framed by the process of poor relief as they decided *when* to apply for support. This was not an easy decision with an inevitable outcome, as I have already begun to suggest. Even people with severe or chronic sickness appear to have struggled to get by *before* they applied to the overseer.[1] Those with less clear moral or customary cases – the unemployed or underemployed, for instance[2] – were likely to have struggled even longer.[3] Chapter 8 revisits this matter at length. For most writers, it was a deterioration in illness or some other unexpected event, an unpayable bill, ubiquitous "little debts," or rent arrears that catapulted them into a relationship with the poor law. It is unclear whether the apologies for writing that framed many letters were genuine or simply reflected the unacknowledged but implicit agreement between officials and the poor on the conduct of negotiation – their epistolary ethics. Yet, given the range of consequences, guessable if essentially unpredictable, that might emerge out of an application in a discretionary welfare system, it seems unlikely that the decision to apply in the first place was a straightforward one. Indeed, the rhetoric of instigatory applications was partly aimed at hiving off the most negative potential reactions from officials, a point to which I return throughout this study. As Maarten van Ginderachter has concluded in the context of begging letters, the very decision of the poor to write was meant to convey misery.[4]

Once claimants had – on their own or in tandem with others[5] – taken the decision to engage with the poor law, the first major point in navigating the process of poor relief was *where* to send an instigatory or interspersing letter. Table 1.1 suggests this was not an easy or obvious matter. Indeed, Anne Crowther reminds us that for the out-parish poor "the decision on where to seek relief was a delicate one."[6] Some poor or prospective poor people had genuine doubts about where their settlement lay, particularly if that settlement was derived through marriage.[7] Mary Heywood, in an undated letter from Lambeth in London to Lostwithiel in Cornwall, claimed to be a widow with six children in hand, one of whom was disabled, and asked, "If you will please to send me thirty I hope I shall not be obligd to apply to you a gain." A draft of the overseer's reply,[8] again undated, threw doubt on the validity of the claim at the same time as its emendations suggest how complex and time-consuming overseers might find the epistolary framework in which they were engaged:

> In reply to your ~~request~~ letter the oversees have no power to grant you the assistance you have requested We ~~shall~~ do not ~~altogether~~ acknowledge you as belonging to this parish and before we are satisfied it is the case I will be necessary you should be examined by the officers of the parish in which you now are as we wish to know ~~what your husband has~~ how your husband has supported himself since he left this neighbourhood and to what acct he has rented.[9]

Other writers quite literally made up a settlement in order to apply for support in a parish that they had heard was generous, exploiting a yawning and (for parishes) expensive loophole in the law that in effect put the onus to prove someone was not settled on the parishes rather than the poor. Between these two contrasting poles, prospective applicants had to decide whether to apply by letter or in person to the (variously constituted)[10] authorities in their host parish, an epistolary advocate who would take up the initial case, or directly to the magistrate.

All of these options carried consequences for the nature of negotiation and agency that followed. Applying to a settlement parish risked instant removal "home," even more so in certain places or at times of economic stress. The parish of Llanasa in Flintshire, when faced with a request from John Williams and his family for support during illness, adopted the same tack as most other Welsh parishes when its overseer wrote to Hulme in Lancashire on 24 August 1836 to say,

> I understand John Williams and Family is still troubling you there-fore if the allowance they now get will not satisfy them I shall be obliged to you if you will when they are ready to come to the Parish of Llanasa to give the old people as much as will pay their way here as the Parishioners are determined not to give them any more than 3/ per week. They must live in their own Parish and will let them please themselves.[11]

Applying to a host parish, either initially or after a conversation had been started with a settlement parish, added a further layer of conse-quences. The official involved might immediately seek removal, either by instigating a settlement examination or by writing to a home parish to demand that it remove the person. If the case was a desperate one, and notably after changes to legislation in 1795, the overseer of the host parish might obtain a removal order but then suspend it, allowing him to provide support to the individual or family until the desperate condi-tions had resolved themselves, after which he would charge the settle-ment parish for this relief.[12] Or officials in the host parish might write on behalf of or about the individual, making the case for an allowance to be paid that would enable the claimant to remain in situ. This case is certainly what most applicants sought to argue and to get officials to argue on their behalf, and the regularity with which overseers did so is really very striking.[13]

A negotiation starting off in this fashion may have imbued a level of confidence in the home parish's view of the claimant that would not have been there had one applied in person. Indeed, some overseers' letters to claimants and officials in host parishes specifically refer to variants of recognition of the "worthiness of the signatures" appended to instigatory letters. The prospective poor might also apply to an advocate to make the case on their behalf for the same reasons, following up themselves with an interspersing letter. This common course of action, however, also carried dangers, not least the prospect that officials might call the bluff of the applicant *and* the advocate and dismiss the case, in effect putting two reputations on the line. These sorts of risk multiplied manyfold where poor people applied to magistrates before they applied to local officials or did so in defiance of local officials once a negotiation was begun. Magistrate orders are a common part of the source scaffolding in this project, and some overseer and vestry accounts are replete with allowances made "by order" of particularly interventionist magistrates. But magistrate support for individual paupers had distinct limits and major risks.[14]

These individual choices are well established in the historiographical literature. What table 1.1 makes clear, however, is that for most communities and at most times, there would have been multiple families and individuals struggling with the decision of where to apply, all shaping their stories accordingly. These same people would have neighbours, kin, and friends who had confronted the same decision, and they might approach advocates who had made multiple cases before. There was, in other words, inevitably a stock of community knowledge on these issues akin to the guidance manuals purchased by overseers in ever greater volumes from the later eighteenth century onward.[15] Having drawn on that knowledge, the poor and prospective poor, as the next stage in navigating the negotiation process, undertook to actually write or obtain a letter and then to send it. In the case of the middling sorts and aristocrats who have underpinned the burgeoning historiographical work on early modern epistolarity, the practical issues involved in these acts were an afterthought.[16] Paper was purchased from travellers, by mail order, or increasingly in a variety of fixed outlets such as the shops of booksellers. Ink and quills came from similar sources.[17] Elite groups set aside specific times and areas for writing and inscribed acts of love, resistance, power, and friendship in what they wrote. Letters might be sent by post, servant, or confidante. Mary Favret has labelled the accoutrements of composition "these mundane articles."[18] Yet, for the very poor, questions of where to obtain paper, ink, and quills were much more complex and consequential, as were questions of where to find the time and space to write, how to convey letters, and how to be sure of receiving replies.[19] How and where the poor found paper probably affected what they wrote. Compared to lengthier and more considered instigatory letters, hastily written notes took less time and dedicated writing space but might influence the way that the recipients then thought about the writers throughout their subsequent engagements. Letters that came for free, conveyed by carters or coachmen, were probably better received than those for which parish officials had to pay, especially where a correspondence was sustained. All of these things might touch upon the tone of negotiation and the breadth of the ground for pauper agency, implicitly influencing what was recorded in the end-of-process overseers' accounts that still, as we saw in chapter 1, shape our perception of the nature and role of the Old Poor Law. For the poorest, and thus for those on the lowest rung of the English and Welsh literacy ladder, nothing was mundane in this next step of the negotiation process.[20]

Against this backdrop, the focus of the current chapter is on the basic materiality of letter writing. The next section asks where the poor found their raw materials for writing and shows that sourcing paper and ink was by no means a simple task. Nonetheless, surprisingly few narratives were written on low-quality scraps of paper with bad ink. In turn, finding the right paper took poor people into the public domain, such that the act of writing became a public rather than a private event even if a letter was composed by a single person. The chapter then moves on to consider the time dimensions of letter writing, arguing that the poor set aside dedicated time for writing. They also put considerable thought into the timing of instigatory or renewing letters, understanding that timing and reception were strongly interlinked in a discretionary welfare system. The final section of the chapter moves on to acts of conveying and receiving replies. It shows that both procedures shaped the negotiation process and what was written in the letters themselves.

## PAPER, INK, AND PENS

It would be easy to assume that claimants wrote on any scrap of paper they could find. This was not the case. Figures 3.1 and 3.2 locate the two ends of the material spectrum, the first being a short note on a cropped piece of clearly recycled paper of the poorest quality and the second being a longer letter on heavy paper that retains the original folds after almost two centuries of storage. Most letters fell toward the better end of this spectrum, written on discrete (rather than cropped) sheets of paper with no evidence at all of recycling. This is perhaps not surprising when we understand that scraps of paper themselves had a value for things like the wrapping of cheese and butter, such that they were in fact worth stealing. Scrap paper, in other words, was unlikely to have been plentifully available in a form – that is, not already printed or written upon – useable by poor writers.[21] Moreover, although there are good logical reasons to expect spatial and chronological variations in the nature and quality of the paper used – paper might have been harder to come by in rural Wales than in London, and the proliferation of potential paper suppliers by the early nineteenth century might have made decent paper cheaper and more accessible – there is no sustained evidence for this assumption. Indeed, there is little material difference between the paper used by the poor and that used by most of the advocates who wrote on their behalf where they exist in the same archive. In fact, the narratives of the poor as material objects resemble emigrant or other personal letters.[22] The one exception to this observation is notes or testaments from doctors on the state of sick people, which seem to have been commonly written on scraps of recycled paper akin to receipts sent to overseers by local tradesmen acknowledging payment for supplies of bread or tea.

Once a poor person had made the decision to apply for support, where did the paper for the letter come from? This is more than a mundane question since the act of seeking out paper might bring the poor person into contact with those who would contribute to such a letter. Not finding paper would necessitate a journey to the settlement parish in person or might require the potential writer to locate an advocate.

Finding the wrong sort of paper – too high or low in quality, for instance – might convey an unintended but obvious message to the recipient. The simple act of sitting down with a sheet of paper, then, had symbolism and meaning for the process of negotiation and the ability to exercise agency.[23] Against this backdrop, we can be clear that the poor did not usually "keep by" stocks of paper even if they had quills and ink available. Joseph Harley's analysis of pauper inventories from Dorset provides no evidence at all of the existence of paper stocks.[24] This finding is perhaps not unexpected given the often damp, overcrowded, vermin-infested, and chaotic housing conditions described by the poor in their own letters or by outside commentators.[25] Preserving and renewing paper in this context would have been a significant task. This observation can be set against the sustained writing of individuals like John Swails of Leicester in Leicestershire, who "has constantly been writing for some allowance for the last 2 years," and like John Lines, who was warned by the overseer of Oundle in Northamptonshire in November 1834 that "in future One letter will be sufficient without having to pay postage unnecessarily our exp[enses] are great enough without adding to them."[26] These instances, which could be reproduced hundreds of times for diverse parts of the country, point to the fact that the poor *could* access supplies of paper. Some of these sources are obvious: claimants and applicants wrote from ships, prisons, hospitals, work-houses, army barracks, and other institutional contexts that one might expect to have kept stocks of paper.[27] With surprising frequency, they also wrote from the offices of overseers or other local officials, who clearly provided paper, ink, pens, and a desk.

Three other means of obtaining paper emerge subtly from the corpus or the surrounding scaffold of sources. The first was from advocates. Perhaps not unreasonably in deciding what to analyse or reproduce, historians have made a distinction between the narratives of poor writers and the letters signed by advocates.[28] This distinction, however, misses those situations in which writers encountered landlords, doctors, employers, and others, told their stories, and were then encouraged to write them down in their own hand. In these cases, it seems clear that the pseudo-advocate supplied the paper. Thus Mark Illif of Leicester "stated

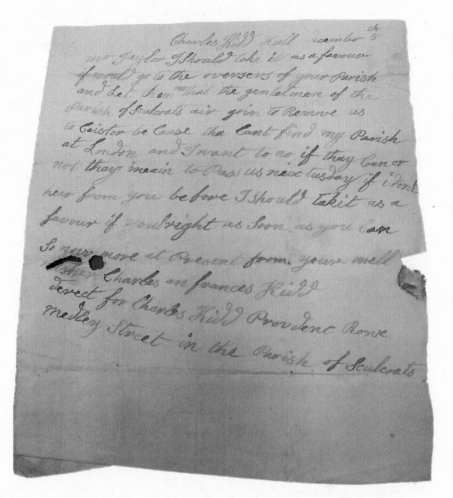

3.1 A cropped note with an unsharpened pen. LIRO 13/2/57.

3.2 *Opposite* A letter written on higher-quality paper. LIRO 13/2/23.

my Case to my Landlord Mr William Harrison, who advised me to apply to you for assistance," which he did and on paper resembling that used by Harrison himself in advocate letters.[29] Other landlords might be more aggressive. John Pearson could not "lay aney blame to my Landlord for going to distris me for" unpaid rent when he wrote from Whitehaven in

to the Overseers
of Caistor

Over

December 23  1831 Louth  in a very poor
Sir I write to let you  in a very
bad State of health I have been confined
to my bed a 11 weeks and is not likely
to get any better and my wife is a very
poor creature we can hardly do for our selves
I hope you will be so kind as thank god
is very thing so re dent and we have so
so every thing do we re dent and as for me cannot
tell I do without ell her week to attend me
is left I am almost ell her week you must
and my wife is never fort week you must
thank how we are likely to the poor with
we so hard is to think they is be so kind as
to send by the likely they have come for
to yourself they will make us pray old and
we have enough to pray with we cannot get
we have received by pound and
what any remains to pray got
I hope you will remember me
best for themes Smith gentlemans
your humble Servt
J Smith

23

Cumberland on 16 February 1812, and it is hard to escape the sense that the letter was written with the landlord standing behind Pearson and on paper supplied by him.[30] When Stephen Dickman wrote from Pembury in Surrey on 21 May 1821 on the subject of John Batchelor, he noted that Batchelor "sits by me and says he woud come & see you but he is too lame to Ride or Walk."[31] Nor should we neglect the possibility or probability that people left the homes or premises of advocates clutching paper for follow-up letters, as for instance did James Howe of Birmingham on 1 June 1800.[32]

A second important, although more amorphous, source of supply was the leisure and business spaces that paupers encountered in their everyday lives. John Payne, an innkeeper of Southampton, revealed something of this in a 1771 letter to the overseers of Stockbridge in Hampshire on the subject of "the Poor Widdow Froud." Implying that her letters had been constructed at the inn, he sought to prick their conscience, noting that "she is attended the Inn Severiall times & as Rec$^d$. nothing therefore is Doubtfull weather you Rec$^d$. the Letter otherwise She thinks you whould have considered her Deploreable condition."[33] Elizabeth Brown wrote from "Mrs Terrys Eating House, High Street, Gosport" to Lyndhurst on 24 October 1828, "being totally destitute of every necessary of life ... which prevents my going about as usual with my Basket for a livelihood."[34] It seems clear that Brown found her paper at the eating house. At the other end of the country, letters by or about Joseph Nelson were sent from or received at John Nicholson's stationary shop, a substantial hint at where the paper for letters may have come from.[35] In Essex, David and Sarah Rivenall asked in their letter of 27 February 1826 that payments of relief be sent to the cheesemonger Charles Savill, a man who might be expected to have copious amounts of paper for wrapping.[36] Although direct statements are relatively uncommon in the corpus, the implication that a significant amount of paper for the letters of poor writers came from commercial premises is clear.

Finally, some of the poor took opportunities to garner paper when they came across it by chance. Joseph Bailey of Hammersmith in London "Took this opartuty" to write to his parish asking for help with clothing when he was passing Mr Green's bookshop in Hammersmith, and he directed the overseers to write to him there in their turn.[37] William Smith wrote to his father at Nuffield Cross in Surrey from a coaching inn on 16 April 1830 while en route to Guy's Hospital to have his hand amputated "next Tuesday."[38] Samuel White had previously taken advantage of an encounter with the bookseller Mr Bass of Halstead in Essex to obtain both paper and help with writing, noting in his interspersing letter of 26 January 1826 that "as I am now able to write myself I thought I would not impose on the kindness of Mr Bass by troubling him to write to you again."[39] Finding paper thus took effort and imagination. The act of finding some was an important navigation point for claimants. Just as the letters they wrote were public documents, the need to find the paper on which they wrote tended to take prospective paupers out of the domestic context. Whereas for middling women "letters linked home and household with other spaces or networks of exchange," the need for the poor to leave home to obtain paper separated the domestic space from the act of writing and made writing a more planned task.[40] Necessarily, then, writing was also a public or semi-public act in a significant number of cases.

Unsurprisingly, where authors found paper, they also tended to find ink.[41] Jane Hills must have actively sought out people who would have paper and ink as well as literacy, noting in her letter of 7 July 1824 that "I can neither Read nor write and ham Abbot to Trouble some body every Time to write."[42] Matt Younge, writing from an unknown address to Tilehurst in Berkshire at 5:30 PM on Friday, 19 March 1823 – details that were intended to show the urgency of the case and his precision in addressing officials – was even more explicit. He wanted to "write you a hasty line which I go into a Shop to do lest I miss the Post," a clear indication that ink, pens, and paper were to be had in even ordinary shops.[43] Such avenues were clearly tried, tested, and of no mean standing. If one allows for the fading associated with the age and inadequate storage of letters, the corpus shows remarkably little variation in the quality of ink. The letters of poor writers look in this sense much like those sent by overseers and advocates, although the ink is rarely as sharp as in some of the middling family letters that form the bedrock of the construction of epistolary communities in England during this period.[44]

The colour of ink occasionally varies within letters, but this almost always reflects emendation in another hand. By way of example, an unknown person added "Dec 1829" in red ink to a letter wholly written in black and in a different hand purporting to be Elizabeth Millard, writing from her hospital bed at the Gloucester Infirmary.[45] In contrast, pens were potentially more portable and durable than either ink or paper.[46] The Banbury shoemaker George Herbert noted of the 1820s that "there were no steel pens then, and every boy used to carry his penknife in his pocket, and all were taught how to make and mend his own pens."[47] Sometimes, this process can be seen in action. In another letter from Mrs Terry's Eating House on 14 August 1829, Elizabeth Brown clearly sharpened her pen midway through writing so that she was able to insert superscript notes, thereafter writing in a hand that was finer and more regular than in the opening lines.[48] The claimant John Davis of Blandford in Dorset probably carried his pen with him. Noting in a series of letters that his family had been reduced to living in one room with no furniture, he had clearly left the confines of the domestic situation to write. However, his letters very deliberately drew attention to the fact that he was taking up "My pen to Address you" and sought to convey "the Case Wich We are at this Moment that I now Write."[49] Writing implements might also be borrowed. Ann Viner borrowed hers from the baker Mr Purcey, implying that she would have no use for one of her own because "I am sorry to say my hands are so contracted that I can hardly hold the Pen." She had hoped that the overseer of Windsor would "Call on you on my account I thought it wold be the same as writing," but having been disappointed in such an expectation, she now wrote a letter that represented a considerable task and sacrifice of pain as well as emotion.[50]

The corpus in turn demonstrates little chronological or spatial variation in penmanship, at least insofar as such variation can be distinguished from that caused by the confidence injected into the act of writing. Most community collections contain a spectrum of examples, from the strong flourishing strokes associated with sustained literacy and a good, regularly sharpened nib to the weak hand associated with poor confidence and poor implements. Occasionally, as with Jane Gosney, who wrote from Southampton to ask her father and mother to chase up an allowance from the overseers of Brockenhurst, both in Hampshire, on 7 March 1812, writers can be seen running out of confidence or time. After saying that she "know not what I shuld do," the hand runs out and the letter is continued to a conclusion in a different, more confident, but not more literate hand.[51] The material, physical, and emotional experience of letter writing thus posed common problems for the poor across the spectrum of our material. They did write, but the act of writing itself entailed investments of time, energy, and perhaps credit and reputation as well as investments of cost, such that writing was not an act lightly undertaken.[52] Sometimes, poor writers themselves elaborated upon this matter, as did Matty Lewes, writing from Forton to Kirkby Lonsdale in Westmorland on 4 October 1809 to remind the overseer that he had not sent her allowance and to ask that he be punctual in the future so that "I need not have to Rite about it a Gain as it is truble Both to you and me."[53]

## TIME(S) TO WRITE

How long it took to write an average letter is unclear, a tripartite function of the skill of the writer, the emotional and physical context of writing, and the degree to which others were involved. Even if one allows for physical material decay over time, some letters were clearly written swiftly given the text size and the negligible imprint of the nib upon the page. Such letters feel essentially breathless when read aloud. John Taylor's undated letter from Portsea in Hampshire is representative: his four lines contained an apology for writing, the cause of his need, which was unemployment, sincere thanks for past favours, a note on the condition of his family, and a request "for a trifell more."[54] Occasionally, authors indicate that they wrote and dispatched in haste. William Addison's letter from Lancaster in Lancashire on 1 February 1817 was written because his creditors "have sent [the] bailiffs to day to my house," and he urged rapid action by the officials of his settlement parish, marking the outside "with speed" to emphasise the perilous situation in which he found himself.[55]

In most cases, however, we can see more deliberation inscribed into the production of the documents. Only a small minority of all letters provide evidence – differences of strength of line, different impressions on the paper, variation in handwriting, or different quality or shades of ink – that they were written in stages as opposed to a single sitting. The light presence in the letter corpus of crossing-out, subscript and superscript additions, and smudging suggests a more considered and concentrated writing experience.[56] Although many letters had postscripts or testimony by others attached to them prior to sending or contained text written onto them subsequently, the writers themselves seem to have had few substantive afterthoughts worth a formal postscript. And unlike the writers of similar sorts of document on the Continent or some familial correspondence in England and Wales, the poor did not generally write into margins or attempt to squeeze too much text into the foot or head of pages.[57] They also seem to have been able to maintain a straight(ish) line across the page, unlike the "ordinary" autobiographers, letter writers, and diarists encountered by Martyn Lyons for Continental Europe.[58] There is, in other words, a sense that poor people saw writing a letter as an event of a sustained nature that required them to carve out time from their everyday tasks.[59] In a modern sense, setting aside concentrated time for a task inscribes it with more meaning and perhaps emotional significance than something done "on the hoof." There is no reason to suppose that the experience was any different for our poor writers. They assumed, as chapter 2 suggested, that the act of writing was in itself evidence of the intensity of their need. The reactions when officials did not reply or reply promptly – ranging across a spectrum from outright anger to incomprehension – were thus more than mere rhetoric.[60]

The importance of time for, and the timing of, the negotiation process does not, however, end here. Nor was it an issue just for the out-parish poor. Controlling for national trade crises and local smallpox epidemics, there is a clear and unambiguous bias in the dating of letters of all sorts toward the autumn and winter months. This finding is perhaps unsurprising and also applies to the volume of business at vestries. Bad weather disrupted work, particularly where that work was casual, exacerbated the impact of poor housing, caused and intensified illnesses, and magnified the perceived and actual burdens of old age. Similar biases in the seasonal distribution of relief as recorded in end-of-process overseers' accounts suggest that officials themselves *must* have expected a seasonal surge in instigatory, extending, and other writing. Positively or negatively, their mindset over how competing obligations to ratepayers and recipients were to be balanced must have changed on a seasonal basis. It is for this reason that we see letters replete with seasonal rhetoric. Jane Buckeridge, writing from Lambeth in London to Pangbourne in Berkshire on 22 February 1827, is typical. Her instigatory letter begged

> to be excused for troubling you but old age and the Inclemency of the wether as compeled me to do it. I should be verry thankfull if the Gentlemen Overseers will be kind enough to allow me a little Money to Purches some Extra Covering for my Bed for the wether is so severe I am nither warm night nor day God knows I shall not trouble you long for any thing, as I am confined to the house and Death I hope will soon release me from all trouble.[61]

It would be easy to see these references as essentially calculating, reflecting a general sense that winter had come and the purse of the overseer might thus be more liberal. Nonetheless, where we have series of letters from the same writers, there is no obvious patterning to precise months of application, suggesting that authors did in fact tell the truth about weather conditions. Some went even further, timing their letters to the state of the weather in the home parish, part of a wider process by which claimants at a distance sought, processed, and used intelligence from "home" to increase the bite of their negotiations. Charles Wild, writing to Lyndhurst parish in Hampshire on 11 February 1830, is typical of this group of claimants. He told the overseer that it was "well known that I have been Drove to every Distress and Wretchedness in Lyndhurst" and that he had "Experienced More hardships and hunger – This Winter than ever I did in my livetime," such that he been forced to decamp to Brighton, from where he now wrote.[62]

A second aspect of timing centres on the question of when a letter – or for in-parish claimants, an approach in person – was best received. It is tempting to regard the arrival of letters as essentially random, not least because some overseers saw them in this way. Yet the content of narratives often suggests more sophistication. Sarah South wrote an ending letter from Brighton on 10 September 1825 to ask for relief because "my little Children now lays dead and they must be inter'd on Monday as we Cannot keep them any longer, the One Died on Monday last, and the other yesterday." She noted that "the Expence of Burial &c. is so Expensive, that I cannot Clear it Without assistance." Acknowledging that she had missed the last scheduled vestry, South was taking "the liberty of Writing to you as you might wish to call a Vestry."[63] That South had an understanding of the schedule of vestries in her settlement parish is important and clearly both influenced the timing of her letter and informed a sense that extreme need ought to make the rules of parish relief malleable and movable. Moreover, some writers seem to have known when overseers would be in the locality of their host community. They occasionally admonished these officials for not calling to check on them but also took these opportunities of missed visits to write letters that sought to extend a case. Thus Robert Lawson wrote to his settlement parish from Lancaster on 17 March 1813 to say that he had heard that the overseer "have Been over at Lancaster and I should have Been vere glad to have seen you." As the overseer had not had the courtesy to call and as Lawson had "allweas don my endevers for to pot the Gentelmen to as Letle expence as I posebely Could," he now made an extended case for permanent relief based upon his age, contribution, and persistent sickness.[64] In part, the prospective poor knew this information because, from the late eighteenth century onward, their host and settlement communities were connected by significant networks of carriers and other regular travellers who conveyed news and gossip as well as people and goods. The arrival and departure of this group, as seen below, affected the timing of conveyance and writing. It also influenced what was written, giving poor claimants like Robert Weale connectivity to their home community and a basis for strategy and rhetoric that they would not otherwise have had. Writing from Matlock in Derbyshire to Rothersthorpe in Northamptonshire, Weale had heard from the paper seller "John Pratt that you are Bowed Down with the claims of the Poor." He wanted to assure his co-respondent, John Davis, that "I am not a Poor Man by choosing and want to Call on My parish to the smallest Part." Closing, he once again referred to Mr Pratt's intelligence and asked that "My Parish do not at this Moment forget me."[65] Of course, the best laid plans of poor applicants went awry, with letters lost or delayed in the post or sometimes sitting unopened in the overseer's office.[66] Yet it is clear that some writers at least could and did understand the importance of the timed arrival of their letters.

Poor writers also, however, had to consider the frequency and spacing of correspondence. Doing so was not easy. The corpus of overseers' correspondence and vestry minutes contains more than forty examples of officials expressing exasperation at the intensity of correspondence from individuals. Thomas Ward, the overseer of Earls Barton in Northamptonshire filed a letter – probably because it was given to him as evidence or for advice – from Oundle dated 12 July 1834. Directed to Widow Gamly, it said, "If you will call at Messers Barclay & Co Lombard Street you may receive one sovereign. Our vestry has desired me to say they think you ought not to have troubled them as soon as you have done."[67] Unsurprisingly, the cost and trouble of receiving multiple letters posed a threat to the credibility of writers in the eyes of officials, and the analogue of the letter retained by Ward is frequent apologies from the poor for sending follow-up letters where no reply had been received or for writing again so soon after they had received their last allowance. An unnamed claimant wrote to "Mister smith" via the "Croft Nigh[t] Barge" asking for help with buying clothes. This was one of a series of undated letters to the parish of Croft in Lincolnshire from the same person, or at least in the same hand, and its writer asked, "ples dont be angry at me sending it [the letter] by the post" so soon after the last writing.[68] Not all correspondents, however, were apologetic. In her letter of 21 October 1825, Hannah Mills noted that she had been ill and was thus writing for prompt payment of her allowance. She went on to say, "you Spoke in your last letter why i wrote so soon, you might see by the letters i sent that i did not write before the proper time I would not be so troblesome now but i ham very much in want at the sooner you can ~~send the~~ send if you would be so kind the better."[69] Mills was instituted in a relationship involving the exchange of self-referential letters; she remembered the timing and content of letters from her side of the relationship and assumed that the framework of exchange was contestable and organic. Indeed, most of the serial letter writers seem to have assumed that frequent exchange of letters with officials was acceptable, and they found the limits to this assumption only when their letters went unanswered or when they were admonished by officials.

Those involved in sustained correspondence also struggled with a related issue of timing, which is how much they could and should expect officials to remember. Where writers knew that an overseer had left office since their last letter, they could legitimately, although not extensively, recap their case and relief history.[70] Agnes Gilbert, writing to Crowland in Lincolnshire on 26 April 1814, is representative. Addressing the new overseer, John Harts, she had taken "liberty hopeing no offence in so doing for my Case is been verry harde" and proceeded both to outline the basis for previous support and to request that he "Ade mee soam Assistance" to reflect new burdens.[71] A variant of such letters consisted of those sent to former officials to protest that the writer did not know the new officials – which was almost certainly untrue given the information networks into which most poor people seem to have been fixed – and to ask that the recipient either convey the writer's request or intercede with the new officials. The situation was rather more uncertain where officials remained in office. In these cases, a considerable interlude between letters always occasioned the remaking of a history, usually with the positive tone occasioned by having made do for a period without parochial support.

Shorter correspondence periods were more difficult to deal with. Some writers took up the broad thread of prior letters, and insofar as they referred to their history, it was to simply remind the overseer that he already knew an unspecified combination of burdens faced by the applicant. Other letters – notably those that followed the prior letter of an epistolary advocate or a visit in person to the parish and those that told of a sudden deterioration in the writer's circumstances – might recount a lengthier history. Stephen Orrill, for instance, having attended Mr Jackson the carrier, wrote from Nottingham on 16 April 1829 expecting some relief from his settlement parish. Being disappointed, he retold his own story of unemployment and sickness but noted that it had been much worsened by the fact that his "wife and Children are very ill, through coming from Mansfield in the rain they have caught cold," forcing him to pawn everything to pay for their treatment.[72] In many ways, Orrill was working out his case for relief as he wrote his back history – in this case, for a third time – which is consistent with a sense that letters allowed the poor to construct themselves in emotional and identity terms, much as they did the same for other social groups.[73] I return to this issue in chapter 12. Other applicants had a rather keener grasp of their stories and the utility of telling them; "history" was deliberately rather than randomly placed, and it was shaped by what the writer expected the recipient to want and by the place of an individual letter in a train of correspondence. Timing, then, shaped what was in these letters, how they might be received, and the nature of the negotiation process that followed.

## ACTS OF CONVEYING

Once prospective and actual claimants had written their letters, the next act of navigation was the decision over how it was best conveyed. Clare Brant argues that "the rich, the poor and the impatient sent letters by various kinds of messenger."[74] To some extent, and particularly in the earlier part of the period covered by this study, the decision was situational. Proximity to transport and postal infrastructure widened or narrowed the options for conveyance. Whether writers were housebound or mobile had similar effects.[75] Urgent letters would have fewer carriage options than those that could wait. Writers who were closer to their settlement parishes probably had more options than those who were more distant. Those writing from Wales, particularly North Wales, seem to have had fewer options than their English or South Wales counterparts. And prior negative experience with one form of conveyance – particularly the loss or delay of post – would inevitably shape or constrain its use thereafter. Indeed, the poor and prospective poor set great store in their writing on the reliability of transmission given the insistent need their letters often outlined. Nonetheless, that any given letter sent by or about a single person usually contained narratives arriving through a variety of avenues suggests the existence of a complex experiential framework across a spectrum from sheer chance to planned postal events.

Some forms of conveyance were unusual, such as barges and steamers in eastern England or Welsh coastal areas, Smithfield porters in London, wagons carrying foundling children to nurses in the home counties, butter and butcher wagons, unspecified "private hands," the showmen of the Kingston Fair in London in 1824, and pinned to woolsacks. Three more familiar methods, however, dominate the sending of letters: hand delivery by a trusted carrier, usually referred to as "the bearer" in overseers' correspondence, vestry minutes, and the notes of epistolary advocates; paid-for postal delivery by carriers, horsemen, or coachmen; and, whether paid for or otherwise, conveyance through networks of tradesmen, officials, and retailers. Although it is tempting to view these as equivalents in terms of the simple collection and delivery of material objects, they in fact carried different time and organisational implications for writers, differing significance for the way that writer and recipient understood agency and the nature of negotiation, and very different symbolic value for both parties.[76]

Around 13 per cent of all letters arrived in person by bearer. There seems to have been little variation in this approach by letter type or area, although it is clear that communities with a cohort of poor people at greater distance tended to receive fewer letters of this sort. Narratives arriving by bearer sent an important and multilayered message. This mode of conveyance simultaneously emphasised the connectedness of writers to their host and settlement communities, applied an extra indicator of legitimacy to the message conveyed, and emphasised the urgency of the case. The in-parish poor might also send bearers to deliver written notes or to make their case, as I argued in chapter 2. Indeed, this is a generic mode, common to correspondence between overseers themselves and between overseers and epistolary advocates, allowing writers to apply pressure to recipients by asking them to reply by the bearer. How often officials did in fact succumb to pressure for an instant reply is not clear from the corpus, but the lack of immediate follow-up correspondence in most cases of bearer letters suggests some susceptibility. This matter is revisited in chapter 4. The rhetorical structure and content of these sorts of bearer narrative were not systematically distinctive compared to those sent by other means, but they often elaborated upon the onset of a sudden or enhanced need that had left the person in a dark place. For instance, rent arrears and sickness were particularly likely to be referenced in ending, extending, or desperate letters conveyed by hand. There was, however, no systematic relationship between the nature and scale of the "ask" and the mode of conveyance.

The number of letters sent formally by paid-for post increased absolutely and relatively in the later years covered by the corpus. This finding is consistent with existing chronologies for the developing scale, reduced costs, and increased reliability of postal services.[77] Brant thus argues that "labouring-class people found money for letters they could ill afford," and Susan Whyman suggests that ordinary people had a "deep knowledge" of postal practice.[78] David Vincent, as we saw in chapter 2, is rather less convinced. He notes that as late as 1839 the number of letters delivered annually per capita was only four.[79] This view finds resonance with contemporary memorialists. George Herbert, encountered earlier, suggested that even by 1836 being a postman was "an easy berth" because sending letters was expensive and volumes for ordinary people were therefore low.[80] Yet, if the penny post and the true democratisation of correspondence lie beyond the period covered here, it is clear from the complaints of overseers about the costs of receiving letters, noted above, that the potential and actual poor had a firm grasp on the value and use of postal services.[81] This is not to say that conveying letters by post was unproblematic. Those charged with organising the censuses for early-nineteenth-century England found a "bewildering mosaic of administrative units" and hence postal addresses. The 1811 census identified 10,674 parishes but almost 5,000 further hamlets or townships and numerous extra-parochial places as well. By 1841 the census organisers had identified 25,000 separate places, most of which administered some form of relief and required an address if they were to receive correspondence.[82] The scope for misdirection is clear, and both officials and the poor episodically complained of lost post.[83] Nonetheless, poor writers seem to have invested real confidence in the post, as did Joseph Wheeler, writing to Pangbourne in Berkshire in January 1829, who asked that "you may send it [relief] by post I shall be *sure* to Receive it ... you will greatly oblige by sending by Saturday as we are quite out."[84] Where directions for a rapid reply by return of paid-for post went unrealised, writers were enabled to respond with an extending narrative of the time and emotional energy taken up by waiting.[85] Letters by post, one might argue, placed a framework of formality around the appeals of the poor, even as they lacked the symbolic urgency of those carried by hand. They also focused the nature of agency much more keenly on the relationship between the writer and official, without the intervention of third-party bearers or other carriers.

A third method of conveyance was deeply inscribed into the wider social and economic networks of parishes and communities. Just as officials used tradespeople, carters, coachmen, bankers, innkeepers, and market traders to convey their own messages, cash, and formal documents, claimants had access to exactly the same networks and people. This co-usage extended into requested and invited surveillance, and there is a clear sense from the scaffolding of overseers' correspondence that officials placed sustained trust in this network of individuals and firms. Arranging carriage of letters via these same networks and asking for relief and further correspondence to be returned in like manner thus carried symbolic importance for all parties. The relationships between poor writers and individuals within this network of conveyance could be both extended and intensive. It might even include those who conveyed letters proffering opinion on the legitimacy of the claims made or the intensity of the need they had witnessed. These individuals might also tacitly agree to have their opinions requisitioned for the purpose of a letter, as in "so-and-so thinks that." Thus Ann Slater wrote from an unknown host parish to Horncastle in Lincolnshire in 1799 to call attention to the missed payment of allowance, noting that "the carier called for it" and was annoyed at being inconvenienced.[86] A failure to reply using these informal channels of communication also occasioned letters from epistolary advocates. Most were actively sought and planned, but some were solicited as a result of chance encounters of people who had gone to seek news or relief that they had assumed would be coming in with tradesmen or carriers.

Conveying letters, then, was not a simple or insignificant act in the process of poor relief and the exploitation of spaces for agency and negotiation. It was the first step in formalising the tripartite relief relationship between poor applicant, official, and parish.[87] How letters were conveyed carried symbolism and might have shaped the way they were received as acts of negotiation even before they were opened. The groans of some officials when confronted by another letter from serial writers such as Frances Soundy are almost palpable, and the temptation not to answer must have been strong. Yet most officials did answer, a fact revisited at length in chapter 4, because they knew that saying nothing extended the reach and impact of the writer's agency and intensified and widened the ground for negotiation.

## ACTS OF RECEIVING

The act of responding to the claims of the poor was not without symbolism and consequence for the ways that writers understood and navigated a discretionary welfare system. Sending responses or resources was not always easy. Officials had to confront the myriad parish names, settlement forms, and spellings that faced early census staff. Moreover, rapid urbanisation and associated transport development meant that addresses could appear and disappear with considerable speed. John Gunnell wrote from Manchester to Oxendon in Leicestershire in the early 1830s to ask for help with rent and ongoing support. A letter of 23 June 1831 noted his address as 60 Portugal Street, Oldham Road, Manchester.[88] On 1 December 1833, another letter stated, "I therefore hope you will have the Goodness to Relieve my Necessitous situation." Asking for an answer by return post, Gunnell directed the overseer to write to him at 117 Portugal Street. In explanation, he noted in a postscript that

"I am still in the same house but the Street is much enlarged and the number augmented from 60 to 117."[89] Even without this sort of development, the poor changed their addresses regularly, either voluntarily or under pressure from poor law officials, landlords, and advocates.[90] Perhaps the biggest problem for officials, however, was the nature of direction from the poor themselves. Some, as seen below, offered precise and clear instructions on where they might be found or where they might receive letters and money. At the opposite end of the spectrum, letters of all types contained no direction at all, with correspondingly vague addresses being used by officials when they sent replies. Clearly, some poor people assumed that, given the prior exchange of letters, officials would simply remember them. This expectation was occasionally referred to in letters like that of Jacob James, whom the overseer had authorised to move from London to Sheffield in order to lodge with his brother. Announcing on 26 November 1829 that "I have got to Sheffield," he asked for temporary relief and assumed the official would remember where his brother lived, giving his address as "Sheffield."[91] To be knowable in these terms gave a veiled signpost of connectedness to a host community, something that was also continually elaborated upon directly in letters themselves and, for the in-parish poor, sometimes in face-to-face encounters. There was, however, a risk with badly specified return directions, and poor writers sometimes struggled to understand whether their letters had not been attended to or whether an outgoing or incoming misdirection had left a letter languishing elsewhere. Misdirected and lost correspondence was also a feature of epistolary relationships between parish officers themselves. As one respondent archly noted upon not receiving a reply to persistent letters, "I do think that common politeness will now demand an answer."[92]

Even where addresses were clear, the cost of postage was frequently elaborated upon as a problem.[93] George Herbert noted that in the early 1830s postage for a single "sheet of foolscap" cost 1 shilling from London to Banbury and that "if the sheet happened to be a thick one they would charge it as a double letter."[94] Poor writers were acutely aware of such costs. John and Ruth Smith, writing from Blandford in Dorset on 28 May 1833, closed with the apology "I am very sorry We Cannot pay the postedge of this."[95] Many others were less apologetic, as I have shown, and sent letters in the expectation that officials would simply pay on receipt.[96] This arrangement, however, also worked the other way round. Claimants and their advocates frequently pointed to the dent that having to pay for postage made in the allowances that letters contained, as did William McWilliams, receiving a letter in Carlisle on behalf of an unnamed family in the town and "conveying notes 7.6.0. deducting Postage 7.4.10."[97] Similarly, William Heberden, writing from Bookham in Sussex on behalf of Widow Vinall, noted he had advised her not to acknowledge receipt of relief given that "a considerable portion of her miserable pittance is frittered away" on the costs of letters and parcels.[98] Most commentary from the poor themselves was rather less nuanced. John Haley, writing to the overseer of Kirkby Lonsdale in Westmorland on 18 December 1814, noted in a postscript that "Every Duble Letter from you is 1s/8d [so] I think you had better send 4 or 5 pounds at this time" to save repeated payment of postage charges.[99] Sometimes, the costs proved simply prohibitive. The widow Hannah Buckman wrote to Hurstpierpoint in Sussex on 20 December 1828 to say that "the post girl brought your letter to my house but i do not know the contents, for i have not the Money to pay i think you could not think it posible i had."[100] She returned to the theme in an undated but clearly later letter, telling an overseer, "Sir this day the post girl Cald at my house with a small note which i supposed to be from you as it had the Brighton stamp on it but i told you before it is of no youse to send me a note without you pay the post for i cannot take it in it is returnet to the Bright[on] post."[101] These are important observations, and they point to the deep complexity of the process of poor relief in relation to the out-parish poor in particular. Nonetheless, it is clear that by saving, borrowing, or begging, most poor people did receive and open letters from their settlement parish. Moreover, they *expected* to do so, writing ubiquitously to officials to ask them for the favour of an early reply and thus a postal charge. This request gave real weight to the act of providing a contact address, and the vast majority of writers seem to have grasped that not to be visible in terms of the act of receiving invited questions of honesty and acts of surveillance or continued surveillance.

Against this backdrop, three forms of direction dominate the corpus, and this is consistent across time, space, and community typology. Some 38 per cent of writers directed officials to send correspondence or resources to third parties, as for instance did Thomas Spalding, who asked on 14 January 1768 that the overseer of his settlement parish send him a year's worth of allowance "at Wm Westmoreland Milk Shop in Little Windmil Street Ney Broade Street Carnabe Market."[102] It is easy to think that such direction was given merely for the convenience of poor writers, and indeed they sometimes elaborated upon this very thing in their letters. George Boothman, for instance, wrote from Little Corby in North Yorkshire to his settlement parish and requested that, "As I get my Shop good on Mr. Hugh James Carlisle, it would oblige me if you would have the goodness to transmit my next three Payments to him as it would save postage and likewise oblige me."[103] Yet a different reading would see direction to a third party as essentially strategic. Letters and payments sent to an advocate, overseer, or known and trusted third party would increase confidence in the truth of the original narrative. The act of direction in this sense might be read as a matter of trust, a sentiment and experience that in effect dominated the daily lives of poor people who accessed aspects of the makeshift economy "on trust."[104] In similar fashion, directing letters and resources to individuals to whom the writer owed money reduced potential fears that lies were being told or money misapplied. Later in the relief process, when additional resources were requested or allowances questioned, these same people involved in acts of receiving suddenly became co-opted advocates for the paupers with whom they had become so familiar.

A second and related strategy was to direct replies to a third party *address*. The reasons for doing so were complex and situational, but a significant factor must have been whether the applicant knew "trusted others" in their host community. Elizabeth Speller, writing from Wigan on 16 June 1807, asked that letters be sent to her at the Black Boy Inn, "I not being known here in these parts."[105] As well as public houses, recipient addresses included, as we have seen, those from which applicants wrote their letter in the first place, the addresses of landlords and landladies, or identifiable places like post offices. Sarah Hughes asked that overseer Holmes of Pangbourne in Berkshire send her relief to the "General Coach Office Balt in Tun Fleet Street till call for."[106] Widow Peney likewise asked the overseer to send her allowance "to the post office Totton as I am not Able to walk so Long a gorney."[107] Some addresses have an essentially random feel to them, as for instance that of Hannah Loft, who "patiently waits the result of her application & requests they will make it known to her – at Mrs. Bailey's near the Swan – Swan Alley Twickenham."[108] Other writers chose places with truly symbolic importance. Elizabeth Buckeridge in 1827, for instance, asked that the overseer "be so kind as to send an Order for me to receive it [relief] at Lambeth Workhouse."[109] Relatively few of the letter series that underpin the corpus exhibit a single uniform place of address from beginning to end. Equally, however, almost none of these series failed to carry direction in most or all of the letters, perhaps a reflection of the fact that an address equated to rootedness in a host community to which writers invariably claimed to belong.

Direction to the actual residences of paupers – a third strategy – was less common. This fact reflects in part the impossibility of finding people in remote hamlets or crowded urban parishes and in part that some residences simply did not have addresses.[110] Where such direction *was* made, it could be finely detailed, as for instance with John Nurse, who noted that he could be reached "at Joseph Hadgers – near to the Toll Bar Gate, Thorney, Cambridgeshire," and with James Boothman, who was to be found "at the Back hill without the English Gate Carlisle."[111] Nan Kenney had a very distinctive address, asking the overseer to send her relief to the "Standing Stone Near Wigton Cumberland."[112] William Lang struggled to set out his own address accurately enough in a letter of 16 July 1814, asking "Please to direct for me ~~No. 25 Collingwood Street Blackfriars~~ (turnover) – Wm Land No. 25 ~~Great Charlotte Street~~ Collingwood Street Great Charlotte Street Blackfriars road Surry."[113] Of course, there are striking examples of vague addresses given by claimants. Abraham Robinson directed the overseers of All Hallows Lombard Street to write to him at "Rawcliff by Doncaster," and William Brook simply asked his home parish to find him at "Birmingham."[114] Yet these instances were in the distinct minority and in any case were matched as examples by indistinct directions given by both officials and advocates, suggesting a wider problem with inexperience of addressing letters. Ultimately, to be findable meant, as we have seen, to be knowable, and this is something to which I return in chapter 12.

## CONCLUSION

The complexity of these initial acts of navigation brings the flat categorisations of table 1.1 to colourful life. Communities would have been full of people writing. The potential and actual poor had to seek paper, pens, and ink, as well as sometimes people to write or contribute to letters. They would likely have drawn upon friends, neighbours, and work colleagues. In coffee shops, booksellers, the offices of the overseer, and a variety of inns and coach houses, people would have been seen writing letters of appeal, information, response, and thanks. Letters had to be sent and received, and when they were received, notification had to be given. Allowances had to be claimed and paid, and where they were not forthcoming or were reduced or less than was asked for, more letters would have to be written. A network of conveyance carried letters and gossip in both directions and shaped the timing of engagements between the potential and actual poor and their home parishes. There is a clear and unambiguous sense in which the dependent poor were engaged in a rich epistolary interchange, one that should lead us to question existing models and chronologies of literacy and illiteracy. In their turn, the letters of the poor were just one aspect of an epistolary culture that was richer and more extensive than any current analysis has allowed. The corpus used here contains letters to friends, neighbours, daughters, parents, and others, some ending up in the hands of the overseer because they were evidence that no one else could help and others ending up with him by sheer chance. Whether in the largest cities or small rural communities, applying for and receiving relief were decidedly acts played out in public and largely in public spaces. In terms of chronology, typology, and space, there is little evidence of this public culture varying. Thus, when poor writers stated that their cases were well known in the community, this was not idle talk but concrete reality. The public nature of application, decision, and action had implications for how paupers navigated a discretionary welfare system. It seems not to have been a matter of shame, as it was elsewhere,[115] but in many ways to have been a resource on which the poor could draw in their negotiations.

Yet the groundwork for the negotiative process had to be laid subtly. The nature and quality of the paper used to appeal to overseers mattered. The paper and the way the letter was conveyed had symbolic value. There is evidence that most writers took time to craft their narratives and tell their stories.[116] They certainly had to think carefully about the timing of letters and about where they would ask officials to respond. Each decision shaped who the poor negotiated with, the rhetoric that they might use, and the strategic modes of appeal that were possible. This assessment does not overstate the situation. Officials realised, and sometimes noted with candour, that they *had* to respond to the letters received. Not doing so could push them into the welcoming arms of the magistrate or force claimants into extreme measures, such as selling off their possessions to come home or emigrating, the latter invariably leaving expensive family behind. But these were in fact extreme measures. In practice, faced with delays or worsening poverty, the poor wrote again and again, interspersing their own letters with those of advocates and overseers and sometimes visits in person as they sought to bolster "relationships rendered especially vulnerable by separation."[117] All of these things might touch upon the tone of negotiation and the breadth of the ground for the agency of the poor, implicitly influencing what was recorded in end-of-process overseers' accounts. The next chapter, then, moves on to the question of how the claims of the in- and out-parish poor were received by officials.

# 4

# *Official Receptions*

How the words of poor writers were received by the differently constituted poor law authorities of the study period is important for a number
of reasons. First, the act of opening and reading a letter started, continued, or reconfigured the relief process from the parish perspective. Such
letters might elicit an answer by the hoped for "return of post," or they
might demand weightier and lengthier consideration, information gath-
ering, and consultation. The latter seems, across the corpus, unrelated
to the nature and size of a claim; suggestions of a tiny increase in pension
often occasioned much more consultation than the need to meet a doctoring bill of 7 pounds. Requests (and occasionally demands) might be
met, refused, or modified. It is this process of poor relief that the in- and
out-parish poor and their advocates sought to influence, and its uncertain
final outcomes are, as chapter 1 argued, the basis of most historiographical understanding of the character and role of the Old Poor Law. Second, in common with most other epistolary communication, how poor
writers and advocates expected their letters to be received may have
shaped the style, tone, content, and rhetoric of the writing.[1] We should
beware of the sense that authors *simply* wrote what they thought would
be most palatable to their readers or what epistolary practices and their
conventions demanded. A series of correspondence by or about the same

person usually became self-reinforcing in terms of the narrative core and the telling or rhetoricisation of histories, and the variety of rhetorical modes – on a spectrum from aggressive demands to passive statements of dependence – undermines any easy assumptions that the poor were, and were supposed to be, humble, deferential, and grateful.[2] Equally, we should not simply assume that out-parish writers had to spend more of their time "filling in the gaps" on their state and history compared to the in-parish poor who applied in person. Although by their nature vestry minutes are summaries of business, those used here do not suggest that people who could be seen made more superficial cases than others who could not. Nor was there any inevitable or systematic relationship between the size and shape of the "ask" and the nature and length of the case or its rhetorical features. Requests for very large sums in rent arrears were often shorter and less strategically and rhetorically sophisticated – concentrating, for instance, on the prospect of homelessness and homeless children – than those that ultimately ended with a plea for a "trifle." Nonetheless, writers did not construct their letters without giving thought to the expectations of overseers and vestrymen.

Third, it is important to understand how the letter as a material object, and the case it carried into the process of poor relief, took on a life of its own once read by officials. Authors, whether the poor, advocates, or scribes, were clearly the first readers of a text, but they could not control how it was invented and reinvented by others once it had been conveyed. Understanding this experience is important not just for the character of the process of poor relief and the nature of the ultimate outcome of an appeal but also for the way that a self was constructed or imposed, something to which I return in chapter 12. Fourth, reception was also important because an outcome required correspondence that inevitably established the groundwork for the agency of the poor, on the one hand, and identified the common conceptual and linguistic ground between parishes and claimants, on the other. It must have been tempting for officials to neglect the letters of serial correspondents, but they could not, as argued in the previous chapter, systematically ignore the need for signals as to how an appeal had been received.[3] It is through this process of co-respondence that we can come to understand the degree to which state power at the local level was, and was meant to be, malleable. Finally, the issue of reception is intimately related to local, county, and regional patterning of relief outcomes measured in central government surveys from the 1770s onward.[4] As chapter 1 suggested, historians are unable to agree on whether we can see macro-patterns in relief outcomes, but there is broader consensus that local variation reflected a composite of financial constraint, the situational nature and causation of poverty, and the richness or paucity of makeshift economies. Investigating reception and its aftermath refocuses the debate: local, county, and regional variation was the outcome of thousands of individual relief processes, and the need for clarity on the considerations of inclusion, exclusion, and entitlement that underpinned that process is compelling.

This chapter, then, starts our search for clarity by looking at official reception of the claims of the poor. Its primary focus is on the out-parish poor, but vestry minutes show clearly that the reception of the cases made by their in-parish counterparts shared much common ground. Against this backdrop, we should not make the mistake of assuming that the effort to detect and understand acts of reception for the letters of the poor is any easier than it is for novels, didactic literature, or chapbooks.[5] That these letters were written tells us little about their reception, just as a decision on the case made reveals little about the thoughts, deliberations, emotions, and agonies of the person making that decision. Unlike book historians, we can rarely read anything into the dog-eared feel of the material object. The lazy contempt or disinterest that one might read into doodles or other ad hoc augmentations of the text (and there are many of these) is diluted by the fact that almost all of this material afterlife was added by those through whose hands the letters later passed or even by modern archivists.[6] We do, however, find contemporaneous annotations on a spectrum from simple notes that a claim had been granted or denied to extensive commentary on the case. And in places, we can find copies of letters sent to claimants, advocates, and officials, some contemporaneous and others made later as officials imposed conceptual order on their archive. The fact of frequent co-respondence is also evident in – and aspects of reception can be implied from – letters written by the poor or advocates that reference or recount prior correspondence from the settlement parish. In this sense, we can think about reception in terms of the afterlife of an initial response.

Drawing on this sort of material, the next section of the chapter considers some of the basic mechanics of reception, arguing that the elongated and complex process of considering appeals once they arrived in the hands of the overseer shaped the meaning of both those appeals and the outcomes eventually recorded. The chapter then moves on to consider the spectrum of receptions encountered by poor writers, which included out-of-hand dismissal, being turned down after consideration, delayed payment, generous response, information seeking, time-limited help, and modified support. That an individual might encounter a wide range of response and nonresponse, or action and silence, over the course of a series of letters is the focus of the third section of the chapter, which argues that binary labels such as success or failure do not adequately encompass poor people's experience of the relief process. Nonetheless, most letters did achieve some outcome, even if not the one originally requested. In this sense, the reasons for the regional patterns that we see in spending on poor relief require reconsideration. Finally, the chapter turns to the issue of co-respondence, suggesting that poor writers expected to receive replies, if not action and relief, and that officials expected to provide such replies. Both parties had clear understandings of the character and limits of their epistolary conversations, but these variables were also organic and contestable.[7] The fact of being involved in such a network of co-respondence, I suggest, gave the poor a valuable currency over and above the relief that they might have garnered.

## MECHANICS OF RECEPTION

Our knowledge of what happened after a letter left the hand of the writer is surprisingly patchy. Some letters went astray because of misdirection or incompetence in the postal mechanisms, as seen in prior chapters. In such cases, officials often went out of their way to explain the situation to claimants. James Benson, writing on 8 June 1827, is typical. He noted that a payment was delayed because he "unfortunately had omitted on the Directions (Staffordshire). The consequence was after a long elaps I

93

received a letter from the Dead Letter Office" asking for payment to return the letter and the notes enclosed.[8] Occasionally, those tasked with delivering letters into the care of officials or intra-parish advocates, such as family, ex-employers, and friends, could not complete their job because the intended recipient was away or sick. And sometimes letters from the poor or officials in other parishes simply sat on the desk of an overseer in a settlement parish while he attended to other business. Even so, such instances were relatively rare, and the "plodding competence of the many" officers that James Stephen Taylor has found for Devon is writ large across this corpus.[9]

Once letters were received, their recipients became the second readers of the text, the third if an advocate had written on behalf of the poor person, or the fourth where a carrier had seen the letter, as some did. The act of reading might not, however, be simple. The oral nature of many letters meant that there was almost certainly an element of basic translation to be undertaken even before officials set about discerning the intent of the author or decoding the secondary meanings with which the text was freighted.[10] There is little reason to think that once this translating was done, officials would not have brought to their reading the scepticism, frustration, anger, compassion, or (dis)interest that might have coloured their attitudes toward other texts. We have already observed officials expressing immense frustration at a further letter from a pauper recently given relief. On the opposite side of the spectrum, some officials were so absorbed in the emotion of a case that they wrote eloquently in return. Thus James Jones, the overseer of Essington in Staffordshire, wrote on the subject of Richard Richards on 10 April 1827, "I scarcely know what measures to take with them [Richards and his wife]. The poor old man has been ill and incapable of working all winter," such that he might have starved had it not been for the "human benevolence of neighbours." Jones "well knew Parishes are heavily oppress'd but they are now poor old people and you can augment their pay a little."[11]

Whatever the emotional canvas shaping initial reception, officials had to decide how to act, how to record their actions, and what the material afterlife of the letter would be. In this context, we should be cautious about assuming any correlation between these variables and the nature or size of the claim. At the individual level, most letters did not actually "ask" for anything. They hinted that a "trifle" would help the writer or that an unspecified increase in allowance was requisite, or they simply left the decision about what was best to the discretion of the overseer. Advocate letters and official correspondence follow the same pattern. On the opposite side of the spectrum, some individual narratives might contain several specific but essentially random requests, such as quantified allowances, clothes, rent, and so on. Across a series of letters by or about the same person, unspecified requests for support dominate the "ask" but might be interspersed with huge requests for rent, apprenticeship, or payment of a doctoring bill. In this sense, it is impossible to provide any remotely meaningful visual or quantitative representation of requests made, and perhaps as a direct function of the vagueness of requests and their fractured nature across a series of letters, we are unable to relate the detail and rhetoric of the case made to the monetary value of the relief requested or eventually given. As I observed above, some of the very longest and most rhetorically dense letters in the corpus relate to requests for a trifle, whereas a doctoring bill of 7 pounds might barely merit more than a couple of factual lines. The poor, in other words, did not feel that the tone and content of their letters had to be tailored to the request made, or at least not in any simple way. Similarly, there is little evidence from overseers' correspondence that officials expected to be approached in certain ways according to the nature and scale of the request.

Just as with the in-parish poor, some officials had the power to take independent action due to the lack of a regular vestry or simply assumed this power whether or not there was a vestry. It is unclear whether the short decisions – granted, not granted, or subject to conditions – recorded by some officials on letters themselves speak to this sort of independent action, but they likely do. Perhaps decisions of this sort were copied directly into the accounts, either contemporaneously or in summative form slightly later. Some parochial officers, however, went to greater lengths to record what they thought about letters, writing either to the author or to fellow officers and advocates about the case. The overseer George Lees is a typical example. Writing from Kimberworth in Yorkshire to Peterborough on 17 January 1804, he conveyed his thoughts on "the old sinner Hutchinson," who "happened to be the very person that wrote the letter you shewed me." Noting that Hutchinson had *seemed* to abandon his wife, thus allowing her to obtain "relief from different townships [and] keeps them in suspence" while he was still living close by, Lees suggested that his counterpart in Peterborough should dismiss the latest letter from her.[12] In fact, Peterborough eventually made a small payment. Such examples suggest that even where officials had the power to act in their own right, the decisions they came to were often interim parts of a longer process framed by the relative expectations of official and writer. In this case, the simple recording of an allowance for Jane Hutchinson does no justice either to the request in the original letter or to the reception and decision making of the recipient. I revisit this matter at greater length in the next section.

Such actions did not, of course, mean that either the case or the letter remained anchored in the private sphere of the overseer's parlour. These documents were no more private than other letters or texts. Even when they had discretion to make decisions, officials recorded sharing letters or reading them aloud to others as they consulted on the best course of action.[13] In similar fashion, they discussed the merits of applications by the in-parish poor with others in the parochial community. Authors sometimes intended just this eventuality, attaching greetings that they wanted passed on or referring officers to others in the parish for their good opinion of the writer or the veracity of the case they made.[14] The question of the material afterlives of texts in situations where officials had discretion is thus difficult to address. Some letters were clearly filed, never to be looked at again, but officers were often more methodical, viewing letters as part of the history of local welfare to be used subsequently and passed on to other officers in due course. Thus William Pullin of Rothersthorpe was not unusual in quoting the promises of Elizabeth Martin's previous letter when he wrote to her denying further relief on 1 December 1788.[15] Occasionally, such filing meant the letters were pinned into overseers' accounts or other books. Most, however, appear to have been kept loosely in parish chests or, as at Hulme in Lancashire, casually consigned to the pages of books meant for other purposes.[16]

Where officials *did not* have discretion or where they required affirmation of their actions, letters seem to have been routinely summarised
or read aloud at vestry meetings, as for instance when the overseer of
Oundle in Northamptonshire wrote to his counterpart from Sawston in
Cambridgeshire on 17 April 1833 to note that he had been delayed replying in the case of Widow Naylor and family because "we have only
a select vestry once a fortnight and all these things are laid before them
before they can be paid."[17] Some of the texts from poor writers seem to
have been sent with the idea that they might be read before vestries. If
claims were refused, follow-up letters often noted that if the gentlemen
of the vestry had really been aware of the situation – that is, if they had
read or heard the letter itself instead of a summary – their humanity
would have swayed them to action. It is a leap to agree with Stephen
Colclough that reading a letter out enhanced the authority of the words,
but such reading would certainly increase the immediacy of the case.[18]
The potential outcomes of this collective consideration were many and
are explored at length in the next section. That they sometimes failed to
accord with the views and wishes of the overseer himself can be seen in
episodic demands in vestry minutes that parochial officials implement
decisions in full. Having reached a decision, officials had to decide how
to turn reception into reciprocal acts. Positive, negative, and interme-
diary positons might be conveyed to advocates or officials in a host
parish, who would be asked to read out or convey letters and their material and rhetorical content to the poor. Correspondence might also be
sent directly to claimants. Sometimes, no text at all was sent, merely
bills, money, or a direction that successful claimants should apply to a
particular person, bank, or trader in order to realise their allowance.

This brief review of the mechanics of reception is important. It suggests how decisions could become elongated, how claims for particular
amounts or types of relief could be modified, and how the administrative
machinery of the parish itself could be split on a proper course of action.
Such mechanics, of which we must assume in- and out-parish paupers
to have been well aware, also help to explain why poor writers were so
eager to personalise their approach to the settlement parish, particularly
by claiming that they were known at "home" or had a connection with

those making decisions. Letters, notably extending and renewing letters, were more likely to be given a hearing or reading where the writer shared a history with the parish and its officials. I return to this issue in more depth in chapter 6. However, the mechanics of reception are also important for other reasons. Overseers and vestrymen did not read in isolation but approached texts with expectations and preconceptions founded on earlier letters and longer histories of dependence and independence. They might misread the text and fail to take up the threads of silence and rhetoric as intended, in effect reconstructing its intent and content. And when they were part of an "interpretive community" through the sharing of letters by or about the poor, officials implicitly accepted direction and restriction on how such texts might and ought to be read.[19] These mechanics, in other words, were important for constructing and inventing meaning. Written responses, in their turn, invited further correspondence and potentially generated a recognised and shared territory of strategy, rhetoric, and language. Viewed against this backdrop, the letter of the poor writer becomes less a flat statement of appeal embellished with various rhetorical and factual flourishes tailored to the nature and size of the request and more a stepping-stone in a dynamic process underpinned by agency and assumptions about the malleability of the local state.

## THE SPECTRUM OF RECEPTION

The outcomes emerging from this dynamic process were, at the individual level, complex, fluid, and unpredictable, not least because of the vagueness of the original requests in the majority of letters. Indeed, some writers talked about the inconsistency of parish positions in relation to how other claimants had been treated, to promises made, and to their standing and accumulated credit "at home" or in a host parish. William Lloyd, writing from Oxford to Wallingford in Oxfordshire on 1 December 1829, is typical. He noted, "The Gentlemen at the Vestry agreed to allow me 3s 6d per week and if that did not suit me I might come home, but as I have not received that I am verry uneasey." His rent now due,

Lloyd thought "the gentlemen are acting verry <u>inconsonsistant</u> the[y] will surely fiend me more burdensome at home than here ... the[y] cannot flinch from what the[y] agreed to allow me without giving me notice to that affect."[20] At the level of applications, this sort of fluidity – a decision taken but not implemented and in other cases a refusal made but then reversed or an allowance applied for but transformed into something else – can also be observed in vestry minutes when the cases of the in-parish poor were considered and reconsidered. In turn, these complex individual decisions cohered to generate the outcomes recorded in overseers' accounts. The nature of the decision making, the spectrum of outcomes – all of which could be experienced by an individual over a very short period – and the fragility of some decisions also shaped the process of poor relief and the way that poor people could exercise agency and deploy rhetorical and strategic engagements with officials. It is above all an understanding of that process and the reactions of the poor to its dynamics that lie at the core of the rest of this chapter and study.

Given that the Old Poor Law was, as we have seen, essentially a discretionary system, it would be easy to assume that the experience of Ann Hughes, writing from Storrington in Sussex on 10 December 1781, was representative of the nature of reception. She would "beg pardon for troubling" the overseer but noted that having been told by "Mr Bishopp" to expect relief, she was in deep trouble:

> not hearing any thing from you Since I am drove quite to Distress I have been oblidge to part with Some things to Support my poor helpless mother & myself for Some time Consider Sir it is almost a Twelvemonth ago that I first applyd. to you for relief and many times Since but never receivd. any thing but once which was sometime before Last Easter the Overseer Mr Hewatt calld. to see my mother and gave me half a guinea with a promise to send me more at Easter after there had been a Vestury but I have never had any thing Since Mr Bishopp told me you <sup>thought</sup> we had no security but I can assure you my father had one many yeare ago from your Parrish.[21]

Unfulfilled rumour, unanswered letters, tokens at a time when need demanded more, and a hint that the parish had failed to act because the
officials did not recognise the settlement of Hughes or her mother had
forced Ann to pawn her goods and left a dutiful daughter and a dependent mother hanging by a thread at the will of the parish. Complaints
from claimants or their advocates that officials had failed to either act
or reply can easily be found in the corpus. Writers in their turn became
anxious at not hearing, just as in-parish applicants did when vestry enquiries and orders were not followed up. Thus, when Ann Slater wrote
her extending letter to the overseer of Horncastle in Lincolnshire from
Hull on 2 November 1803 to "let you know that we intend to come to
horncastle next week," she added in a postscript,

> you said that you would rite to us but we never got a letter and it
> is a fortnight since you was at our house so I thought that you
> would have sent if we was not to have comed away be so good as
> to send answer by the Carrier for we have sold all our goods but
> what we intend to bring with us.[22]

Whether or not the Slaters had really sold all of their goods is unclear,
but the overseer of Horncastle had melded together a personal visit and
a promise to write, testimony to the multilayered relationship that the
out-parish poor had with their parishes. The fact of the *expected* letter
not coming both generated an admonishing letter and ostensibly pushed
the family to radical action.

Other writers were even more direct in reminding overseers of their
part in the drama and process of poor relief. Hannah Mills, a serial correspondent from various addresses to her settlement parish of Phillack
in Cornwall, wrote on 8 September 1824 to Mr Berriman,

> I have not heard from you now since the 20 Feby which is now 6
> months and I, have sent severall times and can get no Answer I have
> bin very ill for some weeks and if I do not hear from you Next week
> I must apply to the Overseers hear and draw Money and likewise I
> must have more pay or you must Send me Cloaths.[23]

Attached to her account of Berriman's failure to answer her letters, this threat by Mills to apply to her host parish for relief, and thus become removable, made clear her demands of him. James Stephen Taylor's analysis of sojourner experiences in Devon, in which he suggests that "denials and delays were common" under the Old Poor Law, would appear to have some traction.[24]

Yet not all delays were deliberate. Although vestries met regularly, relief decisions or instalments had to reach the person concerned once dispatched. The latter was not always certain. Sarah Hughes wrote from London on 18 November 1829 to tell the overseer of her settlement parish that "last time you sent up my Moneys but you sent it to the wrong Office."[25] And if it is clear that some claimants and their advocates met with persistent delay or refusal, focusing only on this group does little justice to the diverse spectrum of potential outcomes for individual letters. Delays in considering a letter or forwarding relief must be balanced by cases where officials responded with extraordinary haste, as for instance when faced with requests to meet the costs of burying the dead.[26] Instances in which parishes responded to specific requests for support from both in- and out-parish poor by paying less than asked or in a form different from that requested by the claimant were common. Yet when asked to respond with a "trifle" or to send what could be spared, officers could be strikingly generous. And instances of harshness must and can be more than balanced in a quantitative sense by cases where officials acted with remarkable generosity and sentiment even when there was no legal reason for them to do so. A typical example is the treatment of John Gann's wife by Oundle officials. Understanding from Mr Strong, the overseer of York, that Mrs Gann was extremely sick and required both cash and a nurse, Oundle granted both allowances. However, the overseer was "to add that it is not usual for the Parish to do so where the man has 12/- per week, in a constant place and only one child But in their case they do it on account of the good character given by you of the man & the unfortunate situation of his wife."[27]

This complexity of outcomes is magnified when we consider the responses occasioned by a series of letters from or about the same person, who could and generally did experience different points of this broad spectrum even when receiving letters of reply that were chronologically close. Two examples highlight the importance of this observation for understanding the process of poor relief. Thus tables 4.1 and 4.2 trace the outcomes of letters sent by Ann and Isaac Curtis – it is unclear which of them authored the texts – and by William Lloyd, the latter already encountered above. We can see that it would have been difficult for writers, and equally for those who attended vestries, where similar patterns can be observed, to have predicted the outcomes of their engagement with parish officers. Because poor relief entailed a process of application, consideration, exclusion, renewal, and extension for both in- and out-parish poor, it is impossible to understand an outcome in the stark and definite terms implied by an entry of 2 shillings and 6 pence in the parochial accounts. These tables show firmly that the story of claimants and their relationship with the relief process was, and was meant to be, continuously reconfigured and reinvented, although not obviously in relation to the form or scale of relief requested. There *were*, however, other nuances to this picture. It is certainly true, for instance, that letter series dominated by the writing of advocates achieved more continuity of decision making than did series where the voices of the poor dominated. But even here, the intervention of landlords – either for their poor tenant to ask settlement parishes to aid the family or for themselves to ask for direct payment of rent arrears – seems to have been uniformly counter-productive in terms of favourable responses. It is also clear that letters written to smaller rural communities, with the stark exception of Wales, and to small towns achieved more rapid responses and more continuity and longevity in relief outcomes than did those written to areas that we might define as broadly urban. That said, the sentiment of John Small when writing to an unnamed widow on 12 July 1834 that "Our vestry has desired me to say they think you ought not to have troubled them so soon as you have done" is almost exclusively one seen in official correspondence from these smaller rural communities.[28]

Lynn Hollen Lees argues that "common understandings of citizenship and social rights ... became intensely class divided during the early nineteenth century," to the detriment of the claims of the poor.[29] Yet the key lessons of the corpus and its scaffolding sources do not tend in this

Table 4.1

*Letter outcomes for Ann and Isaac Curtis of Twerton, near Bath*

| Date and author | Letter type | Core concern | Outcome |
|---|---|---|---|
| 6 December 1817, overseer of Twerton | Instigatory | Ann Curtis "extremely ill" | No apparent reply |
| 28 December 1817, couple to "Father and Mother" | Interspersing | Family desperate, asks for the mother and father to plead their case to the parish | Relief given |
| 30 January 1818, Mr Whitehead, vicar of Twerton | Interspersing | Ann still ill and the family wanting "proper necessaries" | Delayed consideration |
| 4 February 1818, assistant overseer of settlement parish | Interspersing | Decision of the vestry | Renewal of allowance |
| 15 February 1818, overseer of Twerton | Interspersing | Ann Curtis is dead | None expected |
| 25 April 1818, Isaac Curtis | Extending | Left on his own with children and requires an allowance to avoid removal | Ad hoc payment rather than an allowance |
| 30 June 1818, Isaac Curtis | Extending | Cannot pay the rent and belongings might be sold | No reply |
| 27 January 1819, Isaac Curtis | Renewing | Again cannot pay the rent and belongings might be sold | Relief given |

*Source*: Hurley, *Longbridge Deveril Poor*, 4–7.

Table 4.2
*Letter outcomes for William Lloyd of Oxford*

| Date and author | Letter type | Core concern | Outcome |
|---|---|---|---|
| 18 July 1818, Lloyd, with attestation by Dr Hitchings | Instigatory | Distress due to "an attack of fever accompanied with violent pain in the the "head" | Delayed consideration |
| 24 July 1818, overseer of Caversham | Interspersing | Granted 1 pound at the vestry | Relief given |
| 7 August 1818, Edward Whitaker, surgeon | Testamentary | Lloyd unable to work due to sickness | Delayed consideration |
| 12 August 1818, overseer of Caversham | Interspersing | The parish is surprised at getting another letter so soon but sends 1 pound | Relief given |
| 26 November 1818, Lloyd | Renewing | Requires an allowance and help with rent | Relief given |
| 17 February 1819, Lloyd | Renewing | Wife confined and needs help with rent | Relief given |
| 6 March 1822, Lloyd | Extending | Debilitated constitution requires an ongoing allowance | Relief given |
| 1 December 1829, Lloyd to his brother | Renewing | Has written for help with rent but received no answer and hopes his brother will intervene | No answer |

*Source*: BRO D/P 162/18, William Lloyd letters.

direction. It is unclear what a matrix of success or failure would look like, either for individual parishes or for the whole sample, given the complexities of reception and the need for constant reapplication and renewal, which is a central lesson of the study for the process of poor relief. Yet most of those who wrote, as well as the majority of those appearing before vestries in "normal" years, did eventually get something. It may have been less than they asked for and felt they needed. Indeed, claimants frequently took officials to task on this matter, as did Charles Smith of Hull, who acknowledged gratefully the 4 shillings per week recently granted by his settlement parish but noted that "we cannot subsist on it." His wife had been very ill, and "the small trifle we get is not sufficient to obtain even common food and she at present is kept ill in consequence of it."[30] By contrast, some writers got more than they could have imagined when submitting their open-ended requests, proof of the capacity of overseers to raise taxes on themselves and their fellow ratepayers to a much higher level than the central state could ever achieve. There were delays, of course, but we can also find significant delays in officials acting upon vestry directions. Moreover, despite the regularity with which payments were recorded in the accounts of overseers, there were universal delays in the actual payment of allowances to all of the poor. Out-parish claimants were less likely than their in-parish counterparts to have their allowances converted from requested cash to allowances in kind, but they were also more likely to request the direct supply of clothing rather than the cash to buy it or to buy the materials to make it at home. Expensive sickness cases and casual allowances paid to wandering vagrants occasioned more local concern than did small payments to the familiar poor, but even here parishes were capable of extraordinary compassion. Indeed, I have argued elsewhere that the sick poor posed a systemic moral conundrum for officials.[31]

Just as Taylor sees the persistence of paternalism in Devon parishes during the crisis of the Old Poor Law,[32] the corpus points to an administrative class motivated by more than blind economy and informed by considerations other than simply the size of the rate base versus the scale of spending requested. In this sense, it is quite clear that two names next to each other on the recorded relief lists and with the same allowance were not in any sense alike. One payment may have been grudgingly given after much delay and negotiation, whereas the other could have been granted with the flourish of a pen the moment an appeal arrived in the post.[33] The meaning of the two allowances was wholly different, and the process by which these allowances had been negotiated is central to our understanding of the Old Poor Law. In turn, probably a large part of the solution to the problem of how we should understand acknowledged variation in the level and form of parochial spending – whether it reflects the independent activity of thousands of parochial welfare republics or was part of a wider and deeply ingrained regional framework – is a clearer understanding of how the in- and out-parish poor strategically, practically, and rhetorically navigated the welfare system.

## CONCEIVING SUCCESS AND FAILURE

We can begin this process by revisiting claimant concepts of success and failure rather than focusing on recorded outcomes. This is a surprisingly complex issue both because success or failure was contingent on personal perception of how others had "done" and because the in- and out-parish poor possessed imperfect yardsticks through which to characterise an outcome. What might success look like when an individual had requested a trifle, left the amount and form of relief to officials, or simply asked for unspecified help? Only a handful of claimants wrote back to officials thanking them for their generous or sustained relief, although the fact that any at all did is perhaps significant. At the other end of the spectrum, some writers and vestry applicants thanked officials for their interventions but noted that the amounts sent were modest compared to the needs outlined, as we have seen. How might writers have interpreted a situation where only one out of three of their letters achieved a response or where they were obliged to turn to an advocate because their own letters had been dismissed or ignored? What was the perceived value of an allowance that was requested to help keep poor people in their home by paying rent arrears but that arrived only after a family had been distrained for rent and thrown into the streets? Would poor writers and vestry attendees have counted as success the continual renewal of allowances in old age in response to their letters and those of advocates, or would success have been achieved only when officials accepted the representative importance of the case and acknowledged that old people needed support in the form of a continuous allowance? Would women caring for sick children and having requested an ongoing allowance have deemed receipt of a one-off cash payment to be success or failure? These questions – all of them based on real cases drawn from the corpus and played out many times in different configurations – have no easy answers. Only occasionally did writers or their advocates relay their direct opinions, as for instance did John Grant, writing from Leeds on 24 January 1830. Noting that his settlement parish had responded to his continuing unemployment with 1 pound, he said, "Sir, think what 3s7d a Week can be among 8 Souls to find them in Food, Clothing, House-room, Fuel to warm them in this inclement season of the year."[34] Similarly, Jane Pate wrote a renewing letter from Kendal in Cumbria in September 1821 to acknowledge receipt of an allowance of 2 shillings. She noted that "though the sum was not great yet it was of much benefit to me at the time." That the overseer of her host parish witnessed the letter could be read as her co-opting the voice and opinion of an official in confirmation of the inadequate allowance.[35]

These examples suggest that the poor had fluid and situational views on concepts of success and failure. Indeed, it could hardly be otherwise. Almost none of the writers or vestry attendees engaged with officials to get a full subsistence, and it has often been forgotten that both the recipient and the donor understood that poor relief was, and was meant to be, only a contribution to the makeshift economy. In relation to eighteenth-century begging, Tim Hitchcock states that the poor "could and did insist that something was given, that the rich live up to their obligation," a situation that was also played out in the context of the process of poor relief. For individual writers, the value of that "something" was intrinsically linked to the background makeshift economy, as were wider notions of success and failure.[36] This implied meaning is embodied in the majority of letters written by the poor themselves and in almost all advocate letters, the latter usually setting out in some detail the prior efforts of a claimant to make ends meet and how a current allowance might be supplemented or might open up other possibilities for achieving independence. These issues are revisited in chapter 9, but for now the situation is well illustrated in the letters of Stephen Dickman writing on behalf of John Batchelor, already encountered in the previous chapter. Writing to Oxted St Mary in Surrey on 12 May 1821, he noted that Batchelor, who was seventy years old, had been turned out of his house and remained lame. Batchelor nonetheless wanted to do for himself, and "he has been picking up a trifle other while at the Mill near Hawkwell dressing their Oat Stones (he cou'd not see well enough to dress their Wheat ones)." In addition, "Mr Merchant a Neighbouring Gentleman has employ'd him a few days … but this is nearly 3 mile off and what he gets is a meer trifle." The family sold small bags of flour, and they had pawned all things of value before approaching the parish.[37] Against this backdrop, success may have been any sum at all.

Notions of success and failure were also shaped by the intangible aspects of the process of poor relief. The immediate purpose of letters to settlement parishes was to gain, keep, or extend relief. There was also an important supplementary motive to achieve what Issac Land has styled as a "street citizenship" or "a community recognition of who you are, where you belong, what is expected of you and what you can expect in return."[38] In this sense, the fact of an overseer's reply, irrespective of the material outcome, denoted exchange, recognition, and acceptance of an ongoing conversation and might thus well have been constructed as a success.[39] Letters that were sent and received also bought time from irate landlords, butchers, and bakers who had run out of patience with accumulating credit and from friends who had reached the end of their willingness to extend financial or emotional support to the writer. In some cases, the very fact of having written to a settlement parish was enough for officials in a host parish to extend further ad hoc relief and avoid removal. Where letters were passed on or read aloud to others in the settlement parish, supplementary sources of making ends meet might open up, as for instance Luke Faulkner must have hoped would happen when he wrote from Hull on 1 June 1803,

I hop that you for give my fridom in Ritin to you not nown wither
My master Morley was Livin her no, I was prentice a Long with
your doathree and Marred my wife frome your hous and nown that
you wil Reclet me Liven in your famely you wood give your Self
the trobel to speke to the hoverseys Let them now that I have maed
Apleckhin to the Govner of the workhouse and he Rit a Letter to
the hoverseyer and no hanser his Comd yet as I ham in Gret want
of Rilif as I have Been hill all most a year and my wife as Been hill
allmost a Quarther of a year and we have got five Smal Children
and as we have ad Sekens So Long in the famely we hir beaient with
hour Rent and in Coas that the parrish doath not give me Sum Littel
Rilef that I must thou my Self on the parish that as I have Bin hill
so Long that I carnt Seport my famely with Bred, If I have not Sum
Rlif till i get Better and I hop Sir that you will be so good as to speke
to the hover Seares hor to M^r Carrinton and if M^r Carrinton will
Be so good as to Rit M^r Loft of March Chapel he will till M^r Carrinton of my drisce I ham in at present pleas Sir to giv my duty to
my Master and Mstres if they be in the Land of the Liven I treat Sir
that in a Littel time that we shall Be wear Sour and pain will be a
flicked us on moer for money hir the trobel of the Bities but the
Lord doath deliver them out of them all.[40]

Although the ultimate purpose of Faulkner's letter was to achieve an intercession with the overseers, its claims to personal connection with the
recipient give it the textual feeling of a begging letter.[41]

Many writers ended up "disappointed" – with nonresponse, inadequate relief, irregular payment, the need to keep writing to renew allowances, and the conditions imposed upon their relief – even if this
sentiment was to some extent automatically correlated with the purpose
of letters. Yet the language and sentiment of disappointment also speaks
to a sense of expectation as to the obligations of the parish, something
that we see embodied in letters themselves. William Dixon of Sedbergh
in North Yorkshire is typical. His letter of 15 June 1818 expressed surprise at having heard nothing from his settlement parish in response to
a prior letter. Given that he was in great distress and had been sick "for

many weeks," he had expected "something more." He hoped the official would "take into Consideration too let me have something weekly as A temperly reliefe will not do." Demanding that the overseer reply by return with a local carrier, he expected the letter to come with "some mony withit some support I must have as Provisions is very high."[42] More often, a sense of expectation that officials would react is constructed in the language of hope, whether the desired outcome was a reply, relief, partnership in returning to independence, or supplementary action when officials were confronted with stories of extra need. There was substance to this rhetorical tool. As we have seen, most writers and vestry attendees got something even if the getting of it implied constant renewal of appeals and the retelling and reconstellation of the stories that underpinned them. In this sense, the process of poor relief perhaps demands that we jettison binary concepts of success and failure in favour of experiential and mutable indicators such as hope and disappointment.

## A PROCESS OF CO-RESPONDENCE?

The need for greater conceptual flexibility is emphasised when we understand that obtaining cash was not the only impetus for claimants. Rather, writers and their advocates wanted to establish a relationship that, despite their almost ubiquitous protestations to the contrary, was or could be ongoing. Writers variously requested replies; asked officials to contact other people who could provide evidence of the veracity of the case; followed up broken promises and delayed payment in writing or in person; reserved the right to return to the parish if their circumstances worsened or other exogenous influences came to bear; outlined a personal history with the co-respondent or people they knew, thus effectively claiming a right to reply; promised to send further updates; and as seen in chapter 3, outlined their waiting experiences when expected replies were not forthcoming. John Haley is typical. Writing an extending letter from Horton in Lancashire on 10 September 1821, he took his co-respondent to task, noting that "I answered your Letter Imeadiately I am surprised you do not Write again Before this time you promised to

Remitt Either every fortnit or Month but you have not."[43] Even writers for whom only one letter survives envisaged themselves as engaged in a process of co-respondence, whether subsequent letters were written or not. Moreover, some 2,000 letters in the corpus begin at a point in the process of poor relief when prior claims had already been considered and attended to.

There is thus a significant danger of underplaying the extent to which the out-parish poor in particular *were* actually engaged in a process of co-respondence. This is an important observation. Complaints that replies had not been received, suspicions that letters had been lost in the post or misdirected, the profusion of follow-up letters, and the accidental or deliberate survival of copy letters to the poor themselves show that poor writers *expected* officials to reply or to acknowledge their letters in other ways, such as arranging for the arrival of an allowance. The poor, as Geoffrey Taylor states, could not simply "be herded out of sight," and their voices could not simply be stifled.[44] This expectation is emblematised by Jane Adams, writing from Padstow in Cornwall on 28 November 1822. She apologised for "a gain take the liberty writing you" and explained that she had received "no answar from the last letter I send you as it is 1 month since I send the first." Thinking this delay unusual, she assumed the letter had been lost in the difficult terrain of Cornwall and added, "if that did not reach to you I hope this Will."[45] Similarly, Martha Lowas, writing from Forton in Cumberland on 10 June 1809, belaboured the overseer because "this is the sechand time I have Ritt to you have not Recvd either money or letter since your first."[46] The clear message of the corpus is that officials in their turn *usually* felt obliged to reply. Indeed, parish officers were sometimes remarkably sensitive to charges of epistolary inaction, as we have already seen. Letters were received, read, deliberated over, and acted upon. Even if few of the actual replies to claimant letters have been preserved, the corpus provides unambiguous evidence that overseers, the poor, and their advocates had a shared understanding of the reciprocal arrangements that framed their relationships of co-respondence. These arrangements included matters such as the acceptable intensity of correspondence and forms of address (both explored in chapter 3), the acceptability or otherwise of requests for certain forms of material help, such as payment of rents, and the need to minimise actions and words that might bring the settlement parish into disrepute. Similar well-understood expectations framed the relationship between in-parish applicants and the vestry. The shared understanding becomes visible when conventions were breached, as for instance in the case of Dorothy Dickinson. Thomas Darwen, the overseer of Lancaster, wrote an exasperated letter to his counterpart in Manchester about Dickinson on 31 October 1817. She had, he noted, "repeatedly by letter and through her acquaintants been *teasing* us to allow her a shilling a week."[47]

For agency and negotiation to exist in any sustained form requires that both parties speak similar languages and share accepted grounds for and limits to contestability. These issues are explored further in the next chapter. It also requires the hope of expected and actual response, which created a firm foundation for rhetoric, strategy, and dispute. The corpus is literally littered with confirmations that such an epistolary conversation both existed and was continuously renewed. This renewal, especially when in the form of a written reply, was particularly important. It gave individual writers the basis for a further and more active correspondence, encouraging them to reflect, for instance, on the contents of a letter the next time they wrote, and it gave them greater confidence in their own agency. A sequence of circular correspondence might also build trust, and we occasionally see this acknowledged in letters from both officials and the poor. Sarah Pooley clearly intended that her letter of 20 November 1809 to Stephen Garnett acknowledging receipt of an allowance with obligation should convey that she could be trusted to act well.[48] John Winder, writing from Kendal on 19 June 1810, was more explicit, sending a hurried note to his settlement parish to the effect that "The Reason of my not sending you a Statement of our earnings [as presumably requested] was Because my Wife did not Perceive What was written on the Back of the note till it was to Late."[49] More widely, action and replies in effect constituted a stock of community knowledge, confirming which rhetorical and tonal strategies worked and which ones did not, a knowledge that would then be diffused through the collective consciousness and appear in subsequent letters of others. Successful or unsuccessful engagement with vestries and overseers by the in-parish poor had a similar effect.[50]

Just as Steve Hindle has traced a "common fund" of ideas about the poor in seventeenth-century England,[51] so too did the later process of co-respondence traced here create a shared meaning of appeal and response. This allowed the poor to "challenge the illusion of a stable organic social hierarchy," which some historians have argued had become impervious since the 1790s to the traditional claims of the poor on their wealthier parochial neighbours.[52] The fact of co-respondence highlighted, embodied, and made real the malleability of the local state. In effect, a sequence of replies by officials – with the recognition of belonging, however tenuous, that such replies conveyed – was a currency much like the character of writers, their ability to access credit, and the support of family and friends. This sense that replies by officials carried value over and above the words and cash conveyed has an insistent if subtle place in the corpus. Landlords were often pacified by letters from overseers, even if the full rent was not paid by parishes. Letters back to the poor that asked them to collect relief via a third party created new relationships that might be useful in the future or changed the way that an existing advocate or contact saw the claimant. The arrival of correspondence might give a writer credit in the eyes of a carrier. And, to revisit the core conclusions of the previous section and of chapter 3, letters gave hope for the future and made it worthwhile to invest time, energy, monetary resources, and credit with others in the sending of further narratives. The latter sentiment is never stated in the corpus, but its analogue – the waste of time, energy, resources, credit, and hope when no replies were forthcoming – is persistently elaborated upon in letters that did not immediately achieve an outcome. Very occasionally, this sense of currency is captured by the poor themselves, as for instance when Sarah Blade wrote a testamentary letter from Nuneham Courtenay in Oxfordshire on 11 August 1784 in which she noted that her creditors would be "Much the more satirsfied on they'r securitie" now that she held a letter from her settlement parish and had shown it to the local overseer.[53]

## CONCLUSION

Few of those who wrote or attended the vestry elaborated upon absolute rights to relief, a theme to which I return in chapter 8, but it is clear that they expected at least to have their case considered and some form of acknowledgment issued. The process of receiving, considering, and acting upon such letters and appearances was, of course, complex – indeed, more complex than the existing historiography allows. Vestry appearances were a matter of public record, at least when notes taken at meetings were converted into formal minutes, whereas letters were both private documents and public property once placed in the hands of officials. In this sense, the public and private considerations of officials intermelded, and individual letters might accrete outcomes across a wide spectrum from the anticipated and the expected to the unintended. Where multiple letters by or about the same person survive, it is absolutely clear that poor writers, much as poor vestry attendees, could expect to experience a many-shaded canvas of these outcomes across a "history" with their settlement parish. I have suggested, in this sense, that binary distinctions between success and failure are unhelpful. Nonetheless, most of those who wrote three or more letters did achieve an outcome or pattern of outcomes that was positive. Even a majority of those who wrote single letters appear to have received relief or at least further consideration that is now absent from the public record. Moreover, many letters pointed to a pre-existing history with a parish or officer, suggesting that they were, or were intended to be, part of a wider and more prolonged series of correspondence. In their turn, rather than merely filling in the gaps of a case where the person could not be viewed, such letters were also part of a wider complexion of agency shared with the in-parish poor. The end-of-process outcomes recorded as who got what in the overseers' accounts thus tell us little about the meaning and intent of relief or about the role and character of the Old Poor Law.

Focusing on the process tells us that parochial obligation was fluid and that the power of officials was, and was meant to be, malleable. A discretionary system remained discretionary in terms of the amount of relief given – something recognised in the fact that the majority of writers did not ask for specific amounts – but less so in terms of the ability to lever even the most disreputable and disrespectful people out of dependence or consideration. In this sense, the regional and intra-regional patterning that we can map on the basis of end-of-process poor law spending owes less to the numbers relieved or the size of the rate base and rather more to the typological patterning of those who applied, to what they asked for in the first place, and to the kinds of relief – whether limited to a single point in time or granted over a relief cycle – that adhered to different forms of belonging. Above all, these patterns reflect the susceptibility of officials and vestries to the rhetoric and strategies of poor writers and vestry attendees, as well as their ability to engage officials in a process of co-respondence. Success in the latter area, I have argued, created a currency, something that partly explains why a request for a small increase in pension could warrant many more words than a request for payment of a large one-off bill. The rest of part 2 of this book explores how poor writers built the foundations to employ this currency. Chapter 5 focuses on the question of where the poor found words, dealing with issues of literacy and intertextuality but mainly with the idea that officials, advocates, and poor writers shared a common linguistic register. Chapter 6 argues that individuals involved in the tripartite epistolary world of the parish understood and operated in a broadly consensual borderland where the process of poor relief and associated questions about matters such as the scale, duration, and form of welfare could legitimately be contested. There was, the chapter argues, a broad understanding of and tolerance for fiction in the narratives of the poor and their advocates.

# 5

## *Finding Words*

OVERVIEW

On 26 May 1808, Mary Horwood wrote an instigatory letter to Newnham in Gloucestershire. She was "under the Nesity of Trublein with these few Lines to Let you no that I am very hill not able to do aney work this month & I hope that you will have the goodness to seend me some money of 2 pounds ..."[1] Horwood struggled to convey her situation, quite literally running out of words, as indicated by the ellipsis with which she concluded. This sort of letter gives form to a sense that for ordinary people the act of writing could be physically, intellectually, and emotionally challenging.[2] It is unclear whether strategic decision, desperation, illiteracy, or lost literacy led to some poor people writing curtailed letters in this fashion.[3]

It is important to note, however, that most of the out-parish poor, as well as in-parish claimants who attended vestries in person, were *not* like Horwood. They found words. These words were inflected with situational nuance. Former ratepayers and teachers navigated a wider linguistic canvas than, for instance, casual labourers. The range of language was also dependent upon one's life-cycle stage, with older writers exhibiting and using wider linguistic registers than younger people simply because of accumulated experience of both language and its employment in story and personal history telling. We also see development over time.

Poor writers were never cut off from the expansion of the linguistic register on the national stage as the growing circulation of reading materials, new genres of fiction, industrialisation, the increase in world trade, and urbanisation drove new referential forms and democratised others.[4] In the very broadest sense, the letters of the poor from the 1830s onward were linguistically richer and more complicated than those from Oxford or Somerset, which constitute the earliest parts of the corpus. And the words of these poor writers constantly remind us of the strong overlap between oral and literate cultures in the period considered here.[5] Horwood's oral writing, like so much in the rest of the corpus, was dominated by the informal register and deeply inflected with the dialect and speech forms of the region where she had grown up. The substitution of *u* for *ou*, the use of the double *e*, and the dropping of the letters *g* and *c* are all core signals of the Gloucestershire accent. More widely, writers drew upon ingrained regionally specific speech patterns, mannerisms, and conversational routines. Thus authors growing up in midland communities begged pardon for writing, whereas their West Yorkshire counterparts talked of an obligation to write. Letters written by those who had grown up in small rural communities tended to have the "ask" inserted late in the text, whereas those written by Lancastrians tended to get to the point rather more quickly and bluntly. These patterns and routines were shared by officials and advocates, and we also see them played out fleetingly in the mediated record of vestry minutes.

Part 3 of this book explores *how* poor writers used the words at their disposal – the way they deployed rhetoric and strategy in order to negotiate relief and shape the system to which they were notionally subject. The rest of this chapter focuses on key aspects of the question of *where* such writers found their language. In the next section, I look at the nature of education, on the one hand, and at the overlapping oral and literate cultures of the period, on the other, arguing that common experiences and structures generated a shared linguistic register for both applicants and recipients.[6] The third section of the chapter investigates referential platforms – or perhaps tropes – both traditional ones and those that emerged during the period considered here. I will show that a shared register was underpinned by a common and accepted frame of reference, or a shared corpus of values, that created the ideological and practical groundwork for the exercise of agency by the poor.[7] The final sections of the chapter deal respectively with the borrowing and appropriation of language by some subgroups of the poor and with the question of whether we can detect intertextuality, with the poor and potentially poor incorporating literary, petitionary, or radical references into their letters as the period developed. Ultimately, it will become clear that writers could draw on a stock of words that was not so very different from that used by the majority of the rest of the population, including the middling sorts in most places. They did not have to consciously pitch their language in a form that they thought officials might find acceptable because both writer and recipient shared a linguistic currency. This commonality made the letters of the poor something more than socially constructed appeals or confections written mainly with their consumer in mind.

## SHARED LINGUISTIC FOUNDATIONS

As many other historians have shown, the penetration, depth, and length of schooling in England and Wales between the later eighteenth century and the 1830s was haphazard.[8] In a situation where the technologies of writing remained crude, writing literacy for ordinary people was gained through a situational mixture of accident, determination, and luck.[9] Maintaining literacy required practice, and in this sense it was also situational and accidental, arising out of variables such as an apprenticeship or job that required reading and writing skills, participation in a religious or other network that encouraged writing literacy,[10] and exploitation of the increasing range of self-improvement opportunities that had opened up, particularly in urban areas, by the early nineteenth century.[11] Diaries, autobiographies, and memoirs for this period provide clear evidence of individual and familial aspiration to sustained literacy.[12] Nonetheless, we have generally equated oral writing and episodic or partial literacy with the very poorest elements of society, and there is a rich literature, as chapters 1 and 2 showed, suggesting that literacy rates among the poor were low, heavily gendered, and subject to easy reversal before the 1850s.[13]

A sustained consideration of the corpus shows that this account is misleading. In fact, the nature of schooling and the penetration of literacy for the lower and middle ranks of the middling sorts were not so very different from those for the rest of local society, at least outside the biggest urban areas. Middling parents certainly had aspirations for their children, but the constant augmentation and renewal of this stratum of local society from below, as well as movement in the opposite direction within and between generations, probably means that the *stock* of literacy among the middling sorts did not change very much until the very end of the study period.[14] In turn, these people comprised the vast majority of overseers, vestrymen, and even epistolary advocates writing for the poor.[15] It is for this reason that the range of writing quality among advocates, on the spectrum from illiterate and highly oral to a tightly written and educated hand, matches more or less seamlessly the same spectrum for the prospective and actual poor. To be sure, the frequency of oral writing among these groups dwindled over time, first among officials and then for advocates, but the same is also true, even if different in degree, for poor applicants.[16]

It is perhaps unsurprising that shared schooling, writing traditions, and oral cultures were matched by common linguistic platforms.[17] Some, such as languages of custom, personal and epistolary conduct, economy, fair dealing, duty, religion, and philanthropy, were long-established and thus essentially backward-looking at the start of the study period.[18] Others, such as the languages of life-cycles, sickness, and gender, underwent an important process of extension and deepening between the later eighteenth century and the 1830s. Finally, we see the emergence of new linguistic registers – always inflected with regional nuances arising out of dialect, traditional speech patterns, and routines – as part of the socioeconomic, demographic, and cultural changes of the Industrial Revolution proper. The nature of these registers and the extent to which they were shared by different parties in the epistolary networks of the parish are fundamental to the rhetorical framing of the words of the poor (discussed at length in part 3) and to their reception by officials in the negotiating spaces of the discretionary Old Poor Law. The remainder of this chapter thus reviews some of these linguistic and referential platforms.[19]

---

It is important to start, however, by highlighting two notable absences. First, very much in contradistinction to petitions and other writing by ordinary people on the Continent,[20] there is an almost complete absence of references to or the language of patriotic service and the duties of the state to veterans.[21] This is the case not because ex-soldiers and ex-sailors are missing from the corpus. Indeed, many people with physical impairments can be identified as former servicemen. Yet George Hailes is one of the few people to refer to this matter. His instigatory letter from Castletown on the Isle of Man on 17 September 1826 said that he had been "discharged from the 5th Veteran Battalion commanded by Lieutenant Col Paulett" because of illness, and he asked his settlement parish to provide relief in addition to an army pension. He enclosed a lengthy supplementary statement pointing to long and varied service in defence of his country:

> This is to certify that *George Hailes* the Bearer hereof, was examined on the 24th day of *January 1816* before the Commissioners of the Royal Hospital at Chelsea, and that he is an Out-Pensioner of the said Hospital at *9d* per day, having served as a *Soldier 16½ Years* in the *5th Roy'l Vet. Battalion* Commanded by *Lt Col Paulett* and in other Corps according to the following Statement.
>
> [Table showing that he had also served in the 3rd Dragoon Guards and in a cavalry regiment whose name is illegible, for a total service of twenty-one years and four months.]
>
> And to prevent any improper use being made of this Certificate, he is *46* Years of Age *5* Feet *6½* Inches in Height, *brown* Hair, *grey* Eyes, *brown* Complexion, by Trade a *Labourer* was born in the Parish of *Aldermarston* in or near the Town of [blank] in the County of *Berks* and was rendered incapable of further Service by *a large Family and by order of Commander in Chief is also ruptured.*[22]

The absence of more examples of this sort suggests very keenly the essentially local roots of the Old Poor Law and its decision making, as well as the existence of alternative petitionary routes through which such people might make their claims on the nation.[23] In turn, a second absence concerns women bearing illegitimate children. Because illegitimacy was increasing during the study period, we might expect that the morality of single women with children would be subject to particular scrutiny and that such women would have to shape their narratives accordingly.[24] Yet, despite the fact that the scaffolding sources include hundreds of bastardy-affiliation orders and warrants for the arrest of absconding named fathers, few poor writers refer to the matter outside of persistent letters written to chase up missing allowances for bastard children or from errant fathers. In this sense, *female* moral culpability, unless it was insistent or egregious, remained on a plane separate from the negotiability of relief and from the ability of the poor and prospective poor to exercise agency.

Moving from absence to presence, long-established linguistic registers, usually inflected as I have observed with nuances arising out of dialect or regional speech patterns, have a substantial footprint. At the most subliminal level, the intertwining languages of custom and duty continued to have a powerful hold in the writing of advocates, the poor, and officials throughout the period.[25] I consider these issues at length in chapter 8. In the meantime, four further backward-looking platforms are important for this study. First, all writers shared a sense and language of *conduct*, as we have already seen through the brief discussion of openings and closings in chapter 2.[26] A brief consideration of the letter corpus for Berverley in Yorkshire throws this observation into sharp relief. Overseers here would "take the liberty of writing," much as poor writers would themselves. Advocates would "beg leave to solicit relief" for a prospective claimant, much as the poor would "beg the Gentlemen to send me a trifle." Just as "necessity forces me to discover the nakedness of my circumstances to you" in the letters of poor writers, overseers and advocates constantly conveyed urgent necessity to each other.[27] Officials, advocates, and the poor were collectively humble servants and petitioners who were much obliged for swift attention when they signed off. At the other end of the spectrum of intent, they also shared an accepted language of threat. Claimants and their advocates noted that they would have to be brought home with heavy hearts, and officials suggested that they would have to apply for orders of removal and suspend these orders, at a cost to the settlement parish, with an equally heavy heart.

Where such conduct norms were breached, any party might be sent a sharp reminder. The overseer of St Mary's Harrow, for instance, admonished Ann Cockerill for a letter from Bicester in Oxfordshire when he replied to her on 29 September 1829, noting that "You are requested when you again trouble the officers of this Parish to use a little more civility than you did in your postscript to the Overseers Letter written by him for you, your addition to the letter is not to your credit."[28] This short note speaks to the existence of a shared and understood language – as well as highlighting a mechanism for its transmission and reinforcement – that locates narratives as something more than constructions of what the writer thought recipients might most want to hear.[29] Honesty was also an insistent part of the conduct language, as we began to see in earlier chapters. Applicants, advocates, and officials all wrote about the truth of the case made and about the justice of action in relation to the conditions described. Their words were in many cases remarkably similar. Thus Elizabeth Bunbrick wrote an instigatory letter to her settlement parish of Shere in Surrey on 20 February 1830 to ask for an allowance because of slow work, telling the overseers that her statements were both true and "honestly stated as others can testify." The "others" attesting at the bottom of the letter included Mrs Chalcroft, who gave Bunbrick her washing to do, John Woods, Isaac Wick the Baker, John Green, Ceaser Baker, and G. Pickness. They all spoke of the truth of the statement, with Pickness noting that "I consider the above statement to be true and just as I have Lived Nex dore But one for more than 10 years and many times have Witness her Distress."[30] The question of honesty and probity is revisited several times in succeeding chapters.

Second, the parties in the tripartite epistolary world of the parish shared a remarkably similar language of *economy*, the *timeliness of action*, and *fair dealing*. Poor writers had and evinced an implicit and sometimes explicit knowledge of the essential balancing act – how to reconcile the interests of taxpayers and claimants – that lay at the heart of all discretionary welfare systems. John Fullbrook, for instance, noted that he did not wish to "offend you or any of the Gentlemen" by writing an extending letter to the parish of Blockley in Gloucestershire on Sunday, 30 January 1839. Asking the overseers to pay for several of his children to go into service as a way of relieving his familial burden, he reminded them that "I do not wish Sir to be troublesom, I am not A Stranger to the weight of Poor Rates."[31] Although Fullbrook is by no means alone in the corpus, most other poor writers referred indirectly to this balancing act, noting inter alia that returning to the parish of settlement and breaking the networks of work, charity, and credit in which an applicant was enmeshed would be expensive; that the cost of carriage would be expensive, with one parish for instance charging another for a horse that had died on a removal journey; that not acting when the opportunity arose, as with child apprenticeship, would end up costing more; that spending now, as with sickness, might avoid higher bills later; that the relief requested was the minimum possible; and that the claimant would do everything in his or her power to be and remain independent, such that this would be the last letter to the officers, at least for a while. John Sargent is emblematic of this linguistic framework, noting in an interspersing letter from his residence parish of Frampton Cotterell in Gloucestershire in 1817 that he was "Greatly Disapointed In your Not sending according to your promise." Threatening to "Imploy an attorney about the Business" of an unpaid doctor's bill that would result in the distraint of his goods and the breaking-up of his family, Sargent said, "Please to Observe as I Do Not Want to Put you to any Unnessary Expence But something must be done."[32] In turn, officials used exactly the same language as the poor both at the aggregate level, as in our parish is poor and so we urge economy, and in individual cases, as in we have acted with utmost economy, please act with economy consistent with our duty to the poor, and please act now to avoid further expense. So did epistolary advocates, who urged the economy of acting quickly or promised to protect the interests of the parish to which they wrote. Repeated applications by or on behalf of the poor challenged the logic of these arguments, but the tenacity of this shared understanding is made evident by its persistent place in the language of letters across both the spatial and chronological dimensions of the corpus and by the fact that the same language was recorded as being used by those who made their cases in person.

Third, other long-established linguistic registers, such as those associated with religion, have a more episodic place in the corpus. Some dissenting groups seem to have taken the poverty of their members very seriously, providing aid outside the poor law structure and thus diverting claims that would otherwise have come to the parish.[33] More widely, although historians disagree on the exact timing of the decline in the purchase of the Church of England on the culture of everyday life in England, it is clear that by the early nineteenth century the rise of alternative networks of belonging and identity based upon occupation, sociability, or neighbourhood should have begun to feed into the language of relief claimants.[34] There are, however, counter-indications, not least the fact that some 36 per cent of all letters from epistolary advocates were written by clergymen of different stripes, which suggests a continuing link between welfare, advocacy, and religion. Across the corpus, references to God or the Bible are uncommon. Giles Bull was one of the few writers who framed his appeals in terms of God's will, arguing in an extending letter of June 1804 that "God hath wrought his pleasure and a poor man and his parish can have nought to say on the matter."[35] One reading of this sort of absence is that writers wished to avoid the confrontational language implicit in references to godly commandments about the duties of the rich to the poor. Yet, even in letters from the 1750s, a period when we might expect the language of religion and godliness to have more traction, we see a similar absence. Writers did not, however, shy away from vaguer languages associated with Christian paternalism, and for some letter types, places, and life-cycle stages, the linguistic register of belief has a more insistent and sustained footprint. Thus, if there are no systematic spatial patterns in the use of religious language in England, the same cannot be said of Wales, where it was common.

Across the entire sample, writers who felt themselves or a family member to be in the last stages of an illness leading to death placed their fate in the hands of God and the alleviation of immediate suffering in the hands of the overseer. Indeed, their ending narratives might be suffused with biblical references, as was that of John Bayley, writing from Moorgate in London on 16 June 1830 to explain that only now could he "Bee restord to perfect health" by "the Blessing of god," who would also determine whether Bayley would be "aney more Trouble to you as the Doctor informes mea" to expect mortal danger "iff I leave [the hospital] wen my time is upp."[36] Where writers were seeking aid in the burial of a deceased relative, which was a common experience during this period, religious references were expressed even more keenly.[37] Mary Simmonds, writing from Nottingham on 5 January 1787 to obtain 2 pounds toward the cost of a funeral for her husband, asserted that "God has Led up through the Vale of Death and into the Vale of Tears and his Mercey as left my children in the gratest of want that no child before God Should See."[38] The in-parish poor used similar language when they appeared before vestries or when their words were constructed in cases made by officials, and praying – whether for relief, action, or the health and welfare of each other – was a common feature of the linguistic register employed more widely by all parties in the epistolary network of the parish. Overseers were particularly likely to use religious references when they contested the humanitarian duties of settlement parishes with their fellow officials, often deploying Christian obligation much more forcibly than poor writers themselves.[39]

There is also a more subliminal language of this sort, one that melds seamlessly into a fourth traditional referential model: necessitous Christian philanthropy. A shared linguistic register in this area encompassed claimants having previously drawn on the charity of unspecified "friends" and the linkage of dire conditions such as nakedness, starving children, and impending death to the need for parishes to recognise an essentially Christian duty.[40] Thus, when Thomas Webster wrote an interspersing letter from Bedford Row in London to the overseers of Staines on 29 September 1808 on the subject of the aged Widow Purday, he noted,

I have endeavoured to furnish them with a little money from my own Pocket & have obtained some for them from a few of the members of the congregation who are *ready to every good work* – their supplys must of course soon fail – for unless some prospect of support appears I must recommend them to claim the benefit of permanent benefit may be expected to occur – But should you think proper to add them afford tis poor Woman relief I shall be always ready to contribute a little extra assistance whenever any sudden pressure of calamity comes upon them.[41]

Webster, then, evoked a historic Christian duty to act and emphasised the continuing purchase of this model on his future actions. The poor, too, named supporters of this type and very frequently incorporated the language of their Christian charity into their appeals. They were not, in other words, seeking to avoid linguistic reference points that they feared might offend the recipients of their letters, as all parties in the epistolary world of the parish shared the same currencies.

These older and more established shared linguistic registers helped to shape the balancing by officials of (potentially) competing duties to ratepayers and the poor. We also, of course, see significant evolution during the period of this study. References to and languages of "the law," for instance, take on particular force from the early 1800s onward. I return to this issue in chapter 8. Meanwhile, four other new linguistic and referential platforms have real importance in this study. The first relates to ways of describing and conceptualising illness, which was a ubiquitous feature of poor law correspondence. Throughout the study period, the poor and officials operated along a spectrum of description for sickness that ranged from the generic "ill," "sick," "very ill," or "very sick" (and variants thereof) to precise and sustained description of symptoms and causation. By the 1820s, however, a rapid increase in parochial resources devoted to medical welfare coincided with a definitive move by all parties to the more precise end of this spectrum.[42] Thus, when the parish of Lymm in Cheshire surveyed its poor in 1823, sending officials house-to-house to ascertain the scale and causation of sickness, poor households entwined traditional "fuzzy" markers of sickness causation, such as fever, costiveness, indisposition, and ailment, with accounts of more precisely defined diseases, including asthma, phthisis pulmonisis, hysteria, peptic ulcers, and cholera.[43] This increasingly precise language of disease was repeated in the letters of advocates and officials and was mirrored in vestry minutes that cover the cases made by the in-parish poor.

A second and related development of the linguistic register over the period 1780 to the 1830s can be seen regarding those with mental and physical impairments. Constructed in terms of what such people could *not* do in the 1780s and 1790s,[44] the letters of advocates, the poor, and officials for all age groups and both genders are replete with a shared language of ability and progressive inability by the 1810s. This linguistic register encompassed and elaborated upon three essential experiences:[45] disability since birth or over the long term; temporary disability or inability linked to disease, accident, the nursing of others, or, increasingly by the early nineteenth century, mental perturbation;[46] and for all age groups, creeping inability melding into disability. The poor, even the most physically impaired individuals, constructed themselves as having residual ability to work and to live independent lives.[47] Adults whose physical capacity was temporarily compromised or who wrote of a downward physical spiral nonetheless used the language of longed-for independence to indicate a desire to do *something* toward their own care. Once this intention had been abandoned, however, the language used by the poor, their advocates, officials, and even vestry minutes to convey creeping disability shows remarkably striking similarity. Thus William Collings wrote an instigatory letter from Watteringbury in Kent to Farnham in Surrey on the 18 December of an unknown year to say that he was "ought of Emploighment" and unable to support a sick wife and unemployed son. An overseer had previously written on his behalf, but not having had an answer, Collings "tak this opertunity to Right to you hoping you will Settle mee some Rlife." The allowance was necessary because "I am Declining in years and ... I Cannot subsist any longer." A prior overseer's letter had noted in similar language and tone that Collings was "incapacitated for any work whatever and has been obliged wholly to give up his situation" due to illness and old age.[48]

More widely, advocates and officials shared with the poor the same language of abilities rather than disabilities. Thus those writing for children who had been blind, deaf, or encumbered by some other impairment since birth emphasised their belief that independence could be achieved if parishes invested in the future when they could and should.

Frances Soundy, already encountered in chapter 2, wrote in these terms to the overseers of Pangbourne on 10 October 1823. Asking them to pay the apprenticeship fees and to provide a new suit of clothes for her son John so that he could become an apprentice to a barge builder, she was "sorry to say if he his not bound I shall have him at home all the winter on my hands a gain as he as empediment in his speach so that he can not go Service as he can not vary wall be understud." Frances appended a note in her own hand but signed by her husband, James Soundy, that held out the prospect of a good return on the requested investment: "he his quit incapable of giting his living other mens So gentillmen we umblely pray you to assist this poor lad in giting his living."[49] Even those with mental impairments from birth short of dangerous lunacy found themselves constructed on a spectrum of ability, with most parishes, for instance, recognising different categories of "idiot" and tailoring relief and policies to these categories.[50] Although there was no systematised package of allowances associated with different degrees of ability, the shared linguistic register points to a mechanism by which certain groups of the poor came to garner de facto rights to welfare that had no legal basis but were widely recognised and respected.

Completely new pools of language and associated referential frameworks also emerged during the study period. Particularly important for the meaning of the process of poor relief were depressions in agriculture and trade, which comprise a third platform of the linguistic register. Almost nonexistent as a reference point in the 1780s, the claim that need was caused by local or national market disruption had become common among advocates, poor writers, and officials themselves by the 1810s. Moreover, writers increasingly assumed that such exogenous events and processes were common knowledge. When John Harley, the overseer of Monks Bretton in Yorkshire, wrote a renewing letter to his counterpart in Earls Barton on the subject of Benjamin Wooding on 10 September 1829, he noted that Wooding

> still remains so [dependent on poor relief] on account of the depression in Trade together with a dispute between the manufacturers and the weavers which adds greatly to the calamitous state of this

neighbourhood as neither the masters nor the men who are willing to work dare attempt to work at a reduced price. I need not trouble you with a long statement as you will see by newspapers accounts.[51]

National events in farming similarly became associated with a new language of factors beyond the control of the individual. Local trade or market disruptions could also mark a reason for writing and provide a language of reference. One aspect of this situation was the seasonality of agricultural and manufacturing work, a common claim in official and poor correspondence, as we saw in chapter 3. Expanded industrial and service sectors also brought with them the disruption caused by the bankruptcy of individual entrepreneurs or cash flow problems attendant upon credit squeezes. In the north, mills were burned to the ground or closed by industrial action. Production might be stopped by delays in getting raw materials, quality control problems, or a sudden change in the fashion of the market. In agriculture, sheep rot and other animal diseases could devastate the farming economy. And sustained competition could drive some occupational groups to utter penury. The Preston handloom weaver John Keller wrote on 18 June 1816 to say that "piece rates his now so low that no man can get enough threw his labaur to meet the needs of his family."[52] Although the question of what to do with the claims of the unemployed or underemployed was in essence timeless, the post-1780 period witnessed a change in the scale of the problem and the intensity of the question.[53] The Speenhamland system and other parochial interventions in labour market architecture were one solution.[54] In northern England, in particular, vestry minutes and the correspondence of overseers are replete with instances where claimants were asked to detail individual and family incomes and where relief was given notwithstanding collective earning that would have looked like a king's feast to the average agricultural labourer in Dorset at the same date. Recent research from Henry French and John Langton suggests that the susceptibility of parishes to the claims of the unemployed could vary radically, but this situation should not blind us to the fact that there appears to have developed a common linguistic register for unemployment across the whole range of writers and the typologies of letters they sent.[55] I revisit this matter in chapter 11.

A fourth development – the language of administrative memory – also has important consequences for the linguistic register within which appeals and negotiation could be framed. I have argued elsewhere that overseers increasingly came to understand their role and the nuances of their local practice in relation to other officials and other parishes in their area and even outside it. The statisticalisation of the poor law in the form of provision of comparative information and national guidebooks for overseers stood in the place of state attempts to create a uniform welfare system, a sort of do-it-yourself version of standardisation.[56] Within this framework, the corpus exhibits a growing and insistent language of administration, confirming that poor people did not write only what was uncontentious or acceptable to officials. The poor and their advocates urged officials to look at their books when allowances did not arrive or were less than expected. Thus Widow Mitchell, writing from Kingston in Surrey on 21 September 1824, asked her co-respondent to pay the arrears of a widow's allowance. Suggesting that they look to their books, she said, "it appears to me to be Ten Weeks from the 18th of July till the 25 day of Sept 1824 Both days inclusive – being £1.0.0."[57] Equally, officials were urged to consult their books in order to understand why, in an extending letter, an episodic relief history might turn into a case for a sustained weekly pension. Officials, too, urged each other to look at their books when securing payments or deciding what to allow, using exactly the same language as other parties in the tripartite correspondence network of the parish. Yet this linguistic register also went further. Notwithstanding requests for economy, officials increasingly asked each other to treat out-parish paupers "as you would your own," recognising local norms and administrative processes. The analogue for the poor and their advocates was to remind officials what would be allowed in particular circumstances for the settled poor in the host parish, as did Michael Willis, writing on behalf of John Chandler in an undated interspersing letter from Egham in Surrey. Noting that Chandler had a family of thirteen to provide for and was too sick to make such provision, he said, "Having been a parish Officer myself a short time ago, I have some little knowledge of what our Parish allows under such circumstances to our Poor, and I consider that what you are kind enough to allow him is not sufficient to keep them in bread, let alone any little extra thing."[58] Unsurprisingly, we also see by the 1810s the emergence of a powerful language of precedent, as opposed to custom, something considered at greater length in chapter 8. That the employment of this language was not generally considered hostile by officials is clear testimony to the shared referential world of the parish.

The corpus bears the linguistic imprint of a number of traditional, developing, and emergent referential platforms that were shared remarkably closely by the different parties involved in parochial correspondence over the process of poor relief. Of course, regional linguistic styles and registers and the uneven survival of a petitionary tradition, notably in Wales and the English borderlands, can be seen. Nonetheless, it is clear that the basic linguistic register *was* shared between places. This shared framework – almost a foundational language – shapes what we find in letters and the nature of the expectations that bound them. It also locates the grey area in a discretionary welfare system where negotiation could take place and agency could be exercised. The poor did not, it seems, simply write a language that was "acceptable." Against this backdrop, it is important to understand that the poor and prospective poor also drew on two further sources of language that were more particular to *their* role in the epistolary world of the parish, and it is to these areas that the chapter now turns.

## APPROPRIATED WORDS

First, then, the poor appropriated words from other parties in the negotiation process. The idea that people learned linguistically from each other should not come as a surprise. We have already seen that letters were written for claimants and in their presence by officials and epistolary advocates, even in cases where the poor could in fact write for themselves. Drafts were inevitably read by or to the potential applicant, and it would be hard to argue that language and strategies were not taken on board. Moreover, we have already seen instances where letters written by the poor were taken to officials and other advocates so that the justice and accuracy of the case could be endorsed, suggestive of a further avenue through which language and histories could be shared. And even if it is difficult to trace in the archive, Keith Snell is clearly correct that letters might be written collectively, such that poor writers borrowed from each other and created a common frame of reference within and between communities.[59]

A wider sense of how the words of others might simply be appropriated into letters, or indeed into vestry minutes where the poor presented their cases in person, can be seen in the extended correspondence of Henry Roper, the overseer of Oundle in Northamptonshire. His letter to Mr Strong of Stanground in Derbyshire on 17 April 1833 asked whether the pauper John Gann was an employee of Strong:

> He [Gann] having referred us to you I beg respectfully to request the favour of your Informing us if he is likely to continue in your employ & what amount of wages he is getting per week as we of course expect him to support his wife & family also what length of time he has been working for you or in case of not being employed by you if he has had any work during the last 3 months.[60]

It is easy to surmise that the text of the reply would then have been re-cycled by both official and claimant. In other cases, there was explicit acknowledgment of this intent, as for instance when Roper wrote to the overseer of Sawston in Cambridgeshire on 12 May 1835 and added a postscript that read,

> I should have replied to you before but wished to lay it before the Select Vestry for their orders. In my last I requested the next time you wrote to inform us as what [are] the names, ages & occupations of the children [of the Naylor family for circulation to the vestry] and expect you will favour us with a line by Return of post for that purpose.[61]

Yet, as the study period progresses, an additional form of appropriation begins to resonate more firmly through the corpus and to shape the language of negotiation, particularly in testamentary and extending letters. That is, the prospective poor, officials, and advocates increasingly incorporated the voices of third parties, directly and consciously, into their own correspondence. This practice took three guises. First, writers simply summarised the views of other stakeholders in the case, as for instance when landlords wrote about the inability of tenants to pay rent given the illnesses and prognoses outlined by named doctors or when officials summarised the actual or likely views of magistrates if a settlement parish did not wish to take action in a particular case. Thus Richard Palmer wrote from Kendal in Cumberland to Billington in Lancashire on 26 January 1829 in the case of James Ormerod's wife, whose current relief "is thought by all who are acquainted with her situation to be quite insufficient." Palmer noted,

> I have consulted Mr Hesmondhalgh on the subject and we have come to the following conclusion: "That the overseer give a ticket to Richard Hesmondhalgh for 11s per week to furnish the old people with milk until such a time as they can provide for themselves." James Seed [the overseer of Billington] had, therefore, better send a ticket to that effect with J. Ormerod to R. Hesmondhalgh.[62]

The poor also incorporated summative voices into their correspondence. Frances James wrote from Leicester to Uttoxeter in Staffordshire on 1 November 1834 on the subject of the long illness of her husband. She reminded the vestry that "the berrden has been much more mine" than theirs and co-opted the words and authority of the overseer of Leicester, claiming that "I have named the Circumstance here to the Overseers of this parish and they think I am taking a proper step."[63]

A second variant of this appropriation can be seen in instances where writers actually appended to letters attestations of their veracity by third parties, examples of which we saw in chapter 2. In some cases, the confirmation was in the same hand as the letter and simply signed by someone purporting to be the person named. The more usual approach was for witnesses to write their own text. Such additions appeared in the narratives of poor people, advocates, and officials. These attestations varied in length, comprising the one or two confirmatory lines usually appended by doctors as well as the much more extensive cases often made by landlords or employers. It would be easy against this backdrop to understand these additions as akin to the enclosures that sometimes accompanied letters and that often seem to have served the same purpose of assurance and honesty. The assumption would be wrong. Additions to an otherwise self-contained text were different in intent and meaning from supplementary documents. They conveyed and were intended to convey a message of the proximity of the parties involved and suggested that the person making the addition had read the case rather than merely hearing of the conditions that it announced. Just as textual amendments and extensions are important to literary scholars in elaborating the meaning and use of texts, in the context of the epistolary world of the parish, they were supposed to signify more "value" than the ephemeral insertions of disembodied notes into the folds of letters.[64] It is also important to remember that an inserted testimony presumed a case where the testimony had already been made in the core letter, whereas an addition could compensate for silences in the text itself as the poor became strategically or actually speechless. Whichever way we construct these additions, the writers of the core document clearly intended to appropriate the words of others, and they believed that the practice carried weight. Dr J.W. Donald, for instance, attested twelve letters for the sick poor across a number of parishes around Pangbourne in Berkshire in the single year 1829.[65]

Third, some subgroups of the poor actively appropriated and quoted the words of others. Nowhere is this clearer than in the letters by, on behalf of, or about the sick poor, for whom prescriptions, the visits of doctors and apothecaries, and discussion of symptoms and treatment provided a rich reservoir of language. The frequent precision of these quotations is notable, but even if others adopted vaguer statements about their never being well, their recovery being delayed, or the causation of their illness being uncertain, the act of appropriation is clear. It was also a shared act. Officials appropriated to their correspondence with each other the words and opinions of doctors in particular cases, even claiming that their actions had been solely determined by the case implicit in those words. Thus Samuel Doman wrote an instigatory letter from Basingstoke in Hampshire for Robert Pummell on 10 October 1827. Having taken the advice of the parish doctor, he advised his fellow official that Pummell "has been confined to his bed nearly a fortnight with the Rheumatic Gout and cannot get up, there is no likelihood of his being able to work for some time and on that account he stands in need of Immediate assistance." Pangbourne parish immediately remitted 1 pound. When Doman wrote again on 27 October without the advise of the doctor and in his own voice, he merely noted that "Robert Pummell is no better is more of a cripple than ever. I think it will be some time before he gets better, cannot get on without your further assistance."[66] Epistolary advocates, too, appropriated the words of doctors. James Trindell, for instance, wrote an instigatory letter from Reading in Berkshire on behalf of a "lad by the name of W House about 13 years of age" on 8 January 1828. Trindell had

> been at a little expence on the part of the Medical Gentleman who attends him, which is Mr May, our parish surgeon, wherein he informs me his complaint is such, that it might be 10 days or a fortnight before his might recover from his illness, (it is the Rheumatic fever), the purport of my writing is, for you to give an order to Mr May for his future attendance, & in the mean time any thing I can do, in a little way by way of sending him nourishment during his illness I shall feel much pleasure.[67]

Of course, this sort of appropriation was not confined to doctors. In some places, for instance, the poor systematically incorporated the words or personae of neighbours and "friends" into their texts. Frances Morel, for instance, wrote from Paddington Green in London on 1 February 1823 to ask for payment of arrears of an allowance from Wallingford parish in Oxfordshire. She commented archly,

> Perhaps you may take me for a Lady of Fortune because some of my Friend got the Bishop of Durham to write to Mr Flamank about the payment of the Money. I must therefore undeceive you – and inform you – that my Income is a very small one and that it is a

great inconvenience to me to be kept so long out of my money as well as the advance the 2s6d weekly out of my own pocket.[68]

These are important cases, exemplifying the complex negotiation strategies pursued by poor writers in their engagement with parishes. The words, however, also evidence a common linguistic platform and provide a sense of how that platform might have become common and how it might have grown. Appropriated language must have been circulated. It was certainly repeated, and it provides a clue to how certain subgroups of the poor came to obtain a widely understood, accepted, and defended right to be heard favourably. The process of appropriation, passing without comment and challenge anywhere in the corpus, also suggests the wide foreground of negotiation that underpinned the sustainability of a discretionary welfare system. Moreover, acceptance of the fact that poor writers, officials, and advocates appropriated the voices of those who in other forums might be labelled actors of the state – overseers, doctors, employers, ratepayers, and vicars – also points persuasively to the intended malleability of state power in its local form.

### BORROWED WORDS

If correspondents could consciously appropriate the words of other parties in the relief and claims-making process, they might also borrow them from a wider range of sources.[69] Intertextuality is never easy to prove for poor authors,[70] not least because eventual writers might pick up from other texts the confidence to write and mastery of the techniques of writing rather than the linguistic register itself. Thus, although we see little evidence of the language contained in nineteenth-century petitions to government feeding into the corpus, there can be no doubt that the poor and prospective poor were touched by the mushrooming of petitioning culture.[71] In similar fashion, we know that ordinary people populated coronial juries, read reports of inquests in the newspapers, and often appeared as witnesses. Such experiences may have improved their storytelling and story structure, but there is little direct evidence in the corpus of their borrowing the formal language of the court.[72] There are also some surprising absences. Unlike for the epistolary cultures of the mid-dling sorts, there is little evidence that ordinary writers, their advocates, or officials borrowed novelistic or poetic languages and tropes.[73] John Sayer of Oxford is unusual in literary references like "Death is certain to all Men the King to the Beggar" and "Necessity is the Mother of in-vention."[74] Equally, there is almost no evidence that writers borrowed from the political pamphlets and radical texts that were circulating at the time. This is perhaps surprising given the deep involvement of poorer people in radical movements like Chartism and in wider episto-lary acts of resistance.[75] Moreover, there are few concrete elaborations of ideological duty, and there is no evidence at all of class-based analysis of the position of the poor.[76] One reading of these absences is that the poor sought to convey texts that fell within the acceptable bounds of contestation and did not question the basic social order. Yet writers were not, as we will see in later chapters, averse to strong and antagonistic statements that parish inaction had led to compromised dignity. The lack of reference to radical texts in particular might thus really reflect a disconnect between the structural and class analysis of radicals and the way that ordinary people thought about the nature and remediation of their poverty. Perhaps most surprisingly of all, reconciling the advice given in popular letter-writing manuals of the period 1800–1830s with the linguistic content of letters by the poor and prospective poor reveals only the most tangential overlaps, themselves focused on traditional models and languages of deference and philanthropy. Didactic literature in its narrowest sense thus has only limited purchase on the language of the corpus.

There *is*, however, evidence of the borrowing of words from other sources. First, we can clearly see references and language from traditional oral and semi-oral culture of the period peppered throughout the texts. The importance of chapbooks and balladry as staples of popular culture was on the wane by the 1790s, but their imprint on the language of the writers in the corpus can be seen in cases like that of David Rivenhall.[77] In his testamentary letter of 24 August 1827 from Cold Bath Fields prison, where he was confined for debt, Rivenhall sought to construct himself as a God-fearing, honest man unjustly confined to the detriment of his family, much as some contemporary balladry focused on unjust imprisonment.[78] Perhaps surprisingly given a widespread sense that literacy in Wales lagged behind that in England, there seems to be no systematic spatial patterning to the employment of such language.[79] Other traditional frames of reference and language also left an imprint. Evidence of the penetration of folktales is less strong than it appears to have been on the Continent, but poor writers did return persistently to the concept of the just outlaw.[80] Thus John Salisbury, writing an instigatory letter to Preston on 27 April 1824, noted that his wife had just given birth and referred to the struggles occasioned by the well-known decline of the weaving trade. He had "nothing to turn to but my hands" and asked "what can a weaver earn" even using every exertion? Salisbury begged "for Gods sake allow me something in this time of need" and warned darkly that "I cannot nor am not able using *honest* means to support my family."[81] Here, then, was a man who had struggled against the dual tyrannies of sickness and underemployment and now found himself driven to the very edges of honesty if he was to prevent his family from falling into starvation and nakedness. The framework of the just outlaw is unmistakeable, and although it is particularly well drawn in this example, some 300 letters in the corpus contain similar elements. Officials did not generally adopt such a clear set of references from traditional storytelling, but even they frequently noted that the efforts of the poor to maintain themselves within the limits of the law ought to make their cases compelling.

Second, officials and the in- and out-parish poor also shared an evolving model and language of begging. The early construction of vagrants and beggars as somehow godly and a necessary part of the web of philanthropic duty that tied together social groups is often assumed to have waned rapidly in the early modern period.[82] Unlike on the Continent, licensed begging in England and Wales in the form of charity briefs and in Scotland as sanctioned by the church declined rapidly as a practice from the eighteenth century onward.[83] Yet, if there was much subsequent public commentary on the ills of beggars and begging, there is also much counter-evidence that ad hoc giving in the street remained an important facet of middling, particularly male middling, identity.[84]

We find no heroic beggars or respectable vagrants in the letters of the corpus.[85] Indeed, the wider scaffolding sources are replete with attempts by vestries to suppress both groups. Nonetheless, the accumulation of stories about them leaves a mark on the language used in the very many cases of itinerant people about whom we have (often single) letters. In particular, poor writers, advocates, and officials shared a language that had three strands: *expediency*, understood as the need to give a small amount now in order to avoid further cost; *blamelessness*, such as when wandering because there was no choice or because it had official sanction; and *urgent necessity*, which was largely due to sickness, something that exacerbated the positon of the wandering poor and brought them to a standstill. Thus Joseph Thompson wrote from Lanchester in Northumberland to Greystoke in Westmorland on 28 June 1826 to recount the story of William Miller, a travelling broom maker. Having pitched camp on the public road, the family set a fire, and upon their "leaving it for a few moments with 3 children," the fire spread, destroying their camp and burning "to a cinder" a one-year-old son. Thompson concluded that the family were "greatly necessitated" and that their presumed settlement parish ought to act immediately for these "poor miserable persons."[86]

These unfortunate events made it into the local newspapers, and particularly later in the period we can clearly discern the poor themselves engaging with newspapers as a third source of words. Samuel Parker of Rothersthorpe, for instance, threatened his settlement parish with published exposure of his case, which would "show the Publick all the perticulers of the matter and it will be a shame on you."[87] There is no evidence that Parker recycled the words of the newspaper back into his later letters, but instances like this one point to the fact, now increasingly well established, that poor people could get to know the contents of newspapers.[88] That this encompassed more than passive reception is suggested by the appearance in letters of statistics and other information that could have come only from this source. John Grant, for instance, wrote an extending letter from Leeds on 24 January 1820 "to inform you of our present Circumstances." Prior relief had been insufficient "among 8 Souls," and Grant quoted material from an article in the

*Leeds Mercury* that showed hopeless work prospects and "500 Shear-men out of work and all other trades in proportion."[89] In similar fashion, Samuel White of Halstead in Essex quoted cases back to the overseer that he had "myself saw in your Printed list of the out Door Poor for Chelmsford."[90] The poor and prospective poor shared this borrowing of newspaper material with their epistolary advocates, who variously noted newspaper headlines about the opening of hospitals, the state of trade, new treatments, and local goings-on in their efforts to suggest a course of action to overseers. John Harley of Barnsley, for instance, outlined the case for a poor applicant and noted that "I need not trouble you with a long statement as you will see by newspaper accounts" the state of the manufacturing districts in September 1829.[91] And as we have already seen, officials themselves were not averse to referring to newspaper coverage of local and national events in their dealings with each other.

There is more substantial evidence of a fourth source of words for poor writers. From the later eighteenth century, as suggested in chapter 1, an ever-larger corpus of scientific or medical knowledge and literary works appeared in the public domain, along with medical advertisements, advice books, and prescriptions.[92] Ginnie Smith reminds us that even by the late eighteenth century, "there was a large reservoir" of vernacular medical works available for ordinary people to read and communicate to others,[93] and the popularisation of medicine could not have left the poor behind.[94] We begin to see evidence of this in letters like that of Elizabeth Taylor, who wrote a testamentary letter to James Daydde, the overseer of Shelton in Norfolk, on 11 April 1764. The core of her narrative was a claim that "I have been so much afflictet since Michelmas with the St antinis Fire that I have had 5 holes in my thighs and I have had no health since March nor no my child." She begged "you to send me sumthing more to subsist me til I gett sumthing Better."[95] This very precise description was unlikely to have come from a parish doctor because Shelton had not at this point engaged one, suggesting that Taylor had picked up the language and diagnosis elsewhere. By the early nineteenth century, direct and indirect references to precise medical knowledge were much more common. Samuel White borrowed the language of "no Common Affliction" from one of the many dozens of self-dosing manuals circulating when he wrote in 1826; Rody Joliff had a bad breast and was informed enough that "I am Nothing else to expect but what it is a cancer"; and Margaret Howell understood the aetiology of "Cholera Morbus," clearly copying from a medical book or newspaper when she wrote on 16 April 1832, but she reverted to the language of "Cholery sickness" when she wrote again on 3 October 1832.[96]

Finally, there is also a sense in the corpus that poor writers and their advocates drew on the language, content, and structure of other sorts of letter that came into their possession. Advocates sometimes wrote to each other on the subject of individual claimants and before they wrote to officials. They may also have drawn on the copy letters of previous advocates, especially in situations where these letter caches were likely to have been preserved, such as when clergymen succeeded each other. And of course both advocates and poor writers could draw upon the letters of officials, quoting back language and sense in order to enhance the impact of the case. William Dunkley was one of 540 writers who came back at some point in their correspondence to the words of officials in this way. His renewing letter of 11 April 1806 opened, "I hope you will be as good as your word in regard of what you told my wife when she was over and that is to Pay our ret for us wich is not in my power to do myself. Sir you said you wuld pay it at Lady Day."[97] Moreover, we know that emigrants entered into sustained correspondence with family and friends "back home." Such letters form a distinctive genre of letter writing,[98] but in the sense that the majority were, and were meant to be, read aloud and read by others, they form a reservoir of language and tropes for wider correspondence. Published letters, too, could be drawn upon as a source.[99] And we should not understate the extent to which the poor and prospective poor kept in touch with families and the degree to which letters of relatives might therefore inform current writing.[100] The avenue might sometimes be a postscript in letters to the overseer asking that he show the letter to family in the host parish or pass on its sense. Yet there are 164 examples of more substantial and sustained correspondence comprising a mixture of pleas for help and requests for the intercession of local family with overseers in the settlement parish or simply for the conveying of information. An undated letter by William Hopkins retained in the archive of Farnham in Surrey is a colourful but not unrepresentative example:

> My Dear ~~Sister~~ Girl
>
> I now wright to you to say that I wrote A Letter to you A fortnight Ago yesterday I ham very Sorry you did not get it my Dear girl we are all quite well But my dear girl we are all quite well But not happy you may depend your Husband wrote to the club – 5 weaks a go But he did not send them the money he owed them and at that time he was at Salsburay in Wiltsheer and I wrote to him the folowing day and sent him your Letter and he returned it back to me with too more and they caunt A Half Crown But I did not take them in Ben wishen you to wright of to the club House with all Speed I think my dear girl you had Better Let the Genteelmen See this letter or Prehaps you had Better wate till you have wrote to him and hear wat he says and if you wright to him and he Answers your Letter I hope you will wright to me and let me know from me you Loving Mother & Father.[101]

Hopkins, then, struggled with whether to write a more or less formal letter, as indicated by the crossing-out of "sister," as he sought to emphasise family solidarity in a text that he intended to be made public. But the broad narrative content – struggle, costs of postage, seeking to make do through membership in a friendly society, and a family at the end of its wits and resources – could clearly be recycled subsequently by any who read it.

## CONCLUSION

Those involved in the tripartite epistolary world of the parish – officials, advocates, and poor writers – spoke and wrote the same language and exchanged the same "linguistic currency."[102] This was not the staged language of the courtroom or the petition to government. There is almost no evidence that words were "emulative and recitative" in the sense of being copied or adopted, or at least not unthinkingly copied, from printed texts, manuals, or other letters.[103] Nor was this language, despite the temptation to think that letter contents were shaped to what the recipient wanted to hear, solely the product of the artifice of those who wrote.[104] It emerges out of a common education experience, a long-shared linguistic register, and a set of referential platforms – old and new – that were well understood by all parties to the correspondence of the corpus. These factors were associated with a stock of language that provided the bedrock of appeal and response.[105] There was some typological and spatial variation, and we can see strong traces of regional accents and speech patterns in the informal registers typical of the oral writing that dominates the corpus. There are also some developments of the breadth and depth of this linguistic register over time, what Roy Porter labels a "new linguistic coinage."[106] Nonetheless, it seems clear that even by the 1830s, when it is argued that ratepayer and public opinion had turned against the claims of the poor, the process of poor relief was one conducted in a shared tongue and pen.[107] The fact of this shared process no doubt informs Nick Hopkin's sense that most letters from poor writers in East Yorkshire "show a confidence that relief will be granted."[108] At the corpus level, as we saw in chapter 4, not all of the poor would have been so sanguine, but there is much evidence that writers knew the difference between plain and polite writing and varied their language in an effort to gain advantage in the negotiation of relief.[109]

These observations are an important vantage point for the remaining chapters of the study. Part 3 explores the ways that a common stock of language and referential platforms was built into the rhetoric of negotiation. Meanwhile, chapter 6 returns to an earlier observation about the remarkable lack of crossing-out in the writing of the poor. I have suggested that putting these stories on paper must have required considerable care and the commitment of much time. But the lack of crossing-out also suggests that the poor had marshalled and developed their stories over time and well enough to tell them coherently and that they broadly knew what sorts of story to tell. It is to this process of constructing an acceptable story and history that the next chapter turns. I argue that officials and the poor understood and accepted a series of shared rhetorical fictions that together generated considerable agency and made relief under the Old Poor Law into a genuinely negotiated process. The existence of a common linguistic register and set of referential platforms means that the word "shared" as I use it here is not mere casual adornment. Rather, it points to a mutual expectation that the power of the local state could and would be constrained by the agency of the poor.

# 6

## *History and Fiction*

On "Monday Morng" of an unknown month and year, the *in-parish* claimant Henry Rutter wrote an extending letter to the former overseer of Farnham in Surrey in the following terms:

My Dear Sir,

    Will you have the goodness to see the Overseers agreeable to *your kind promise*, and use all your interest and eloquence in my favour – Have the goodness to tell them that if they will advance me the sum of £15 on my Promissory note [i.e., a loan], I shall be certain after seeing my friend at Lymington (many of who are very respectable, and would if they knew my distress compassionate and relieve me) of being able to repay them, before the termination of the present year, but under my present circumstances, and appearance as regard Apparel, I am unwilling and ashamed to see, or make any distress know to them, My intention is to take out a Hawker's License, and to travel with light Articles of Stationary – My chief Business will be with Attorneys, many of whom I know, who will feel it their interest to deal with me. Trusting to your Exertions & friendly representation of my Case, I remain Dear Sir,
          Your Sincere Wellwisher,
           Hy. Rutter

P.S. As Mr. Fraser [the new overseer] is well disposed towards me, and as two strings to a Bow is better than one, perhaps you seeing him, he will act in conjunction with you, and I think your united efforts will have the desired effect. I have said nothing to him, but leave the matter entirely to you.[1]

Rutter's story is compelling, rehearsing the languages of honesty, dependability, struggle, and desire to be independent – he asked for a loan, not a gift – that have begun to unfold in the background of earlier chapters. His prospective employment as a hawker of stationary also throws important light on key navigation issues, such as where the poor found paper. Since Rutter was an existing relief recipient in Farnham, it seems likely that his tale had developed over a number of tellings in the forums of the vestry, neighbourhood, and overseer's office. The story was also somewhat fluid, even false, as later correspondence shows. A self-justificatory letter to the overseer of Farnham on 19 November 1832 noted that he was in an "awkward and distressed situation" because of "The unkindness, calumny, and ingratitude of the Bennett Family," who had clearly accused him of falsehoods. Rutter noted that "through their Misrepresentations of me," his hopes of improving his lot had been dashed, and "I much fear, that unless your friendly interposition does not prevent it, I shall, such is the present state of my feelings, be induced to do something, that others as well as myself will long have to deplore, My present state of mind is such, that I cannot add more."[2] The threat of violence is clear. By 23 April 1833, Rutter had reconstructed his story, asking that the overseer

will from the Parish Funds, grant me a Loan of Twenty Pounds [an increase of his first request by 5 pounds], on my Promissory Note, for 3 months, at the expiration of which time, after having seen my friends in my native Place,[3] who are many of them respectable, I shall be able to repay it. The purpose I want it for is, to supply myself with a small stock of light Stationary, and therewith to get my Living, without further Parochial Assistance. I am confident that at the time specified, (3 months) I shall be able to repay it.[4]

---

Tapping into ongoing disputes over the costs of church maintenance in Farnham, he would "assure you Gentlemen, that a recent discovery of a most unpleasant nature, in which a functionary of the Church is concerned, has rendered Farnham most disgusting to me, and has had at times, such an effect on my mind and spirits, that I am when under excitement of feeling, almost driven to desperation."[5]

The parochial officers of Farnham were unconvinced and did not pay. Rutter disappears from the record, only to surface again at Lymington in Hampshire, where he made the same sort of case. The similarities to the character Wilkins Micawber in Charles Dickens's novel *David Copperfield* are unmistakeable. Rutter, then, was part of a small but entertaining group of the poor first encountered in chapter 2 who, usually over a series of letters, tried to actively deceive the officials, whom they knew would change office regularly. Adopting a complex pattern of letter origination – their own writing, scribed narratives, letters purportedly from other family members, and narratives from advocates – these were the words and stories of "the unworthy."

There are many reasons, as we have already seen, to think that most other poor writers and their advocates were honest. The room for embellishment was limited. Nonetheless, whether embodied in letters or inscribed into personal appearances before the vestry, all stories were developed over several tellings and often with multiple participants. Thus no one teller or receiver could and did hold a "whole" account in their hands or memories, as opposed to more or less accurate and comprehensive fragments. The letters of the poor, in other words, share with diaries, autobiographies, personal or familial letters, and other so-called ego documents an "element of fiction."[6] This might be deliberately engineered, as in the case of Rutter, but more often emerged out of partial statements, silences, the act of forgetting, and unconscious decisions about what information was important to convey and what not. Moreover, the multipurpose nature of the claimant letter, extending even to a means of conveying information and greetings to relatives via the overseer, was bound to shape the nature of inclusion and omission in individual narratives in a period with a "written-cum-oral" culture.[7] Alternatively, fiction might creep in because of the exigencies of the law and custom.[8] It would be easy in this context to suggest that writers confected partial stories on the basis of what they thought officials "most desired to see," as for instance does Patrick Joyce.[9] In practice, however, there is little evidence of the sort of sustained deliberation and creation that this view would imply. Letters were fictive but not necessarily fictional.

There is of course nothing new in these broad observations. European scholars dealing with ego documents, or ordinary writing, have long recognised the existence of multiple fictions in their material.[10] Jeremy Boulton's rich reconstruction of the competing and partial stories told in the settlement examinations conducted by the London parish of St Martin in the Fields also points to the scope for fiction in the setting of courts and petty sessions.[11] It is unclear whether the letters of the poor were more or less susceptible to fiction than either other ordinary writing or stories told in person by in-parish claimants.[12] Except in the most sparsely populated rural areas, officials could hold only a partial picture of the lives of those who applied in person, such that it is possible, even likely, that those appearing to make their cases used exactly the same fictions as their epistolary counterparts. In this sense, an understanding of the rhetoric and strategy of the poor – of how they operationalised their words in the territory of negotiation emerging out of a discretionary poor law, the core theme of part 3 – must be underpinned by an understanding of the fictive landscape of story and history construction, as well as by an awareness of the degree to which officials and others involved in the process of poor relief also peopled this landscape.[13]

The rest of this chapter is thus concerned with the particularities of how claimants constructed the groundwork of their stories or had it constructed for them. I am less concerned with the rhetoric of pauper letters than with the nature of the stories to be rhetoricised. For poor writers, the decisions about what to put in a story, what to leave out or "fudge," and which "facts" to attach to the different types of letter outlined in table 2.1 speak, inter alia, to what they deemed most current and relevant, their accumulated experience in the negotiation space, their experience of storytelling, the nature of their memory and that of the parish, and the ways that they understood and sought to operationalise agency. There is no sense from the letters that certain "facts" and approaches were tied to different sorts or magnitudes of request. *But* their stories were often *more* than what a reader can mine from the text, even if there are multiple letters to cross-reference. Rather, in the majority of cases where we see sustained correspondence, third parties also constructed a version of the story. Putting this material back together again lays bare the decisions by the poor about what to include and what not.[14] Where epistolary advocates or officials wrote instigatory letters and thus in some respects "started" the version of the story that was to inform the negotiation process, the situation could indeed become very complex, explicitly shaping what subsequent writers thought was appropriate or even reasonable to say.[15] Officials, too, remade the stories they received, as we began to see in chapter 4, by undertaking further enquiries and by entering into correspondence with the poor or their advocates, thus shaping the interpretation of what was written and extending it into a new story that could take on a life of its own.[16] In turn, how parochial representatives understood the obvious or discovered fictive elements of the stories told to them speaks to the character and scope of the negotiation process, their acceptance or otherwise of agency, and their conceptualisation of the system of which they were part. It also, of course, feeds directly into the technical question of what end-of-process overseers' accounts actually mean and into the wider matter of the quality as well as the quantity of welfare.[17] Nowhere is this issue more keenly played out than in their reception of the claims of shifty applicants like Henry Rutter.

To understand how stories were constructed, the next section of the chapter looks at the influences that shaped what poor writers included, did not include, or "fudged" in their narratives. A detailed review of letters by or about the widow Hannah Buckman, already encountered fleetingly in chapter 3, from various addresses over the period 1826–1834 will show what officials could have known about an individual at different stages of a correspondence. The section also deals more generally with the issue of how poor writers kept track of the histories that they told. Subsequently, the chapter switches perspective to that of the recipient of constructed histories, suggesting that officials, advocates, and the poor shared a fictive landscape, or an acceptance of the fluidity of "truth," which means that negotiation lay at the very heart of the intent of the poor law process. Finally, I return again to the question of the unworthy and what their experiences of welfare and the reception of their fabricated histories tell us about agency within a discretionary welfare system.

## TELLING AND NOT TELLING[18]

Chapter 2 argued that we should understand the letters of the poor as essentially truthful in terms of the material conditions and causation of deprivation described. This veracity does not mean, however, that recipients of such letters knew the complete story of their co-respondent.[19] Writers might not include "facts," experiences, or views that did not seem relevant at the time of writing. Where circumstances were fast-moving, as for instance when the poor moved from health to ill-health, the case outlined in a letter might become redundant as soon as it was sent, or even as it was being written. And authors might be deliberately silent or vague on contextual matters that could reflect negatively on their case – although, as I have observed, poor writers did not simply deliver what they thought officials would most want to hear.[20]

There is a need to distinguish between narrative truth that "assists in establishing continuity and coherence" and literal truth, with the difference between the two often constructed via silences rather than outright deception.[21] Thus the poor might fail to mention kin who could – and in certain circumstances should under the law – provide support for their destitute relative.[22] They might alternatively overplay or neglect to mention the prospect of finding work or be rather vague about whether children were co-resident or had been farmed out to relatives and others. Reflecting modern concerns over entitlement to welfare, it is clear that single people were generally opaque about their exact residential arrangements, although generally short of determined deception.[23] Letters – even those of the poor and their advocates – invariably call attention to character, and they do so deliberately as a way of fabricating an image of self as one would want to be known rather than as a hapless petitioner for welfare. In this sense, it was perfectly possible for authors to claim to be telling the truth – as well as for advocates and officials to confirm such truth telling – and yet for the information they conveyed to be hedged round with invention. The same observation holds true for the settled poor who made their case in person. Once again, there seems to be no systematic relationship between the stories told and the information withheld, on the one hand, and the nature and size of the "ask," on the other, not least because most letters did not make specific requests.

In turn, recipients were not unknowing victims of deception. Rather, they appear to have understood and, to a degree, accepted that they were engaged in a process that both had a fictive element and was actually a process of unfolding knowledge and action. The letters of the English poor, as with their counterparts in nineteenth- and twentieth-century Europe, were part of a framework that made people of *ostensibly* unequal social standing known and knowable to each other.[24] That the stories they told were, and were meant to be, cumulative perhaps explains why officials did not by and large target particular sorts or magnitudes of claim for additional scrutiny. This fact has important implications for the meanings of the welfare given, for denial or exclusion, and for the way that parishes balanced their potentially competing obligations.

The corpus employed in this study allows us a unique window onto the process of telling and developing stories. As chapter 2 suggested, the majority of letters were from or about poor people for whom we have multiple letters and for whom we can thus trace the accretion of stories – those told both by the poor themselves and by advocates and other officials – from the perspective of the overseer recipients. This possibility assumes, of course, institutional and individual memory and triangulation, and I return to this matter below. The widow Hannah Buckman is emblematic of the potential of this process. We first encounter her as a by-line in two letters requesting help with rent arrears written by her husband, William, in September 1820.[25] Hannah's instigatory letter when applying in her own right to her settlement parish of Hurstpierpoint in Sussex is missing. A testamentary letter written on 1 April 1826, which was clearly soon after her first approach to the parish had gone unanswered, forms the start of the storytelling process and is noted here in full:

Sir i am sory i am under the nesesity of riteing a second time But i beg pardon for the liberty i wood not have done it on aney account had i not have been drove to ask the favour which i mentiend in my letter which i trust will not give aney ofence now my Rent day was last Saturday and i have got 10 days more granted me as i told the gentlemen that owe my house i had rent to Beg the pardon of the Comity to plese to stand my friend i do not ask it in aney other way than this to have the goodnes to send me all 5 pounds from the first of march which was the day my mony was dew i wood not have mentiend i could i have made up my rent my having so mutch afliction which is well known to all around me if i can but settle my rent this time the spring is giting up and my [illegible] will soon come in and i trust your goodness gentlemen one and all as i have reson to say you have all behaved like a friend in deed to me i turn you many thanks for every favour that i have recivd plese to favour me this once if you never do again for i should by the rite of it pay my rent every 3 months it is a favour indeed to let it go 6 months the parish suficent knowing my case advised me to state the particulars as they said they had not the smalest dought as it will save the expence of letters as ill as it will be some time before sir i shall have to trouble you again please sir have the goodness to lay this before the Comity your Humble St. Hannah Buckman

[Below, same hand:]

Sir
I shall be at my Brother [illegible] who keeps the King and queen inn Brighton at the latter part of the summer i shall have to come with a lady for a month and then i hope to have the pleasure of seeing you sir and state to you [four illegible words].[26]

---

Here, then, Hannah Buckman assumed through omission that the over-seer recipient would remember her address and place from previous cor-respondence, reminding him only that she would be in Brighton over the summer. The rest of the text rehearses themes that were to snake through the other thirty-two letters from or about her: the need for lump sums to pay arrears of rent, an appeal to the overseer and parish to stand as her friend, thanks for past favours, a history of making do and not troubling the parish, sickness (or "affliction"), reputation and visibility in her host community, and a desire to be free of dependence upon her parish. I re-turn to these rhetorical vehicles in part 3. The letter is remarkably unin-formative about the contextual story that might have allowed the overseer to make a considered decision. The presence of a brother of substance appears as an afterthought, and there is little detail on her wider family situation, the nature of sickness, why the arrears of rent had been accrued, or the scope of her work. Rather, these things emerged, and were meant to emerge, in a series of co-respondence that throws considerable doubt on her claim to want to be independent of the parish. Table 6.1 takes subsequent letters by or about Hannah Buckman and traces how new el-ements of her story emerged and how existing knowledge was augmented or varied across the series.

The complexity of Buckman's story and its gradual emergence is clear, as is the value of considering all of the letters in an epistolary world rather than simply ego documents. The full details of Buckman's family – her co-resident children, the existence of two brothers, and a periodi-cally co-habiting lover[27] – are finally revealed only in the last two con-solidating letters of the series.[28] Between 1826 and 1834 her co-resident family structure was remarkably fluid, and although much of this context is flagged by Buckman herself, that a brother had taken in one of her fe-male children was referenced only in the letter of an official. We do not learn Buckman's age – and the overseer of Hurstpierpoint is equally likely to have been ignorant of this – until March 1830, and we would not have known that she had become pregnant by John Marstone at the age of forty-four without his own father's letter to this effect in 1829. Al-though Buckman episodically refers to her desire for independent living,

Table 6.1
*The development of the Hannah Buckman story*

| Letter date | Sent by | New story | Variation |
|---|---|---|---|
| 18 September 1826 | Hannah Buckman | First mention of family | Change of overseer co-respondent |
| 7 April 1827 | Hannah Buckman | Existing allowance of 4 shillings per week Widowed in March 1821 Left with 7 children at widowhood, 3 still at home | Change of overseer co-respondent New town in Ipswich in Suffolk rather than Harwich |
| 17 June 1827 | Mr Hatch, overseer, Ipswich | | "3 small children and the eldest only ten years of age" |
| 4 October 1827 | Hannah Buckman | Unspecified chance to take her and her boy off the parish | New address in Ipswich |
| 18 October 1827 | Hannah Buckman | Chance of marriage to a man if she can "be Clean of all debts" | "3 children *under* 10 years" Her unspecified work is "slow slack" |
| 21 October 1827 | Mr Hatch | Buckman has got a letter informing her of discontinuance of the allowance | |

| Letter date | Sent by | New story | Variation |
|---|---|---|---|
| 21 August 1828 | Hannah Buckman | Eldest child still at home is a boy and can be apprenticed to a shoemaker for a fee<br>Eldest boy apprenticed to a cabinetmaker for past 4 years and doing well | Eldest child "not 13"<br>Discontinuance of allowance puts off her suitor<br>New town of Woodbridge in Suffolk |
| 5 September 1828 | Hannah Buckman | | Boy now on trial with a shoemaker and no fee paid by parish |
| 13 December 1828 | Hannah Buckman | 2 girls at home<br>Parish allowance of 2 pounds used to pay fee for the boy<br>Prospective work as a bookkeeper and housekeeper for Buckman in a local family<br>A friend will care for 2 girls at 1 shilling per week | All household goods sold<br>New address in Woodbridge |
| 16 December 1828 | William Ellis, vestry clerk, Hurstpierpoint | No more allowance | |
| 20 December 1828 | Hannah Buckman | Promise never to hear from her again as long as she has her health | Youngest girl 9 and eldest 10 years 3 months |

| Letter date | Sent by | New story | Variation |
| --- | --- | --- | --- |
| 31 December 1828 | Hannah Buckman William Kemp, overseer, Woodbridge | Bailiffs have arrived for rent arrears | |
| 10 January 1829 | Hannah Buckman | | Widowed now in March 1822 Prospective work as a bookkeeper and housekeeper for Buckman in a local family if she can get the clothes A friend will care for 2 girls at 4 shillings per week rather than 1 shilling of December 1828 |
| 17 January 1829 | William Kemp | Buckman "ill in bed" Rumours of her remarriage are false 1 girl of "about 9 years of age" still resident | |
| 28 January 1829 | William Kemp | | Buckman better |
| 5 February 1829 | Hannah Buckman | Asks that the overseer pay for her wedding to John Marstone, a lodger in her house | Kemp had failed to notify overseer of a second girl resident |
| 4 March 1829 | Hannah Buckman | Potential work as a fruit seller if she can get back to Ipswich | New address in Woodbridge |

| Letter date | Sent by | New story | Variation |
| --- | --- | --- | --- |
| 17 March 1829 | William Kemp | Case made known to a magistrate | Kemp not mistaken over the girl, who had been at relatives in Ipswich Boy apprenticed to a gem maker but still resident at home |
| 2 April 1829 | William Kemp Hannah Buckman | Buckman's illness has passed – first reference to her intention to remove Harwich | "My boy is 13 Hannah 12 Sarah 10" |
| 24 April 1829 | William Marstone Ipswich | Buckman pregnant with the child of Marstone's son | Buckman has "lately left Woodbridge" |
| 22 March 1830 | Hannah Buckman | Buckman 50 years old Renewed offer of marriage | Son back with her Brother had taken in the 12-year-old girl, but he is now dead, so the girl is back in residence |
| 24 March 1830 | William Ellis | Hurstpierpoint refuses further support | |
| 22 May 1830 | Hannah Buckman | Continued offer of marriage | Eldest boy has been found a place "in the last fortnite" |

| Letter date | Sent by | New story | Variation |
| --- | --- | --- | --- |
| 28 June 1830 | William Kemp | | New town of Dover Court, near Harwich |
| 3 August 1830 | Curtis Plumb, overseer Ipswich | Eldest boy, aged 15, has a badly broken leg | New town of Ipswich |
| 21 December 1830 | Hannah Buckman | Living with her proposed husband Idea to take the family to live with her second brother Illegitimate child by Marstone is dead | Boy's leg broken in 2 places and confined to bed for 16 weeks Eldest girl 13 years old New address in Ipswich |
| 2 December 1831 | Christopher Wright, overseer, Ipswich | | New address in Ipswich |
| 23 January 1832 | William Kerridge, overseer, Ipswich Hannah Buckman | Buckman is ill | New address in Ipswich |
| 13 December 1832 | Charles Baker overseer, Ipswich | | Buckman "very ill" |

| Letter date | Sent by | New story | Variation |
|---|---|---|---|
| Undated but 1832 | Hannah Buckman | | "what I have said his honest" New town of Woodbridge |
| 11 June 1834 and 24 June 1834 | Thomas Bonton, landlord of John Buckman, Hurstpierpoint | | John Buckman is second brother to Hannah Buckman and caring for the two girls named above |

*Source:* SURO Par.400-37-122-1, 7–9, 19, 21–3; Par.400-37-123-2, 16, 18–20, 25, 33–6, 43.

her work opportunities move lightly in and out of focus as she invites the overseers to invest in clothing or childcare. Frequent changes of town and addresses in the same town go unremarked, and we learn much more about Buckman's ill-health and restoration from the letters of officials, advocates, and third parties than we do from her own writing. In turn, it is clear that Buckman knew about the contents of the letters of these advocates because on two occasions she was invited to write her own text as an addendum to their contents.

In the case of serial letter writers, then, officials who were engaged in the process of negotiation and poor relief made decisions on the basis of partial and organic stories in which silence and imprecision were tools of agency as well as reflections of innocent omission. The officials of Hurstpierpoint recognised this situation in their letter of 24 March 1830 to William Kemp, the overseer of St Margaret's parish in Ipswich. Responding to Kemp's enquiry about whether he should make the sick Hannah Buckman an allowance, the vestry clerk William Ellis noted, "I am directed to inform you the Parish Officers cannot do any thing more for her as they have sent considerable sums to her & she has lately continually been writing for more *sometimes under one circumstance & then another* They cannot send any more relief & therefore must abide by the regular course to be pursued."[29] This subtle letter is important. Hurstpierpoint could have dismissed Buckman's case, variously made by herself, advocates, and officials, on any number of grounds: her moral standing, undisclosed family of some means, moving towns without the assent of the parish, funds meant for rent that were misappropriated for the payment of an apprenticeship fee, imprecision over who was co-resident and when, a failure to properly exploit work opportunities, and the multiple fictions and partial or cumulative renderings that make Buckman's storytelling so compelling. In fact, Ellis was told not to act because the letters lacked narrative consistency rather than because overseers doubted the truth of the case made, the views of advocates, or the deservingness of Buckman herself. Indeed, before and after its letter of 24 March 1830, the settlement parish paid significant sums in her support. Officials in Buckman's host parishes also made episodic "gifts" to ward off utter destitution, notwithstanding their likely appreciation of her contradictory "cosmological fresco."[30] Most of the time, they accepted her words as essentially authentic because they were plausible even if fictive.

In turn, we can see that serial letter writers strived above all for narrative consistency, even if the narrative itself was adorned and augmented with emerging information that might have shaped the case if it had been revealed early in the process of poor relief. Such consistency depended in large part, as I have already suggested, upon how poor writers remembered their story across multiple letters and years and how much of that story they assumed their co-respondents remembered. Buckman implicitly assumed some institutional memory and (temporarily) paid the price when this assumption strayed into narrative inconsistency. The majority of other writers more carefully marshalled, managed, and controlled their stories, especially as the period progressed. This fact is perhaps not surprising. The claims-making strategies of both the in- and out-parish poor drew on a common heritage of remembering, fashioning, and repeating stories.[31] From the late eighteenth century, as chapter 1 began to argue, the poor were exposed to many more forums where their "stories" might be developed, told, demanded, or recounted, where their petitioning and rhetorical skills might be developed, or where they might hear the stories of others. Case histories taken in voluntary hospitals, witness statements, petitions to charities, meetings and subsequent public petitions to Parliament,[32] briefs, appeals for assistance via newspapers,[33] and migrant letters[34] all provided forums in which the poor could fashion themselves and their lives. Those resident in medical institutions were likely to have become familiar with detailed complaint procedures, and we know that some at least actively complained about their medical care or about the food, drink, and washing attendant on a stay in hospital, thus fashioning a wider appellatory culture.[35] Providing evidence via depositions or in the forum of the coronial court also gave an increasing body of ordinary people experience of organising "their memories of events into a suitable form: narrative becomes the form of *truth*. But narrative is also the form of *reality* in these cases because of its capacity for illusion."[36] However we interpret the process, holding, refining, augmenting, and reinventing one's story became central to the process of poor relief for both the settled and out-parish poor in the discretionary world of the Old Poor Law.

## FICTIVE LANDSCAPES

If the storytelling of the poor contained a certain degree of fiction or more deliberative illusion, the wider question becomes why those who received and considered such stories did not turn more forcefully and frequently to the control mechanisms that were built into the Old Poor Law, particularly for larger or potentially more contentious claims. These mechanisms included enforceable requirements for certain degrees of kin to care for or otherwise support poor relatives, clear channels for the prosecution of dishonest or disruptive claimants,[37] disciplinary processes such as removal, and the signals implicit in the exercise of powers such as the forced apprenticeship of children. It is, of course, important not to "elevate the text above its purpose,"[38] but a reading of the corpus as a whole and of its scaffolding sources suggests three important reasons for the tolerance of fiction.

The first is that officials – engaging with each other, advocates, and ratepayers – were themselves deeply involved in creating fictions. A consideration of the remarkable correspondence books for the township of Hulme in Lancashire, near Manchester, reveals something of this situation.[39] Some fictions were minor: officials wrote to each other claiming not to have replied previously because they were away from home, even though other material in the archives shows them to have been in situ; incoming and outgoing letters were ostensibly lost in the post, even though we know that they were not; officials would write to host parishes when a pauper had transferred residence and provide a testament of character for them, omitting to mention problem experiences; and letters of advocacy from overseers might contain the affirmatory signatures of other respectable members of the parish who in fact had never heard of the prospective pauper. Other fictions had more far-reaching consequences and might include allowing a host parish to pay for an out-parish claimant and then disputing the scope of authority originally given; promising to exercise utmost economy and then submitting bills that clearly point to a more generous treatment than was typical for the local poor; asking for out-parish paupers to "come home" in the full knowledge that the costs of such a return would be considerable, thus placing the burden of the day-to-day management of poverty in the hands of the overseer in a host parish; noting to ratepayers that decisions had been taken "by order" of magistrates even when they had not; and persistent nonpayment of bills.

The mutual tolerance of these various fictions – perhaps because they were so universal – was remarkable. Yet all of the significant collections of official correspondence in the corpus also contain evidence of threshold points beyond which such tolerance was sharply curtailed as fiction began to undermine the public reputation of officials.[40] In Hulme, irritation with Welsh parishes failing to pay bills or to sanction relief in the first place was palpable; a letter from the overseer James Moore to Llanasa on 15 January 1809, for instance, noted that the Welsh parish "has behaved very shabby towards us."[41] North of Manchester, the overseer of Spotland, near Rochdale, wrote to his counterpart in Colwich in Staffordshire on 18 December 1830 having tried multiple times to obtain reimbursement for payments made. Complaining of the "shameful conduct" of Colwich, he would be "sorry if the Overseer, Churchwarden and Parson are all Dead in some Epidemic disorder" and threatened formal action if his irony did not work.[42] Officials could hardly require complete honesty from claimants when they were not themselves honest with each other.

The second driver of tolerance was an implicit acceptance that the stories told by *all* parties in the epistolary world of the parish would be fluid because the conditions causing need were also fluid. It is partly for this reason that we detect no patterning in the sort of fictions attached to different sorts of request. This once again suggests the importance of understanding the process of relief rather than simply its outcome. Crudely, the prospective poor could not at the outset of a case know what to tell, and overseers could not know what to ask. Consequently, allowances were frequently given and accepted with time limits, after which a review of the situation would be undertaken. As one Welsh overseer put it when writing to his counterpart in Hulme on 4 January 1803, "It is impossible for our Vestry to judge his case into perfection from here."[43] Even in-parish paupers had fluid stories, something that is clear from frequent reapplications and from the continuance of allowances beyond their expiration date. Officials thus asked their counterparts to update them as and when a situation changed, advocates promised to keep up a flow of intelligence, and writers yoked together assurances of the truth of their case and a rhetorical desire to remove themselves from dependence as soon as the conditions shaping their applications were alleviated. On 9 September 1835, William Hudswell, the minister of George Street Chapel in Leeds, wrote to the overseers of the poor of Hulme on behalf of the aged pauper and widow Jane Higginson. He noted that an allowance had not arrived, sending her into considerable unease because "She has contracted debts in dependence on the 2/6 per week that you allowed." Hudswell claimed, "I have written twice to Mr Sandiford about it but no answer has come to hand." Inviting the overseer to send the allowance to him, he pledged to let Hulme know if circumstances changed.[44] In a follow-up letter of 2 October 1835, Hudswell added in a postscript that "Jane Higginson is more than 80 years old and very infirm, if she die I will immediately write to you."[45] A further fifteen advocate letters provide a running commentary of the deterioration of Higginson's condition until a final note in 1837 confirms her eventual death.

Updates were no doubt much appreciated, but it nonetheless seems clear from the corpus that officials assumed that the letters they received from the out-parish poor and the cases made in person at the vestry by the different sorts of resident poor identified in table 1.1 contained a backbone of truth irrespective of the eventual "ask." This was especially the case where interspersing narratives by advocates were present in the correspondence series, the questioning of which would undermine the structures of trust, order, and civility that underpinned eighteenth- and nineteenth-century society.[46] We should not, of course, assume that overseers or advocates were incapable of detecting deception or acting when it was brought to their attention. On 25 July 1831, William Emmant, the overseer of Farnham, wrote to his counterpart in Guildford, both in Surrey, on the subject of Eli Hillyer,

> who is in the parish this morning informs me that he will not work for a farmer at 12s per week but would rather remain at parish pay I having about 10 acres of grass to cut applied him and the answer I received from him this morng Monday that he would not work after Tuesday with much insolence I think it right to inform you as the guardian that he should be discharged from the poor Book in consequence of his refusing imployment I do not wonder at his refusing when he can go and return at any hour from parish labour.[47]

Hillyer – whose attitude seems to have epitomised the dependency culture that was at the heart of public disquiet about the Old Poor Law in the late eighteenth and early nineteenth centuries – was duly removed from the parish relief list.[48] He had crossed an important threshold by actively seeming to favour parish welfare, and I return to this matter of critical thresholds in the next section.

The third reason for tolerance is the analogue of the Hillyer case. For officials to find and then proactively keep abreast of the literal and whole truth in the stories told to them would be costly. It might involve regular inspection, more frequent enquiries of advocates and officials by letter, episodically calling the bluff of the out-parish poor who threatened to return home, and drawing up definitive allowance rates attached to different types of poverty or different claimant locations. Tolerance of a certain degree of fiction, then, was a mechanism for containing the monetary costs of administering the relief system, acceleration of which would have deprived both ratepayers and the poor of free resources. Surveying the settled poor was not necessarily any cheaper in urban parishes or in the large and sprawling rural parishes of northern England, which perhaps explains why this tolerance can also be seen for the fictions of the settled poor as recorded in vestry minutes. Parishes also faced heavy administrative burdens. Officials and vestrymen could claim expenses for their work, but the spread of paid overseers was patchy and at the parish level inconsistent.

---

In the vast majority of places captured by the corpus, the office of overseer remained an unpaid task for which ratepayers were lotted or elected. Actively reconstructing and policing the stories of the myriad categories of the in- and out-parish poor present in most parishes were tasks beyond the administrative and time capabilities of officials, who also had to fulfil their existing familial, social, and work duties. Prosecuting those found to be lying was also a considerable task, one with an uncertain outcome in terms of conviction and punishment. When the overseer of Spotland reminded a counterpart that "I am relieving for about seven or eight and twenty Townships or Parishes besides our own and we have about seven Hundred families of our own on the Books," he was thus voicing a much wider burden faced by officials.[49] Against this backdrop, and as we saw with Hannah Buckman above, the stories of the poor had to have a degree of narrative consistency in order to keep below the threshold that would demand action.[50] This threshold was not consistent across the country. Officials in Welsh parishes in particular seem to have had a lower tolerance of inconsistency and ambiguity than did their English, even northern English, counterparts. When Peter Bailey Williams, writing an interspersing letter to Caernarvon on 29 March 1830, noted that William Owen had obtained relief despite having good health, two houses, and a garden and that "this Parish was greatly wrong'd in having him & his family saddled upon it," he was expressing a scepticism felt and practised across a much wider canvas of Welsh communities.[51] Even in Wales, however, levels of tolerance for all forms and magnitudes of the "ask" were such as not to alter the basic process of poor relief or to bring into question the local purpose of the Old Poor Law.

Officials, the poor and prospective poor, and advocates shared a fictive landscape in which their own and interrelated self-interests created a tolerance of partial truths, silences, ambiguities, organic cases, and inconsistencies emerging out of the telling of stories by different parties in the epistolary world of the parish. There is little evidence for the "gnawing suspicion of deceit" on the part of recipients that Stuart Woolf identifies in relation to the giving of out-relief in Continental Europe.[52] Indeed, such tolerance might mean that certain groups of the poor, such as the old or sick, gained relief more often than they should have or remained on relief for longer than would have been the case with more active policing of their stories. For others who strayed beyond the limits of acceptable fiction or narrative consistency, relief could be cursorily removed even though the underlying case had not changed. Constructing a story and remembering it were thus by no means casual and inconsequential acts. Hedging it round (or failing to do so) with an effective rhetorical structure – one that might speak to the permissions of the law, custom, markers of absolute and relative need, humanitarian imperative, and the requirements of masculinity and social order – could also carry fundamental consequences and is the focus of part 3. For now, it is important to note that the issue of how officials located, measured, and communicated the depth of their tolerance for the stories of the in- and out-parish poor is intimately tied up with their experiences of the unworthy, and it is to this group that the chapter finally turns.

## THE UNWORTHY

For the most part, a shared fictive landscape sits in the background of parochial business, whether conducted in person or by letter. Uncovering this landscape requires, as we have seen, the reconstruction of different stages of individual stories. Some people, however, stretched the definition of fiction, and little of their definition was shared by officials. Henry Rutter, whose story opened this chapter, was one. Another was Elizabeth Brownlow. Henry Roper, the overseer of Oundle in Northamptonshire, wrote to his counterpart in the nearby town of Peterborough on 23 May 1835, clearly in response to a now missing letter asking for authority to give her relief. He said that Brownlow

> was in our workhouse some short time ago & derived great benefit from the treatment. Indeed got as she herself said quite well & left it. She has been for some years constantly on our Parish Books & we were much astonished at her <u>very</u> quick <u>recovery</u> from her treatment at the workhouse and my orders were not to allow her any more money or relief out of the house but from your own signatures

which as sure me that it is right. I am willing to allow what you ask. Two shillings per week for the next four weeks.[53]

Roper added mournfully in a postscript, "We considered that she came the old soldier over us to use a Common phrase for the last year or more."[54] Although Henry French and Jonathan Barry argue that agency "tended to be mediated through and restrained by socially accepted pathways," there seems to be little evidence for this view in relation to Brownlow.[55] It is not hard to imagine the vestry meeting where the term "old soldier" was used, or the gritted teeth through which the relief decision was taken, given that the social standing of those who signed the now missing letter trumped parish doubts over the honesty of the applicant. At the opposite end of the study period, the overseers of Oxford St Martin clearly doubted the word of Ann Lapworth. She wrote to them from an unknown host parish on 17 August 1754 to refute a charge made in a letter of 28 September to her now dead husband:

> I do assure you that neither my late husband or Self ever had any estate at Caversham or elsewhere nor has he gained any other settlement than the parish of St Martin's in Oxford. He has left me with 4 Children 3 Boys and a Girl – namely Wm about 10 years old, Thos about 8, Eliz 4 and Francis 2 in a very poor condition. Now my request to you is that you acquaint the parishioners with the Death of my husband and with my poverty (which upon Enquiry you will find to be true) and if they will be so good as to grant me a certificate to St Marys where I now live and allow me 4s a week for the support of myself and Children I will do my utmost to breed them up.[56]

The overseer's letter had obviously contained a rumour of undeclared wealth, and Lapworth was careful in her reply to deny the rumour, provide detail of her family, and invite officials to make enquiries as to the truth of her statements. It is unclear whether Lapworth and Brownlow were of the same ilk, but Lapworth certainly entered into sustained correspondence and an uneasy relationship with her settlement parish over the next four years.

There are no sustained typological or spatial patterns in the incidence of lying applicants in the corpus, although northern, midland, and Welsh overseers seem to have reserved their bluntest language for this group. Moreover, it is important to remember that concerted lies, deceptions, and bad behaviour were not the preserve only of the out-parish poor. Vestry minutes and correspondence also reveal a colourful parade of the unworthy, as for instance in the case of George Earle. Charles Morris, the vestry clerk of Brentford in Middlesex, noted on 15 July 1833 that he had "in consequence of the repeated complaints of the Females of the neighbourhood, as well as my own observation [and] ... under sanction of the Overseers &c taken him before the magistrates." Earle's lies and contempt for the directions of overseers and the vestry had not prevented him from receiving continued relief, but here, when his bad behaviour became a public nuisance, the parish reached a threshold point.[57] Such examples remind us once again of the dangers of drawing sharp distinctions between in- and out-parish paupers. Henry Rutter, Elizabeth Brownlow, and almost all of their equivalents conducted negotiations in person, in their own letters, and through advocates and officials. More widely, most of the unworthy sojourned in their settlement parishes at some point. Thomas Joint, a resident of Derby but settled in Rothersthorpe in Northamptonshire, is a good but not unusual example. He had a regular time of year for arriving at his settlement parish, and when he did not appear there in September 1787, the overseer of Rothersthorpe wrote a letter to his counterpart in Derby enquiring whether he would be lucky enough to learn from him "before my time [as overseer ends] and to tell the Gentlemen [of Rothersthorpe] that Joint has died."[58]

There can be no doubt that this sentiment of ill-will was widely shared or that officers and ratepayers reacted with considerable ill-humour to the claims of those who were clearly abusing the system. Such people might find officials granting less than was asked for, delaying payments and responses to letters, or not paying at all. The unworthy poor might also see their requests for cash transformed into some other form of relief or their requests for open-ended pension payments becoming in practice time-limited casual relief. Indeed, some officials clearly enjoyed the game that the unworthy poor invited, as for instance did the overseer of Tile-hurst in Berkshire. He continually delayed sending allowances for Mary Hamilton, whom he heard had local kin to look after her. The overseer of her host parish of Egham in Surrey struggled across a series of letters in the early nineteenth century to rehabilitate her reputation. His letter of 13 May 1806, for instance, noted,

> About two years since you allow'd a poor woman of the name of Hamilton on shilling per week which belongs to your Parish – since which you have not paid it for what reason I don't know I can assure you you have not a Pauper more deserving than she is she is over 70 years of Age and does a little washing and the Neighbours are very good to Her – otherways she must have been brought home before.[59]

In such circumstances, and as chapter 1 noted, the meaning of end-of-process poor law payments matters as much as their value.

Yet, as some of these letters have begun to imply, welfare historians have focused too keenly on binary divisions between the deserving and undeserving poor and on top-down debate about how such labels might be defined. The unworthy could be rehabilitated, and the deserving might move in the other direction if fictive texts were transformed into unacceptable fiction. Alex Shepard's contention for a rather earlier period than the one considered here that "the divide between the idle and the industrious poor ... appears to have been paper thin" should perhaps have gained more sustained traction.[60] In the corpus, the clear and clanging fact is that the unworthy *did* continue to get relief and to re-establish their claims if for some reason they were dismissed. This relief may have been grudgingly granted and residual, but judged over a letter series in which writers pulled well-understood rhetorical levers – the subject of the rest of this study – parishes rarely maintained a consistent exclusionary stance.[61] Their officials accepted certain fictions, even from this group. Exactly the same is true of the unworthy who appeared before the vestry, where members can often be found implicitly or explictly questioning their morals. Such people could not easily be passed off to other parishes under settlement legislation, not least because they tended to have the most fluid stories of all claimants. Indeed, attempts at passing the buck could result in the crumbling of the mechanisms of inter-parochial trust that made the out-parish system, and hence the Old Poor Law in its later stages, work. In any case, the removal of the unworthy was very often accompanied by their immediate return to the host parishes from which they had first written. William Lloyd was removed five times from Hulme between 1793 and 1816, each time returning after a short sojourn in his Welsh settlement parish and with, the overseer of Hulme suspected, the connivance of the Welsh parish officers, who seem to have provided him with the funds for transport.[62]

In turn, the inability of parochial officers to simply refuse allowances and to stick to that decision where they doubted the veracity of the story told is a consistent feature of the process of negotiation. These in- and out-parish claimants employed complex patterns of interspersing, testamentary, and extending letters once an epistolary conversation had begun. We clearly saw this practice in the case of Jacob and Sophia Curchin, outlined in chapter 2. Moreover, memory of their own stories seems to have been particularly strong compared both to other poor writers and to the officials with whom they were in co-respondence. Only if behaviour reached a threshold point did officials act. Admonishing and warning letters sent directly to this subgroup of the poor or conveyed by advocates survive episodically across the corpus. Thus Thomas Darwen of Lancaster sent a consolidating letter to Mr Heelis, the overseer of Bolton Le Moors, both in Lancashire, on 14 March 1809. Reflecting on the cases of all of the Lancaster poor resident in Bolton, Darwen reserved especial venom for Betty Booth, who "deserves to be a little punish'd for not acting honestly."[63] Yet such statements seem to have had little purchase on the activities of the unworthy poor, who applied again and again and again, even when they were in receipt of regular relief. As Mary Fissell reminds us, power relations were inherently unstable and were "always being acted out, tested, represented and rearticulated."[64] Nowhere does this view have more traction than in parochial attempts (or, rather, failures) to contain the unworthy.

People like Henry Rutter existed in all the conceivable subgroups of the poor, and vestry minutes make it abundantly clear that they took up a disproportionate part of the parochial space for administration. The unworthy simultaneously highlight the capacity for agency that the poor possessed in a discretionary welfare system and emblematise its limits. Dishonesty did not inevitably result in the full or permanent removal of the right to apply for welfare or to receive it given that there was a fluid spectrum of deservingness. The threshold between a shared fiction and one imposed on parishes by claimants or their advocates was in this sense a high one. Drawing on the lessons of the wider historiographical literature, it might be argued that officials were afraid in these cases that they would be ordered by magistrates unfamiliar with the character of the applicant to pay even more if the case made it that far. Certainly, some of the unworthy poor – along with other groups of claimants across the typological spectrum – did threaten to go to magistrates. Nonetheless, it is also quite clear that magistrates in many areas did not simply grant relief and were sensitive to arguments about the worth of applicants.[65] Rather, the experiences of the unworthy speak to some of the basic humanitarian and philanthropic beliefs woven into the fabric of the Old Poor Law. These beliefs were given strong voice by Miles Craston, the overseer of Manchester, who noted in a letter of 20 February 1803 about George Bainbridge that although he "is not a man that Can be much depended on," the family "must have what is necessary" because extreme sickness had resulted in his being bedbound.[66] In practice, officers were wary of adopting policies that would exclude the unworthy but simultaneously establish precedents that might then affect the worthy or rehabilitated poor. Of course, there were periodic drives to shed claimants from relief lists, and there are numerous acts of callousness at the individual level to be found in the corpus, but this does not seem to have been the modus operandi of officials even though it could easily have been. In fact, two distinct fictive realities – one agreed and the other appropriated and contested, as in the case of the unworthy poor – shaped the nature, form, longevity, and depth of the allowances recorded at the end of the process of poor relief.

## CONCLUSION

Sandra Sherman has argued that the Old Poor Law "made outdoor clients into entrepreneurs, negotiating with overseers for services and supplements," a fact that drove increasing attempts to statisticalise and depersonalise public understandings of poverty and welfare.[67] At the heart of this process lay the core story of the poor person, one that had to be forged, remembered, supplemented, reinvented, and defended in order to make applicants and recipients knowable and acceptable to each other.[68] In this sense, writing a letter or series of letters carried deep material *and* symbolic connotations.[69] Yet there were rules. Although older models that structured the behaviour of unequal parties in formal relationships, such as orderly sociability, were passing at the start of the period covered by this study, the intimate workings of the Old Poor Law were built on backward-looking concepts of trust.[70] This situation did *not* mean that those involved in the epistolary world of the parish, or indeed in its face-to-face aspect, told the truth or expected to have the truth told to them. Nor did it mean, in contradistinction to the early modern period, that applicants invariably had to inscribe their stories with gratitude and respect[71] or to create an ordered "consensus of social knowledge."[72] Rather, the stories conveyed and received had to exist within the fluid and movable boundaries of a shared fiction – an acceptable level of silence, omission, or partial statement – that simultaneously contained the costs and administrative intensity of parochial administration and led the poor themselves to suppress their demands on the parish.[73] A sense that in the seventeenth century "the administration of social welfare presupposed the practice of vigilance among overseers and surveillance among ratepayers" gave way to episodic surveillance and a broader concept of trust in the epistolary world of the parish as poverty and the costs of poor relief expanded.[74] There is little support for Dorothy Marshall's assertion that the discretion afforded to local officials led them to "have bullied the helpless, corrupted the children, and polluted the moral life of the country-side."[75] Rather, an implicit acceptance that cases were inevitably fictive at some level signals a much more understanding relationship and a less obvious ability to exercise state power.

The unworthy challenged these arrangements, and their stories occur with sufficient frequency in the corpus to point to significant change compared to the early modern period, when "The poor were sorted and ultimately came to see the advantages of sorting themselves, into the moral categories approved by the overseers."[76] Faced with people like Henry Rutter, officials were not powerless. They could delay responses or payments, fracture entitlement, and make life uncomfortable for the individuals concerned. Outright refusal was rather rarer, and where it did happen, it is not uncommon to find advocates or officials subsequently writing in support of applicants, a clear indication of the difficulty of disentangling fact from fiction. The spectrum of deservingness was thus fluid. For the in-parish poor, the same conclusion can be reached through the observation of how frequently refusals of support in vestry minutes melded into allowances at a later date. An acceptable fiction for the vast majority of applicants – even for the majority of the unworthy poor – was thus manufactured by degrees, and different sorts of benefit became at-tached to these degrees. The shape of that fiction and its acceptability to the recipient were not patterned onto what was asked for and how much a claim might cost. Yet the process of poor relief and thus the meaning of end-of-process relief allowances were not just a function of the core stories set down on paper or told at the vestry. Rather, stories were, and were expected by their recipients to be, framed by rhetoric and strategy. It is this observation that drives the agenda of the chapters in part 3.

PART THREE

# Rhetorical Structures

# 7

## A Rhetorical Spectrum

### OVERVIEW

On an unknown date, John Pratt Sr wrote an extending letter from Durham to Tweedmouth, both in Northumberland. He hoped

> you will forgive my freedom in troubling you at this time – belive me its from real necessity – My helplessness and many infirmities increasing daily – and I am a greater burden to those I stay with – and they being much in the same circumstances Oblidges me too solicit your favours for a small addition to my Mite. In doing so you will much oblidge Your Humble Petitioner.[1]

Although short, Pratt's letter is packed with rhetorical signals and signatures of deservingness and (parochial) obligation. He noted that his eligibility had already been established – he had a current "Mite" – but that it was insufficient. As an honest man of good character, he now applied for a little more, indicating that the overseer should believe him, as he had been straight with the parish before. Pratt had tried his best to make do without troubling the ratepayers, but his own capacities and the resources of those with whom he stayed had now been exhausted. The letter was dressed up in the opening and closing of supplication and deference

– apology and the humbleness of a petitioner – but in the end the inevitable infirmities of age had drawn him low. Pratt appealed to the Christian paternalism of the parish and its officials to save him from further suffering. The discretionary power of the overseers was duly acknowledged in his request for an unspecified amount of support, but custom – "Mite" was a strongly customary concept as well as a dialect form deeply rooted in the northeast of England – and humanity demanded action.

Some of this language will be familiar from letters dissected in earlier chapters. It should not be unexpected given my argument that officials, advocates, and poor writers inhabited a space of shared linguistic and referential modes. In the tripartite epistolary world of the parish, officials and poor claimants both spoke the same language *and* used the same rhetorical currencies. Against this backdrop, my understanding of the term "rhetoric" for part 3 of this study steps beyond classical definitions. These renderings have at their core "an antagonistic process of persuasion based on logical proofs" and forensic analysis, and they utilise the fixed reference points of logos, pathos, and ethos, which are framed in formulaic and ritualistic language.[2] Rather, I understand it as a cooperative process of persuasion, in both written and oral forms, that is played out in a public forum and draws on a complex amalgam of logical, rational, emotional, and strategic thought and language. In the context of letters from poor writers – with their essentially oral foundations, frequent appeals to amicus or paternalistic protection, fluid or partial representations of "truth," and interspersal with the testimony of others – I share the reading of Jennifer Richards and Alison Thorne, who argue for a strong overlap between rhetoric and eloquence. They see the latter as the culmination of practice both in a general sense and over a series of letters. Like early modern women writers, the poor sought eloquence (even if they did not achieve it), consistency, and subversion of some of the potentially repressive and antagonistic structures that frame classical understandings of rhetoric.[3]

In this context, the rhetorical ecology of poor writers and their letters is complex, ranging across a spectrum that includes the highly situational, rhetoric that was particular to subsets of letter types or their writers, and more general rhetorical modes that were shared by the majority of those who approached the parish and, in many cases, by advocates and officials. This chapter, then, is about the way that rhetoric was constellated. At its heart sits an attempt to understand the common and distinctive rhetorical currencies that can be observed in the letter types summarised in table 2.1. Through summative tables, this chapter traces substantial common threads that cohere into four wider infrastructures of rhetoric – anchoring, character, dignity, and concepts of self – that are shared between all parties in the epistolary world of the parish and are not systematically correlated in any way to what a writer requested in terms of relief. These issues are the subject of extended discussion in chapters 8, 9, 10, and 12 respectively. The life-cycle stage or gender of writers also shaped the colour and margins of these core rhetorics, and chapter 11 explores both issues in depth. The function of this chapter, over and above the identification of broad rhetorical infrastructures of this type, is to understand some of the highly situational vehicles that arose from the personality or position of writers and that gave the feel of eloquence to some of their letters. In this sense, the chapter is a fundamental foundation for the whole of part 3 of this study.

## RHETORIC AND LETTER TYPES[4]

In chapter 2, I argued that existing models for classifying and codifying pauper letters are inadequate. Such models separate the writing of the poor from that of others in the epistolary world of the parish. They also tend to fuse the type and function of letters with rhetorical and linguistic content in a way that obscures as much as it reveals. Table 2.1 suggests that we can identify several broad letter types, with any extended series of co-respondence likely to include several or all of these types by the time the writer or subject passes from observation. A detailed reading of these letters – that is, minding the story – reveals particular but also general rhetorical threads that were shared across the canvas of letters written by or about the poor. The words were not, in short, simply expedient. This (considerable) exercise is summarised in tables 7.1 to 7.6, and the lessons of these tables are explored throughout subsequent chapters. Of course, a rendering of rhetorical ecologies, and their underlying classificatory structure, is in some ways misleading. I leave some rhetorical avenues, such as aging, disability, respect, and gratitude, largely off the page. Such language was simply so ubiquitous that it might crop up in letters of any sort and indeed multiple times in the same narrative. I also leave untouched, at least in this chapter, the issue of silences in letters. In a rhetorical and strategic sense, such silences were themselves a language intended to convey as well as obscure meaning, and they were deployed persistently in ending letters but also across the typological canvas.[5] Chapter 6 considered these matters in more depth, suggesting that stories were, and were meant to be, made up of various degrees of fiction or, turned on its head, silence. More widely, a single letter could fulfil multiple purposes – it was perfectly possible, for instance, that an ending letter could also take the form of a desperate note – and thus meld together a rich and colourful rhetorical canvas that is done little justice by my tables. Nonetheless, the schematic approach is important for understanding the basic regularities of the way that poor writers and their advocates constructed rhetoric from their shared linguistic platforms and referential modes.

The lessons of these tables are subtle and numerous. It is not, of course, the case that every ending or instigatory letter contains the same range of rhetoric. Regional dialect and conversational patterns inevitably shaped the expression of language in oral writing, as I have already observed. Moreover, the tables show that it mattered whether the letters being considered were written by women, men, the aged, widows, widowers, and so on. Each sort of writer brought his or her own colour and emphasis to common rhetorical vehicles. Because such letters were often part of a series of co-respondence in which officials and advocates might also participate, these subtle differences could slowly give form to a very different sort of case from that put forth by others who might, on a casual view, use the same sort of language. I revisit this matter at length in chapter 11. Meanwhile, it is important to note that if the rhetorical footprint attached to each letter type could be relatively distinctive and letter types did share a core rhetorical thread, there were nonetheless small but important differences of emphasis. The summative tables highlight this in a way that would be less accessible in an extended discussion. Thus

Table 7.1
*Instigatory rhetoric*

| Type | Form |
|---|---|
| Contribution | Previous payment of rates, previous employment, kin and friends in the parish, contribution to host parish, wise use of past parochial relief |
| Prospect of burden | Threats to "come home," impending death, threat of job loss, sending children "home" unaccompanied, threat of spreading disease if forced to return |
| Independence or sharing | Promises of independence, assurances that claimants have done all they can before writing, prior selling of possessions, support of families now exhausted, neighbours and others willing to complement parish resources |
| Thresholds | Agedness, disability, sickness, family burdens, lunacy, widow(er)hood, unemployment |
| Yardsticks of dignity | Nakedness, starvation, homelessness, unpleasant disease, lost goods, inability to play the role of mother or father, inability to attend church |
| Struggle and sanguinity | Prior efforts to make do, approaching the parish in extremity, trying to make do on as little as possible, the impossibility of doing so (notably in old age or for large families), patience |
| Custom | Local practice, need and relief inevitably associated with particular conditions or life-cycle stages, normal practice (for instance, to support childbirth), the need for parishes to "do something" for those who belong |
| Law | Elaboration of legal belonging, suspended removal orders, legal precedent, legal opinion, threat of magistrates |
| Exogeny | Trade downturn, expensive provisions, unemployment or looming unemployment, want of family, demographic crisis, war |

Table 7.2
*Extending rhetoric*

| Type | Form |
| --- | --- |
| Right | Reference to analogous cases, disappointment that parishes had not acted, appropriation of the voices of others, statements of right and associated parochial responsibility |
| Law | Quotation of the law, implication that the law has been breached, threat to go to the magistrate, quoting precedent |
| Precedent or custom | How host parishes deal with similar circumstances, knowledge of how settlement parishes have acted, customary senses of duty, no wish to set precedent |
| Honesty | A story honestly told, yardsticks of honesty (including invitation to inspect and testimony of others), prior history with the parish confirming the writer is to be trusted |
| Sanguinity, struggle, and independence | Writers have told only half their suffering, credit due for contending with suffering and reducing the burden on the parish, writers reconciled with their fate, hopes for final return to independence (often through partnership and friendship) |
| Humanitarianism | Officials co-opted as Christian paternalists (often in gendered language), the need to act because of exigency or the natural consequences of conditions such as aging, officials asked to have feeling and to think how the writer must feel |
| Shame | Applications against better inclination, shame and pain at continuing dependence, detail of compromised material world, the shame of pawning and scratching about, shame in host communities |
| Support and advocacy | Statements of support from doctors, officials, and so on, handing case over to epistolary advocates, implication or statement of current and prior support from neighbours, religious imperative |

| Type | Form |
|------|------|
| Parochial reputation (and subtext of dignity) | Officials or parishes will not be trusted subsequently, current reputation is compromised in the eyes of a host community, reputation will be enhanced by acting |
| Time running (and subtext of dignity) | Fundamental consequences of not acting quickly |

dignity or its yardsticks constituted a common theme across the different typologies, but those writing instigatory letters tended to talk in terms of threats to dignity and the *prospect* of nakedness, hunger, or homelessness, whereas those writing desperate notes talked in terms of a dignity that had already *been* compromised and that threatened to be beyond repair and revival.

These observations notwithstanding, there *were* important and insistent common threads, as these tables powerfully show. They cohere, I suggest, into four broad rhetorical infrastructures or ecologies. The first and most obvious one was anchoring rhetoric, which appears across and within letter types with such clear regularity as to be part of the wallpaper of the epistolary world of the parish. This anchoring rhetoric appears to have been relatively well known, well used, and *shared* between officials, advocates, and poor writers. This sharing confirms that poor writers did not *simply* write what was likely to be most useful in advancing their case. Anchoring rhetoric included models of struggle, custom, precedent, right, duty, law, humanitarianism, and friendship. Although not always sufficient to swing a claim in the direction of the poor applicant, anchoring rhetoric was the core building block of entitlement within letters and, even more so, across sets of letters by or about the same person. It is the subject of chapter 8. The second rhetorical ecology was that of character. Its presence is perhaps unsurprising in an eighteenth- and early-nineteenth-century social system where character was, for all men (and some women), the true

Table 7.3
*Renewing rhetoric*

| Type | Form |
| --- | --- |
| Support and advocacy | Apology for renewing approaches but unavoidable (particularly due to exogeny), co-opted words of professionals and stakeholders like landlords, active statements of support (particularly from officials), presence of friends and potential parochial partners in relief |
| Yardsticks of dignity | Writers drawn to extremity, compromised material circumstances, threat to parochial reputation, accumulated suffering cuts writers off from normal life |
| Certainty of burden | Prospect of burden turns to certainty of burden, a little help now will postpone long-term dependence (particularly that associated with old age) |
| Honesty | The need for renewed allowance honestly stated, public knowledge of the plight of the writer, approach to the parish only when needful |
| Suffering (with struggle and sanguinity) | Severe suffering compounded by struggling to make do, put off until the last extremity, the inevitability of certain conditions (such as decline or the return and intensification of sickness), burdens (particularly nursing, dead partners, and young children), exogeny |
| Compromised gender roles | Inability to perform the roles of mother or father, being seen as unable to fulfil these roles, requests for officials to think of themselves in such situations |
| Being ordinary | The universal burden placed upon people by ordinary life-cycle conditions such as aging, the sense that recipients of letters were just like their writers |

| Type | Form |
| --- | --- |
| Exhausted makeshifts | The impossibility of getting more credit, the limits of patience of landlords, kin, and friends no longer able to help, possibilities that a little help now might renew this makeshift economy, coming home would make things worse |
| Custom and precedent | It might be seen as normal to renew, others in the same situation, the language of trifles, past parochial practice |

signifier of worth and respectability. Framed with the ubiquitous signifiers of respect – deference, submission, and gratitude, even if these were actually appropriated for the positive assertion of agency – the rhetoric of character was built from notions of honesty, probity, suffering and responses to it, partnership, and the desire to be independent. Chapter 9 picks up this theme. The third rhetorical ecology, perhaps the most common thread across the letter types, was that of dignity or its absence. Whether constructed in terms of direct and stark indicators – nakedness, starvation, and the inability to hold up one's head in public – or in terms of more subtle inferences of "normal" behaviour and experience, dignity has a powerful place in the rhetorical ecologies of the corpus and could often be the tipping point for the acceptance of the shared fictions that these letters embodied. Chapter 10 takes this discussion forward. Finally, although almost always unacknowledged directly in tables 7.1 to 7.6, these poor writers suffused their texts with the rhetorical infrastructure of the pauper self. Fusing the languages of belonging, sanguinity, shame, pain, self-awareness, and self-reflection with the status of simply being ordinary and having normal experiences, writers sought to show themselves rhetorically as a "fellow." The poor writer *and* vestry attendee embodied a plight that could befall anyone. In requests for officials to think what they would feel in similar situations, the poor constructed themselves not only as fellow citizens and

Table 7.4
*Testamentary rhetoric*

| Type | Form |
|------|------|
| Honesty and character | A story honestly told in detail, its telling a matter of character, the canvas of suffering should elicit humanitarian duty, checking the facts should not be required |
| Crisis and suffering | Writers brought to a tipping point by exogenous crisis, the elaboration of intense suffering, the sense that the individual has nowhere left to turn, suffering should elicit paternalistic duty (especially when endured by women) |
| Yardsticks of dignity | Crisis brings writers to shame and humiliation, compromised material circumstances that lead to lost employment and local identity, starvation |
| Support and advocacy | Others can provide testimony if needed, the offer of more information (for instance, names and ages of children) than in other sorts of letters, co-opted voices and quoted voices, the sense that acting now will enliven "friends" |
| Compromised others | The suffering of the writer pales to insignificance when compared to the associated suffering of wives, husbands, and children, the need for the parish to stand as a friend, mothers and siblings left on the edge of living and dying, injustice |
| Accumulation of misfortune | Writers could not have done more, misfortune is glued to them, writers are drawn low by exogeny, seasonality, and natural life-cycle conditions, the accumulation of misfortune is natural, parish officers must realise that for ordinary people the accumulation of misfortune is as natural as the seasons |

Table 7.5
*Ending rhetoric*

| Type | Form |
| --- | --- |
| Shame and pride | The shame of a prospective ending dependent upon the parish, pride at the struggle, a life well lived, compromised gender roles, fear for those left behind, litany of attempts to prepare for the end |
| Living an ordinary life | Men and women who could not have done more, the sharing of this fate by others, struggle in the normal run of things, sanguinity, a desire to be remembered |
| Yardsticks of dignity | Need for a dignified burial, the parish should of course act generously in these last hours or days, particular requests of a dying man or woman, their demise has drawn families low, the dignity of parish officers |
| Character | Suffering honestly and ferociously borne, planning for the end, regret that the writer never managed to return to independence, the shame of decline and death "on the parish" |
| Resignation and self-reflection | God's will, the inevitability of this outcome, a life well lived, how those left behind might return to independence, memory of the writer, belonging and the duties of the parish to one who had a history |
| Precedent and duty | How parishes ought to act in cases of last illness and death, Christian paternalism and the need for humanity here at the end, normal responses to acute suffering |
| Friendship to those left behind | The parish must substitute for husbands, wives, mothers, and fathers, spend now to get dependants over the worst of things in order to reduce future bills, requests to think how dependants will be situated, co-opted voices of advocates and officials |

Table 7.6
*Desperate rhetoric*

| Type | Form |
|---|---|
| Struggle, suffering, and humanitarianism | Exemplary struggle, the need for parish to act out of humanitarian duty and human empathy, bone-breaking need, lack of reference to independence or the makeshift economy |
| Parish shame | The situation of the writer is so obviously common that parishes should feel shame that it has reached this point, officials who have failed in their duty as men, the travesty of inaction when other parishes would have met their duties |
| Honesty | The statement is itself a testimony both of crisis and honesty, the claimant has no other chance, by implication the situation described is checkable |
| Law and belonging | An assumption of eligibility through belonging, occasional quotation or assertion of law, the duties of the parish when faced by the conditions described, recourse to the law |
| Pain | Physical pain, the pain of seeing loved ones suffer, parishes causing pain and suffering through inaction, emotional turmoil and mental suffering |
| Anger and right | Anger at the world, anger at parish inaction that has led the writer to this point, the right to expect relief, anger at rights being ignored |
| Friendship | Friendship has run out, the parish must stand as a friend, the need for friendly action, co-opted voices of friends |
| Time has run out and hopelessness | The final limits of tolerance have been reached, the time for action has passed, the material circumstance of the writer is little better than that of an animal, the writer has no hope for the present or future |
| Dignity | Starvation, nakedness, homelessness, inability to show oneself in public, mental perturbation, living as a shadow of oneself or between life and death |

residents but also as fellow humans. They had the same capacities for emotional turmoil, hope, pain, gratitude, pleasure, and crushed dreams as the parish elites whom they joined in the epistolary world of the parish. I revisit these matters in chapter 12.

## SITUATIONAL AND PARTICULAR RHETORIC

These regularities should not be allowed to mask a second important feature of tables 7.1 to 7.6, which is that each broad letter type exhibits, as I argued above, at least one rhetorical signature that does not occur elsewhere, or at least not in a regular pattern. The fact that such signatures were closely shared by poor writers, advocates, and officials in their different correspondence suggests that they might have had particular purchase on the process of poor relief as triggers for action. In instigatory letters, for instance, the vast majority of writers constructed in the minds of officials – just as officials noted when corresponding with each other – the prospect that bringing them "home" to a settlement parish would increase the burden on parish finances. This construction might take the form of observations that the claimant was too sick and would thus have to be put under a suspended removal order, delaying his or her return and costing the settlement parish even more because of such a delay. More positively, the poor, officials, and advocates reminded each other that the writer was known in the host community and could expect to find employment, credit, and friends there and that upending an individual would lead to all sorts of unexpected cost. Relatively few officials, as we saw in chapter 4, tested this rhetoric by demanding that the person return home, although they might offer less than was asked for or invite the person to return home if he or she was dissatisfied. I do not argue, of course, that the prospect of burden is absent from other letter types, but its use in instigatory letters was particularly acute because their writers could not know whether they would be removed. By contrast, those writing extending letters had already received relief, or at least entered into sustained co-respondence about it, so they could have a decent inkling that forced removal was unlikely. Thus, as table 7.2 shows, the authors of extending letters used a very distinctive rhetoric of ticking time in efforts to press their claims for more parish resources. Advocates and officials shared this rhetoric. They reminded each other that there were costs to not acting when the time was right and before the situation became critical. Denuded material lives and crushed dignity were expensive to repair and might carry fundamental consequences for the reputation of parishes and their officers. Many of the claims made in such cases were themselves time-limited, such as when landlords had given those with arrears a matter of days to pay before they threw the poor into the streets. Such time limitations explain in part why letters back from advocates could themselves be a material and rhetorical currency for poor recipients, particularly where there was an inference of expected payment. If time ticked for all of the poor, most notably for those who wrote desperate notes, the elaboration of time in extending letters is singular.

Those who wrote renewing letters, coming back to the parish after a break of however short a time, also imparted a distinctive veneer to a more widely shared rhetorical vehicle. For such writers, the language of an exhausted makeshift economy was a modus operandi of their claims. This theme spoke to the expectation that those who claimed a share of the parish bounty should have exhausted their own means first. How far this was a real experience, as opposed to a confection of the rhetoric that writers expected officials would want to hear, is not always clear given the fictive qualities of letters explored in the previous chapter. The testimony of officials and advocates along the same lines in their interspersing letters should, however, give us confidence in the veracity of claims. The writers of renewing letters invariably pointed to their (characterful) attempts to make do during breaks in their engagement with the parish. Always unwillingly and against their better inclination, they were driven back into dependence by the disintegration of these structures, whether they could no longer obtain credit because debts had not been paid, they had tested the patience of landlords, small jobs had dried up, disability had reduced earning capacity, or friends and relatives had reached the end of their means. On the more positive side, the fact of the parish acting quickly, even if only with a trifle, would perhaps allow writers to revive their support networks and thus prove no long-term burden on the parish and its finances. Those writing desperate notes, instigatory letters, and extending letters also referred to compromised makeshift economies, particularly where sickness prevailed and produced extra costs as well as fewer resources, but for the authors of renewing letters, the question of what had changed was always in the background of their thinking and writing.

Makeshift economies were also invariably part of testamentary letters, whichever party in the epistolary world of the parish wrote them, but the distinctive rhetorical emphasis in such narratives was actually on the suffering of others. Writers constructed famished children screaming for bread, wives giving birth without a bed to lay upon, naked children running around the streets, leaky hovels giving husbands and children incapacitating illness, and family members clothed in rags not fit for the dog kennel. The suffering of the author was dread to behold, but the suffering of others would make an ordinary person weep. In such situations, the parish was invariably called to stand in friendship with the family concerned in order to prevent a grave injustice that could tip honest people over into dishonest means. Such rhetoric of the suffering of the other seems to have had a particularly powerful grasp on the actions of officials, as chapter 4 implied. Of course, "others" suffered in all typological categories used here, but none did more so than in testamentary letters. In some cases, the rhetoric extended to the religious – as in for God's sake act, act in God's name, and we are in the vale of darkness and relief will mean you are greeted in heaven – but nowhere was God's will played out so extensively and intensively as in desperate notes. Those who wrote them invariably constructed themselves as resigned to their fate in a way that we simply do not see elsewhere. God was the originator of troubles laid upon individuals, and only God could relieve them through death or, with a little help from the parish, through redemption.[6] Although exogenous influences like a trade downturn or seasonality could be managed, there was an inevitability in desperate notes that a writer would end up in this position when all hope vanished. These writers threw themselves on the mercy of their parishes, and one can, when closely reading the parish archives, feel recipients wondering how to act, itself an affirmation of the depth and reach of the agency of the poor in its effect on the process of poor relief.

In turn, the hopelessness that desperate notes embody is also to be found in ending letters. Writers felt themselves to be at the end of a journey, one that they often constructed in the language of the seasons – as in winter is coming and it is autumn with me – a clear footprint of conversational routines from the oral tradition. Such hopelessness, however, was positively inscribed into self-reflection on a life well lived and a fight well fought.[7] It was balanced by hope for those left behind, especially where the parish would play its part as a friend or substitute father or mother. For those drawn low, to the point where their material conditions were little better than those of pigs or sheep, we find anger and bitterness, but most ending letters were not written in such a vein. An end was to be borne, and there could be individual and parochial pride in such bearing.

These distinctive rhetorics – a function of the particular situation of the writer, their take on the universal condition, or the exact function of the letters they wrote – point to the complexity of the world of negotiation that shaped the process of poor relief. They also, however, begin to construct poor writers as autonomous and reflective individuals who were capable of taking control of the depiction of their lives and shaping the relief system to which they were notionally subject. This constructed self was much like that of others involved in the epistolary world of the parish in the eighteenth and early nineteenth centuries.

## CONCLUSION: THE EMERGENCE OF ELOQUENCE

Tables 7.1 to 7.6 and the succeeding discussion encourage us to deconstruct the letters of the poor and their advocates, atomising them so as to mark out both distinctiveness and regularity. This process is deliberately continued in chapters 8 to 12. Such an approach, however, deflects our attention from a further important feature of the corpus: the sheer eloquence of some of the letters and the fact that almost all of the writers seem to have grasped that there was a performative – but as we have seen, not fictional – aspect to accessing the resources of a discretionary parochial system. Not all could be like James Harris, who wrote to Sandal Magna in Yorkshire on 25 May 1815 to say that in consequence

of the deranged state of my Affairs I am under the painful Necessity
of leaving pledwich, I was led to Suppose that that practice in that
Neighbourhood would be considerable as also beneficial, but I
have found after an anxious Trial, that any future Exertion would
prove fruit-less and unavailing, this, along with a train of other
Disappointments in pecuniary Matters have actuated me to abandon a Concern which by further prosecuting, must unavoidably involve me in greater difficulties and consequently tend to injure
rather than alleviate. I hope I have it in my power to produce a
sort of Statement which will entitle me to that indulgence from you
which is seldom witheld from one who is equally unfortunately situated with myself. I shall immediate-ly proceed to ~~my~~ an arrangement of my Affairs – A little time will be necessary for the Purpose
of adjusting them, which I hope you will have the ~~purpose~~ goodness
to grant me, assuring you at the same time that I will most faith-
fully give up what I possess in the world, for the mutual Benefit of
all my Creditors, I am desirous & willing to make an immediate Assignment to any 1
or 2 of the Principal Creditors as may be approved with infinitely less Expence than any other, and of course make my Estate more produc-
tive, it is my wish to satisfy or explain any inquiry you desire, or
may have to institute or ask of me – All that man can do, I will do
to the advantage of my Estate.[8]

This beautifully crafted but still oral writing clearly challenged Harris
both in terms of the words themselves and how they should be presented.
He was by no means unique in his eloquence, as we have seen in earlier
chapters and will see subsequently. Even those with less skill and determination, however, exhibited an awareness of the need for more than
mere reportage. Authors sometimes apologised for their poor lettering
as they wrote or when they finished. More often, they apologised for the
struggle to convey in a sufficiently colourful fashion their exact predicament. For some, this struggle descended into silences or simply running
out of words, as we have already seen in earlier chapters. But in the sense
that eloquence, performance, and confidence were inextricably yoked,
we often see the development of colour, argument, and representation

during letter series. Poor writers, in other words, learned as they wrote and aspired to be better than when they had begun, key markers of selfhood for this most marginalised of groups. They did not simply "write up" in an effort to even out the power relationships implicit in the process of poor relief or to fulfil the expectations of officials. Rather, they actively sought to better their rhetoric and extend it beyond their intensely personal circumstances. In the joint construction of meaning and knowledge that underpinned the epistolary world of the parish, it was the poor themselves who developed and deployed the most substantial and sophisticated rhetoric.[9] I explore this theme and others in the rest of part 3 and in part 4.

# 8

## *Anchoring Rhetoric*

OVERVIEW

On 5 December 1833, Anthony South sent an instigatory letter from Brighton to Peterborough. Confidently written, relatively well punctuated, and in a strong hand, South's letter noted,

> It was my intention to have address a letter to you for some time past, but I was averse to give you trouble while I had hopes of it being unnecessary – Now however I am sorry to say it becomes an imperious duty, as my wife, who has long been in a declining state but whose recovery, till now, I had flattered myself would have taken place, is so much worse that my hopes and expectation, and those of the doctor who attends her, are almost at an end.
>
> In this situation I am under the necessity of applying to my parish, without which I am unable to support myself and her and a helpless child. I am the son of Anthony South who served his apprenticeship with Dr Spalding and Mr White know my father well – I was myself at home six years ago last July, but never received any parish relief except about a fortnight of that time. I think it necessary to mention these circumstances in the first place that you may have an opportunity of informing me, whether I may expect relief from *my own parish*, or put myself on the parish of Brighton, which

I shall be under the necessitiy of doing unless you are free to allow me something for my own. My wife is at present in that state that she is totally unable to do anything for herself or her family, and indeed we have been compelled for some time past to keep a girl to attend her, at an expense which I can no longer support. In the hopes of being forward with your Reply in *acquiescence* with *my very untoward situation* I remain Respectfully sir your mo. obe. servant Anthony South.

[Note on opposite page:]

Mrs South living at no. 55 Chesterfield St in this town is suffering with severe inward disease. Geo. Buttercock Surgeon.[1]

This letter embodies many of the rhetorical signposts that are repeated regularly across the corpus and letter types, as well as in vestry minutes. South opened, and then infused his text, with the rhetoric of struggle. Brought to a bad place by the continuing illness of his wife, he had the "imperious" duty as a husband and the legal and moral right as a person who belonged to Peterborough – indeed, he had recently been "home" to where he belonged – to apply for welfare.[2] Although he did not make direct reference to the law, South knew very well that a threatened application for relief in Brighton would trigger either a letter from the overseer there seeking out-parish relief or the commencement of removal, which would be suspended because of the keenly emphasised sickness of his wife.[3] South explicitly noted that he had told his story so as to give "my" parish the chance to act before it was forced into more expensive solutions. This detail was an implied indicator of his honesty and concern for the parish finances. He called on mutual acquaintance and friendship – Mr White was either the overseer or a vestryman – as a backdrop to his claim and subtly but definitively acknowledged custom, precedent, and the balancing act between claimants and ratepayers that had to be achieved, asking his co-respondent whether he was "free" to act.[4] Finally, South must either have taken the letter to Dr George Buttercock or have had it ready for him to sign when he visited the house to treat Mrs South. In effect, the doctor's voice was appropriated to imply the humanitarian imperative for the overseer to act given the "severe inward disease." The voice of an unnamed doctor had also been appropriated earlier in the letter to emphasise lost hope of recovery.

Notwithstanding the rhetorical sophistication of this letter, Peterborough failed to respond. On 24 December, South wrote a second – testamentary – letter emphasising the "impossibility of my being able to procure the requisites which her [his wife's] situation demands and at the same time to maintain and pay a person who *necessarily* attends her without some relief from *my* parish."[5] Although he did not employ the language of right, entitlement, and duty, the use of words like "requisite," "demands," and "necessary" tend in this direction, as does the fact that a nonresponse to such a clear case "surprises me very much."[6] South went on,

> I did not however know when I wrote that you are at present acting as head overseer of that Parish, otherwise would have addressed the letter to you as being well aquainted with my father and which you told me when I was last at Peterboro about six years ago. May I therefore request your kind attention to the contents of my letters soon as possible.[7]

Claiming personal connection with the overseer on top of his belonging to Peterborough, he asked that the unnamed official treat him kindly, much as a friend would. The letter ended with the rhetoric of running time, noting that his wife was "every day declining in strength," and sought to change the basis of his relief from ad hoc to regular.[8]

Anthony South was unusual in terms of the quality of his writing, as earlier chapters show. Nonetheless, his correspondence provides numerous insights that are important for this chapter and for this part of the study. At the core of his writing, it is possible to identify a basic anchoring rhetoric – a set of arguments, proofs, and claims – that frame most appeals in writing or in person at the vestry and that are continually restated within and between letter sets and types. As chapter 7 began to suggest, such rhetorical models – struggle, custom, law, right, duty, friendship, and humanitarianism – stretch across the spatial, chronological, typological, gender, and life-cycle dimensions of the corpus. The rest of this chapter thus analyses how the poor understood and used different components of anchoring rhetoric. How, in other words, did claimants navigate rhetorically a canvas primed by a linguistic register that was common to officials and advocates and by a shared understanding and acceptance of the fictive and fractured nature of individual stories? How did an anchoring rhetoric foster agency? And how far was this rhetorical territory and process shared with the other parties who comprised the epistolary world of the parish?

## STRUGGLE

The vast majority of all letters, whether as individual documents or part of a series written by or for the same person, were framed with the rhetoric of struggle in an effort to freight the text with "moral authority and affective eloquence" and to elicit, in a framework of reciprocal obligations and mutual understandings of the means of claims making, the "moral duty of the strong."[9] I return to the suffering occasioned by struggle – a different rhetorical matter altogether – in chapter 9. The conceptual vocabulary of struggle itself is vibrant.[10] Wives struggled against the pauperising effects of absent, violent, neglectful, or useless husbands, and (rather less often) husbands struggled with drunken or feckless wives. The poor at all life-cycle stages struggled with the economic troubles occasioned by sudden or chronic illness or by the death of a family member. Inclement weather, as we saw in chapter 3, invariably fostered the rhetoric of struggle with the seasons. Lack of clothing saw the poor struggling to keep or get jobs, and a lack of food left mothers and fathers struggling to fulfil their familial duties or roles as mothers and fathers.[11] Sometimes the poor, both in- and out-parish, struggled against the neglect of relatives or the actions of parish officers, as for instance if individuals found themselves slated to pay rates when they did not have the means to do so. Across the sample and all of its spatial and typological divisions, the poor and prospective poor, both settled and out-parish, struggled with their landlords. It was essential, then, for poor claimants to have, and to be able to rhetoricise, a burden so that the balancing action of altruism on the part of officers had a basis of recognisable "fact" in the eyes of their constituents, the ratepayers. There was, as we saw in the previous chapter, a performative element to these narratives. Against this backdrop, three particularly powerful and intertwining rhetorics of struggle thread their way insistently throughout the sources.

The first was the struggle of writers and vestry applicants to make do from their own resources. Ann Jones, writing an instigatory letter from Newcastle Street in London on 18 January 1825, noted that her husband had been stranded overseas with the East India Company and that

> since the absence of my husband, my Eldest Daughter and self supported the family by working at worsted embroidery – that work having failed for some time past we have been totaly out of employment – my eldest son, has been two Voyages to China in the Honble Companys ship Vansittart – but his health prevents him from entering the service – he is Now endeavouring to obtain a situation on shore and my eldest Daughter has lately been ill not making – she has the promise of some employment from Mr Edwards No. 85 Hatton Garden as soon as the Trade will permitt – by that period I shall be enabled to work at the business likewise and am in hopes to support my family by this means.[12]

For Jones, this complex ecology of efforts to make do, allied with a promise – ubiquitous in the wider letter set and vestry minutes – to be independent in the future, was an indication of her deservingness, on the one hand, and a signifier of parish duty, on the other. Some poor writers painted an even more desperate picture of the struggle to make do. William Townsend wrote from Leeds on 25 November 1820 to say that he had been ill and under the care of doctors for nine months and thus "Not bene Able to yearn one Peney." Notwithstanding such a long illness, "Rather then Troble you I have Pledge all the Close Belonging to my Self and Wife and Now as Nothing to Suport ourselves on I ham Oblig^d To Troble you wilbe [illegible] I Get Better and be Able To work as I hope Sir you will do the Best for me."[13] For Townsend, then, the struggle to make do had come down to parting with the very clothes on his back, and he now employed a well-understood rhetoric of entreaty in an effort to obtain remedy.[14] As yardsticks of their personal struggle to avoid dependence, other writers employed rhetorics of going hungry for days on end, trying to mend their own health with sojourns in the country and at the seaside, or exhausting the resources of kin and neighbours. Nor was this rhetorical device peculiar to the out-parish poor. Vestry minutes are replete with cases of in-parish claimants such as John Winsworth, who applied to the vestry of Oundle in Northamptonshire on 11 January 1835 for "some assistance" in the case of his niece, who "resides with him she having left her service from severe injury and her mistress having promised to take her back again as soon as recovered." The overseer noted that "the girl has been with him 3 weeks" prior to the application and that Winsworth had struggled with her condition at his own expense.[15]

The second universal form of struggle was that against exogenous circumstances, including sickness, trade depressions, war, and the distraint of goods by landlords in lieu of debts for rent. For some poor writers and vestry attendees, the rhetoric of such struggle was an art form. Richard Broadhead wrote from South Hindley in Lincolnshire in an undated instigatory letter to seek relief because of unemployment. This was never an easy task given the ingrained belief that unemployment was at least partly the fault of the individual.[16] Noting that he had "ben Seeking Work at Difront places and Canot Light on," he claimed that "I Do Not Want to be a Common pauper Upon you pleas to send Mee Som Money to Soport my famley a few Wekes praps Work Will turn Out after Crestames if please god I have Onley Arned $^{S}$11 Shilings this 3 Weekes, and Credet is Run Out from Yours."[17] Here, then, Broadhead fused a confident self-regard, which was framed in a strong local dialect form, with a sense of struggle and a definitive yardstick that the struggle had come to an end because his credit, both financial and in terms of his standing, had run out. The aged were notably skilled at portraying multiple layers of struggle in relation to exogenous factors, none more so than Walter Keeling, who in December 1784 was hopeful of obtaining work in Hull so that he could "stay while I live." Sustained work was to become a distant prospect. In November 1786 his family was in a "deplorable condition" because of a lame son and fever in the house. By July 1787 his son had died, fever had returned, Keeling had funerals and doctors to pay for, and the family had fallen behind with the rent. Seven months later, in January 1788, unemployment had added to his troubles, and by February 1791 his legs and eyes had both deteriorated, such that "I have Been Sumtimes all most Blind for this 2 Months." At the time of his last letter in March 1798, exogenous struggles and tests had washed over Keeling and his family. He was "in grate Distress as my wife Has Been Verrey Bad In a fever for this Two months and me a old man Verrey much Trobled with a pain in my side Verrey unable to work."[18] For Keeling, then, a struggle to make do, allied with a struggle against powerful exogenous causes, equated to a strong case for relief.

A particularly striking rhetorical variant was the exogenously derived tipping point or threshold that pushed individuals into initial dependency or into a request for a different form of allowance. James Halford Jr is typical. He wrote an instigatory letter from Spratton in Northamptonshire on 9 April 1821 because of the death of his wife and the problems he now faced balancing work and the need to care for a young family. Noting that his employer had already helped him a little, he was "Now in Debt Very much" and hoped that "the Rest of the Gentlemen and you will consider mine A Case of Real Nessity." He had, he assured them, "Been Very much tried Before But I Always Kept from troubling you And I Assure you Sir I am very sorry to Do it now But I Am obliged."[19] At the other end of the period of study, Richard East wrote from Henley to Wallingford, both in Oxfordshire, on 24 March of an unspecified year (but almost certainly 1755) to say that his wife had been under the doctor "long before I sent to you last" and that she remained unwell. Now "I have been lame with a bad foot and Can't work and if you don't send me sum assistance I rely can't live."[20] Here, then, struggle reached its ultimate conclusion in impending death and a presumed need to go no further in describing the impact of the tipping point.

The third rhetoric of struggle, which we can increasingly locate across the chronological period covered by this study, was centred on the continuing difficulty that individuals had making do even when they *had* a parish allowance. Thus John Maltman, writing from Boston in Lincolnshire on 26 January 1836, suggested that he "needed a Little *more* Assistance," a request that "i have Drove it off to the Last Befour I Made" it.[21] The claimants William and Mary Mann, resident in Bethnal Green but settled in Colchester in Essex, provide a striking but not unrepresentative example of this sort of rhetoric. Their letter of 21 March 1814 offered apologies for writing and then noted that "the Money that you was So kind to Relive me with I Layd outt to the Best Advantage." This concern for economy and the resources of the parish was, at least in the view of the Manns, to their great credit. Nonetheless,

> Every thing in London is So very Dear that theire is no Such a thing as Living at all the Couls are 3 Shillings a Bushell And very thing is Dear in perpeotin and I have Gott so Litel work to Doe that wee Are almost Lost out stand at 3 Shillings a week therefore Dear Gentlemen I Hope that You will be So Good as to take it into Consideration to Be So kind as to Send ues Some thing to help use in our Distress.[22]

Acknowledging the discretionary nature of the system with which they engaged, invoking exogenous circumstance and an element of pathos – they were almost lost – and detailing a creditable struggle, the Manns claimed that no one living in London could subsist on the allowance that the parish had so generously provided.

Claimants like the Manns were not, of course, operating in a vacuum. The intertwining rhetoric of struggle and tipping points was also shared by other participants in the epistolary world of the parish. Advocates and officials frequently deployed stark histories of struggle in their engagement with each other over the proper course of action in the case of the actual or prospective poor. James Call is a good example. Writing from Skipton in Yorkshire, where Call was the parish clerk, to the Rev-

erend Westerman on 11 February 1828, he asked Westerman to inter-
vene in the case of George Thompson:

> a resident in my Neighbourhood, who I'm convinced is in very
> indigent Circumstances at present, he has been out of Work a con-
> siderable time but has at present a prospect of getting employ at
> Manchester, but being nearly barefoot & having no Money for
> either Shoes or travelling expences renders it almost impossible for
> him to prosecute his Journey without the Charitable aid of his
> Parish, I am not fond of writing upon such occasions when I'm not
> fully convinced of the propriety of making the claim upon any
> Parish, knowing that there are many will make false claims to make
> up for their own improvidence, whatever his circumstances might
> have been before time I'm not able to judge, but at Present I believe
> he is very ill off.[23]

Asking for charitable aid rather than an allowance, Call acknowledged
the essential discretion of the parish. Noting the prospect of work in
Manchester, he outlined a possible solution to parish dependence. The
essence of his approach to Westerman, however, was Thompson's long
struggle to make do without trouble to the parish, which had resulted
in his being barefoot and "very ill off."

Examples like this one can be seen repeatedly across the corpus. In
turn, although it was rarely a sufficient cause, a story of struggle was a
necessary and accepted basis – even if fictive – for a positive decision. It
is for this reason that vestries railed against applicants, both in- and out-
parish, who were not seen to have struggled enough. Thus Sandal
Magna, in a letter to the same George Thompson on 15 December 1826,
had written forcefully, "The Select Vestry think it very wrong of you to
ask for Relief when you have £15 in the Savings Bank to mention nothing else – Relief is for such Persons as are destitute and not for those
who have Property."[24] We also see the strong traction of this shared
rhetorical foundation in (the relatively few) cases where parish officers
*systematically* failed to acknowledge and account for prior struggle.

Nowhere in the corpus is this clearer than for Billington in Lancashire. Here, the overseer, John Seed, was known for late payment, not answering his letters, paying less than was needed or promised, and pursuing every avenue to contain parochial relief costs. Yet he was consistently challenged by other overseers, such as Thomas Heath of Preston, who on 29 November 1825 noted that Elizabeth Shuttleworth was "lying in, in a most deplorable state." Seed had "sent her 3/ 13d. just and [unfulfilled] promises to call on her on Saturday." Heath warned his counterpart sternly that to avoid a suspended removal order, he must "take her situation into your serious consideration, and give her such further Relief – as may be necessary for a person so situated."[25] Heath's letter, of course, also highlights a further anchoring rhetoric – custom and precedent – and it is to this theme that I now turn.

## CUSTOM AND PRECEDENT[26]

Anthony South asked that the overseers grant support "in acquiescence with my very untoward situation," implying perhaps that relief would, or ought to, be a customary parochial response for people faced with his afflictions.[27] For contemporary critics of the Old Poor Law, the development of customary allowances and attitudes toward the poor had become corrosive by the early nineteenth century.[28] Subsequent historians have come to question the reach of custom as a structuring relationship between people and a framework for action, variously locating the 1810s, 1820s, and 1830s as the last major reference points.[29] In the context of the Old Poor Law, Sandra Sherman points to the progressive extinction of a system of parochial social relations and "customary dignifying rights" that had "accorded the poor nominal choices and recognized their prerogative, however slight, to bargain face to face for what they claimed to need and deserve."[30] In terms of local practice, however, evidence for the decline of customary attitudes on the part of parishes and for the decline of claims from the poor embodying custom and precedent is contradictory. Henry French has shown persuasively that for Terling in Essex by the early nineteenth century, the claims of those customarily seen as deserving and claiming

such deservingness were outpaced by the insistent and increasing presence of un- and underemployed men on the relief lists. In other rural
places equally beset with low wages and overpopulation, we do not see
such definitive shifts.[31]

Nor do custom and precedent dwindle as a rhetorical mode in the corpus. William Timpson wrote an extending letter from Prestwich in Lancashire, near Manchester, on 20 June 1808 because of the "deranged
state of my Affairs." Unable to find work, "along with a train of other
Disappointments in pecuniary Matters," he resolved to try his luck in
another place with the support of his parish, and "I hope I have it in
my power to produce a sort of Statement which will entitle me to that
indulgence from you which is seldom witheld from one who is equally
unfortunately situated with myself."[32] Such assertions of custom are repeated in letters across the geographical and chronological range of the
corpus and in letters of different sorts. Thus, when John Hall wrote from
Chelmsford to Colchester, both in Essex, on 6 May 1816 to note that
"you know Sir Every Poor has a Doctor Allowed them," he was eloquently expressing a sense of customary right and analogous parochial
duty, one that we see played out in an almost universal engagement of
doctors under formal contract to parishes by the 1810s.[33] These are important emblematic examples both of agency and of the continuing reach
of custom as a rhetorical vehicle.

Other writers and vestry attendees adopted a more inferential language to place moral pressure on officials. William Thackeray Sr, writing
an instigatory letter from Sheffield on 21 December 1818, asked the
overseers of his home parish for their "favour" in paying his sick club
subscription, which proved beyond him because of unemployment.
Having sought work, moved to a smaller house to conserve money, and
joined a sick club as a precaution, he fused struggle with an implicit
marker of precedent when he stated that he would "Wish to get through
this World if Posable I can I have troubled you bfore but I hope you will
not think amiss I have to Inform you that there his men that has been
before the Overseers of this parish for 2 or 3 years But Gentelmen I wish
to Do without Been so Troublesom."[34] Thackeray, then, constructed
himself as a man who did not wish to create further precedent and who

would avoid doing so if helped a little in his extraordinary situation. Precedent, however, might also be used more aggressively, as for instance when poor writers or the settled and proximate poor noted what would be allowed for a similar circumstance in their host parishes or what had in the past been allowed for similar experiences by settlement parishes themselves. One such writer was Samuel White, who sent an extending letter to Chelmsford in Essex on 25 February 1826 in which he claimed that, despite huge afflictions and loss, he had received from his parish only "seven pounds while if I am rightly informed there is a Family in this Place that is receiving more than Double that sum from your Parish" even though the family also had a child working in the local tan yard.[35] This example is important, too, because it suggests that as well as re-membering and marshalling their own stories, which was the subject of chapter 6, the poor also knew, discovered or uncovered, remembered, and could use the stories of their peers.

As might be expected from chapter 5's focus on finding words, rhetorics of custom continued to inform the starting point for the process of poor relief throughout the period covered by this study. Indeed, it could hardly be otherwise given that poor writers were tapping into a rich seam of official and semi-official rhetoric along these lines from other participants in the epistolary world of the parish. The advocate Joseph Kennedy, writing from Lincolns Inn in London, is a strident but not untypical example. He would, in an interspersing letter, "beg and earnestly impress on the Overseers of St. Clements the justice & good policy of attending to the letter sent herewith. Mr. Kennedy believes the writer to be a most industrious man but it is impossible under his circum-stances to do without the Relief which was promised him & has been so unjustly withheld."[36] As with the poor, officials and others sometimes fell short of mentioning custom but employed its yardsticks nonetheless. Robert Ferris, for instance, wrote an interspersing letter from Dawlish in Devon on 13 April 1828 in the long-running case of Widow Attack. The seventy-three year old was living with her eldest son, whom "you may depend that he is not able to assist his Mother in any way more than he does he gives her her Lodgings." Citing a now lost letter, Ferris called attention to precedent in his own parish as a way of inferring the customary duties of Sandal Magna: "you stated that you had relieved attick with 370$^£$ we have a person in Dawlish have had 400 and upward."[37] Custom, then, retained its constraining power over the actions of the parish for much longer than it has been conventional to think.

## RIGHTS AND DUTIES

Custom did not, of course, equate to absolute right. Chapter 1 suggested that even if we can accept the view that the right to apply for relief from a settlement parish was as valuable to ordinary people as property, poor applicants had no right to receive welfare, and parishes had no blanket duty to give it.[38] Writers were carefully attuned to circumstances in which this issue was uncertain, as for instance when parishes were confronted with requests to help the families of those drafted into the militia. Robert Galpin, writing in a strong dialect form from Shaftesbury in Dorset, epitomises the rhetoric associated with such approaches. In his instigatory letter, he sought to remind the co-respondent that

> it es very harrd that I shuld Sarve for your Parish and not for my wife to have herr money as others do wich i hope that you wold Sent to Marnhull to Sune as possbel for my wife is in a great want of et if not I will Come to London my Self and have et my Self for *the money do be Long to mee as well as others that Serve for the Parish* of Roels Leberty.[39]

There is also a clear sense from the corpus that the actual and prospective poor, both settled and out-parish, felt that extended sickness conferred upon them the right to a favourable hearing of their case and resulted in a de facto duty on the part of the parish to act in areas like cash allowances, access to doctors and midwives, and sustaining nourishment.[40] In their ending letters and desperate notes, those for whom all hope was ostensibly lost were also likely to assert rights and duties, as for instance did James Cook, writing from Bramley in Yorkshire on 19 March 1821:

[W]here is the man in Sandal that would Oblige me or any of mine, I recollect when and not long ago that John Cook with such others went to ask of your honorable Paritioners at the Church for a little Bread and what was the answer by one of your very feeling and charitable Brethern with a stern Look, No you may go where you belong you don't belong to us.[41]

The implicit assertion of parish duty by pointing to neglect and thus a worsened prospect for Cook and his family was a dramatic gambit but one justified by his reaching the very depths of despair. Among in-parish applicants who felt they had reached the end of the road, similar cases were made in person or (more often) by their representatives.

Outside these sorts of example, however, direct and plain reference to rights and duties was rare. This situation is perhaps understandable. For poor writers, the assertion of right and duty not only constituted agency but also represented a questioning of the very nature of discretionary state welfare and a direct challenge to the balancing act between rate-payer and poor claimant that officials had to engineer. Faced with the direct or implicit claiming of rights, officials often pushed back, as for instance in the case of William Thackeray Sr, first encountered above, whose persistent claims resulted in a note from James Firth to "inform you that the Gentlemen and Officers were very unwilling to do this a second time, as they say it *looks like as if you claimed a right* to have it paid for by the Town, and therefore you must not repeat it, and what nonsense to let it go to 3 Quarters, and have the forfeit to pay."[42] By contrast, both advocates and officials were prone to using the rhetoric of right and duty in their correspondence with each other. Thomas Wilkinson, the overseer of Knottingley in Yorkshire, wrote on 2 January 1827 in the case of the unemployed Francis Sawyer, noting that the family "alas have no Credit, and they Cannot subsist of air alone – you will take these hints into due Consideration; and have the goodness to write what you intend to do."[43] Even more directly, Thomas Moore, the overseer of Wakefield, told his correspondent on 13 June 1807 that Jane Howe had a "right to our Due consideration and [this parish] will not let her run to final Ruin."[44] As I suggested in chapter 5, it is inconceivable that these sorts of rhetorical vehicle and the sentiments that they embodied would not spread to the wider community and to the dependent poor.

Thus, even if the direct claiming of rights and associated duties was problematic, the poor in person and in writing were not shy about asserting the implications and yardsticks of rights and duties, often in ritualistic rhetoric.[45] One vehicle was disputation of the way that the scale and duration of relief had been calibrated by officials to the detailed circumstances of individual and family need. A typical case is William Thompson of Skipton in Yorkshire, who noted in an extending letter of 2 September 1826 that he had "received your note which I was very thankull for." Nonetheless, "it was but very Little considering the time I have been out of work you must send me som more relief."[46] He returned to the theme in a renewing letter of 13 September that year: "I write those few lines to inform you that I have got no Work and that we have nothing to eat the money which you sent is *only* five Shillings per week for house Rent and fire and to keep the three of us alive."[47] Most writers and vestry attendees avoided such confrontational language, but more subtle vehicles for asserting rights and duties could also be very effective. Across the corpus, both local and distant parishioners sought the "protection" of the parish, which might in turn be read as an assertion of parochial duties. John Ellis is typical. He wrote an instigatory letter from York on 17 January 1821 to say that he had been unemployed for weeks despite his best efforts to travel as far as Hull. He sought to remind his settlement parish of Darrington that "I am not Like them that is always Laying on you and it is Nesesity that oblidges me or I would not." He concluded with a veiled appeal to the basic duty of the parish: "I have no were to find Pertection but under your Walls But I hope you will have the Goodness to take it into your concideration and do a little for me at this time."[48] In turn, the analogue to protection was the rhetoric of neglect or at least its inference. In some cases, this rhetoric was embedded in a wider sense that officials lacked humanity, and this issue is considered at greater length below. Finally, some claimants sought to enhance the impact of their implications of parochial duty by balancing them with an explicit assertion of personal obligation to the parochial authorities. This assertion is well rehearsed in an undated letter of William Jones, who wrote from an unknown address to state "in plain words I am anxious to do my duty to society by taking that Station that Providence may be pleased to assign me" and to ask that his parish offer him "necessary support" for a short duration.[49]

We should not, however, ascribe more uniformity to the corpus than really exists. As the discussion of sick paupers above suggests, certain groups of the poor more often asserted rights and duties or their equivalents than did others and also found a more ready reception. The particular rhetorical strategies of some of these groups, such as the aged and women, are dealt with at length in later chapters, but few of the unemployed, young, or recently migrated seem to have rhetoricised any form of right. There were also other subtleties. It was easier to assert individual rights and parochial duties where experience taught writers and vestry attendees that the local system was, and was meant to be, more than simply residualist. I have argued elsewhere that residualist sentiment – and thus a more cautious rhetorical approach by the poor to their parishes – and conversational routines were particular features of northern and western counties.[50] In practice, however, intra-regional variation in sentiment could also be marked. Nor should we forget that this rhetoric was unevenly distributed across letter types, with rights and duties more forcefully and frequently elaborated upon in extending and renewing letters than in those of the other typologies outlined in table 2.1. Poor writers, in other words, tailored their rhetoric to the stages of their engagement with officials, much as we might have expected from their sensitivity to the season and from the intensity of their writing, both outlined in chapter 3.

## LAW AND PRACTICE

A further component of the basic rhetorical infrastructure used by vestry attendees and letter writers was explicit or implicit reference to "the law," changes in the law, or ambiguities of legal interpretation.[51] This finding is not unexpected given that the poor had always had a good grasp of settlement law. Moreover, officials, poor writers, and advocates had always threatened each other with the law by way of the magistrate, as chapter 1 noted.[52] The language associated with this threat could be direct and forceful. Both officials in their dealings with each other and the poor in their letters to settlement parishes noted the inevitability of a judgment in their favour if they were forced to go to a magistrate. By the 1800s, however, we see significant development in legal rhetoric. When Robert Galpin, already encountered above, noted that parishes had a duty to support the families of militiamen, he was demonstrating an important knowledge of black letter law. This knowledge extended powerfully, as we have seen, to an increasing awareness after 1795 that removal orders could be suspended in cases of sickness and that the bills for treating the sickness of people with suspended orders could then be charged automatically to settlement parishes. William Ellis of Brighton in Sussex is a particularly good example. He asserted in an extending letter to his parish that the "Act of His Majesties Parlement of 1795 means that you must take into consideration my case and remit me some relief."[53] Written in 1798, this letter suggests that familiarity with individual acts spread rapidly from London to become part of what writers across the corpus often styled as "public knowledge." Moreover, we know from increasingly sophisticated work on the relationships between applicants and magistrates that the poor were keenly aware of the *process* of the law.[54] John Lovegrove is a good and typical example. He wrote from London to Pangbourne in Berkshire on 1 November 1816 to ask where his money was for looking after his mother. Dealing with a new overseer, he suggested that "the other overser aloud her 3 shillins per week I know a magistrate would alow it her if you do not send the mony soon you may expect to hear from me a gain,"[55] presumably via a magistrate's order.

The poor and prospective poor also, and increasingly, demonstrated an appreciation of, and deployed associated rhetoric to exploit, the grey areas of welfare law. These areas might arise because of the poor drafting of black letter law, the tendency for new legal measures simply to sit on top of existing legislation rather than repeal it, the fact that many eighteenth- and nineteenth-century legal statutes were enabling, and the continuing interface between law, custom, and case law at the local level, which determined how new statutes were read and applied. One grey area, for instance, was whether family members were responsible for pauperized relatives.[56] Richard Talbot is typical of more than 300 similar cases. In a letter to his father of 25 November 1817, he set out why he was unable to offer him support, clear in the intention that the father could use this letter as evidence when dealing with the overseer, in whose archive it has ended up. His letter, a masterpiece specifically designed to demonstrate his willingness to help if he could but at the same time designed to evade the law of responsibility, is worth quoting at length:

Honoured Father
I received your unkind letter today and am very sorry you got no more thought recollect I wrote to you above a fortnight ago the state I was in that I could not get out of doors if you had gone through what I have you would be another way of thinking you well know that when I have got money I never fails sending I have not earned by 13s6d for this 5 weeks how am I to send must I go on the highway and rob for it parhaps you would not care if I did so that you had it here is this letter and the one I have received has cost me sixteen pence I was obligded to borrow the money to pay for them I owes for a months lodging and washing beside this week I have not got a sixpence in the world at this time I have been under the Doctor's hands and I have him to pay some time or other but thank God I am better and could work if there was any we are now waiting for stuff which you know I mentioned in my two last letters though we expect it every hour we have heard it is on the passage I shall not be able to send any thing before the week after this if I have ever so good luck the Job wont last above a month when it comes please to show this letter to Mr Cotterell and ask him if he will be so kind as to let you have a few shillings till I can send I should not have desired any thing of him if it had not happened as it has
I remain your dutiful son
Richard Talbot.[57]

Sons might also use the law in a much more proactive way, as for instance did Joshua Hindle Jr, who wrote to the overseers of Sandal Magna on 19 October 1793 to complain that his father had double-crossed him in a business deal, leaving his family destitute, and "he all ways made a Baster^d of me." In this light, Hindle reminded the overseers that "by the Law my father as an Oblidge to mentane my famly as long as he as any property & as he is the only motive of them trobleing the Town I thought it my Duty to let you Now that."[58] The underlying corpus is rich with similar missives dealing with the way that the poor understood the grey areas of law on things as varied as the rights of vagrants, on the one hand, and the responsibility of claimants for finding work, on the other. Women showed a keen appreciation of the process of the law in relation to illegitimacy cases, and the aged appear to have had the most developed sense of the legal requirement to establish an inability to work as a precursor to a regular allowance.

Rarely, if ever, did these writers get either the law or its grey areas badly wrong. A glimpse of how this might have been so is to be had through an analysis of the correspondence of Elizabeth Tanfield, resident in Birmingham. Writing twelve letters between 1829 and 1835, she drew firmly on the law in her very first correspondence. Noting that she was sick and unable to earn a living for herself or her children now that her husband was dead, she "wood reminde you that Mr Walkers booke [i.e., Samuel Walker's *Manual for Overseers and Other Parish Officers* (1824)] that I got off Mr Roberts for a week sais that you should hinspect in such cases and give suche allowance as will pervent dstertution." In a later letter, she went further, quoting a letter written by Joseph Cranborne, a magistrate of Birmingham, in the analogous case of Mary Hatcher, a Birmingham widow who had appealed to Cranborne when refused an allowance. The judgment, she noted, "said that There can be No Basis in Law for refusing an allowance to this unfortunate woman whose case should excite both Christian feeling and legal duty." Clearly taken from an original letter or from something reported in local newspapers, this intervention is a rendering of the strict letter of the law in the case of widows with young children.[59] Knowledge of the law was, in other words, easy to obtain and reproduce.

To some extent, the employment of direct or indirect references to the legal framework of the Old Poor Law should not surprise us since it was possible for poor writers to draw on a wider narrative of "the law" in their communities. At its broadest level, from the late eighteenth century onward, changes to statute law in a whole range of areas – weights and measures, poor law, criminal law, and so on – were well publicized in newspapers, handbills, and oral proclamations. Indeed, beginning in 1797, we see the systematic transmission of sets of statutes to the provinces,[60] and "information about law and legal proceedings became a staple" of newspapers from the 1780s onward, generating an almost "virtual" engagement with legal processes.[61] The contentious nature of some of these new laws, such as regulating traditional leisure pastimes,[62] and the fact that they often gave secular courts a jurisdiction that was not exclusive but concurrent with the jurisdiction of bodies such as the church and manorial courts generated numerous ways for ordinary people to engage with the law.[63] Moreover, in common with aspects of the criminal code, the written and oral circulation of "judgments" by magistrates or prominent court cases at the supra-regional level created a well-known body of "local welfare law" that the poor could weave into their narratives, negotiating tactics, or rhetoric. And of course individual cases would have occasioned wide local comment. Local legal disputes might drag on for decades and involve much of the community, yielding a "powerful sense of The Law" and a situation in which a "remarkably wide range of people had first-hand knowledge of legal processes and concepts" and of "low law."[64]

Above all, however, it is likely that the poor obtained specific knowledge of welfare law and precedent from the words and actions of their advocates and from the officials with whom they corresponded. In this context, the rhetoric of legal argument was deployed with surprising frequency. The interspersing letter of an unnamed correspondent who wrote from St Werburgh parish in Derby to the vestry at Earls Barton in Northamptonshire on 1 December 1829 is an emblematic example. The correspondent asked why no allowance had been sent for Sarah Robins according to an existing agreement between the parishes and would beg if you have any mercy in you that you would send the money immediately and not suffer a poor old woman of 74 years of age to die of starvation she has no means of support but the small pittance you have allowed her and if the statement of Mr Moody's [the St Werburgh overseer] is correct I think you are very much to blame in not remitting the money when due ... if you do not think well to send the money the magistrates here shall be applied to and they will compell mr moody to do something for her for it is impossible for her to be removed and I trust the magistrates will give the poor woman that full support that her case requires but I trust you will save all that trouble and expense to yourselves by remitting the money due.[65]

This sophisticated letter combined an implication that the law was being broken, given that parishes were not legally allowed to let people starve to death, with a sense that the morals of the Earls Barton overseer were suspect, as he had not fulfilled his agreed obligations to St Werburgh parish, and a specific threat to go to a magistrate in order to compel favourable treatment of the individual. Under settlement law, the position of the two parishes was clear: Earls Barton was not obliged to pay, and St Werburgh could have removed the claimant given that there appeared to be no sickness in the case. In fact, this letter, suffused with a broadly defined concept of the law, prompted Earls Barton to pay. It would be a short imaginative step to think that advocate letters such as this one might have been read aloud to the subject prior to sending and thereby generalized to the wider poor community so that a background narrative of the law might be appropriated into mainstream rhetoric.[66]

Equally, the letters of epistolary advocates pale numerically compared to the correspondence between officials themselves. Such officials worked and wrote in an environment deeply influenced by legal rhetoric. Thus, when William Clarke, the master of the Oxford House of Industry, wrote an interspersing letter to Samuel Lucas, the overseer of Tilehurst in Berkshire, on 5 November 1832 to ask about nonpayment of relief for John Meller, he noted, it must be recollected that an Order unappealed against is conclusive to all the World* & their order was not desputed.

[Written sideways in margin:]

* Rex v Kenelworth 4v. Burn or 2VNP 14th where an order, though in error, unappealed against was conclusive – I hope you will look to this case.[67]

It is not of course surprising that officials had and used a detailed knowledge of the law, but the wider point is that the language and meaning of these sorts of narrative must have leeched into holistic communal knowledge. Thus, where overseers wrote on behalf of claimants to their settlement parishes, legal embellishment often crept in, and the subsequent reading of the letter to the person provided a mechanism of transmission. Even more directly, claimants themselves sometimes noted that they had been instructed to write to their settlement parish by the overseer of their host community, and it is likely that such officials coached writers in what to say and how to say it. It is thus unsurprising that either black letter or case law became part of a pool of resources for the poor.

Formal disputes between parishes of the sort that developed in the case of John Meller above were often played out at the parish level rather than in the closed community of knowledge that was supposed to be the vestry. The whole process of out-parish relief depended upon tolerance by parishes owed money and upon administrative and financial efficiency on the part of those who owed it. Most were in the position of being both debtor and creditor.[68] Nonetheless, a second aspect of overseers' correspondence was the scope for minor disputes to mushroom into legal events that gained wide publicity in all of the parishes concerned. When the overseer of Gedney in Lincolnshire wrote to Oundle on 31 March 1835 regarding a dispute over Oundle's liability for a lunatic called Burney, he reminded his counterpart,

I recd yrs acknowledging Burney as yr Pauper but you in it do not say what you wish us to do with him. The Act requires 21 days no-

tice on the majority of the Parish Officers signatures to yr acknowledging him – which I must request you to send by return of post
signed by yourself the other overseer & one churchwarden or otherwise I must confine him under the Clause stated ... The signatures
of one other overseer does not comply legally with the act to which
I desire your attention.[69]

In similar fashion, Oundle turned the tables on the overseer of Old
Weston, writing to him on 31 March 1835 to warn,

I received a letter by your man with only the initials of "W.R. Overseer." This is not a legal recognition of the Pauper and I therefore
on the part of this parish require a proper acknowledgement of him
& his wife agreeable with the Act of Parliament before we can send
them home before the end of the 21 days required by the Act. The
Act requires the signature of the *Overseers* & majority of Parish officers therefore the letter should have been signed by the two overseers & one or 2 churchwardens.[70]

Nor were officials averse to using the judgments or threat of magistrates
in their relations between each other. On 25 April 1833 the Oundle overseer wrote an interspersing letter to William Strong, the overseer of
Cambridge, on the subject of allowances for John Gann, noting that
"the magistrate only allowed him 9/- during the severe illness of his wife.
We therefore are not called upon to allow anything during the time he
is in receipt of 12/- weekly."[71] Magistrates could also be used in the
claimant's favour, as for instance in the case of Widow King, a resident
of Christchurch in Surrey. The overseer of Christchurch wrote to his
counterpart in Pangbourne on 3 October 1829 to acknowledge a letter
that had withdrawn her regular weekly allowance, but he added,

I cannot help, for the sake of the poor woman, expressing my regret
that you should have sent me such an order, as I feel confident that
should she be incapable of reaching your parish her days will be
shortened for nothing was wanting to complete her miserable situation

that the withdrawal of this pittance. However I have communicated to her, your determination, & advised her to apply to the magistrate, at Union Hall for advice under her very distressing circumstances.[72]

These individual letters exemplify a wider body of evidence that points strongly to an essentially legalized out-parish relief system. In turn, both settled and out-parish claimants were unlikely to have been insulated from either the language or the practice of these legalistic relationships if, as seems to have been the case, they were keenly attuned to parochial politics and shared a common linguistic platform with officials when negotiating relief.[73] It was this shared understanding that James Lock tapped into when he wrote an interspersing letter from Oxford to Blockley in Gloucestershire on 5 May 1831. Seeking relief to allow him to look after his mother-in-law, Mary Jeffs, he asked the overseers to "extend charity, where it is needful & more especially where the Law, of this land doth order it." Warming to his theme, he reminded the parish that paying an allowance was of no consequence to them, "for it is not a far thing from out your pockets, but from the Parish stock namely poor rates of what is collected by Law, for the sole purport of & for to relieve the distressed of which she is one."[74]

## HUMANITARIANISM[75]

At the opposite extreme to the law in the basic rhetorical ecology of poor applicants was the sense that officials should act, whatever the law said, out of humanitarian concern and fellow feeling. The question of whether the eighteenth- and nineteenth-century poor had "natural" rights to parish relief – rooted in biblical and philanthropic models, in residual obligations associated with rank and order, and in their function as a variable that balanced the poor's loss of common rights during enclosure – is as complex a question for modern historians as it was for contemporaries.[76] Only a small handful of the writers in the corpus or their advocates used the rhetoric of natural rights, and even then sometimes obliquely. Robert Mawman wrote from Lombard Street in London on 9 December 1832, and upside down at the bottom of his long self-justificatory letter, he noted in a moment of supreme logos the concept of natural rights, such that "I wish my case to be Put to the Authority in this way, Suppose I were to die there are four of my children who are unable to defend themselves in any way and the natural consequences would be that they must become a Fixture on the Parish, but if I had the means of Emigrating to America this possibility would be avoided altogether."[77] More broadly, the rhetoric of humanitarianism or its equivalents has a persistent place in the corpus, and one reading is that, at the most basic level, both the settled and out-parish poor assumed "natural" rights.

Some writers and vestry attendees questioned the humanity and feelings of the officers, as did John Owen and his wife, Maria, who wrote a joint letter from Southwark to St Clement Danes, both in London, on 9 April 1824 to say that "it is the last time I shall Appeal to your tender feelings, If you have any belonging to you."[78] William Sutton, writing a long series of letters from Bath in the late 1820s was also forthright. In his letter of 16 August 1828, for instance, he noted that his wife had pawned her wedding ring and asserted, "it's most cruel of you to prevent her by your silence, in my unfortunate situation, in keeping her from obtaining a shelter and food for her children." He resumed the theme in his next letter three days later, noting that he would "trouble you till you send me an answer," referring again to "your cruelty" and ending with the rhetorical flourish that "It is a cruel piece of business."[79] James Sykes, writing from London to Tilehurst in Berkshire, was equally forthright after failing to get either replies or the action he expected. Reminding the overseers that his children "of course cannot subsist on air," Sykes demanded that he must have relief when faced with the "pressing calls of nature."[80] The in-parish poor would also occasionally question the motives and feelings of the vestrymen and officials they encountered.

Such cases, however, were unusual and highly situational. Rather, applicants used humanitarianism in a much more positive way. Some writers were very direct. They might refer to the "humane goodness" of officials who had granted past favours, ask them to extend benevolence and humanity to starving children, or ask them to act humanely in the face of inevitable life-cycle conditions, such as old age. John Nash, writing from Potovens in Newcastle on 18 September 1833, is a good example of this much wider signature in the corpus. He asked for forbearance of his extending letter and "hopes your *humane feeling* for Old age Not able to do aney for my Self with out your and Town assistance I haveing no other means to depend on the allowanc[e] I now have is but threepence half penny Day."[81] He returned to the theme in his extending letter of 14 February 1834, in which we learn that Nash was seventy-eight years of age and that he hoped the vestry would "have the Brotherly Humanity to place me in some place a bit longer till please God to Remove me," and "I will endever with our Hevenly Father assistance to be able to be able to be Reday hopes you will not fail your affectionate poor Brother."[82] This deliberate elision of humanity with the claims of fictive kinship constitutes a powerful rhetorical tool whose roots were deeply embedded in older religious and moral constructs of amicus.[83] James Sykes, already encountered above, followed a different path, enjoining the overseer of Tilehurst in a letter of 6 July 1818 to give him relief because it was "impossible to exist without it ... I must have relief by some means or other and which I hope you will not for humanitys sake refuse."[84] The underlining of "exist" in this sentence subtly elides the basic duty of the Old Poor Law to prevent starvation and death with the humane act of one man to another.

More common than these very direct rhetorical and moral claims on the parish, however, were letters that *implied* humanitarian, and often godly, duty. Joseph Himsworth wrote an undated extending letter from Milnthorpe in Cumberland in which he tried to establish the ground for an inevitable later supplementary claim. Regarding the vestrymen, he hoped that "God will reward you all for you Charit$^y$." As for himself, he noted that "I know My Duty to God is to worship Him, truly every Day and Hour, so long as I shall live. (except I be asleep)," and he hoped that "you will excuse Me. for My Days are almost consumed & vanished, away." Although Himsworth never asked for humanitarian consideration, the framing of his letter could not have made the case more plainly for humanitarian treatment of a godly man at the very end of his life.[85] The widow of William Thackeray Jr is also an emblematic example. On 19 December 1831 she wrote from Sheffield hoping that the vestry would "have the goodness to be so good As to Remember me." Throwing herself on the humanitarian mercy of the overseer, even though "you now that I am a great way from you," she pleaded that he "not forget me this Charatable Kindness And ... What you please to give me I will thank You."[86] The subtle but frequent elision of crisis and humanitarian duty that we also see in much of the wider corpus is well illustrated in the texts of William Bromley of Shrewsbury. Writing on 26 May 1817, he apologised for "addressing you with thees lines" but was forced to do so against his inclination because his wife was close to giving birth and he was out of employment. Against this backdrop, they had been obliged to

> pledge [i.e., pawn] the whole of our nessarys to Support us so that we have not one thing to Shift our selves with nor at this time we have not one bite of Vituals to Eate nor one half penny to buy nor have i the least knowledge wher we shall have any from for i have been forty one hours upon one meal of Vituals and my Children Crying Round me for Vitual and non to give them it grives me wors than all Nor can we scarce keep our selves free from Vermin for want our nessarys.

Asking for help to redeem his clothing and bedding and to buy flour, Bromley sought to elicit a natural humanitarian response to a dreadful set of conditions and the utterly hopeless state of his children. The suffering of children had particularly intricate connections to backward-looking traditions of godly paternalism, Christian philanthropy, and humanitarian or biblical duty.

As with other parts of the basic rhetorical ecology of appeal, the poor who wrote to or attended vestries and made claims on the humanity of parishes shared much in common with their own advocates and with officials. Advocates appealed to or requisitioned the humanity of their correspondents with phrases such as "kind officers – and to your own good offices,"[87] "being Eyewitness of his distress moves me out of Compassion to his family,"[88] "a proper object for your Compassion,"[89] "the worthy and humane Consideration of the Benevolent Gentlemen," "cries of Suffering and distress,"[90] and "you may depend on it they are Miserable objects."[91] A classic example of this genre was written by Dr Robert Macleod at his house on Dean Street in Soho in London on 8 August 1821. He appealed to a Mr Whitaker "to deliver the enclosed note to the Gentlemen of the Committee for the relief of the Poor, with thanks for their very polite and humane attention to the case of the poor miserable woman to whom it refers."[92] Particularly when they had been asked to apply multiple times or over an extended period, such advocates yoked together ongoing entitlement and a requisite humanitarian response from parishes. More widely, and perhaps surprisingly against the backdrop of a historiographical literature that has seen a waning of favourable sentiment toward the poor in the latter decades of the Old Poor Law, officials themselves often used the language of humanitarianism. William Crouch of Axminster in Devon is typical. Sending a testamentary letter on behalf of an unnamed widow – whose circumstances he clearly assumed would be familiar to officials in the town of Chard in Somerset to whom he wrote – Crouch relied on "your goodness" to respond to a woman in desperate need and with six "fatherless children." He was "convinced that from your humanity you will step forward."[93] This shared understanding of the link between crisis or tipping points and necessary parochial duties points once again, and forcibly, to the sense that poor relief was, and was meant to be, negotiated.

## FRIENDSHIP

A further part of the anchoring rhetoric for poor writers and vestry attendees was the concept and practice of friendship. Claims that the poor would have made approaches to their parishes much earlier if not for the actions of friends were ubiquitous in the letters of poor writers, vestry appearances, and the letters of advocates – who were sometimes the very same friends – and officials.[94] This elision of friendship and partnership with the parish was particularly strong in letters from urban areas. Jonathan Gregg, writing an undated extending letter to the officers of the Liberty of the Rolls in Chancery Lane, noted that "I am in great difficulties in consequence of none of my friends being yet in Town."[95] Sometimes, the benefits of friendship were very directly stated and summarised, as for instance with Jonathan Roberts, who wrote from Nottingham on 12 April 1818. Asking for relief during his continuing sickness and payment of a doctor's bill, he noted,

> I must have quit this place was it not for mye goode freynds and neibours who ave elped thos old man of near 80 yrs of age and not done nothing but goode for him and they have sent thar children with fireing and given me such food and clotheing as was fit for a Prince and I Pray Gentlmen that you will be so king and generus to help mee bee fitte again and I have no dubte that but my neibours will be willinge to put thare backs once more into my care.[96]

This powerful rendering of direct support simultaneously emphasised that Roberts belonged to his host community, offered the prospect of lower future bills for his settlement parish, and created the groundwork for later appeals when the ability of friends to provide support had petered out. This rhetoric might also become forward-looking, as in the case of Theodosia Buck, who in an undated letter from Oxford noted that if she were given an allowance, "I hope I shall be able to get some of my friends to assist me that I may not be Obliged to come into the house."[97] We see, of course, similar rhetoric in letters sent from rural communities, but in general rural residents elaborated upon a more general sense of belonging, one less rooted in individual connections.

Even where friends could apparently offer little by way of direct financial or material support, they might be practically and rhetorically linked to a case for relief. Thus Robert Galpin, encountered earlier asserting a legal duty for parishes to pay allowances to militiamen, wrote to his friend John Smith of Drury Lane in London, this time from Gosport in Hampshire, on 28 June 1826 to ask, "Dear Smith do you go to Mr Jenins so sun as possbel I Sent them 10 Leters you sent me Leter to Gosport derectley what thay to say bout it dont fail senten to mee for I wold go ten mills for you at aney time my Love to you and your wife so no more at Present from your Loven frend Robt. Galpin."[98] Smith, then, was enjoined to act on his friend's behalf. Other writers noted that named and unnamed friends had or would receive and distribute the allowances sent by host parishes, had written or witnessed letters on behalf of claimants, or might in the future offer employment to writers if they could recover from illness, become properly clothed, or become well fed. Thus the serial writer William James noted in his letter to Colchester in Essex on 13 September 1827 that he had been "Living, or half Living" on borrowing from friends and neighbours. Now, however, he had reached the limits of his strength and age, and "Friends Advise me & would write for me, if it would do me any good, by so doing." James ended his letter with a rhetorical flourish by stating that he would "commit myself to you," much as one would commit a body to the earth, foreshadowing the early death he had talked of in the letter itself.[99] Here, then, connectedness, friendship, suffering, and a proud independent spirit undone by the natural infirmities of age and sickness were conjoined to create parish obligation.

The analogue of these sorts of supporting activity was, of course, that writers had no friends able to come to their rescue, which in itself was a reason and justification for parochial action. William Bateman, settled in Thrapston but a resident of Bury St Edmunds in Suffolk, is a particularly good example of this episodic rhetoric. His letter of 26 March 1826 said,

It is with painful feelings I have to address you upon this subject after I got to Bury [St Edmunds] my wife was confined about 14 days after and the House being intirely New Birth it has taken a great deal of caoles as we were obliged to keep good fires the weather being cold after my wife got about two of my children were taken ill and kept their beds some weeks a Nurse and a Doctor I was obliged to have and Trade being dull the situation a new one and myself a stranger to Bury it is brought me very low in circumstances my rent being due on 25 March and other bills to pay which I am not Able to meet I am under the Necessity of asking Thrapston Parish for assistance and you being the overseer I address myself to you – Therefore must beg of you to show my case to the Gentlemen and unless they will render me some Assistance I shall be Obliged to sell all I have and my wife and Family must come home to Thrapston where I belong as I lived there 4 years and 4 months and what the Gentlemen think will do for me will be Thankfully received ... you see what I have suffered I have had a bad beginning but I hope I shall [have] a better ending my Trade begins to increase there is 13 Houses built Joining mine and 8 more going to be built 13 will be occupied by the 25 of this month and hope by what I shall be able to do in my Gingerbread Trade and confectionary in the Town and the Buildings around me I shall be able to get a living.[100]

Bateman talked about his belonging to Thrapston, but the rhetorical heart of this letter was a positive assessment of his long-term independence in Bury St Edmunds, which he associated with the building-up of the urban fabric. However, in the short term, he faced trouble, not simply because his wife has been confined but also because he was a stranger to the town; he lacked friends. A little relief in this situation would, he assured the overseer, not lead to long-term dependence.

Poor writers and their in-parish counterparts across the corpus also sought to rhetorically construct officials themselves as "friends," as we have already begun to see. Writing from Sheffield on 30 July 1809, Sara Wadsworth signed off, "so Conclude with my Best res[p]ects to you and remains your Sincere Friend and Wel wisher."[101] Similarly, writing from Catworth in Hertfordshire on 13 June 1825, Joseph Richards addressed the overseer as "My dear friend." When officials did not reply to previous letters or did not respond to the pathos embodied in them with the expected generosity, writers often resorted to letters that co-opted officials as friends who might provide protection. Catherine Whitlock, for instance, wrote from Liverpool on 30 October 1836 to ask for further relief because her husband had been "unable to earn me & my family a farthing this last 20 weeks through illness." Distrained for rent and turned out, she now urgently applied to her husband's parish, opening her letter, "Dear friend i take the liberty of writing for to let you know my situation." In a similar vein, the illiterate Thomas Weire got John Dempster to write a desperate note to his settlement parish sometime in late 1782.

Co-opting the overseer from the start, the note stated, "Friend Robert Moffet I Desire you will send me the small trifle of money."[102] Whitlock and to some degree Weire fused together concepts of and appeals to paternalism, protection, humanitarian duty to a supplicant, and the claims of amicus in an effort to draw their parishes into a relief relationship.

A renewed historiographical focus on the importance of ties of friendship and neighbourliness to everyday life in England during the late eighteenth and early nineteenth centuries, and on the lasting ties thus generated, finds resonance in the epistolary world of the parish.[103] Kin were present more often in the letters of poor claimants than we might have imagined from the historiographical literature on demography,[104] but the consistent presence of those in kin-like or kin-substitute positions as actors in the lives of letter writers is truly striking. Poor writers subtly melded acts of patronage, pity, philanthropic service, love, friendship, employer support, and neighbourliness into a wider and more amorphous rhetoric of friendship. This rhetoric conveyed a sense of belonging, rootedness, and support that could tilt the balance of the relief decision in their favour and extend and deepen their agency. The valediction of friendship was, like being called to give evidence in the early modern courts, "a subtle test of credit," but it was also one of the indicators that officials could use to locate the boundary between deserving and undeserving individuals on what we have already seen to be a fluid spectrum.[105]

## CONCLUSION

The poor exhibited a basic – anchoring – rhetorical ecology of claim and appeal. The scope and nature of this ecology changed subtly over time, particularly with respect to the increased rhetorical presence of the law observed here, although it varied little between areas, the nature and scale of the "ask," or community typology. The ecology was a complex one. Reference to the law or appeals to humanitarian sentiment were, for instance, rarely enough on their own to swing the relief decision, but in absentia they could be fatal to a claim. Unsurprisingly, writers frequently sought to yoke together in a single letter all of the rhetorical strategies that have been the focus of this chapter, subtly changing only the central emphasis according to the type and purpose of the correspondence. In doing so, they followed the lead or practice of both their own advocates and officials. Thus the letter of Frances Fleetwood from Kensington in London on behalf of Rachel Gardner, written on 20 May 1823, is worth quoting at length:

> I beg to address you on behalf of a poor woman named Rachel Gardiner, to whom you granted relief for more than a twelvemonth (I believe) up to Jan. 7 last, when early in that month she was admitted into an Alms House belonging to the Friendly Female Society for the relief of Aged Women; – <u>Situated</u> in the Albany Road Camberwell – she at that time waited upon you and (with thanks) informed you that she should no longer need your assistance, <u>thinking</u> that the same allowed by the Society would be sufficient to supply her future wants; but she soon found that <u>three shillings & sixpence</u> per week which is all that the present funds of the Society will enable them to grant was totally inadequate to procure <u>food, fuel</u> and <u>clothing,</u> and as she has only the <u>occasional</u> assistance of friends it was with difficulty she struggled through the late severe winter – I am induced to make this application to you Gent., because upon enquiring of an Officer of the Parish which I reside (Lambeth) I understand that you will not be departing from <u>established rules,</u> in authorizing the Parish of Camberwell to dispense to Rachel Gardiner that relief, which she as greatly needs at the present time as when actually residing in your Parish.[106]

Here, then, we see the deft combination of the rhetoric of precedent, custom, struggle, friendship, humanity, law, and practice. It is a useful reminder of the need to avoid trying to impose structural expectation on documents that, despite their basic regularities, demonstrate a powerful individuality of style and content.

More generally, we have seen that, in most aspects, the poor shared their basic rhetorical ecology with officials and others. This situation is unsurprising. Without any reliable mechanisms to distinguish the deserving from the undeserving, the costs of surveillance of the relief process would have been wholly prohibitive in the absence of a common rhetorical and fictive structure, as chapter 6 argued.[107] This context had important implications for the operation of the relief process itself and for the likelihood that appeals would be favourably considered. In particular, the discretionary world of the parish narrows somewhat when we understand these shared platforms, accepted fictions, and borderlands of negotiation. Ultimately, the notorious discretion of parochial officials was not used as often in the negative sense of turning people down or ignoring their pleas as it could have been if a purely economic logic had driven decision making. Anchoring rhetoric may not have been sufficient cause to give relief, but it was an essential precondition, as shown by instances where officials wrote doubting letters to the poor in response to their stories. Against this backdrop, the ultimate outcome of an epistolary or personal case was crucially dependent upon how the basic ecology was embellished to reflect the exact purpose and form of the appeal or the very situational circumstances of the writer. The rest of this section, then, explores the *particular* rhetorical strategies of poor writers, starting with the rhetorical assertion of character.

# 9

# *The Rhetoric of Character*

On 9 April 1834, the eve of the instigation of the New Poor Law, James Leggett wrote to the overseer of Worthing in Sussex from his bed at the Brighton Hospital to say,

> Sorry to Troble you But am Compeled as I am unable to Help my self at Precent But thank God I am getting Better I am Compeled to keep myself Clean and I have no money to pay for my Washing I have Been oblidge to Borrow money to pay for it some time past as my Frends are unable to help me any longer as you know thay have been at a great Expence with me for a Long time Past therefour if you will be so kind as to send me some money I shall be very much oblidge to you.[1]

This short letter is laden with rhetorical and linguistic complexity. It opens and closes with the formulaic language of respect and submission that might be expected of a respectable applicant, which we have already encountered in chapter 2. Some of the anchoring rhetoric outlined in the previous chapter – notably suffering and friendship – is also deeply inscribed in the text. And the letter implicitly acknowledges the discretionary power of officials by not stating a fixed sum that was required from the parish. Yet one further reading of Leggett's writing is that he wanted to elide deservingness with personal character. He was compelled by a sense of pride, and no doubt by the rules of the hospital, to keep himself clean, a task that was now beyond his resources. Leggett approached his parish unwillingly and after publicly – the phrase "as you know" being an important signifier of parochial visibility – exhausting the goodwill or resources of his friends. This was something that, as a moral man with an eye to the interests of the parish, he ought to have done. These friends and their public display of support were in turn implicitly yoked into the letter as an indicator of Leggett's standing, reputation, and honesty, much as we would expect from the previous chapter. The officers of Worthing were clearly susceptible to these attestations of character and paid an allowance. On 4 May 1834 Leggett wrote an extending letter to "Return you many thanks for the Half Sovering you sent me." He was sorry to trouble the parish once more and so soon, but "my Doctor thinks a little Gentle Exercize and the Country are will do me a deal of Good so he has Discharged me and I shall be out on Wensday next so I wish you to send Something to Fetch me Home if you Plese as I have no Meens of Getting there Without I shall be out by 12 o clock."[2] Co-opting the authority of the doctor – he would not otherwise, of course, have applied for further relief – Leggett asked to come home to the place he belonged and was clearly known.

We learn no more of this particular writer, but the conjoining of a sense of deservingness and expectation of action – themes familiar from earlier chapters – with an accumulated and worthy personal character is an unmistakeable cornerstone of the wider corpus. What constituted a "good" character in the eyes of the poor and, more importantly, among the officials and parochial communities with whom they engaged is of course a complex matter.[3] It was certainly more than simply writing what the poor person thought would be most appetising to officials, not least because the in- and out-parish poor shared a similar range of rhetoric. We have already seen that it involved claims, expectations, and demonstrations of honesty. A good character might also involve fair dealing – for instance, not asking for more than was needed – recognised standing in the community, civility, sobriety, industriousness, participation in the networks that gave communities cohesion, the ability to co-opt independent witnesses to a case, or respectable forms of address, behaviour, dress, and cleanliness.[4] However we construct it, a broadly conceived sense of the importance of character resonates strongly across all spatial, typological, and chronological subdivisions of the corpus and was a matter of actual and rhetorical importance to both the in- and out-parish poor. We also see it in the letters of the other actors in the tripartite epistolary world of the parish – officials and advocates – and in vestry minutes, where testament to (good) character was almost universal. It does not appear that the nature of a "good" character was tailored to the size or nature of the "ask." This chapter, then, is concerned with the way that the poor and prospective poor sought, on application or during their relief history, to create, maintain, sometimes regain, and use character in their engagement with officials. The wider question of how poor people understood themselves and their position – how they created a gendered, age-related, or locationally specific self, of which actual or projected character was a part – is explored at greater length in chapter 12. For this reason, two ubiquitous and interchangeable components of selfhood and character will be discussed in that chapter. The first is a sense of belonging and contribution, ranging rhetorically across a spectrum that included prior payment of rates, employment histories or contributions in a host parish, and notation of the wise use of past parochial relief. The second is rhetoricisation of personal standing, especially through an ability to recruit epistolary advocates to the cause but also much more directly in terms of applicants constructing themselves as men and women who were godly, law-abiding, and worthy of the informal charity of others. This chapter focuses instead on the way that the settled and out-parish poor sought to construct character through intertwining rhetorics of respect and gratitude, deference and submission, honesty and probity, crisis, and partnership and independence.[5]

## RESPECT, DEFERENCE, SUBMISSION, AND GRATITUDE

As we saw in chapter 1, much of the historiographical literature on the process of poor relief has been underpinned by a sense that parochial officials demanded, and the poor largely conveyed, gratitude, deference, and subjection when as claimants they applied for or received relief. David Green, for instance, argues that in nineteenth-century London, "restraint and submission rather than an assumption of the right to relief" shaped applications to parochial officers.[6] By contrast, the corpus contains first- and second-hand examples of angry rhetoric and confrontation, as for instance when the overseer of Helpstone in Cambridgeshire wrote to his counterpart in Oundle in Northamptonshire in June 1833 to say that he had reduced the weekly allowance to the Prentice family as instructed by Oundle but that "I received a great deal of abuse from the man for making the reduction. To us it has been a very troublesome concern."[7] The settled poor could also be prone to active disobedience and incivility. At an 1805 vestry meeting for Swanage in Dorset, the clerk noted that "William Brine Bower and Charles Benfield having behaved with insolence" were to be "made examples of and the committee are ordered to proceed against them as they think most proper."[8]

These examples notwithstanding, anger and angry confrontation were rare. Most letters opened, as we have already seen, with apologies for writing or requests for forbearance, and almost all closed with formulaic and potentially submissive variations of the phrase "humble servant." The epistolary advocates of the poor followed a similar pattern in opening and closing, with the majority also noting the claimant's gratitude for past favours where they had been bestowed. More widely, poor writers – an amalgam of those in receipt of relief, wanting relief for the first time, and coming back to the parish after a gap – adopted many of the classic linguistic signals of deference and gratitude. They variously acknowledged discretion and the need to provide full information, asked for the favour and charity of officials, expressed thanks for past relief, emphasised the unwillingness behind their applications, wished for the health of officials and vestrymen, promised to pray for those offering welfare, and cast themselves as miserable supplicants willing to make do with the smallest allowance possible.[9] The in-parish poor used similar language where it can be traced in vestry minutes or intra-parish letters. James Stiles, writing an instigatory letter from Eltham in Kent to Bampton in Oxfordshire on 4 February 1818, is an encompassing example:

Gentlemen, I am Sorry to be under the Nesesety of troubling you with this But bee Ashurd I am in destress at present as I am out off work and have had a Pore Afflicted Lad to maintain Many years and Cannot dow it any Longer with out your Astince iff you will Render me a triffell I will Endever to Get on Longer I should not have bee in this persishon had my Master Caried on busness aney Longer I served him 6 and twenty year I have been every ware after worke and Cannot get aney think to dow at present but am In Hopes of some in a short time in I hope you will Comply with the above request Iff not wee must bee Brought home wich will bee Attended with more Expens you off Coarce Now nothing off me at present this is to Informe you my name is James Stiles Son of Adam & mary Stiles pleas to direct for James Stiles Bricklayer Eltham Kent.[10]

Stiles, then, was sorry for writing, did not presume he would receive an allowance, asked only for a trifle, framed his letter as a request, cast himself as a miserable supplicant bowed down by years of struggle, and provided a backstory to allow officials to make a decision. The roots of such letters in the structured and deferential petitionary cultures of the sixteenth and seventeenth centuries are clear and resonate throughout the corpus and even in vestry minutes.[11]

The percentage distribution in figure 9.1 provides a corpus-level overview of the importance of different words or phrases that might be correlated with deference, respect, submission, and gratitude. Only the anchoring rhetorics explored in chapter 8 appear more frequently for the out-parish poor, and their presence in the corpus is consistent throughout the period covered here. In some ways, however, these figures mask as much as they reveal. Rhetorics of gratitude and deference were much more common in instigatory and extending letters than in other types, suggesting poor writers understood that there was a performative aspect to accessing the resources of a discretionary parochial system. These rhetorics were, however, much less frequently deployed in instances where we have three or more letters by or about the same person than they were in cases of single letters. Although there are several readings of this situation, the one preferred here is that extended co-respondence boosted the confidence of writers or provided the territory in which a more informal and familiar engagement could take place. Moreover, if we see the rhetoric of gratitude and deference played out across all of the typological and regional dimensions of the corpus, there were important differences of depth and frequency. Writers from lowland eastern England, from the southwest, and from the far west of the midlands were more deferential and grateful (whatever the "ask"), deploying repeated rhetoric on these matters throughout single letters, than were writers from the central midlands or London, who generally maintained a much thinner veneer of respect. In similar fashion, wherever they lived and wrote from, the poor or prospective poor who applied to smaller rural communities were more likely to use and repeat the languages of gratitude and deference than were those who wrote to larger urban parishes, something that might be read as the disruptive effect of rapid urbanisation on older social and cultural structures as well as on wider cultures of address and civility.

It is also important, however, not to disembody these sentiments of gratitude and deference from the linguistic context in which they were deployed. On the one hand, such rhetorical devices might reflect the "imperfect empowerment" of the poor.[12] On the other hand, as seen in the work of scholars who have reconstructed and reinterpreted the epistolary networks of women between the seventeenth and nineteenth centuries, it is clear that the employment of languages of deference and subordination could in itself be an act of agency and resistance to conventional structures of power and subjection.[13] Used by other groups, such as emigrants, repeated references to gratitude, deference, and recognition of authority masked important silences and deflected attention from partial or fractured stories.[14] Freighted with subsidiary rhetorics of old age, compromised gender roles, or sickness, deference could easily be turned on its head to imply an absolute duty on the part of the parish officers to act.[15] Some sense of this complexity can be seen in the correspondence by or about Richard Wright, who wrote from several addresses in the southwest to Oxford St Michael parish between 1743 and 1769. We first encounter him in a letter of 4 February 1743, but there was clearly an earlier

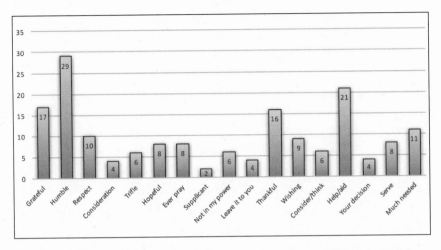

9.1 A quantitative overview of the importance of different words
or phrases that might be correlated with deference.

correspondence because he noted that his letter followed up an earlier
approach, in which "I made it part of my Sisters Letter to prevent being
Chargeable as well as troublesome." Wright asked that the overseer

Excuse my being so troublesome to you on this so unwelcome an
afair but as you know my maner of life here as you have been Informed by Substantiall Witnesses [in a previous letter, presumably
appropriating the voices of witnesses] and nothing I thank god
but the truth I hope you will Relate no other of me I make bold
to lett you know that the mony I told you is to Little for me for
my Creditors are so sharp upon me that I can in no wise doe with
it but I was willing to go as Low as possible but if the Gentlemen
will be pleased to alow the other thirty to make it four pounds I
shall be humbly oblidged to them and to you for if I could once
get clear which if the will be pleased to grant me my Request I
should do with gods blessing in a short time then I will Indeavor
to make my settlement here to prevent my ever being troublesome
to them any more for I will do to the utmost of my power as I

have ever done though fortune has frowned so Sir I would Desier the favor of you to Interseed for me your poor petitioner and I shall be bound to pray.[16]

Rhetorics of gratitude, deference, acknowledgment of the discretionary power of the parish, and a desire to minimise trouble for the officers are interwoven in Wright's narrative, just as they are by the settled poor where we can trace their words. Yet at the core of this letter was the desire to make a bargain: relief now in return for Wright's trying to gain settlement elsewhere so that he might never trouble the parish again. His expression of this desire showed linguistic confidence, included the suitable caveat that his ability to achieve the end was dependent upon God's will, and emphasised his unwillingness to take the blame for his current situation given that "fortune has frowned" on him. Here, deference and gratitude were successfully entwined with a much more penetrating case for support and with a demonstration of character. Wright's stated desire to shift the burden of relieving him to another parish through the settlement laws was not realised, and he remained an episodic and hopeful applicant to the parish until an interspersing letter from an advocate in 1769 brought to an end his visibility in the sources. This letter, from Henry Hawes, the minister of North Bitton, near Bath, was not wrapped up in gratitude and deference given the long history of relief by Wright's home parish. Hawes wrote not "as in a parish Affair, but as a private person, in behalf of the man, whose circumstances according to this acc^t I know to be as represented." He assured his co-respondent that Wright

& his Wife are in a very Weak way, not that they are obliged entirely to lye by, but only in past, He can work some, and has many friends, & as I Know him to be industrious as to His inclinations, so I verily believe with an Assistance from you, He w^d be able to subsist, & to get a maintainance having many advantages in this part of the World, which he must want in your's. But with all his industry & endeavours he can not long hold out, without some Addition Or other made to it.[17]

In the course of the letter set, languages of deference on the part of this claimant and episodically on the part of those who wrote on his behalf shaded subtly but surely into an assumed right and parish duty to act – Wright could not hold out long without supplement of his self-help efforts – given his good character.

It is unclear whether Wright started his engagement with the parish deeply instituted into older and current notions of deference, subjection, and gratitude of the sort that continued in this period to be equated with receipt of charity.[18] Nonetheless, it is certainly true that a veneer of this sort of rhetoric, however thin, was accepted and expected, being a way of establishing a baseline of good character dressed in a garb that was commonly understood. Thus, although few writers maintained a deferential tone throughout their correspondence with parochial officers, equally few discarded all semblance of respectable address and acknowledgment of the discretionary system that they were trying to navigate. In turn, a "good" overseer was himself someone who maintained a respectable form of address to applicants, whatever the provocation that he might encounter. Character in this sense was a part of the relief process that cut both ways.[19]

## HONESTY AND PROBITY

A second core rhetoric of character was centred on honesty and fair dealing. In chapters 2 and 8, we saw that poor writers went out of their way to claim or signify honesty. Making claims from a distance and to places where the writer might not have been seen for some time could magnify the risks of mistrust between ratepayers and officials, on the one hand, and poor applicants, on the other. The poor were not idle in keeping, rehearsing, and writing down their stories as part of their navigation of a discretionary system, even if, as chapter 6 suggested, most parties in the epistolary world of the parish had a tolerance for a degree of fiction. Poor writers, I have argued, were keen to explain (or explain away) any possible ambiguity over their honesty, as for instance did Stephen Hill in an instigatory letter from London to Fawsley in Hampshire on 8 February

1830. Noting that he had been unable to find work, he was "now En-depted to the Landlord 2 months rent on Monday 15 Feby. Next." An-ticipating a parochial question about how he had used a prior allowance intended for the payment of rent, he explained that "On receiving the last money the House we then had in view was let two Days previous and I was gowing to return the Money but the Ague fell upon me I was afflicted for Ten Weeks not able to earn 1/- During the Whole time." Thus an honest man – he *was* going to return the cash – was driven to desperate ends by severe sickness.[20] The synergies between this rhetoric and that of the just outlaw, explored in chapter 5, are striking. Elizabeth Pike's ex-tending letter from Bridport in Dorset on 31 August 1831 was even more complex. Sick and unable to pay her rent, she had been placed in the po-sition of applying for relief because "my Husban [was] taken up and Send to Prison for 3 Months for Standen up for More Wages," as were twenty-eight other workers. Juxtaposing her husband's actions with her own con-sidered and blameless approach, she noted that her letter was "Signed by the Parrish officers to Certify the truth."[21] These are important letters, but it is important to note that those attending vestries or the office of the overseer in person *also* used the rhetoric of honesty. Epistolary advo-cates for the poor similarly deployed yardsticks of truth on behalf of those for whom they wrote. We can thus surmise that the rhetoric of honesty had functionality over and above legitimising the "facts" as set out in narratives. Indeed, honesty and personal character were indivisibly bound together for all of the claimants.[22]

Some writers left this connection latent in recounting and accounting for their stories. John Ellis, writing an instigatory letter to Wallingford on 24 February 1830, for instance, was

> in the greatest distress and in bigest of troble I have lost the best of a Parent my Father is no more and my Mother is a poor afflicted Creature wich I wish to help as longest I can I have lost a grat deal of time pray Sir be my freind this time as to lend me one pound I shall go to work next week and I will pay you honestly I hope you will excuse you Humble Servant.[23]

Asking for a loan rather than a gift, Ellis clearly felt that his promise to repay from his prospective wages was testimony enough of his good character. In similar fashion, the settled claimant Thomas Cleare wrote from Braintree to the officers of this parish on 29 January 1827 to say that he was in danger of having to sell his possessions. Recounting his efforts to make do and to support others, he explained that he did not "wish to bring any Expenc upon you if I can avoid it for I have done to the utmost of my power & trust Gent$^n$ that you cannot say but what I have behaved as a Man." The juxtaposition of a traditional marker of respectability – trust – with masculinity and the struggle to avoid dependence spoke to the very character and honesty of the man himself.[24]

In most cases, however, the essential connection between honesty, probity, character, and deservingness was presented more directly and neatly to officials. For some types of applicant, this was a matter of absolute necessity. On 25 July 1830, Amelia Lorking replied to a letter from her home parish dated 30 June 1830 about support for her bastard child. Although the assumption that the relief policies of parishes would be hostile to the mothers of illegitimate children has often been overplayed, the home parish in this case had clearly proposed to suspend an ongoing allowance.[25] Lorking deployed both explicit and implicit statements of her honesty and deservingness. Quoting the overseers' letter – "you further state that you understand that I am well off to support her my self" – Lorking sought to correct their view of her: "I realy wish it was the case but can assure you on a Most Solomen Oath that I have Not a farthing more than I had at the Washing Tub for or can I live by work more than any other Poor Person." This direct statement of honesty was matched by a sense that she was an honest woman drawn low by the father of her child, Henry Rowlins: "the only regret that I have got is that I should have been so truly unfortunate as even to become aquainted with so base profligate a fellow as he has always proved him self to be."[26] Other groups or individuals with problematic credentials also firmly linked honesty to character. The unemployed or underemployed pointed to a past history of industriousness and honest toil. Those with venereal diseases portrayed themselves as the unwitting and honest dupes of unscrupulous men and women. Men (and some women) burdened with large families argued that they had done their very best to put together a makeshift economy and now required just a little help to keep them in honesty and independence, sometimes pointing to dishonest acts, such as family abandonment, if no help was forthcoming. In-parish claimants who were in full-time work but earned a wage insufficient for subsistence used the fact of work and self-exploitation as a badge of honesty and deservingness, often arguing that officials must know the very bad situation that all people engaged in a particular trade now found themselves in.

These perspectives are perhaps not unexpected under a discretionary poor law, where moral considerations *might* be applied, even if they rarely were. However, other groups with more substantial customary and humanitarian claims also asserted their honesty as part of character building. Nowhere is this clearer than in instances where episodically sick paupers sought to build a case for ongoing relief. John Brooker is a particularly good example. In an undated letter, he addressed "the Churchwardens, Overseers, and Others, the Gaurdians, and Directors, of the Poor" of Tilehurst in Berkshire, contending that his

> business *you well know* is very pernicious to most Men that follow it after they have been a few years in the employ. But there is no doing without Painters, for Paint not only preserves but ornaments a Building without which the best of Structures would soon look mean, and filthy, as well as come to decay. But it is a Misfortune to them who are brought up to such a Trade that in the prime of life, lose the Use of Limbs by a relaxation of their Nerves, attended with Violent Coughs, Asthmas, &c. And have only to *linger out a few miserable Months, or years*, in Anguish, and Pain of Body, which Renders the miserable Objects, unable to get that Relief whereby they might be able to get their bread.[27]

During his illness, Brooker had sought to improve his own health through "a little time in the Country," but finding myself better I came to London last May twelve months, in hopes I might be able to follow my business again, having no other way of getting my living. But I had not long tried to work, when my Complaints returned worse than ever, and I have been above twelvemonths, and only done Seven days work put it altogether. As often as I have tried to work for two, or three hours, I have been so ill as to be oblidged to leaved my work, and take to my Bed, where I am confined most of my time, and am now so Bad, I do not expect ever to be any better in this Life, as no Physition can administer to me the least Relief.[28]

Tilehurst had previously afforded support during the worst episodes of ill-health, and the parish was now asked to renew its "kindness."[29] Brooker laid out his case – inevitable sickness as a result of honest toil, struggle honestly confronted, a genuine attempt to heal himself and not trouble the parish, and ongoing attempts to get back to work – in a way that dripped with markers of honesty and contribution.

Brooker was granted ongoing relief and disappeared from the records. Others – whether granted allowances or not – entered into extended correspondence with settlement parishes, such that the accumulation of letters became in and of itself a testament of honesty and, through the judicious use of prior poor relief as recorded in those letters, probity. More widely, particularly in the context of ending letters or desperate notes, the very act of writing was sometimes constructed as evidence of honesty, with claimants noting that they would not have gone to the very real trouble of writing – as we saw in chapter 3 – if their situation had not looked at that point so hopeless. Honesty and character, then, were deeply and continuously entwined across the corpus.

### SUFFERING AND CRISIS

A further anchoring rhetoric for both the settled and out-parish poor was that of struggle. As chapter 8 showed, those seeking to obtain or to extend an allowance frequently portrayed struggling in the starkest terms, blamed it on exogenous circumstances rather than on personal failings, and sought a balancing humanitarian response. In practice, most struggling also went hand in hand with the pathos of suffering, whether a case was made by the in- or out-parish poor. Some of these circumstances were indeed harrowing. The case of Elizabeth Bull is a good example. She wrote from Gosport in Hampshire on 13 January 1833 to ask for unspecified relief because

> I have had the misfortune to lose my Poor Boy by a sad accident he has been to a Place about three weeks merely for his Victuals untill he could become expert when he would have had a trifle weekly but his master unfortunately sent him into a store where there was some Bit of Tar which caught Fire and he was burnt to Death in a few minutes, I have been very ill and still remain so with the fright it occasioned I have been to a great expence with medical advice and other things.[30]

Bull, then, expected the shocking nature of her case to speak for itself and to draw an appropriate response out of fellow feeling. The implication is that such a harrowing story would be well known in the locality and could not be anything other than honestly portrayed. For Bull, struggling and its elaboration into suffering were rooted in a personal ownership and experience of the problems described, and the two must be considered hand in hand. In other cases, as for instance where parish action was too late to prevent families from having their goods distrained by landlords, claimants consciously attempted to transfer to officials part of the responsibility for the situation and consequent suffering, creating a de facto case for action.[31] In such instances, struggle, suffering, and attendant crisis cannot simply be considered one rhetorical strategy, whereas they might be regarded as such in the case of Elizabeth Bull.

However we read individual rhetorical strategies, it is clear that where we have their cases laid out, the majority of writers and vestry attendees did not simply render crisis and trace the consequent suffering. Rather, they also implied or argued that the nature of their response to the suffering was a test and exemplification of character that should in itself play to the relief decision. As with the anchoring rhetorics analysed in chapter 8, there was a considerable overlap in this area between the rhetoric of advocates and officials and that of the poor, such that one might expect an interchange of language, sentiment, and argument. Thus, on 17 September 1748, at the very start of our period, John Hippersley wrote to Hungerford parish in Berkshire about Anne Bradford and her daughter. Hungerford having failed to respond to her initial request for relief, Hippersley reported that "they are in very great distress (particularly the child) and consequently in danger of Perishing for want."[32] A more determined attempt to link suffering and character was made by William Roberts, who wrote from Truro to Trewirgie, both in Cornwall, on the 28 August 1811 about the case of James Tregoning and his daughter. Production cuts at his tin mine had reduced "The poor Old Man's wages ... & his Daughter is not Employed ½ of her time." This situation and continuing inflation meant that the "Old Man & girl are reduced to the utmost Distress." Not satisfied with this summative description, Roberts went on to say, "were you to go into his house & see the picture that presents itself, you would say he had a poor advocate in me, – I can feel for his Distress, but I cannot paint it out, – In fact the poor Old Mans face tells you he wants." Given Tregoning's character, however, this was not a case of abject dependency: "[I've] known the Old Man very many years – & from the spirit he possesses – I'm sure he would not have given occasion to my writing this, if he had not in very [illegible] wanted." Roberts was sure that this painting of character would be believed, "your ears being always Open to the likes of me."[33] The balancing rhetoric from poor writers was centred on distress that had been borne largely or completely without recourse to the parish up until the point that they were obliged to write by dire need – a threshold of the sort discussed in the previous chapter – which now stood beyond their power as individuals to address.

The rhetorical bedrock of accumulated or deepening distress and characterful response has an insistent place in the writing and vestry appearances of the poor. There is no sense that the out-parish poor had to be seen to suffer more than their settled counterparts or that the starkest accounts of suffering had to be reserved for the most costly or enduring claims. Sarah Hine's instigatory letter from London to Brimpton in Berkshire on 3 September 1822 typifies the approach. Noting that she was "very ill" and asking for an unspecified amount of money, her letter implied that she should accrue personal credit for the fact that "I have not troubled you for this 27 years. I am the wife of Joseph Hine my maiden name was Sarah Champion. Sir I should not trouble you if I had not been ill and *I have been very ill a long time.*"[34] Those experiencing ill-health frequently implied that their long suffering outside the relief system ought to weigh in the minds of officials,[35] although few stated it as clearly as Hine. Women who lost their husbands, men who lost their wives, adolescents who lost their places as servants or apprentices, and the aged in their years of decline all sought to yoke together character, the elongated experience of suffering or making do, and the final need for the parish to act. Yet it is in the letters of the unemployed or underemployed where we find the most determined attempt to paint character in these terms. Writers and vestry attendees facing such conditions usually pointed to generalised malaise in the local and regional job market. The majority, however, detailed their characterful attempts to alleviate sustained individual and familial suffering by finding work through trudging, exploiting contacts, and trying alternative employments in alternative places.

Other nuances of the data are also important. Thus on balance letters written from the largest urban areas, rather than those from the longest distance or embodying the biggest "ask," reference the chronologically longest struggles[36] and deploy the densest indicators of character. Peter Stewart is an emblematic example. Writing from Preston in Lancashire on 3 April 1822, he said it was with

regret and feelings that I cannot express that I send you these few lines to let you know our deplorable situation. It is now nine weeks since I wrought 3 weeks work and just as I was beginning to mend my wife took her trouble and was brought to bed on the 24 of last month and has brought on additional hardship such as must be seen to be believed. We were totally unprepared for any such thing and in my poor state of health and very neare in distraction tried every scheme in honesty to earn some money But to no purpose at last a neighbour advised me to go and sell one pair of our looms and not see my wife and children lost. I went and found a man to buy them and gave me 1 pound for them and he was so good as to give me 3 weeks to pay it back again and keep the looms. On Monday 15 the time will be expired and the money is not and more needed now. Gentlemen, I appeal to you as husbands and fathers to look to our deplorable conditions and prevent the breaking up of a house with 4 little ones under 6 years 2 months the oldest now. If you do not look to this last request that I shall ever make I shall have no other shift left but see what we have and keep my wife and children till she gets better and then she shall come to you Depend on what I say if I am live till she is well I will never starve both them and myself while the law of the land has made a place for her and them, if not for me. I am not fit to maintain myself at present But I shall not come to you I shall never undergo another brow beating by a fellow as fierce as if he had a brief to bleed my life away. I shall die in a ditch first if you think proper to stop this overwhelming torment of destiny. Send what you think good by the bearer of this and you will prove yourselves worthy the character of men with human feelings and forever oblige your humble servant.[37]

This letter is shot through with sophisticated rhetorical strategies: apology and deference, claims to respectability and future independence, threats, appeals to the humanity of the recipient, suggestions of the good value of acting immediately, the implication that Stewart's suffering was public knowledge, anger, and hints that his very standing as a man, father, and husband had been compromised. He threatened the overseers that the consequences of inaction would result in public scandal – he would "die in a ditch" – and stated categorically that poverty was not his fault but the "torment of destiny." Above all, the drama of his situation had been enhanced by the sheer suddenness of a medical situation for which the family was "totally unprepared."

In part correlated with this feature of urban texts, writers who were least well connected to their settlement communities in terms of residual kinship, parochial memories of them as employees, neighbours, and residents, or recent visits "home" clearly deployed more evidence of character in the face of accumulating suffering than those for whom direct observation, rumour, or in-parish advocacy might substitute. For instance, Margaret Proctor of Manchester had been absent some time from Lancaster when she fell into need on 10 June 1812. The overseer of her settlement parish "did not mistrust her but told her (as you know we have a deal of prying folks in our place) that I must have a certificate either from the Overseers or some Professional Man" because he had not seen the child about whom she wrote and thus could not grant relief.[38] Spatial nuances are also clear in the corpus. There is no simple north-south divide of the sort that we see in the scale and duration of Old Poor Law relief,[39] but it seems clear that those in poor upland communities who claimed relief had to work notably hard to link character to accumulated suffering. The sentiment of Edward Pye, the overseer of Lancaster, when writing to an unnamed pauper on 17 October 1818 seems to have been particularly frequent and fervent in these sorts of community. Enclosing a 1 pound note, he said, "it is a most shameful thing that you should apply for any sum."[40] Upland England and North and Mid Wales might be said to share a single welfare regime,[41] so it is no surprise that claimants writing back to Welsh parishes were also obliged to engage in the determined building of character, reflecting Welsh officials' distrust of those who had left for English communities as well as traditional Welsh parsimony in poor relief.

Whereas testament to the accumulation of distress and to the individual's balancing response was *the* core rhetorical vehicle for linking suffering and character among both poor writers and the settled poor appearing at the vestry, another group of letters conveyed and embodied sudden, dire, and overwhelming need and associated acute distress. In part, this need was related to random and disabling accidents but also to a suite of wider experiences, including epidemic disease, homelessness, the theft or loss of allowances, the death of a family member, or the unexpected arrival of sick kin. Some 56 per cent of all such instances were reported by or for people for whom we have fewer than three letters or just a single vestry appearance, suggestive of both the suddenness of the underlying cause and the ability of individuals and families to bounce back once the initial crisis was over. In the case of advocates, their letters were often written in haste and with a presumption that parish officers would show a humanitarian concern for the extraordinary conditions described. Advocates nonetheless usually still found time to imply the worthiness and esteemed character of the people they wrote for and about.[42] Where the poor wrote on their own behalf to describe imperious need, we have already seen instances where the case made was abruptly interrupted in order to get the letter in the post. We have also encountered narratives that were breathless in tone and pace, and even more commonly the corpus is punctuated by cases of speechlessness in which the distress portrayed was so great that words could not convey its extent and depth. Even in this context, however, the construction of character in the face of acute need and suffering is unmistakeable. Thus, when William King wrote to his settlement parish of Braintree in Essex on 30 April 1829, he said, "My Sean of wreachedness appeared in the News and in a Small track [tract] Likewise wich I Now Can Produce if Neads be, and am Happy to Say *My Carricktor will Bear Looking into.*"[43] Some writers returned to set out such a character once the crisis had passed, as did John Corry, who wrote from Whitworth, near Rochdale in Lancashire, to say that having received the benefit of the treatment of the Whitworth doctors, he and his wife were in a fair way to return to independence. Thomas Darwen, the overseer of his home parish, was clearly moved by the letter, sending a reply and further relief because "I am very glad to hear so good an account and hopes you will both of you be completely cured, I would advise you not to be uneasy nor come away to soon." This extraordinary final line simultaneously reveals the advantage of an accumulated good character and gives the lie to a sense that the poor lost legitimacy in the eyes of communities in the final decades of the Old Poor Law.[44]

The intertwining of personal character, worth, deservingness, and responses to suffering is most sophisticated in letters from or about those with physical impairments.[45] This group posed a moral conundrum for parochial officials, as we saw in chapter 5. Impairment and the disability constructed from it might easily be faked or exaggerated by both the in- and out-parish poor.[46] Families might also be tempted to abandon their responsibility to relatives with impairments. Even if the case was genuine, the arrival of a letter from or about such a person invariably occasioned significant new costs or an increase in existing support. Yet on the more positive side, physical impairment had always demanded humanitarian and philanthropic sentiment, and chapter 5 suggested a strengthening of this symbiosis in the early nineteenth century. Against this backdrop, not acting might ill-serve the parish if it led to lifelong dependency or involved whole families in a slide into expensive destitution. Parishes also had reputations to protect, as officials frequently reminded each other when moral duties to those with impairments were neglected. Thus parishes of the later eighteenth and early nineteenth centuries retained a strong, even generous, commitment to the welfare of these people and worked hard to ensure that impairment did not transform into disability and withdrawal from work or neighbourhood support networks.[47] In this complex situation, one of which writers and their advocates were all too fully aware, the dual rhetoric of suffering and personal character was an essential prerequisite and justification for parish action. These observations apply equally to the in-parish poor. On 20 September 1804, for instance, the Swanage vestry determined that "Elizabeth Rawles daughter of William Rawles a blind girl be sent to the Asylum for the indigent blind, Callowhill Street Bath" at parish expense. Anticipating that her character was such that she would be a good worker, the clerk added a note to the effect that "whatever profits or advantages may arise from the labor or earnings of the said Elizabeth Rawles shall be received by the Overseers of Swanage for the time being."[48]

## PARTNERSHIP AND THE RETURN TO INDEPENDENCE

Poor writers and their advocates also sought to establish character in more formulaic ways. Thus two of the most ubiquitous rhetorical vehicles in the corpus were intercorrelated promises that the claimant would return to independence and, as we first saw in chapter 6, that in partnership with the parish, kin, friends, and neighbours and drawing on their own familial efforts, individuals would strive to make do. Even the very oldest writers, at best tangentially connected to the labour market, made such assertions and promises, as did most of the settled poor attending the vestry.[49] In practice, only about 24 per cent of all claimants realised sustained or prolonged independence. Most returned to the parish with extending, renewing, or ending letters, or they wrote episodically because they could not pay rent or meet other lump sum payments, such as for clothing. These life stories point to a substantial seam of unstable and barely functional family economies in most places over and above those supported directly by the poor law.[50] Against this backdrop, it would be easy to construct poor writers' and vestry attendees' rhetorical desires for independence and aspirations for partnership as mere lies, hopeless optimism, just writing what was expected, or a strategy linked to particular types of request. There are, however, other readings of equal weight. That advocates were as likely to point to prospects for independence and partnership as the poor themselves suggests some basis in fact or at least reasonable belief. When Joseph Cheetham wrote from Selby in Yorkshire on behalf of Elizabeth Field on 22 September 1794, he offered Epworth parish a deal that he had personally brokered whereby "If you please to send Her 1$^s$ 6$^d$ pr week for Her Child Her Brother and Sister will Endeavour to Support Her while please God She gets Better and then She will go to Place [i.e., domestic service] as soon as ever She is able."[51] Moreover, both the poor and their advocates also used independence – particularly where it was linked to a personal or familial return to the labour market – and partnership as shorthand for character. Confronted by a renewing letter about Elizabeth Butcher on 29 October 1818 that noted she "is willing to struggle on a little longer," the overseer of Longbridge Deverill in Wiltshire could use the shared fiction of partial independence as a platform to construct a deserving individual. Butcher might have gotten less than she requested and for a shorter time than she might have wanted, but her essential character carried the day in the process of balancing the demands of parishes and the poor.[52]

Three rhetorical forms dominate this aspect of the corpus. The first was the stated desire of claimants or their relatives and friends to pay back the parish for relief given. Judging from the overseers' accounts that overlap with official, advocate, and poor correspondence, such aspirations were rarely realised. Nonetheless, the shared fiction that it was possible in the first place proved powerful in parochial decision making. Richard Godby, writing from the deck of the privateer *The Enterprise* in Falmouth harbour in Cornwall on 8 March 1781, is a typical example of a promise by someone other than the claimant to reimburse the officers. With his "Heart full of the greatest acknowledgements" for relief given to his wife while he had been capturing ships in the English Channel, he would "return you my sincere and humble thanks for the favour," which had been brought to his attention in a letter from his wife a week beforehand. Godby explained that "it's for them & them only that I do venture my life." Constructing himself as a swashbuckling man doing his familial duty, he would

> humbly pray you to spake to the other Gentlemen of the Parish in Behalf of my Wife and Children, and I do hereby assure you & them that whatever [additional] money you do let them have I will most thankfully Repay, for thank God here is now lying a longside our two Prizes & they are estimated at fifty thousand pounds, besides the Chance of the Residue of our Cruse which is nine Weeks more.[53]

There is no evidence at all that Godby returned to his family, let alone paid back the relief that was given on the surety of his letter. Applicants themselves also promised swift repayment, sometimes with interest, as for instance did William Crofts of Crediton in Devon, who expected to "derive the benefit which is expected from the property of a deceased relation."[54] In a period when honest dealing and paying debts were important markers of masculinity and citizenship, such promises and intentions counted almost as much as the act itself.

The second and much more frequent rhetorical vehicle of this kind – often accompanied by a roadmap and timescale – was the promise that an in- or out-parish claimant would return to independence if helped a little in the present. We have already seen many examples of this sort of approach in earlier chapters, but William and Nancy Taylor, writing a renewing letter from Warrington in Lancashire on 7 January 1823, exemplify this issue well. They owed rent but would struggle as best they could, and "should our lives be spared until the next time it will be one pound we return you and all the Gentlemen."[55] The analogue of this sort of rhetoric for claimants, and for some of the advocates who wrote for them, was not an aspirant return to independence but a promise to keep costs down as long as possible in what was an anticipated decline into worklessness and eventual death. Such efforts, a simultaneous recognition of the burdens placed upon parish officers and ratepayers and an assertion of parochial duty, spoke keenly to the character of the claimant.

Third, a large subset of writers and their advocates sought to elide the control of cost and claims of good character by noting past support from friends, kin, and neighbours or by offering an ongoing partnership if the parish would play its part. In chapter 8 we saw that multilayered claims of friendship were an anchoring rhetoric for the corpus. Some sense of how "friends" might be hooked into the applications and relief stories of others can be gained through the barely literate writing of Richard Foxell Jr, who wrote to his friend Mr Elet on 19 April 1767. The letter opened with an assertion that Foxell's daughter had sought sanctuary at Elet's house, having abandoned her illegitimate child with Foxell and his wife:

> I have mad bold to trobel you wonce mor with thes few lines and to lat you no that we do hear that the Chides mother is a tome att your hous and to desire hear to come and take the Child and we will give her haus room and the paresh do say that thay will a com hear anyday for the Child but thay will a low me nothing nor never have and as for me I fear I Shall never be abel to do any work no mor nor I have done none for a grat whil.[56]

Having thus staked the claim of friendship, Foxell's letter then reverted to a text meant for his daughter, emphasising the precarious situation of her child and the wider family:

> So If you have any pity for your Child com to get for I and my wife and famaly is hafe a famished and your Child is a great sufferer for want of food and intendens but lusty anow and lickly to [illegible] if tat food to subsist but I fear threw darter aflictions and you Crulty

and barbas actons and [two illegible words] mind to let your Child we shall be famished all to gether without you help and gods help I have a frind lives in Bristol on the Cay his name is Mr Ching he lives att the Barnstabel all hous and If you have eny mind to help the Child he will safely convay yet to me I desire If you have eny pity compacion Come or send In distres some helps to sucker the Child.[57]

Finally, the text switched back to a conversation with Mr Elet as Foxell signed off, "So no mor att present from a poor helples and Destresed frend of yours Richet Foxell."[58] In turn, the letter was conveyed to the overseer of Camelford, presumably in an attempt by Elet to gain support for his friend given such intense suffering and such a characterful response to a pressing familial situation. Foxell had not sought to shirk his responsibilities under the law and his moral responsibilities as a grandparent but had merely requested some transient support given the extraordinary circumstances.

For some writers, partnership and independence were constructed as a bilateral agreement or aspiration between parish and parishioner. Sarah Christopher's letter from Southampton on 26 May 1830 noted, "I ham Not able to get my Living without help or I wold not send to you."[59] More vividly, Elizabeth Medlin sought to make a bargain with the parish of Budock in Cornwall through her instigatory letter of 4 November 1828. In return for an allowance that would help Medlin in her distressed state and allow her to "right" her daughter, she would try to reclaim "3 fee houses in Came Rack the parish of budock" that her now deceased husband had been inveigled into devolving to "James Deacon [who] bought and he died suddenly."[60] That these rhetorical structures had some basis in reality is perhaps shown by the frequency with which officials chastised claimants for not keeping their side of the bargain and by the hurt, accusations, and sometimes anger expressed in letters from relief recipients to officials when they felt that parishes had not upheld their side of the bilateral bargain. Indeed, as we saw in chapter 4, the failure of parishes in this respect afforded writers the grounds to contest prior decisions and to make a case for extra relief as compensation for the negative impact of parish inaction.

Much more common, however, were attempts by writers, advocates, and vestry attendees to rhetoricise multiparty partnerships that would remove or ameliorate the financial burdens of parishes in the future. The very ability to convene such partnerships spoke to the character and respectability of the claimant. Henry Hayward's letter from Portsmouth on 18 March 1831 noted that his uncle William had recently died. The "expenses of his funeral was paid between *his* relatives, who, Gentlemen, can very hill afford it as they have all large families of their own," a clear signal of both partnership and family worth.[61] Similar to the circumstances of every such death, "there is a family of 6 small Children and the Widow left completely destitute of every support," a situation made worse by the fact that they "have not the support of his Sister now, who was in the Market, for she is married and to a Man with a small family and she has now declined that support which she used to give him." Hayward proposed an allowance of 5 shillings per week, itself "scarcely enough to find the bread they eat," in order to bring the young family to stability and buy the time needed for a longer-lasting partnership of the willing on his uncle's side of the family.[62] In similar fashion, the advocate for Widow Marshall wrote to Kirk Andrew in Northumberland on 24 March 1813 to say that her settlement parish might send relief because its officials "should suppose she would cost you less here among her friends than you could support her for."[63] These examples are a small part of a consistent thread running throughout the corpus and across the typological, chronological, and life-cycle dimensions of the letters. Wherever they wrote from or to, the poor and their advocates proposed partnerships, often in several constellations across a series of letters as background conditions changed. The rhetoric of partnership was itself evidence to the recipient that poor writers realised their obligations under the discretionary poor law. The ability to assemble a partnership – or its rhetoric – in the first place spoke to the character, connectedness, and worth of the individual concerned. We see this clearly played out in the only spatial nuance of these general observations, which is that Welsh writers were more likely to use the multilevel rhetoric of partnership outlined here than were their English counterparts. This difference must certainly have reflected what the officers of poor Welsh parishes wanted to hear, but as Richard Howell pointed out in his letter of 13 June 1800 to Montgomery, "I mun b ya man who stands on is owne too feete and with thee elp of mie frends i will try nor to berden mie parish of Mungumry."[64]

## CONCLUSION

Positively or negatively, the issue of character and respectability suffuses the corpus. Wrapped in a familiar and accustomed rhetoric and structure of claims making, one's having, evidencing, and maintaining a "good" character had an important role in establishing common ground in the tripartite espistolary world of the parish. To draw on the work of David Harley in a different context, the language of character gave coherence to the scene of poor relief and provided a mechanism by which officials and the poor could begin to create an accepted and acceptable – perhaps a reputable – knowledge of each other.[65] Having a good character, on the one hand, and its implicit acceptance by a correspondent, on the other, were not sufficient for relief, but character formed the basis on which the actors in the process of poor relief might have faith in each other. In turn, character had a wide resonance in the world of the parish. To be sure, officials dwelt on the character of poor applicants, but they also reflected positively or negatively on the characters of their fellow officers and co-respondents when they acted or failed to act. Thus, when Joseph Hackney, the overseer of St Ives, wrote to his counterpart Job Berriman in Phillack, both in Cornwall, on 18 November 1825 about the case of John Williams and his wife, he could

scarcely Know how they are alive, incapable both of earning any-thing and destitute of a friend, the times here are so bad & things so dear that their children are almost in want themselves instead of being able to help their father [and] mother – The old man is also very weak and I am aware, that if you Knew their condition, you would send them further relief – I am myself Overseer of the Poor in this place and to persons in their circumstances we pay 3/- p week indeed, we pay one old man 3/3 –.[66]

Hackney gave a yardstick of relief to his counterpart, but at the core of this letter was a matter of character, as Hackney had been moved to write by the intolerable condition of the aged couple and by the lack of opportunity for partnership. He was in every sense humanitarian, compassionate, and a good servant of his parish, recommending nothing that he would not do himself. His letter invited Berriman to define his own character by acting or not.

Advocates often outlined the character – honest, sober, hard-working, and self-reliant – of those for whom they wrote, but they also dealt with their own characters and tried to paint a character for parish officers in their attempts to get them to act. And, as we have seen, although poor applicants – whether writers or vestry attendees – rarely elaborated upon any unified sense of character, they constantly deployed rhetorical indicators and signals of their good standing, sensitivity to the pressures on officials, and the characterful struggle against suffering and need. Character, in other words, left a definitive imprint on the nature of the process of negotiating poor relief and on the wider canvas of the agency of the poor. Such an imprint obliges me to come back once more to a theme latent in many of the chapters: the essentially personal nature of the process of relief even for applicants and officials separated by distance. Just as claims to character drew simultaneously on old and new models of social order and identity, another mainstay of claims making was the fluid rhetoric of dignity. It is to this issue that I now turn.

# 10

## The Rhetoric of Dignity

OVERVIEW

On 13 February 1758, Benjamin Mayor, Charles Bagge, Thomas Hawkins, and William Clarke of Kings Lynn signed a formal statement attesting that the widow Sarah Doe was in desperate need. She "has been an industrious careful Woman" who "in some part of her time lived well & in reputation, and even to the present day, has done every thing in her power, to make herself as little troublesome as possible." Now that she was too old to labour and too sick to be moved, the men asked that her settlement parish increase an existing allowance. The statement was pinned to a letter from Charles Bagge himself, who stated,

At the request of Mrs Doe I have drawn up ye above Certificate, in order to assure you and Others concerned, that she really is an Object of Compassion. I have done This, with design to obviate the Objection in your Letter [now lost but presumably doubting a story told by Doe herself], and I hope it will induce the Officers concernd, to have Pity on a poor old Woman, who, with some failings, is not without her Share of Merit, and who is moreover not likely to trouble you long. If it has the Good Effect I promise myself, I shall think that I have done a kind Office, and You may be assured that in complying with it, the Interest as well as Humanity of your City will be regarded.[1]

The letter is replete with some of the shared rhetoric of officials, advocates, and the poor that we have seen in earlier letter examples: deservingness, honesty, humanity, struggle, suffering, compassion, character, and the requirements of Christian duty and paternalism. These themes continued in a determined attempt by advocates to force the hand of the settlement parish.[2] The statement was followed up by Robert Underwood in an undated but certainly later letter in which he asked that 6 pence per week be added to Doe's allowance given that she was "very infirm and unable to do any sort of work." Underwood warned that "If you refuse to make this small addition, be pleas'd to let Benjamin Nuthall Esq[r] Govern[r] of the Corporation of the Guardians of the Poor of this Town, or me know it, as soon as maybe," giving his co-respondent a clear sense of how little it would cost to alleviate the suffering of the poor old woman.[3] In short order, on 19 February, a further certificate arrived on the desk of the overseer, noting that Doe "is now living and incapable of providing for herself, that her age & infirmities are so great as to require the constant attendance of another Person." Building on rhetoric seen in earlier chapters, the certificate stated that "her present allowance from the Parish – was it not increased by the charitable contribution of her Friends – would be very unequal to her *necessary* wants." Charles Bagge once again appended a personal note to the overseer:

I cant help wishing you [page torn] consider, that however burthensome her great Age proves [page torn] it must be a much severer burthen on her, who has live [page torn] some plenty – & now so reduced (in such an advanced age) to almost war [page torn] – helpless in herself & destitute of all assistance, but what compassion brings her – Do but suppose yourselves Gentlemen (& this is what may happen to any man in Common Life) reduced like this poor old woman at ninety years of age – to half a crown or three shill[g] a week for your *support & help* – and then you will be able to judge whether you should unwillingly contribute a little more than usual to her comfort – She cant – in the Course of things – be long troublesome to you, indeed I am every week – expecting to hear that she is removed from her present state of pain & infirmity – Let me persuade you then to persevere a little longer, & not repine at those additional expences, her additional wants require she cant now be removed, til death removes her from you – I hope you will take in good part – this my little remonstrance in her Favour, I suffer me to say that in complying with the requests of Mrs Doe, you will do and it to yourselves & your own characters.[4]

This was a powerful statement, connecting universal experience, human empathy, the needs of the poor widow, and the characters of the three parties – overseer, writer, and claimant – involved in this epistolary nexus. By October 1758 the rhetorical argument had worked. Robert Dewson, the corporation clerk of King's Lynn, submitted a bill for a further year of enhanced allowance, but he also went further, attaching a certificate signed by five important residents to the effect that "Sarah Doe widow is still living and really is an Object of Compassion, that she is now too infirm to provide any Thing towards her Support, nor can she be *decently* maintained here without some [illegible] Addition to her present Allowance."[5] In this certificate, then, language and rhetoric moved subtly from a focus on forms that were situational or spoke to the individual relationship between claimant and parish – suffering, character, friendship, struggle, and the Christian duty of one person to another – to a more objective sense of "normal" behaviour and the limits to human suffering that could be tolerated by parishes. The language of decency was very deliberately invoked, sending a clear message to the settlement parish that it had a duty to act and must do so in order to secure the dignity of this helpless old woman.

This core theme – how advocates, officials, vestry applicants, and poor writers understood and used the concept of dignity and its normative yardsticks – is an important one for understanding both agency and the meaning of the process of poor relief, as we began to see in chapter 7. Exploring this issue, the present chapter starts with a discussion of contemporary understandings and descriptions of "dignity." It suggests that although the poor *could* use the word and had an understanding of its meaning, the nature of power in the relief system meant that they could not easily or casually link issues of entitlement with open and positive expressions of "dignity." Nonetheless, the corpus is absolutely replete with rhetoricisation of de facto notions of dignity – starvation, nakedness, an inability to perform gendered roles, and the shame of not being able to be seen in public – which appear consistently across the chronological and typological dimensions of the corpus. The incidence and intensity of these rhetorical forms were not correlated with the size, nature, or potential longevity of the claims made, and the subtle development, deployment, and accumulation of these equivalents form the bedrock of the chapter.

## DESCRIBING DIGNITY

Applications of the concept of dignity to poor people were surprisingly contradictory in the eighteenth and early nineteenth centuries. On the one hand, individual commentators – vicars, landlords, employers, and so on – were sometimes moved to describe the dignity, often represented as resignation, with which poor people faced their plight. Thus, when noting his encounter with "old George Adams," the Somerset parson William Holland reflected admiringly on his independent spirit. Approvingly, he recorded Adams's use of the phrase "they are best off who can help themselves."[6] Whether dignity was inherited at birth, something that could be gained and lost, or a status that was constructed out of the actions of the poorer sort, there is evidence that individual advocates had and could apply a notion of dignity to poor people, as we saw with the experience of the widow Sarah Doe above. This notion often went hand in hand both with ad hoc charity – which could confer dignity on the recipient and confirm the dignity of the donor – and with the provision by advocates of work opportunities through which dignity could be regained.[7] On the other hand, reforming pamphleteers of the eighteenth and early nineteenth centuries were often considerably less sanguine. Some of those seeking reform of the Old Poor Law occasionally referred to the indignity of the treatment meted out to the poor by corrupt and amateur parochial administrators.[8] Much more often, they implicitly and explicitly condemned the poor for their lack of dignity and moral fibre, harking back to earlier times and cohorts of the poor who were ashamed of receiving relief and would do anything to keep their independence and thus their dignity.[9] Poverty was not the cause of lost dignity but a symptom of it. Historians have, as we saw in chapter 1, developed this theme.[10] In particular, Steve Hindle argues persuasively that dependence came to be associated with the loss of dignity, submission, obedience to moral codes, the rhetorical and behavioural norms of deference and gratitude, and subjection to the will of the donor.[11] For the purposes of this chapter, whether the poor were truly subjugated in this way or instead found ways to rebel against the norms of submission, as many commentators have argued,[12] is less important than the fact that the existence of this framework of ideological and power relationships may have shaped the rhetoric of both the poor and officials.

In this context, the term "dignity" is almost entirely absent from the corpus of pauper letters and overseers' correspondence, appearing only eighteen times. The term was largely used in one of two contexts: where an overseer of one parish wrote to his counterpart in another to reflect on the death of a nonresident person; and where the poor wrote to the overseer after having already sent numerous letters and received no reply. Thus Thomas Whitlock wrote from Manchester to the overseer of Higher Booth in Lancashire to say, "Think Gentlemen, how it would be if yu too ad lost your dignitie."[13] Clearly, then, although the word "dignity" was known to officials and the in- and out-parish poor alike, they did not use it in their discussions of entitlement or deservingness.[14] For overseers to have used the term would have implied a baseline standard of care for the poor, imparting associated rights to those who in law had none. For the poor to have used the term "dignity" would have implied that such dignity had been compromised or risked being so, which might have been seen as confrontational. It would certainly have implied the existence of legal or customary rights of the sort first explored in chapter 8, entitling the poor to a "decent" level of treatment compatible with the maintenance of dignity. Such rhetoric would have

invited a moral struggle over structures of submission and social strati-
fication that would have been good for neither claimant nor parish.[15]
The nature of poor law decision making might thus have compressed
the linguistic and rhetorical range of officials, advocates, and poor writers and vestry attendees alike.[16]

Against this backdrop, the concept of dignity becomes slippery. If
they did not use the term, how might the poor have described the individualised and generalised concept of dignity,[17] and how might they
have claimed and maintained it in the moral and customary spaces identified earlier in this study? As we have seen, the poor often justified their
appeal for relief in terms of previous and current respectability, honesty,
industry, independence, and reputation in the community – in other
words, their deservingness. Could such concepts act as a proxy for dignity? Or should we regard deservingness in particular as an outcome of
the process of establishing one's dignity? Or perhaps we should define
dignity – and uncover the structures for claiming and monitoring it –
by its absence and learn about it through the language of absence: a
language of shame, contravened norms of living, and public humiliation
occasioned by events that were beyond an individual's control. Alternatively, rather than being claimed, was dignity something that was ascribed by others and framed in terms of both individual indicators of
moral status and global indicators of the range of normal treatments
for the deserving? And when the poor and commentators such as officials and pamphleteers talked directly about, or implied commentary
on, the dignity of the poor, did they distinguish between the dignity of
men versus women, individuals versus families, the old versus the
young, and the immoral versus the moral? We know that the rhetoric
of dignity and its equivalents was not correlated with the scale or nature
of the "ask" for either the in- or out-parish poor, but was the concept
mutable, shifting according to whether the circumstances that caused
poverty were normal or extraordinary? In particular, how were descriptions and concepts of dignity freighted onto explosive situations such
as hunger, starvation, or nakedness where the silences, careworn expressions, fractured intonation, and shabby or disarrayed "look" that
stood in the background of face-to-face encounters had to be substituted

by a letter?[18] Not all of these questions can be explored here, but a focus on the proxies of dignity reveals much.

## CLAIMED DIGNITY OR DIGNITY BY PROXY

If letters by poor writers rarely employed the term "dignity," their multilayered descriptions often embodied its meaning and measure – the ability of writers to participate in "normal" life and to hold up their heads in the company of their peers.[19] Hence George May, writing from Kettering on 18 August 1825, outlined a long episode of sickness that had resulted in his building up debts. He suggested, "Sirs I don't want any assistance when I am well I can maintain myself and the two children comfortably but as I am in the state I am in I cannot hope you will think it over and a trifle from you will be very thoughtfully received by your humble servant." May had, then, been drawn low by sickness, which had compromised his much prized independence and, by implication, undermined his dignity. As if to reinforce the latter point, May added in a postscript, "Sir, if you wish I can have the names of several respectable inhabitants of Kettering but they said they thought not necessary." His state, in other words, spoke for itself.[20] In turn, May wrote again on 28 August 1825 to thank the overseer for 1 pound but noted,

> Sir I have been under the Doctors hands 5 weeks this summer and I am forced to go into trust for every thing the woman charged me 4/ for washing my bed and I have got to pay the woman for attending of us when we was so very bad and how I shall get through them all I do not no. If I get better I must sell my few things to pay some of them because I have been so long bad.[21]

For May, his inability to pay for doctoring and nursing and the resultant threat of having to sell his possessions to make do weighed heavily on his mind. Moreover, it compromised the dignity of a man who under normal circumstances would not have incurred debts or been forced to beg from the parish. Turned on its head, an appeal based upon encroaching pauperism and desperation becomes a positive statement about dignity, whether May used the term or not.

In turn, the implied dignity of claimants and the indignity of their situation suffuse the language of letters in the corpus. Thomas Brown, writing a series of letters from Portsmouth to Earls Barton in Northamptonshire in the early 1830s is a good but not unusual example. His letter of 27 February 1830, for instance, noted that he had been discharged from the military, itself an indicator of standing, but that he had no work and consequently no bread. He reminded the overseer that "I will allow that times is very bad but as I said in my letters to you I shall possotively fulfill what I have said," which was that he would do everything possible to obtain work. His testamentary letter of 13 May 1830 concentrated more directly on the indignity of the situation: "I shall not stay hear to be starved to death for whant of bread [for his children] I have tried all that lyes in my power and see very plainly that you do not intend to relive me."[22] These letters, referring variously to starvation as an absolute yardstick of desperate need, to Brown's dignity as a father wracked by his inability to provide food for his children, and to his promise of good citizenship, constructed a man of dignity and independence. The letter of May 1830 also referred to the dignity of the overseer, asking him to place himself in the same position as a father by using his heart and thus to offer relief, in much the same way as we saw for the widow Sarah Doe above.

It would be easy to regard such language as mere posturing and strategising in order to establish entitlement. Yet the use of this implied or proxy language of dignity is too prevalent in the letters, too consistently replicated for the settled poor, too frequent across the space and time dimensions of the sample, and too loosely patterned onto the nature of the "ask" to be characterised in these terms. As a further example, we see the issue of implied dignity played out strongly in the correspondence of Samuel Parker. His letter of 21 July 1833 to Uttoxeter in Staffordshire, considered fleetingly in chapter 8, is worth quoting at some length. He lambasted the overseers for not having responded to previous letters and noted,

Certainly any Person of a Christian Spirit could not surmise any other way but what there would been a feeling and a great one for us whereby to have relieved us and to Encourage us as we have strove against Poverty and *would not for a moment think of Parochial relief* as I have stated in the Letters to you we have a Spirit above that Provided we was not *really drove to it* ... Now Sir all this Incumberance and Trouble I should reckon you brought on yourselves all through not haveing the *Heart that could feel for another* – that is – for the sake of not sending a Sovereign or such like sum at such a time or times as a poor Family stood so really in need of it as ourselves oweing as I say through badness of times or let it be what it may and what may turn out the Almighty only knows for I am now in a very *Shattered state* my Wife is confined to her Bed through Childbirth and *not one Fourth part to Subsist on* in a Miserable condition Therefore once more I Humbly and Earnestly Solicit you to be so kind as to send a little relief ... for when a *Person as lost the Spirit of Independence* oweing to Degradation through not being a little released out of poverty it brings on every thing that is bad till a person becomes a bad Member to Society.[23]

Parker never used the term "dignity," but his feeling that the failure of the overseers to act had compromised his dignity, their own, and that of Christ is absolutely clear. His family, Parker assured the overseers, was of independent spirit and would not have applied for relief unless driven to do so. The badness of the times compromised his ability to provide his family with an accepted standard of living – which he equated with less than a quarter of subsistence, implying some sort of accepted yardstick, at least in his own mind – and threatened his very status as an upright and honest citizen.

Although Parker may have been an unusually forceful and eloquent writer, those with less skill or courage employed equally strong yardsticks of dignity. Hence Frances Soundy, now a familiar serial letter writer in this study, wrote from Battersea in London to Pangbourne in Berkshire on 2 February 1829 to say, our disstrees is so grate throw the heaviness of our famely that we can not any longer keep a hous over our hone heads wich is vary hard that 2 old people shuld be brote in to the gratest disstrees and trobell throu finding a home for thar chilldren ... Now as I have stated our disstreesed case and not one word more then then the truth and indeed gentellmen not one third part of our disstrees.[24]

Here, silent suffering – a means of protecting her own dignity and that of the parish – was used as a proxy of dignity. But there is another layer of meaning, one implicit in references to the dignity of an aged couple who were just trying to fulfil their familial duty to their children. Such rhetorical devices are woven throughout more than thirty letters from the Soundy family, suggesting that dignity was important to them, that they could elaborate upon its dimensions, and that they expected their yardsticks to bear on the logic and conscience of officials. This was after all not simply the language of struggle and suffering but also spoke to the basic human condition, norms, and obligations.

Nowhere was the rhetoric of dignity equivalents so strong for both in- and out-parish claimants as in matters of clothing, or rather its absence. It will be clear from earlier examples in this study that writers, whether on their own behalf or for partners and children, frequently pointed to absent, pawned, ragged, and insufficient clothing as both evidence of their need and one part of the desired parochial solution to it. Historians of welfare and material culture do not agree on how "generous" parochial responses to such claims were in terms of the range, quantity, and quality of the clothing provided, even if they concur that spending on clothing and cloth for its making was a consistent, and in many places consistently important, element of the end-of-process spending recorded in overseers' accounts.[25] There are, however, two clear and unambiguous rhetorical approaches to clothing in the claims of both the in- and out-parish poor. In the first, writers, their advocates, and vestry attendees pointed to compromised or absent clothing, often noting how they had made do in terms of mending and renewing for as long as they could before approaching the parish. Such rhetoric melded easily with wider claims of struggling, suffering, character, and honesty, and we find it most often in instigatory, interspersing, and renewing letters. Such was the case, for instance, with George Elliott, the overseer of Longtown in Cumberland, who wrote an instigatory letter to his counterpart in Hayton in Westmorland on 7 February 1825. Informing him that George Peel "is in great distress and confined to his bed" and that Peel had survived for more than a year on the charity of neighbours, Elliott observed that "his present distressed situation calls loudly for your assistance." Peel's bedding was simply "filthy raggs not fit for a dog kennel," and Elliott supposed that the Carlisle ratepayers were a "very hardened set of people" to allow their poor to get into such a state.[26]

We have already encountered, however, a second rhetorical form, one that implied normative standards associated with private and public dignity and that was much more aggressive in tone and the demanded response. This was the rhetoric of nakedness. At its most passive, such rhetoric was centred on claims by both in- and out-parish claimants that clothing had been pawned and that they or their family were not fit to be seen in public or to attend public events such as church services. The argument might also extend to claims that children, husbands, or wives were not sufficiently clothed to go into apprenticeship, service, or employment.[27] Such was the case, for instance, with Jane Blundell of Garstang in Lancashire, whose compromised clothing caused the parish to request that the overseer Joseph Seed buy her "a pair of shifts and a pair of shoes and an under petticoat, plain good things such as you would for your own poor."[28] In some interspersing and extending letters and in desperate notes, however, the rhetorical construction of compromised clothing moved into more direct claims of nakedness. For some writers, their personal shame at having no clothing and the shame of the parish for having allowed such a situation to develop were left latent in the observation. The assumption seems to have been that such rhetoric would key into the well-known, universal, and long-established understanding that to be poor was one thing but to be seen to be poor was quite another.[29] Other writers were much more direct, parading nakedness and its alleviation as a normative standard and obligation. John Grant of Leeds in Yorkshire, for instance, argued in his extending letter of 4 October 1818 that unemployment had left him in such a state that "our children has not a morsel or shoes to there feet and Nearly Naked."[30] Poor writers were not, of course, alone in these rhetorical approaches. Advocates and officials also berated each other about the state of pauper clothing, as for instance did William Haydock of Walton-Le-Dale in Lancashire when writing on 22 December 1813 about Robert Newton's children, who were "almost naked and it would be improper to remove them in their present situation." The use of the word "improper" here encompasses both an absolute marker of dignity and a signal that the settlement parish had failed in its core moral duty.[31] The sense that nakedness compromised dignity, and in turn that compromised dignity was not the sort of situation that a "decent" parish officer ought to stand for, is unmistakeable.

Thus poor writers and vestry attendees rarely articulated the word "dignity," but they retained and maintained a notion of how it might alternatively be weighed, measured, described, and claimed. They also appear to have had, and to have elaborated upon rhetorically, a sense that the poor law should act to maintain dignity where it was compromised, complaining of the inaction of officials and often calling them to consider their own dignity as overseers, fathers, and fellow citizens. It is easy to regard as mere strategy the language in which the poor wrapped up their claims; an alternative reading would be that in the grey areas of entitlement afforded by the Old Poor Law, the in- and out-parish poor simply did not have the linguistic freedom to link issues of entitlement with open and positive expressions of dignity. Instead, they offered an alternative, negative, vision of the suffering that poverty inflicted and of the indignity of their position. In this sense, we might regard dignity as a currency that was not only part of the negotiation process and the rhetoric of pauper letters, to be drawn upon as needed, but also something of value in its own right, to be rhetorically developed, protected, and regained when lost. Dignity had benefits that were both definable, such as when it facilitated access to credit and charity, and indefinable, such as when it bolstered self-esteem and standing in the local community. It was also an organic feature of the claims of the poor, both in the sense that its elaboration could develop over several letters and because within any letter set it could be imposed and elaborated upon by others as well as constructed by the individual. It is to this feature that I now turn.

## GIVEN DIGNITY

One of the important features of the corpus, as we began to see with the example of the widow Sarah Doe, is the frequency with which advocates – officials, friends, neighbours, landlords, kin, and so on – employed yardsticks of dignity when describing why relief applications should, and sometimes must, be granted.[32] In particular, there are many examples of appeals where individual indicators of the moral status and need of the claimant are allied with "global" indicators of deservingness, such as extreme old age and an inability to provide "normal" levels of food and clothing. Thus, writing to the overseer of Peterborough on 15 April 1833 in the matter of Joseph Clark, "to whose case I beg most earnestly and respectfully to call your attention," William Howarth, the vicar of March in Cambridgeshire, said,

> He is himself very ill and totally unable to work, and his wife has for some time been confined to her bed with inflamation on her lungs, and the medical gentleman who is kindly attending them thinks the womans life in great danger. I found them and their four children without food, money, or a nurse [i.e., all normal expectations] and altogether in a *most distressed and forlorn condition*. The master for who Clark has worked gives him and excellent character for steadiness and industry.[33]

Howarth, then, developed a multilayered rhetoric of dignity equivalence. The medical gentleman was probably attending Mrs Clark free of charge, as indicated by the term "kindly," a confirmation of their local respectability and a mark of their proper behaviour in saving the parish money. However, Mrs Clark's life was apparently in great danger, and the family was without the money even to employ a nurse, a circumstance that prompted Howarth to make an earnest appeal. This was after all a family that would be independent if not for sickness given that it was headed by a man with a reputation for industry. In this sense, Howarth not only created an impression that the family was deserving and respectable but also pointed to the loss of dignity that was associated with sickness and to the failure of the parish to be sufficiently well informed to at least ensure the family had a nurse, the "normal" – rather than simply customary – requirement in such situations.

Other commentators went further, not just creating an impression of compromised dignity but also stating firmly the duty of the parish to act in order to recover the dignity of individuals. James Neave of Spalding in Lincolnshire wrote to the overseer of Peterborough about Giles Bull and his wife, respectively eighty and seventy years of age, on 12 October 1833. He demanded that "thou will pay immediate attention to the pressing calls of these poor people & to the cause of humanity."[34] Richard Palmer, writing to Billington from Burnley, both in Lancashire, on 26 January 1829, called on the authority of the wider community to draw attention to the indignities heaped upon Mrs Ormerod:

> James Ormerod's wife is very poorly indeed and the relief which they have had is thought by all who are acquainted with her situation to be quite insufficient: I have consulted Mr Hesmondhalgh on the subject and we have come to the following conclusion: "That the overseer give a ticket to Richard Hesmondhalgh for 11s per week to furnish the old people with milk until such a time as they can provide for themselves." James Seed [the overseer of Billington] had, therefore, better send a ticket to that effect with J. Ormerod to R. Hesmondhalgh.[35]

We saw this letter in chapter 5, but in the context of the particular focus of this chapter, it suggests that in Burnley at least there were clearly community-based norms of treatment for poor people, the transgression of which amounted to compromised dignity (as indicated by the phrase "quite insufficient") and not a little shame for the parish of settlement.

Other examples abound. Elizabeth Foxal wrote from Birmingham to the overseer of Thrapston in Northamptonshire on 26 January 1826 to say that

> William Worlidge is now very ill indeed and has been for some time and gets worse every day ... he wants a many comfort and is destitute of *every necessary of life* he has a complication of disorders a strong asma on his lungs and a gravel complaint and the piles severely poor creature I am sorry to see him.[36]

She added more firmly, "poor old man, in his 74th year and so ill *I am shock'd to see him.*"[37] Although the general tone of her letter was conciliatory, Foxal felt that the dignity of the man had been compromised: he lacked "every necessary," his series of illnesses demanded sympathy and sorrow, and his general condition was enough to shock. This was more than simply an appeal to Christian duty or a sense that the overseer ought to act with humanity. The application of normative yardsticks and a measure of the degree to which they had been breached – Foxal was shocked – suggest that although the term "dignity" was not used, its measure was written into the very core of the appeal.

However, it is in a series of letters by or about the same person that we see most clearly the local concern that poverty and an attendant loss of dignity could generate. Isaac Gould, a surgeon of Oldham in Lancashire, wrote on behalf of the Jump family to the overseers of Uttoxeter on 23 October 1832. He argued that the family "has Suffered unaccountably for want of Employ they not having I am Inform[ed] *half Sufficiency to Satisfy the Common demands of Nature* tis therefore hoped you will humanely Consider the unhappy Conditions of the Same miserable family and remit relief by Earliest Post ... your answer is required *Immediately,* fully Stating your Resolutions Concerning them."[38] Here, then, Gould explicitly did not emphasise the respectability of the family or even, at least directly, deservingness. John Jump had had his dignity undermined. Unable to provide his family with half of the food and clothing that would be considered normal or to which he would be morally and universally entitled – "the Common demands of Nature" –

Gould offered a stiff assessment of the family's state, calling on the over-seer to act without delay in order to support Jump's dependants and thus fulfil an undeniable duty. The letter was apparently answered, but Gould wrote again on 12 August 1833 to say that he

> was Struck with *amaze and wonder* when I entered their Miserable abode & Garret where I found the 2 Infants Grievously afflicted with Voilent Inflamation in every part of their Tender Frames Lying on a Bed Composed Chiefly of Rags &c with little or no Covering over them and apparently nearly *without the Coarsest Viands for Life* being the Most Miserable family I have Long time beheld ... I therefore Employed my Pen in behalf of them ... Loudly Calling your Feeling attention to relieve them as Theire Miserable Case re-quire ... the Said family is totally deprived of the *Commonest Com-forts* by Day as by Night and whose *evident Conditions of Distress* will stand the Strictest Examinations therefore I beg your humane and Immediate attention which is hoped for and highly Necessary.[39]

This time, then, Gould had been to inspect the family, and his letter con-tains numerous rhetorical indicators of indignity, from the meanness of the lodgings to nakedness, hunger, and a generalised inability to obtain even the meanest standard of living, or the "Coarsest Viands for Life." Gould appealed to the essential humanity of the overseer and ratepayers, both directly and in his harsh description of the tortured frames of the children, in order to bring the family to a level of common decency and thereby ensure the family's own dignity and that of the settlement parish and its overseers, who might otherwise be shamed by "evident Condi-tions of Distress."

There was seemingly no answer, for Gould wrote again on 7 Septem-ber 1833, this time in alliance with Francis Atkinson, the employer of John Jump. He noted indignantly,

> I am very much Surprised to have cause to address you a second time on the behalf of John Jump and Family of whom I stated to you the most needful particulars of the distress of the said family in

my former accounts I being in an undecided consternation to account for the disregard you latterly attached to my Informations respecting the family of Jumps for whom I have Interceded many years to your Parish and did you at any time discover my accounts founded on Falsehood *no God forbid* ... I therefore again Inform you that John Jump and family are in a State of deepest distress being *without nearly all the required Necessaries of Life* and particularly for the Coming Inclement Season in respect of Bedding Clothing &c the poor Man I am Credibly Informed has not Employ to procure the half needful Quantity of the Coarsest Food for *his daily Starving family* you therefore are desired to attend to the distressed Condition of the Same or I am Inclined to think other methods must be Shortly appealed unto.[40]

In this letter, the *common* necessaries of life and a want of food had been rhetorically transformed into the *required* necessaries and starvation. For Gould, the dignity of this man, his own dignity given that the want of a reply called into question his very honesty, and the dignity of the overseer himself, who might have to be overridden with "other methods," were tied firmly together. No reply forthcoming, Gould wrote again on 20 October 1833, this time in alliance with Isabella Taylor, the landlady of the Jump family, to say,

I have before Stated in Lines of Strictest truth and on Examining their every Circumstance their distress will Evidently appear to any Inspection as before related the Same family is in want of Bedding having Scarcely anything to Cover their Bodies from the Inclemency of the presant Night Air Such help I understand being what they at presant require from you it is astonishing that no reply has been made unto the 2 former addresses which Statements have been undeniable Facts Such you have always proved the Identity of my Pen.[41]

Here, the dignity of the family had been pushed to the background of the drama, and it was the dignity of Gould and the overseer that had become the issue at hand. The matter was seemingly resolved, for we see no further correspondence. Whether couched in terms of respectability, proper behaviour, standing in the locality, or the ability to garner and keep the common necessaries of life, one reading of these letters and those related to the widow Sarah Doe, with which we started, is that advocates and poor writers shared a sense and rhetoric of dignity.

## ABSOLUTE INDICATORS

Two striking rhetorical regularities across the corpus bring the importance of dignity as a navigation point in the process of poor relief and the tripartite epistolary world of the parish into even sharper relief. The first is "starvation." As we saw in the Jump-Gould correspondence above, advocates were skilled at calling attention to a want of food, either as a discrete experience or as part of a wider rhetoric that the necessary elements of life – clothing, bedding, furniture, fuel, and so on – were missing. This assertion of normative standards and an implicit sense that they had been breached extended to the writing of officials and to the poor themselves, in the latter case branching into the rhetoric of hunger and missed meals. Similar language can be traced for the in-parish poor. When John Lambden of Limehouse in London appealed to the vestry on 17 October 1817, he was "very Ill indeed [as] I now am labouring under one of the most Dreadfulest Disorder that the human body can sustain being and has been liable to a violent Rupture for these 30 years past my intestines are now down wich enabls even to walk I am in continual pain day and night." Lambden hoped that his parish would meet the "expence wich I may incur wich I hope will not be thought extraveggant as in my sittuation at present I want some nourishment for I am very weak."[42] This rhetoric of hunger ties subtly into a wider linguistic register of protest in the early nineteenth century where a lack of food and the prices of food constitute a core justification and demand of ordinary people driven to collective action and riot.[43] There is, as we have seen, no simple intertextuality of protest narratives and pauper letters, but it seems clear that the dependent poor could not have been deaf to the language through which ordinary people sought to confront or contain power.

Yet some people – advocates, poor writers, and officials – went further than the rhetorical construction of hunger, particularly where they were engaged in a series of correspondence. Charles Soundy signed a letter written by his mother at their house on Sleaford Street, Battersea, on 14 May 1829. Citing a lack of work, he wished to remind the parish of Pangbourne that "my family are in great distress I may say almost in a state of starving as we are I may say without common surport."[44] A rhetoric that the parish had allowed people to starve was potentially explosive. It spoke to a negation of the basic duty of the Old Poor Law as inscribed in law and moral intent, which was to prevent starvation and death. More widely, it implied that officials had failed to adhere to widespread local practice and obligation, given persuasive evidence that across the country – not just in the food price crises of the 1790s – parishes had been remarkably adept at ensuring minimum standards of nutrition.[45]

The subtext of Soundy's letter was that parish officials needed to take urgent action both to preserve life and to prevent their own reputation and that of the parish from declining. He was not alone in making such claims, with 780 references to starvation, starving, or desperate hunger by poor writers or advocates in the corpus. Thomas Earl, writing from Portsmouth to Bradford-on-Avon in Wiltshire exemplifies this group. His extending letter of 19 January 1835 outlined a litany of sickness and noted that he, his wife, and their daughter were all under the care of doctors. He did not seek to have his parish pay the bills for these medical gentlemen but rather enjoined officials to "help us through the winter ... at present we are in a starving state."[46] At no point did such writers employ the word "dignity." Yet the use of the rhetoric of starvation clearly assumed the existence of an absolute threshold of nutrition compatible with a dignified human life and provided a sense or measure of the extent to which these norms – and thus the dignity of poor mothers and fathers obliged to starve their children, thieve, or scratch around for scraps – had been compromised. We see this powerfully played out in the writing of James Hale of Banbury in Oxfordshire. His renewing letter to Cheltenham in Gloucestershire on an unspecified date argued that with nine children, "all small or Nearly," his wages would simply not suffice: "I Cannot Do it think I say what father can Quietly Look On a Starving family Begging and screeming for Bread & None to give them."[47] A variant of this theme of starving children and compromised dignity is to be found in the memoirs of Thomas Geering of Sussex. Looking back at the experiences of workhouse inmates in the last year of the Old Poor Law, he noted a poem circulating in his district that was "sung to the tune of, and was a parody on, 'The Mistletoe Bough.'" The last stanza told the story of a missing boy:

At length the soup copper repair did need;
The copper-smith came and there he see'd
A bundle of bones lie grizzling there,
In the leg of the breeches the boy did wear.
Ah! dreadful to tell, the boy gave a stoop;
And fell in the copper, and was boiled in the [workhouse] soup,
And they all of 'em said, and they said with a sneer,
He was push'd in by the Cruel Overseer[48]

In turn, we see the rhetoric of dignity deployed even more forcefully in a second arena: the discussion between different parties in the epistolary world of the parish about the question of pauper funerals. The casual assumption of much early historiography that the poor feared and abhorred the pauper funeral is wide of the mark. Indeed, I have argued elsewhere that a dignified burial was seen as both a necessity and a right and that there is much evidence that poor law officials in some (but not all) parts of the country agreed. The spectrum of funeral costs, and thus funeral quality, within as well as between parishes was wide, but on the whole, parishes clearly did *not* coalesce at the cheapest end of provision.[49] Thus, when Joseph Richards wrote from Catworth in Hertfordshire to Thrapston on 13 June 1825, he stated forcefully,

My dear friend I write these few lines to let you no that my son – William Richards is dead and is to be buried to night he died on

Sunday night and he was attended by Mr Shaw of Spaldwick and you *must* pay him and bury him for you had all his nursing and 2 pounds besides and we have that to pay and all his cloathes he is got wont pay all the expenses he lay ten days.[50]

The expectation that the costs of burial would be paid is clear, as it was in the case of the settled poor who attended the vestry. We get rather more detail in a letter written by Edward Landy of Godmanchester in Cambridgeshire on 14 November 1826 concerning Widow Collins, who had been dreadfully burned and had subsequently died:

the daughters husband has been to the Overseer of this Parish the enquire the best manner he was to be provided with the expense already incurred and also with respect to the funeral and such other expenses which will *necessary be incurred* ... if you will send word by return of Coach what is to be done and give any instruction I will on your part take care that every thing shall be done as economically as can be done and your guaranteeing me I will send an account of every expense – there has been already two women attending night and day since Sunday and some attendance from the Surgeon and laying out by ye women so that you will be appraised of the expenses hitherto incurred.[51]

There was, in short, an expectation on the part of the overseer in the parish of residence – and hence presumably on the part of the claimant – that medical expenses in the run-up to death and then the cost of burial would be met. For Collins, the subsequent account included

Cash paid two women attending Widow Collins from Sunday to Friday day and night and laying her out £0:12:0; Provisions for the two women including the time of funeral, use of bedclothes and washing the same £0:8:0; Coffin and man putting her in £1:5:0; Flannel for cap & shroud £0:5:0; Use of the Pall £0:5:0; Bread, cheese and beer for the carriers & women £0:6:4; Clergyman fees taking in Church £0:5:0; Clerk's ditto 3/-; Sexton ditto 4/2.[52]

In total, the funeral cost 3 pounds, 13 shillings, and 6 pence, a significant expenditure as well as an excellent listing of what made for a dignified pauper funeral. The underlying sample of letters shows clearly that officials were highly attuned to the need for dignified funerals, and additional bills collected as part of the wider project confirm that expenditures on individual pauper funerals by parishes may have been above what could be afforded by the independent labouring population.

That said, delays, misunderstandings, attempts at cost savings, misinformation, and a downright niggardliness on the part of officials created occasional fracture points in the process of getting the dead buried. Letters written in response to such fracture points can reveal much about the understanding and use of concepts of dignity by the different epistolary parties. Thus Frances Soundy wrote (again) from Battersea on 14 October 1829 to say,

> I lost every frand that i ad in the world for wan my dear child died i was in hopes that battesea parrish would have assisted me in buring her as thay did all others but they refused me and sayd as i found a home for my chilldren and kept them from the parrish i mite do as i could and gentillmen wen i ad got a undertaker to barer her and to taik [illegible] so that my poor child was a fortnight before she was buried and than i want to them a gain and i told them i would go to a Magastreat and then thay granted it to me so gentellmen it took me 4 months to pay the undertaker.[53]

This letter – a claim for extra allowances given the expenses incurred – made both the moral claim that Frances was being penalised for having provided for her children and the claim that she had been denied basic dignity given that it took two weeks to bury the poor child and that the Battersea vestry agreed to pay only when threatened with a magistrate's order. By inference, it was undignified for Soundy to be pushed to such extremes, a common complaint.

Advocates were equally direct in their criticism of parishes that sought to dissolve their responsibility for the poor in death. When James Sanderson of Higher Booth in Lancashire wrote to inform his co-respondent that "James Driver has had the misfortune to have a child burned to death," he reminded him that the poor unfortunate man was "entitled to your consideration for something to bury him" even though Driver had an annuity.[54] Nor, of course, should we forget that the sentiments and rhetoric employed by writers were duplicated in the forums of the vestry and overseer's office when the in-parish poor applied personally for help with burying dead relatives. For instance, on the 15 June 1820 the vestry of Putney in London ordered that, "consistent with our duty" to William Jones, whose child had died, the overseer must "see that all is done to satisfaction."[55] Such direct rhetorical elaboration finds its balance in cases where select vestries simply ordered that such bills and requests from the in-parish poor be attended to by officials, often with expensive consequences. The process of poor relief was thus intimately entwined with the rhetoric and actuality of dignity and its equivalents.

## CONCLUSION

On 29 August 1810, John Sayer, a resident of Oxford, sent an angry letter to his home parish. Touched upon earlier in this study, it said,

> you very much Sirprize me in Deed at not hereing from you yet when you very well know how Distress I am & have a Long while but Did not Like to throw my self upon the parish till I had seen whether the Doctors that I was under or not could Do me any Good or not but Sorry I am to Say Discharge from the hospital without Receiving the Least benefit in the world which is very Distressing to me in Deed as I have no other way of Support but from your parish & I am Sorry to See that Support that I Stand in So much want of So neglected as I at this present have not a farthing to Do any thing with I Realy Gentlemen must tell you that I have not a bit of bread to put into my mouth which after writeing to you a month back & not to Receive any answer it Shows how unthinkin you are and as Long as you Can Get What you want your Selves you Care nothing about that one in Distress ... Mr

Wolseley will be angry at your Long Delay in not sending to me before as he wrote to me a fortnight back to say he would See I had as much as the parish allowance was therefore he will think it od at you not sending.[56]

Sayer, then, attacked the overseer on two levels, accusing him of selfish and undignified conduct, on the one hand, and calling on the authority of Mr Wolseley's promise, on the other. The letter is shot through with the language and rhetoric of deservingness and rightful expectation: Sayer was sick and incurable, he was hungry, and he had not even been shown the common decency of a reply and the fulfilment of a faithful promise. His respectability and honesty had been questioned, his proper behaviour in turning to the parish only in extremis had not been recognised and rewarded, a reputation had been compromised, and his character had in effect been undermined. Sayer now presented himself as deserving once more, co-opting the persona of a prominent local personality as a mark of that deservingness. He nonetheless "retained the sense of the parish as an extended community and maintained an investment [through continued writing] in the continuance of the fruits of paternalism."[57] Sayer wrote not just for relief but to redress a wrong.

For other poor writers and their advocates, however, deservingness was a product of establishing one's dignity. In this context, "dignity" is itself a relative and malleable term, one that must be understood both in the context of the mechanisms that shaped normality – and hence the boundaries of dignity and indignity – and in the context of the power relations that shaped the claims-making process.[58] Frances Soundy contrasted her experience with what was normal for other poor people, and hence dignified, in the case of the death of a child. Her letter was both a public articulation of private circumstances and an appeal to what she assumed to be well-understood normative standards. Other writers used similar rhetorical yardsticks by which they might convey claims to dignity, even if the nature of the negotiation process militated against using the exact term. Thus compromised dignity was associated with nakedness, threats to housing, starvation, the failure of officials to treat one

poor person like another, and an inability to procure the common necessaries of life, such as a funeral, nursing care, or a doctor. The constel-
lation of such language was in no sense intercorrelated with the scale or
nature of the claim made. To these rhetorical structures, the poor – both
in writing and in person – might attach language that, inter alia, expressed their own shame or that of officials; public humiliation; domestic
confinement and exclusion from the public sphere; heartbreak; and the
despair associated with exogenous events that stripped away household
status and their ability to perform even the basic functions of a man or
woman, a father or mother, or a brother or sister. In turn, this was a
shared rhetorical infrastructure: advocates writing for the poor used similar models, as did officials when trying to influence the conduct of their
counterparts in settlement parishes. In the tripartite epistolary world of
the parish, dignity was something that for the poor could be ascribed as
well as gained, regained, and lost. This situation should lead us to question simplistic assertions that "parish-based authority [was used] to reinforce the power of employers."[59]

Unsurprisingly, then, over a series of letters from or about the same
person, it is normal to see some assertion of dignity or its equivalents.
Such claims might simply *be* rhetoric, reflecting either an accepted convention of application or a version of what poor writers thought officials
in their parish of settlement would best respond to. The poor might, in
other words, have really constituted that sly, dishonest, slothful underclass that some commentators portrayed in nineteenth-century England.
Their essential lack of dignity and honesty would in this sense define
them. Yet, as chapter 2 warned us, we should not take this casual assumption too far. There is certainly rhetorical flourish and development in the
writing of Frances Soundy or John Sayer. Nonetheless, however we look
at the letters of the poor, it is hard to deny that there was an essential
truth to the claims they embodied and that their writers understood both
the basic concept of dignity and some of the mechanisms through which
it might be claimed, regained, maintained, and defended. Similar conclusions might be drawn in respect of the in-parish poor. For this group,
contact with officials or intra-parish inspectors and advocates meant that

compromised dignity could carry a personal or material piquancy, including ragged clothing, freezing empty rooms and homes, pawned wedding rings, crying and starving children, bare beds, gaunt faces, and the hacking coughs and eruptions of blood consistent with advanced tuberculosis.[60] However, despite this "advantage" in their claims making, it is striking how often in vestry minutes or other recorded encounters between officials and the poor, the rhetoric of dignity crops up. Josias Down's report on Richard Maisey and his wife, for instance, found them in a distressed state, he bedbound and she constantly nursing him. With the help of "a Gentleman" who paid their rent and gave a bread allowance, the proud old couple had reached their last extremity before applying to the parish. A universal condition – decline – had in the end overwhelmed them.[61]

That said, as we have already begun to see in the current chapter, the nature of the rhetoric deployed was also dependent upon the situational position of the writer or vestry attendee. Widows wrote differently from mothers with husbands and children, the former emphasising their friendlessness and the need for allowances to compensate for lost men and the latter emphasising their inability to fulfil their socially constructed duties. The aged wrote differently from the young, framing their narratives with very different expectations,[62] and so on. The next chapter, the final one in this section, thus turns to rhetorics of life-cycle and gender in order to understand the nature of agency and the process of poor relief.

# 11

## Rhetorics of Life-Cycle and Gender

### OVERVIEW

On 22 May 1826, Thomas Elsegood wrote an interspersing letter from Norwich in Norfolk to Braintree in Essex asking for "Greater Relief of Solomon Spooner," likely his father-in-law. Citing the hardness of the times and the recent death of Elsegood's own wife, he was

> oblidged to get a Woman to do for him [Solomon Spooner] has he is so infirmed with age that he is not capable of doing any thing for himself for his age is 78 and Gentlemen your kindness at present for the Relief of him is 2s 6d per week but I hope you will be pleased to take it into your most Serious Consideration through the hardness of the times and his infirmed Age that you will be pleased to Allow him as far as You Possibly can he have had a very Severe illness and I have done for him all that laid in my power.[1]

This letter speaks to many familiar rhetorical themes: the respectability of a man doing his utmost to support a father-in-law despite his own devastating loss; exogenous causes of need; gratitude and deference; latent appeals to humanity and parochial protection of dignity; and a due regard for parochial finances, with Elsegood coming to the parish only when his own powers had been exhausted. The letter had an immediacy, logos, and pathos that demanded, at least in the eyes of Elsegood, a swift reply. Its central rhetorical thrust, however, was the need of an aged man who was incapable of independence and whose future had been thrown into doubt by the death of a daughter who had presumably provided his day-to-day care. The universal physical and emotional experience of aging was deftly focused on the particular needs of a single old man and a family driven to extremis by providing the care that society, and the law,[2] expected of them.[3]

In turn, letters or vestry appearances centrally concerned with needs linked to particular life-cycle conditions dominate the underlying corpus.[4] This should not surprise us. In an eighteenth- and nineteenth-century economic context where work by all family members was vital to ordinary family economies as well as being a key yardstick of personal and moral identity, the worklessness often associated with old age, nursing the sick, widowhood, childbirth, abandonment, depression, and melancholy[5] had fundamental consequences for independence. Advocates and officials were in general keenly attuned to such conditions. Yet there is also something more. As chapter 1 began to show, welfare historians have increasingly focused their analysis of the operation of the relief system on particular life-cycle groups, such as the aged or widows. We have begun to garner a complex picture of the sensitivity of poor relief to such experiences and to the malleability of parochial rules on its generosity, extent, and duration. In turn, some rhetorical forms were inextricably linked to the life-cycle condition itself, and it is in this tailoring of rhetorical form that we see the agency and strategy of the poor most keenly played out. The rest of this chapter thus explores how the poor and their advocates understood, rhetoricised, and used life-cycle conditions and gender particularities in their engagement with parish officers. Reflecting the broad concentration of the historiographical literature, the focus will be on old age, widow(er)hood, and abandonment, but I will also investigate the rhetorical and claims-making apparatus associated with orphanhood, childbirth, and the augmentation of large families. Broadly, we will see that the anchoring and extending rhetoric considered thus far in this section was inscribed by poor writers, their advocates, and vestry attendees into well understood, accepted, and universal models of the requirement for parochial action when they were confronted by common life-cycle conditions or deeply compromised gender roles. Once again, we will see that one entry in end-of-process overseers' accounts was not, even if for the same amount and duration, much like the next.

## OLD AGE

The question of what constituted old age in the period covered by this study is extraordinarily complex. We know that by the 1800s the absolute numbers of people reaching higher age brackets were being pushed up by population growth, the decline of the most virulent epidemic diseases, and relatively low background adult death rates even in cities, but it is much more difficult to nominate a particular age or age group as "old." Many studies have used sixty as a core benchmark, but in the underlying corpus relatively few applicants constructed such a milestone as in and of itself aged. By contrast, the age bracket of seventy and older was firmly associated with infirmity, withdrawal from labour, persistent sickness, and the breakdown of alternative care arrangements, whatever the nature and cost of the "ask" itself.[6] However we define the state of being old, an additional complication for understanding its experience, its place in claims making, and the nature of parochial responses is that the extent and robustness of alternative support mechanisms – family, almshouses, age-related charities, and institutions – in any host locality shaped who applied for poor relief, when, how, and with what particular rhetorical flourishes.[7] Thus, when the aged Mary Barnacres wrote an instigatory letter from Chester in Cheshire on 26 January 1796 claiming to have come to her parish only when all other avenues had been exhausted, including the charity of neighbours, work, a "little legacy," and Christmas donations to the poor, she was almost certainly telling the truth as well as conforming to parochial expectations.[8] This was true of the wider set of writers and vestry attendees, as we have seen in earlier chapters. Barnacres was eventually supported in her place of residence, but in other areas the attitude of parishes toward bringing people "home" could also impact which old people wrote, how often, and with what rhetorical position. The relative absence of aged writers in letters to Welsh parishes compared to their English counterparts reflects the fact that Welsh parishes were more likely to simply demand that their old people return.

Meanwhile, how approaches to parish officers were received was partly dependent upon other pressing calls in settlement parishes. As suggested by Richard Smith for the eighteenth century and by Henry French for the early nineteenth century, it was possible in some places for applicants with large families or unemployed younger men to become the focus of the poor relief process, reducing the proportion, if not absolute amounts, of relief distributed to the aged.[9] The ubiquitous fashion in which older writers or their advocates aligned multiple hardships with a central condition of being old suggests that, by the period covered here, applicants were very much alive to these competing pressures.[10] The aged William Smith was keenly aware of this situation when he said in an ending letter written from Shipley in Yorkshire on 15 January 1797 that "I Know Gentlm'n that times is Hard at Home but my Case is Honestly stated and I worse off than Many who have your Favour from the Acc't of Mr Knowles [a distributor of woollen cloth] when he was Last up this Way."[11]

These complications notwithstanding, aging and the status of being old are universal reference points in letters and vestry minutes, both for the period as a whole and across all of the community and spatial typologies employed here. It is impossible to know whether the aged wrote more often than their place in the wider populations of host or settlement communities would otherwise warrant, but as 42 per cent of all letters were from people who implied they were old or getting old, it is likely that they did.[12] Their letters and vestry appearances are overlaid with a consistent rhetoric of worklessness and withdrawal from the labour market, on the one hand, and sickness, on the other. We have seen such concepts deployed throughout previous chapters, and here I take them as part of the rhetorical wallpaper, although it is important to note that labour force participation by the aged almost certainly did come under pressure in the glutted labour markets of early-nineteenth-century England. Three *further* rhetorical constructs are distinctive to the claims that older people or their advocates made and to the correspondence that officials had with each other: the state of being old; the construct of accumulating infirmity, which was sometimes combined with the rhetoric of prior contribution to communities; and the notion of decline, be it sudden or gradual.

I start, then, with the state of being old, rhetoricised either as a certain age or as a state of mind and body. Elizabeth Maunders wrote a renewing letter from Old Brentford in Middlesex to Mr Randall, the schoolmaster of Wootton in Oxfordshire, on 6 January 1827 asking him to approach the vestry in order to see why her allowance had not been paid. Noting that "the Season now has set in so severe," Maunders did not want to return home to Wootton because to do so would "quite put it out of my power of returning here again as I should lose the little employ I have & I trust at my time of Life 65 the Gent[n] will not wish me to leave here as I am content with what they allow me."[13] In this case, then, the age of sixty-five was constructed as a "time of Life" that was deserving of some consideration by the officers of her settlement parish.[14] For other writers or their advocates, the figures attached to what was most frequently called in the corpus "advanced age" varied significantly. The overseer who wrote an interspersing letter on behalf of the widow Catherine Thompson from Durham to Berwick upon Tweed in Northumberland on 21 May 1830 noted that she was "unable to maintain herself at her advanced age (70) and her son who is with her from the poor wages which are made here is scarcely able to Maintain himself."[15] James Rutherford set a higher but more definitive bar when writing an interspersing letter from Livenhoe to Ancroft St Anne, both in Northumberland, in the case of Margaret Nelson, "who is at the Advanced Age of 84 or 5 & is as may be Expected unable to Rise out of Bed or do the least Thing herself." He forcefully asserted the duty of the settlement parish in such cases: "you Cannot Expect her to be supported" by a "Daughtere having the Bondage to uphold."[16] By contrast, John and Sarah Budding of Coventry were "both very feeble and infirm, & *near* 60 years of age" in April 1816,[17] and John Ralph of Warwick noted in an extending letter of 6 November 1801 that as well as illness and a family to support, his parish ought to be swayed by the fact that "[I] am bove fiftey years of Eage."[18] In short, the ability to describe oneself as old or the eligibility to be ascribed this label, as well as the ability to use this standing as part of a rhetoric of deservingness, encompassed a wide range of physical ages. Indeed, many writers eschewed the specificity of age, preferring to use a sense of being old in conjunction with other variables in order to make a rhetorical case.

Maunders and the advocates for Thompson, Nelson, and the Buddings wrote or were the subject of single, but by no means unusual, letters. We get a better understanding of how a particular age or state of mind and body came to be associated rhetorically with deservingness when we look at a series of letters by the same person. William King, writing multiple letters from London to Braintree in Essex in the early 1830s, is a typical and eloquent example, and we already encountered him briefly in chapter 9. After a series of letters where King described the health problems of himself and his wife, lack of work, compromised clothing, and the struggle to make do by pawning everything down to the wedding ring off his wife's finger, we first get a sense of King's age in a letter of 25 February 1830 when he claimed, "I have Bourn the Heat of the Day of forty years Trubble and Painful Distress Without Being Chargerble to My Parrish."[19] Not until several years and letters later did King seek to develop this rhetorical platform. His letter of 4 March 1834 suggested, "I Now Get in years and feel the Nead of what I Cannot obtain."[20] The rhetoric was renewed on 31 July 1834 when King said, "I Get in years and feel the failings of Nature to Be Verl alarming Not only in Boddy But in Mind allso Long Years of Trubble have Bowed Me down as it wheare."[21] By September 1834 he was "Not able to Do as formerly – I feel Great weakness and Sinking Such as I am perswaded all People feel who are told 60 years."[22] Finally, King moved from this definitive statement of age back to a sense of the melancholy consequences of his getting old. In his letter of October 1834, he would "Still hope to hold out My epointd Days wich are Now on the decline Tis October with me."[23] The experienced and rhetorically constructed process of getting old and reaching a certain age was thus powerfully deployed as a source of agency and power in negotiations with officials in the settlement parish. King was by no means alone, and settled claimants adopted a similar rhetorical construction of aging when attending the vestry.

These examples highlight a second distinctive rhetorical strand used by old people, whether or not we ever find out their actual calendar age:

the accumulation of infirmity, which reaches its natural and inevitable conclusion in advanced years. The wife of Robert Mole of Northam in Northumberland had by the time of an interspersing letter of 17 December 1830 been dragged down by half a lifetime of suffering, such that she was "very frail and appears like a shadow."[24] John Pratt, writing an instigatory letter from an unknown location to Tweedmouth in Northumberland on an unspecified date, but likely in the late 1790s, was a humble petitioner who asked that the officers "forgive my freedom in troubling you at this time," but he had little choice because "My helplessness and many Infirmities increasing daily" had created an intolerable burden for those around him.[25] Similarly, Richard Reed, writing from Kidderminster in Worcestershire on 1 February 1790, could "well Asure you sir that I ham in A Distressing Circumstance at thiss time." Implying an accumulation of misfortune, he noted with a flourish that "my Case Requires a Speedy Assistance for I ham in A Lingering Situation Neither Living not Dieing."[26] The elision of accumulated infirmity, increasing inability or disability, and old age is a particularly common feature of the corpus and seems to have played powerfully on the decisions of recipient overseers, as chapter 4 suggested. The aged widow Elizabeth Chapel, writing an extending letter from Malmsbury in Wiltshire on 14 July 1794, is typical. She was "entirly a Creepal [cripple] and I am very Ill in my Consitution and so verry Weak in my Body that I Can Scarce Go about the house without help." She would not, a postscript to the officers stated, "have asked you now If I Could have done Without But tis Imposable for me to Go on any Longer Without ~~Aserstane assitunce~~ Help from you."[27]

Of their own accord, through advocate letters or via vestry appearances and personal encounters with officials, old people using this sense of accumulated infirmity frequently fused it rhetorically with a promise or gloomy prediction that they would not long be a burden on the parish given impending death. Thus an unnamed advocate wrote an instigatory letter from Chester on 27 July 1795 in the case of "Poor old mary Toarance," who was at "this time Very Ill, and to all appearance cannot continue long old age ~~has render~~'d & bad health has render'd Her incapble of Supporting herself any longer."[28] The striking-out of a

phrase in this letter and subsequent insertion of a further variable drag-
ging down Mary Toarance – poor health – is a useful reminder that old
age in and of itself was rarely a sufficient condition for obtaining relief.
That said, the narratives in some of the letters from old people, particularly those concerning the intertwining miseries and accumulated infirmities of a couple, are among the most rhetorically and strategically
sophisticated in the entire corpus, although again seemingly unrelated
to the nature of the "ask." The instigatory letter from George Cleaver
to Tetbury in Gloucestershire on 11 October 1825 is not untypical in
its richness:

It is by the greatest necessity that I am now compell'd to address
you with the following request in consequence of my own age &
infirmity and also that of my Wife together with our affliction which
is altogether very great it is now three years the 8th of this Month
scince my wife was seized with a Parylatic stroke which nearly deprived her of the use of her limbs in short she is become a child
which we may expect she being in her 79 or 80th year, & myself 67
years & on the 2nd of last June she was taken speechless but it came
again & whenever she is taken with her complaint it nearly leaves
her the same way I cannot leave her in consequence of her affliction
& as my employer allows me to work at home I am able to attend
upon her myself and as I cannot do but little work myself and haveing no friend I find my income scarcely able to find us the common
necessaries of life indeed that we never have for nearly 3 year past
I have not done above five score in two weeks and that of the coarsest sort I am sorrey that I should be under the disagreeable necessity
of thus addressing you under the aforemention'd circumstances but
as honest poverty is no disgrace I make bold to solicit your kindness
to take into consideration our case and hopeing you will be so good
as to allow me if it is but sufficient to pay my rent you know I have
been a poor Man all my life in this Town about 30 Years & never
troubled you for any thing before nor would not now was it not a
case of extreem poverty which oblidges me to this step by complying to my request[29]

Cleaver thus traced a catalogue of distresses, the foremost being his own age and ill-health, allied with the caring responsibilities associated with the stroke of his wife, the endurance of which for three long years had been devastating for the family economy, his own health, and his peace of mind. Struggling, humility, an appeal to humanity, and a sense of the fragility of lives in the face of exogenous circumstances like sickness were yoked together with advanced old age to make a compelling practical and rhetorical case for officials to act.

For some aged writers, their own appeals and those of advocates encompassed less colour than in the case of George Cleaver. Rather, they were infused with a third rhetorical strand: a melancholy sense of decline and loss of hope of the sort also exhibited by William King above. This rhetorical vehicle was shared by the sick of all ages and both genders but appears in a particularly sophisticated fashion in the writing of or about the aged. Thus the Reverend Charles Atkinson, writing a testamentary letter from Wakefield to Oxford on 12 October 1771, traced the decline and lost hope of Widow Sims over the five years he had been acquainted with her. She was "in great Distress, being unable to work, as she has had a Stroke of the Palsy, & is not likely to be any long Time a Burthen to you." Noting that "I have a Respect for the Place of my Education," Atkinson undertook "to inform you of the very Day when she ceases to be a Burthen to your Parish."[30] This rhetoric of decline unto death is consistently used across the spatial, chronological, and typological dimensions of the corpus. It also transcends national language. In 1814 Ishmael James wrote in Welsh from Abergavenny in Monmouthshire to Gloucester in Gloucestershire on behalf of himself and his wife, Mary, to "state my situation and my poor olld women at near the age of 70 Each of us in great disstres at Presen wee have all both of us Strove to the utmost of ouar power and noW wee are bound to set beefore you ouar condision." Paradoxically, the letter contained no details at all about the case; rather, James painted a picture of decline and asked for "asmall trifle for to help us to live the short time as wee have hear on earth for it is uncer tain."[31] Other writers gave a stronger sense and rhetoric (or rhetorical equivalent) of decline. Sarah Park, writing an ending letter from Laymore in Somerset on 9 June 1833, for instance, suggested that she would not likely be a long-term burden on the parish, "for I am decaying very fast."[32] Such letters did not often enter into a detailed elaboration or restatement of circumstances, reflecting both the struggle that out-parish writers had in trying to decide when they had said enough and the sense that "decay" and accelerated decline ought to be something that needed statement, not explanation.[33] Increasingly across the period, decay of this sort came to be associated rhetorically with an open expression of depression and melancholy, a clear reflection of the fact that the linguistics of emotion had passed into more common parlance.[34] The traction of this sort of rhetoric is well illustrated in the correspondence of Charles Williamson, the overseer of Whitehaven in Cumberland, who returned frequently to the costs of caring for old people. Nonetheless, he almost always paid up, as for instance in the case of Jane Dickinson, who was "more than 70 years of age" when he commenced relief. He did so because "she had a wish to live in that house [rather than the workhouse] until her death being the place where she was born and had never lived out of it."[35] Such consideration speaks to the de facto rights that the aged managed to garner.

## GENDERED RHETORIC

Whereas old men and old women wrote (or were written about) in similar terms as they tried to establish ongoing and long-term entitlement, other shared life-cycle experiences were rhetoricised in distinctively gendered ways. This finding, and an associated lack of any patterning in the deployment of gendered rhetoric according to the nature of the "ask," the length of time spent away from the parish, or the type of letter written, should perhaps not surprise us. Women wrote all the time in a context full of situational limitation. When writing, they were manipulating a primarily male discourse aimed at men in power, and the outcome of their writing in terms of an offer of support might be read as, and be dependent upon, "an admission of their own inadequacy or lack."[36] Nonetheless, a vibrant historiography of the epistolary world of middling women from the early modern period onward has begun to show convincingly that such writers were skilled in taking restrictive masculine discourse and linguistic registers and using them subtly but concertedly for their own purposes. The normative modelling of female speech and writing as "exuding humility, mildness and deference that signifies the wife's acceptance of her subjugation" was in practice appropriated and transformed as women claimed power and voice in public and private spheres. Such women increasingly established "an authoritative and trustworthy rhetorical persona,"[37] one that was rich at the lexical level as a result of their adopting "new and unusual linguistic forms apparently encountered in everyday speech."[38] It is inconceivable that ordinary women, many of whom would go on to become dependent on the poor law or to write for those who had become thus dependent, would have been insulated from these experiences. Whether in turn we can discern a particularly "female" voice and linguistic register in the corpus is a question worthy of a study in its own right. However, the numerical presence of women writers in the material is, as chapter 1 noted, striking. And although we can certainly find women (and men) conforming to stereotypical norms in the sense of languages and signals of deference, protection, and paternalistic duty, the writing of poor women and sometimes their appearances before vestries suggest that in three distinctive situations, they appropriated language and gendered models just as skilfully as their middling counterparts.[39]

We might turn first to the 494 letters in the corpus from women who were (temporarily or permanently) deserted by their husbands. Although some of these desertions were, or were perceived by contemporary officials as being, manufactured for the specific purpose of obtaining poor relief, most seem to have been genuine cases of abandonment. Indeed, such women and their advocates can often be found exhorting parishes to detect and prosecute errant husbands, even providing information on their whereabouts when it came to hand.[40] Letters from or about such women systematically fused together the rhetorics of worthless men, dependence on the friendship and consideration of the (essentially male) parish, the exhaustion of other efforts to make do, and the worsening of their plight by exogenous factors such as the sickness of themselves or their fatherless (sometimes called "orphaned") children. The case of Hannah Blotheridge is typical. Sent to her home parish of Chipping

Campden in Gloucestershire by the assistant overseer of her residence community of Souldern in Warwickshire on 1 April 1829, Blotheridge carried an interspersing letter by the official in which he stated that he had known her

> many years as a quiett Industrious person, but is now in distress been desserted by a worthless Husband. I believe her to be in want of some assistance for her support – the present price of Bread & scarcity of *Silk* which work she have allways been accustomed to renders it impasable for her to support herself.[41]

Whether this appeal was successful is unclear from parochial accounts, but the case was revisited in a testamentary letter of 7 May 1829 from Mr A. Haines, who noted that Blotheridge was ill "and stands in need of your assistance her husband never comes near her unless tis with the Intention to get some thing of her he is only about 4 or 5 miles of Campdean Will you be so kind as send a Letter by return of post as she is so very ill." Haines added pointedly in a postscript that "she have no friends as can assist her."[42] Faced with this subtle argument that the parish must substitute for friends, a common rhetorical vehicle (see chapter 8) given a gendered tinge, Souldern paid an allowance until Blotheridge later remarried.

Phebe Parker rehearsed many of the same arguments in her own instigatory letter, written to Tetbury on 5 December 1835. Having noted that she and her "three small children" had been abandoned by her husband some five months previously after he had set out on the pretence of looking for work, she said that "he has only sent me one Pound – and it is thirteen weeks this day that I have heard from him – – and sir – I should be glad – if you would send me a trifle to help me and with what little I could get I would endeavour to support my children." By way of rhetorical flourish, Parker implicitly asserted her honesty and no doubt a small measure of revenge when she added that she would "be glad if the Gentlemen of the Parish – would send after him and punish him as he deserves – he his working at Buckfastleigh in Devon shire – but what the Masters name is I dont know he is working there – for his Letter was directed from that place."[43] Parker, then, melded together rhetorics of dependence, friendlessness, struggle, and honesty, and although we might read her letter as conforming to expected gender norms, a different rendering would find that pride, resistance to more forceful parochial action, such as workhouse confinement, and an attempt to keep or restore a reputation were woven into a very subtle communication.[44]

The rhetorical direction and sense of letters by or about abandoned women vary little across space or time. Moreover, the deep roots of this language can be traced in one of the earliest instigatory letters in the corpus, which was written by Anne Grant of Banbury to her settlement parish of Wootton, both in Oxfordshire, on 27 March 1711. She was "in great want and have bin all this winter that I have Sold all my [illegible] that I have nothing Left to helpe my selfe and my husband hath bin gone from me almost Six years and I can in no wise make shift any longer with out sum speedy releife for The hardness of times & the badness of trade." Requesting help with her rent and support for her two children, Grant asked that the parish officers "let the clarke acquaint your own feares of the poor and the in inhabitance of the town that they may take some care of me as [two illegible words] may not starve for I cannot make shift any Longer."[45] This final rhetorical desire that the parish stand as a substitute husband or breadwinner held powerful sway over the decision making of officials in this case and might be read as conforming to long-instituted models of female weakness and dependency. A more subtle consideration of the text might show Grant asserting the personal credit of a long struggle for independence, the vicarious effects of exogenous circumstances – hard times and bad trade – on her efforts, her standing in the host community, and the moral risk of allowing two children to starve. The rhetorical vehicles, familiar in large part from earlier chapters, were given gendered colour and, at least in the eyes of Grant, created a compelling case.

Men, too, were abandoned by their wives, although less commonly. Such men were invariably angrier than their female counterparts[46] and tended to draw on the testimony of a wider range of witnesses to the consequences of their abandonment. Where their wives took the children with them, men constructed themselves as distraught fathers doing all that they could to reconcile the situation. John Osborne of Reading is typical. Abandoned by his wife sometime in September 1829, who took their three children, Osborne asserted in a letter of 3 October 1829 the "Ill treatment, I have received from my Wife, and which has ben proved by many of my neighbours, of her most infamous conduct towars me, I beg to refer you to Mr Warburton Keeper of the Boro' Bridewell, also to my late Landlord Mr Champion Grocer, London Street, also to Mr Wigmore bricklayer Coley Terrace." Outlining his failed attempts to reconcile with his wife and to offer her monetary and in-kind support, Osborne constructed her as a bad mother as well as an unfeeling partner: "I have my eldest son with me which I intend to support as her ill treatment to my son John was infamous, as she actually lock'd him out of doors all night, had not the neighbours taken him in and fed him."[4] These sentiments were renewed in a letter of 10 October, where Osborne asked for a little support to get back on his feet because

> I gave my house up, as for Furniture I have but little. Sir, after all that I have suffered, I am willing, in case my Wife will condescend, to take a lodging for her, myself, and Family, for a few weeks until I can recover myself; for I assure you I have been so unsettled for 5 or 6 weeks past, that I am in a very unhappy state of mind.[48]

A dejected and unhappy father thus asked the parish not to stand as a friend but to relieve a melancholy brought on by his situation.

In practice, the difference in the rhetoric of abandoned men compared to that of abandoned women emerges most firmly where men were left caring for children. In such cases, men invariably pointed to their curtailed independence and earning power, noting the inconvenience of the children and exhorting parishes to provide the resources for childcare so as to allow the claimant to occupy his rightful place in the world.[49] Thus Thomas Albion wrote from Cambridge on 9 November 1833 to say that abandonment by his wife meant that he had to hire a nurse for their four small children. Unfortunately, "having to Maintain her [i.e., the nurse] has hadded much to my present difficulties," notwithstanding a small allowance from the parish. Having pawned his clothes and run out of credit and reputation, he proposed to send three of the children "home" to be boarded out by the parish unless the overseer would send "a Trifle to help my Dear Motherless Babes."[50] Wronged husbands often – although not always, as the case of Albion illustrates – offered more rhetorical invective than wronged wives, but both genders had to use subtle rhetorical measures if they were to avoid the deeper consequences of a rejection of their claim, to re-establish a reputation, and to demonstrate their character and honesty.

Subtle differences between the rhetorical position of men and women continue if we switch our attention to a second life-cycle situation: loss of a spouse through death. It is now well established in the British and European context that widows were disproportionately represented in the highest and lowest socio-economic groups of both urban and rural communities.[51] They are also disproportionately represented in the corpus for both in- and out-parish applicants compared to their likely numbers in the wider population.[52] For widows at all stages of the life-cycle, the loss of male partners was constructed rhetorically in terms of some combination of the necessity of application and relief, compassion, the shortness of remaining time, support for children, a lack of friends, dependence on the paternalism of the parish, and a crushed family economy. Thus, when Mary Stevens wrote from Gloucester to Cheltenham, both in Gloucestershire, on 5 February 1790, she did so because

> my Nessecity obliges me thro the Lost of my Husband who was Drowned about six weeks before Christmas leaving me with 3 small Children and ~~do~~ expect to Lie in with another every Day which makes my Trouble Very Great not being able to do any thing toward the support of my Family and shoud be Glad if you will Please to allow me somthing towards their Support, as I am setled here I hope you will take it into Consideration to allow me somthing as *it will be less expence than for me and the Family to Come to Cheltenham* my Husband name was Edward Stevens Plaisterer.[53]

Intertwining rhetorics of respectability and independence – if she were not about to give birth, she would have been able to do something to support herself – with the fact and consequence of widowhood, Stevens also appears to have been aware of the precarious position of women who depended on their husband's settlement after his death.[54] Notwithstanding an ingrained historiographical sense of the complex sociocultural position of widows as both an object of pity and charity and a threat to local sexual and social order,[55] Cheltenham moved swiftly to support Stevens. More generally, to be widowed and pregnant at the same time seems to have created a universal obligation on the part of parishes, and there is a clear sense that such women knew or suspected this would be the case, even playing on the dual condition in their rhetoric. The heavily pregnant Mary Neworth, writing from Worsthorne in Lancashire on 7 April 1803, was not unusual in noting that "I am unfit to travel being so very heavy & inactive" and in linking this circumstance to the loss of a husband and distressed children in order to argue that "my Situation at present is very pitiable."[56] Such letters give substance to Molly Wertheimer's view that rhetoric was firmly tied into the portrayal of character and into contemporary philosophies of duty and obligation.[57]

Widowed women who were not pregnant but who nonetheless had large families or were of childbearing age used similarly sophisticated constellations of universal and gendered rhetoric. Ester Sharp, writing an instigatory letter from Bromsgrove on 11 September 1794, asked her parish to "read over" her letter "with Compassion towards Distress widoow that – I may now call my-self at – this present period." At the heart of her appeal were "my small and tender offspring as I have 6 Children the Eldest – being 12 years old the 2nd 11, and the – other 4 Children being so small and not able to work at any employment." These "Children being allmost naked for Cloathing as well as – in want of food so I Resin [reason] Gentn you will not fail sending me – an order one way or the other – as soon as posable." This powerful rhetoric of starving children, as we saw in the previous chapter, was designed to appeal to the humanity and Christian duty of officers, to the very basic law of the Old Poor Law, and to wider constructions of dignity. Nonetheless, it was not sufficient. Sharp also constructed herself as friendless and dependent on the male sphere of the parish, noting that she was obliged "to flee to your

Charity[58] to suport me" and that "I cannot – with all the industry that I can make be able to support" herself and her children now that her husband was dead.[59] Here, then, the rhetorics of powerlessness and dependence upon the male parish were appropriated and juxtaposed with the potential of her own industry, which might in other circumstances have generated an independent existence. Feeble dependence, itself rhetoricised so as to carry moral authority, was thus coloured with integrity, standing, and even a touch of heroism.[60] Sharp sought something more than a casual dole, inviting an exchange of support in which she would, if helped, now work for her children and thus support the long-term position of her parish. A language of entreaty had been appropriated subtly so as to become something more than a call to paternalistic action.[61]

These letters have some similarities to those written by or for men in similar circumstances.[62] In particular, old men losing their wives constructed themselves rhetorically as suffering the loss of a wife and the inability of children to take them in or otherwise support them.[63] More generally, however, men emphasised various combinations of the weakened family economy occasioned by the loss of a wife, the accumulated costs of nursing a sick wife now dead, the emotional toll on the man and his children of losing a wife and mother, the way that childcare interfered with the work of men and thus the viability of the family economy going forward, and the hope and aspiration for independence.[64] George Hailes is a good example. We first encountered him in chapter 5 through an addendum to his instigatory letter of 17 September 1826 from Castletown on the Isle of Man to Brimpton in Berkshire emphasising his service to king and country.[65] In the main text, however, Hailes noted that he was in "very Great Distress for these last sixteen Months in Consequence of the Death of my Wife who Died in Child Bed of her Twenty Second Child and left me with A large Family with out Any Employment to suport them." Applying for support of "five out of Seven the youngest who is one year and four months Old Which I was Obliged to send to Nurse and the Eldest Which is Nine years and six Months old," he asked that the parish recognise his loss and inability to labour while caring for children of this age.[66] In a similar vein, the rope maker John Burdock was a "distressed widower" with six children, "the youngest of which re-

ceived life when the cruel hand of death seized its Mother." The cruelty
of death is something that men returned to again and again in their letters. In this case, Burdock noted that he was unable to look after the
other children or to "provide a Nurse for the dear infant" and that he
had lost the income of his wife. Striving for independence and partnership with the parish, he had taken the hardest of steps, proposing to send
three of his children to live with his brother (likely his brother-in-law)
George Ricks in Bristol. Four respectable gentleman of his unspecified
host parish attested to the honesty of the content of the letter and asserted that relief would be "just."[67] In letters written by women, we see
some of the analogue of this rhetoric in the increasing presence of claims
that circumstances – particularly the nursing of family members – had
compromised their contribution to the family economy through wages
earned in the labour market.[68]

A third (and larger) group of married women had not experienced loss
or abandonment but nonetheless found themselves writing letters in their
own right or on behalf of families when sickness or unemployment struck.
As Joanne Bailey has pointed out, in the letters of these poor women and
those who advocated for them, references to dependence, charity, weakness, and the paternalism of the local state melded subtly with the sorts
of rhetorical infrastructure used by most writers – honesty, character,
struggle, and suffering – but also with their compromised roles as wives
and mothers.[69] The latter hardship was particularly powerful, and the
wide corpus of letters, advocate letters, official correspondence, and
vestry minutes used for this study provides depth and colour to our understanding of the rhetorical ecology of motherhood. Thus, although
mothers shared with men a focus on their inability to perform primary
roles in relation to children, they generally employed a much more emotional, emotive, and eloquent rhetoric. This distinction is typified in a letter from Oxford by Ann Bennet on 6 January 1824. A violent cold and
sore throat meant that "I have been almost starved on Account I Could
not swallow any thing to Nourish me." Her own suffering, however,
paled into insignificance when set against the fact that she had "Nothing
to Subsist of for my poor Babes and self but the little that my two feeble
parents Could [obscured by seal] who has but a small pittance to keep

theirselves [obscured by seal] their Own Labour." This dual narrative of parental support in extremis and starving babies was calculated to tug at the heartstrings of male officials. For good measure, and in common with women who approached parishes because of widowhood, she threw herself at the feet of the male parish, reaching out implicitly to ingrained models of female dependence and submission: "Necessety has no Law, therefore Gent lemen I must be left to your Mercy."[70] By contrast, some women offered a much more robust sense that compromised motherhood should be a call to arms for parish officers. Gwen Bassett wrote a renewing letter in Welsh from Caernarvon in Caernarvonshire to Henllan in Denbighshire on 16 August 1836 to say, "I who am sending this to you are witness to the fact that it has been very hard to obtain even a morsel for the children and it is very difficult here for women to earn anything." She threatened that if the overseer did not reply to her immediately, she would throw herself on the host parish, "and if I do then it will probably be worse for you."[71] Ann Jones, writing an interspersing letter from St Pancras in London to her deceased husband's parish of Llantrisant in Glamorgan, was less direct in her letter of 23 August 1818 but constructed a multilayered rhetorical picture of compromised motherhood. Noting that her husband had died when on a visit to Gwent in January 1818, she now wrote for help with supporting her two children. Hearing that her husband had been buried at parish expense, she told the overseer that "his relations promised him that they would bury him at their own expence or at the expence of his Cloaths, which would have sold for enough to have buried him for they were very good." Pointing to her inability to fulfil her mothering role because of illness and widowhood, she layered a further unnatural disadvantage onto the case, pointing to the selfish attitude of grandparents and kin: "I understand they have devided his Cloaths amongst them ... which I expected they would have sent me for the benefit of his two Children Wm & Sarah Jones, as we have great need of them being in great distress."[72]

The complex rhetoric of motherhood emerges most strongly where we consider a series of letters written by, for, or about the same woman. Dorothy Styrin, writing from Leeds in the early 1830s, is a good but not unrepresentative example. The narrative she constructed through her letters portrayed a woman struggling against the caprice of her family situation, illness, seasonal and cyclical fluctuations in employment, accident, and her own misery, all of which combined to prevent Styrin from filling the role of mother, her ultimate yardstick of deservingness. We first encounter her in a renewing letter of 11 July 1832, earlier correspondence not having survived. Styrin had recently been suffering from cholera, which had decimated the neighbourhood and left her weak. She asked the overseer for relief not on her own account but to take care of "the Children Money for it Will Bee of great servise to Me at Present." The first thought of a very sick mother, then, was for the welfare of the children, and this rhetorical ecology was to develop further over the course of subsequent letters. On 23 April 1832 she wrote again from Leeds, apologising for the fact that the person writing the earlier letter may have not written to officials "in a proper manner." Styrin was "sorry for the Misfrotune of not being a scholar" but urgently required the help of the parish with rent. This request was made not on her own account but because of the threat that her "poor Fatherless Children [will] have no plase of shelter." Stitching together claims to paternalism, her own emotionally degraded state, and the indignity of having to beg, she asked her co-respondent to "act the part of a Husband & a farther to us and God Wil Repay you an hundred fold hereafter ... and you will have thanks from a poor Widdow and her Fatherless Children." Whether the letter was simply a rhetorical tool to establish entitlement, as suggested by the fact that Styrin also felt the need to say that she was telling the truth, is irrelevant to this discussion since she believed that highlighting her compromised ability to act as a mother should toward fatherless children ought to elicit a parochial response.

It is unclear whether the parish responded, but another letter arrived on 2 August 1832, in which she noted that if the overseer "New my situation you could not but help pittying me." This rhetoric will be familiar from earlier chapters, but her real reason for writing was that her "youngest Little Boy" was gravely ill and needed an operation, for which Styrin was ill prepared to pay because she had cared for him over such a long period and thus had not worked as much as she would otherwise have done for her young family. Although Styrin stopped short of noting that the situation undermined her mothering role, it was deeply implied, and she closed, "pray Do not Neglect my good Sir." Here, then, deservingness, dignity, deprecation, and motherhood were welded firmly together: the overseers were faced with a woman impoverished by caring for her children and unable to provide them with food, clothing, and necessary medical care. Styrin went on to exploit the complex moral and experiential status of motherhood throughout subsequent letters. In June 1833 she was distressed once more for rent. Unable to prevent her children, all under the age of ten, from being dispatched to the streets, she asked the overseer to feel for her situation given that these children lacked a father. By 13 October 1835, on the eve of the New Poor Law, the family was in receipt of an allowance of 16 shillings per week, a significant proportion of the full-time male wage for ordinary labourers in Leeds at the time, but Styrin was still unable to pay her rent. She now appealed once more to the godly charity of the overseer as a man and a father.[73] Motherhood and widowhood were thus rhetorically juxtaposed to create a multilayered case that the parish officials should act out of duty, humanity, obligation, and above all as family men feeling for the situation of a lone mother just trying to do her best by the family. An allowance of 16 shillings per week suggests that they did just that.[74]

For women, then, dignity, dependence, deference, respectability, and overwhelming moral claims based upon the inability to fulfil the natural role of a mother were powerfully entwined. If, as John Walter claims, gendered prescriptions of behaviour took hold in local communities from the 1760s onward, their effect in terms of the process of poor relief was to give female claimants, both those writing and appearing in person, a rhetorical ecology with which to influence male overseers.[75] It is perhaps unsurprising to find male writers and vestry attendees constructing compromised fatherhood as a rhetorical cause for relief in a way that was very different from that of their wives and female neighbours. William Lloyd, first encountered in chapter 4, outlined the central rhetorical tenet of fatherhood in his letter from Wallingford to Oxford, both in Oxfordshire, on 6 March 1822. Claiming to be in "Extreem distress" because of "my Debility," Lloyd professed himself "Kuite tired of my Miserable

Existance." His core claims-making rhetoric, however, was an inability to support his wife and four children as a father should. He had

> allways don my best Indeavour to suport them but want of trade and ability is my only prevention such a family as mine I find is Verry Expencive Its not Vituals alone that suffice's But there are other Expencive things wanted such as Clothes Bedding &c and all to be depended on from one pair of hands of a Debilitated Concitution is a moral of Impos[sibility].

Prolonged sickness – invariably the simultaneous partner of claims to compromised fathering roles in a way that was not the case for women – had taken away Lloyd's ability to perform his primary role, and he now asked for empathy, humanity, and charity.[76]

Advocates wrote in similar fashion. Christopher Baker's renewing letter to Daniel Cole on the subject of William Gilmore in August 1835 testified to the honesty of the man, his ill-usage by a landlord, and a prolonged period of sickness. At the core of his letter, however, was that "his famley layes verry hard upon him and all thair support must come from his Labour, as it is quite as much as his Wife can do to provide for the famely of Five small Children to keep them clean and mend thair Cloths."[77] The inability of a man to provide the resources needed to feed and house small children and a struggling wife, felt the advocate, should weigh heavily in the decision making of the settlement parish.

Some writers infused their notion of compromised fatherhood with sustained pathos, as for instance did James Hale when he angrily contested a decision to "Stop the Scanty Pay allowed By the Parrish." Hale noted that although he had worked in prior partnership with the parish,

> We are half Naked & Very Barley fed as it Stands Place it to the feeling heart if any thare be how a man is to soport 9 Children all small Or Nearly; with his Bare wages & But very Little Brought in Besides – I Cannot Do it think I say what father can Quietly Look On a Starving family Begging & screeming for Bread & None to

give them; No I will not you and all that knows me; knows that I have fled from starvation and have seen too much of the world to be thought Quite Ignorant Enough To see my Self and Family Starve – Place it I say to your own Breast or any others who knows me.[78]

This heartfelt emotional appeal for the officers and vestry to think of themselves as fathers – just as women asked officials to think how they must feel as mothers – and to ask whether any man could fulfil the societal role required of him with so many children in tow speaks to much wider constructions of masculinity and fatherhood in the nineteenth century.[79] Yet this rhetoric was subtly different from that employed by and for women. An appropriated language of dependence and paternalistic duty allowed women and their advocates to tie together universal rhetorical models, emotional appeals, and firm parochial obligations much more consciously than was the case with fathers and husbands.

### OTHER LIFE-CYCLE CONDITIONS

Distinctive constellations of rhetoric also framed life-cycle conditions other than aging and widowhood. There was, for instance, a common rhetorical construction of the need occasioned by actual or impending childbirth. William Millard, writing an extending letter from Cheltenham on 14 January 1835, assured officials that notwithstanding previous claims, he was "dutifull of employment." On this occasion, he wrote to them because although "I have but One Child – but I do not know One Hour but my Wife will be confined and having no employment regularly lately it have thrown us Back in our Lodgins," such that he owed 13 shillings in rent.[80] It is unclear whether this was an opportunistic application for help with rent arrears now that Millard had some occasion to write to the parish again. Certainly, we can find examples of writers telling falsehoods about pregnancy. However, this and most other claims relating to maternity assumed that parishes would want expectant and recuperating mothers to be secure in their accommodation.

Mothers themselves frequently sent letters noting that landlords threatened them even as they were on the verge of childbirth or that accumulated troubles meant that they did not have a bed to lie on at such an important and dangerous time. More widely, both men and women rhetoricised a right, and corresponding parish obligation, to receive support during and after childbirth. For men, this rhetoric was generally supplemented by other indicators of deservingness, such as a lack of work, or by exogenous factors like high prices or sickness. John Elliot, writing from Twerton in Somerset on 18 July 1801, is typical. His wife had just given birth to their third child, "And the Expence it has put me to Obligates me to Ask for Some Asistence." The rhetorical sense that childbirth was expensive, in terms of both the additional expenditure and the foregone income of husband and wife, was common to almost all letters of this type. Elliot, however, offered further evidence of his deservingness, referring both to his character and to exogenous factors in the form of high prices: "As it tis well known that Ivery Article for Subsistence is, at preasent at an enormas Rate, My particular attention hithertwo has been to keep my self & Family as Independent as possible from any other support them by my ow[n] [damage to document] Industery."[81] Elliot's (correct) assertion that the high prices of the time and their impact on family budgets was well known speaks to the sense outlined in chapter 5 that poor writers drew on other texts and reference points to enhance the standing of their appeals. Women writing on this subject, by contrast, were much more likely to assert a simple right to support with no further rhetorical flourishes other than their own actual or potential suffering at such a pivotal time. Thus Sophia Curchin wrote a renewing letter from Wisbech in Cambridgeshire on 26 June 1826 to ask for "a Trifle more a week in my confinement as every one of feeling will allow it a shocking thing to want at such a time as I expect very shortly."[82]

This rhetorical sense of "right" was also deployed in relation to orphans. The voices of children in general are underrepresented in the corpus. As chapter 1 noted, however, letters *about* them are much more numerous. John Timely, who was keeping the child of the deceased John Lows, wrote a renewing letter from Thame in Oxfordshire on 7 May 1755 to ask for help with shoes and clothes. He reminded the unnamed recipient that "I have keep him 2 years and He has not Cost the parish any thing," a challenge to the parish to step in at this crucial time. Clothing, or a lack of it, is a ubiquitous feature of letters about orphans and their care, creating a rhetorical disadvantage compared to other children: lost parents *and* nakedness. Timely "bedg yooo will Send an answer as Soon as you Can youars to Comand" and threatened that the child might have to be returned "home" if the requisite support was not forthcoming.[83] The de facto (and sometimes direct) assertion of right supplemented by the threat of withdrawal from care and future burden to the parish was also a ubiquitous rhetorical vehicle at the other end of the study period, as for instance in the writing of Mary Barlow of Manchester, who on 28 June 1833 threatened to send her granddaughter home to Tottington in Lancashire because "I Shall not keep it any longer for Nothing."[84]

At the opposite extreme, writers and advocates whose cases were centred primarily on a surfeit of children could rhetoricise few concrete rights unless a system of familial support in the Speenhamland vein was in place.[85] It is now clear that formally constituted (and often extra-legal) bread scales or other forms of support for large families were simultaneously more common across the country than early writers on Speenhamland suggested and much less sustained than has usually been thought.[86] The corpus reflects this situation, with most vestries instigating family allowance systems but none supporting them for anything other than the shortest term. Nonetheless, writers across the typological, spatial, and gender dimensions of the material wrote consistently on the subject of large families. For some, as we saw above and in earlier chapters, the fact of three, four, or twenty-two children was a rhetorical adjunct to cases that were made primarily on other grounds. However, in a not insignificant subset of letters (7 per cent), the number and age distribution of children played a more important rhetorical and strategic role. James House, in an undated and hand-delivered letter found in the archive for Pangbourne in Berkshire, asked for "the Favour of a little Money" because he had ten children, "8 of whom are living and by having so large a Family to provide for I am unable to procure sufficient Nourishment." This bland statement of need without further rhetorical flourish or use of anchoring rhetoric is unusual in the sample.[87] Mary Haywood of Lambeth in London was more forceful and expansive in a series of letters that were undated but probably written in 1806. One letter said that she was unable to make do with her income as a washerwoman because business was dead in the winter months. "You are well a ware," she warned the overseer, "I have five children four of which are on my hands the eldest is a Cripple and quite unable to get her living." With sickness running through the family, Haywood doing her best to "breed them up," and her clothing compromised, she proposed that the parish should "send me thirty."[88] The reticence of applying on the basis of large families that we sometimes see in relation to men was turned on its head in this letter and others from Haywood.

### CONCLUSION

Life-cycle stages and events that have been here characterised as discrete could become combined as experiences, and their rhetorical exemplification could also be combined in single letters or letter series. Thus Hannah Mills wrote a renewing letter from Falmouth Docks on 2 October 1821 to contest the fact that her "pay" had been stopped. The letter represents a complex intertwining of the broad rhetorics explored in earlier chapters and the situational life-cycle rhetoric analysed in this one:

> [My] Son being Very ill in august last I was sent for to come to see him which journey I undertook thinking to have returned at the furthest in a fortnights time But was myself seiz'd with illness And a Gathering in my head which confin'd me a long time for three weeks was delirious and life despair'd of And am now in such a weak state that I feel Incompetent to come home at this present I am now Residing with my Daughter who has three children And excepting sleeping cannot assist me in any thing My age is Sixty Two last time And I Humbly [page torn] That you will be pleased to consider my age and infirmity and that with my Daughter I may have the consolation in my Sickness of having the Kind attendance should it meet your approbation to allow me the pay I have formerly enjoy'd it will sooth my Downhill of Life.[89]

Mills thus entwined in a complex rhetorical infrastructure stories of her taking the appropriate action of a good mother by going to her son when called, exogenous factors like illness, accumulated distress, acknowledgment of the discretionary power of the parish officers, exhausted familial support, aging, the love of a daughter for a parent, and decline during the "Downhill of Life." That the parochial response was to send relief speaks to the fact that for both the in- and out-parish poor there was a very broad understanding of the nature and extent of the contestability of the relief process.[90] In this context, rhetorics that were linked primarily to particular life-cycle conditions or to gender roles provided more power for the exercise of agency and were connected to a very broad understanding that the risks of poverty were, for many in parochial communities, simply unpredictable.[91] Given the "mobility, confusion and sheer messiness" of ordinary lives,[92] the linguistic ecology springing out of particular life-cycle positions provided a backbone around which claimants, both in writing and in person, could draw together the fractured experiential and rhetorical fragments of their lives. The resulting letters sought very purposefully and (to draw on the new language of outcomes suggested in chapter 4) hopefully to exploit the "structural ambiguities in relations between individual and institutional power."[93] They also fulfilled another important purpose, especially when written, received, and read as part of a series by, for, or about the same person. That is, the urgency and (often) raw emotion generated by the intensity of particular life-cycle conditions provided opportunities to obscure, shape, claim, and reshape the offered and perceived self. And it is to the question of how poor writers understood and constructed themselves, and how they were in turn understood and constructed by the other participants in the epistolary world of the parish, that this study finally turns.

# PART FOUR

## Self and Meaning

# 12

## Identity and the Pauper Self

### OVERVIEW

At the very end of the study period, on 6 January 1834, John Gunnell (first encountered in chapter 3) wrote from Manchester. Referring to an unanswered previous letter, Gunnell said that he would

> therefore once more Repeat my Request nothing Doubting but it will be my last. I have for a long time been very ill, not able to do anything at all, and for a considerable time confined to my Bed with not the last hope or expectation of 6 January 1834 ever leaving it in *this Vale of Tears but the Lord's will be Done* I am Resigned to it and it alone for he alone knoweth best what to Do with his Children. With Desiring you to Answer this by return of post I remain Your much obliged servant.[1]

Cholera and unemployment stalked Manchester at this time, and we know from other correspondence that Gunnell's pessimism about personal survival was warranted. More widely, his letter portrays an archetype of the pauper identity and projected persona that some aspects of the historiographical literature might lead us to expect: he was submissive, needed to establish his honesty, was humble, and made no assertion of rights to relief. It is uncertain how the officials who received this narrative understood the identity that Gunnell was trying to convey and, through its elaboration in writing, to create.[2] For other poor writers in the corpus, this matter is rather clearer. Near the beginning of the study period, in 1754, Jonathan Griffen, the overseer of Clewer in Berkshire, wrote to his counterpart in Oxford St Martin to acknowledge receipt of 2 pounds, "which you Seem to make Objection of Given any Weekly Alowance for the Suport of the [unnamed] Family it being so Numerous and in Such a Raged Condition almost Naked the[y] are Mere Objects and the man being Adicted to the Rehumatism in Such a Manner that He Cannot Suport them."[3] His counterpart clearly replied in a now lost letter because on 6 May 1754 Griffen renewed his correspondence, noting that "You Desired me to Inform you what was wanted in, the Family as I Inform[d] you Before the[y] are all almost Naked in, Apparel." Moreover, he added,

> you Write that you was Credibly Inform[d] that he is a very Idle Fellow and wont Work, when he has it to Do – which I have Inform[d] him, the Caracter you hear of him But he Declares that he would not have had any thing From his parish, was he But Able to Earn it Himself, he has Nothing From our Parish, at Present nor will not without Case of Nesessity which, we had much, Rather you will Send Sombody or Come for the Better Satisfaction, of your parish, in, this Case.[4]

This sense that the parish doubted the very honesty of its out-parish poor sits easily with historiographical perspectives that, as we saw in chapters 1 and 5, suggest there was a strong and direct elision between being poor and compromised dignity and believability.

Yet the overseer of Clewer clearly did not recognise the rumoured dishonesty of this unnamed father or sympathise with the parochial response, rattled off as it was without seeing the person involved. This fact is important. We have seen throughout the study that those involved in the tripartite epistolary world of the parish shared linguistic and referential platforms and inhabited a world where the potentially competing duties of the parish to ratepayers, the poor, and other stakeholders were reconciled in part by the creation and acceptance of shared fictive land-scapes. Necessarily, the identities of the poor were partly created by themselves, partly imposed by others, and partly adopted from stock im-ages that might be acceptable and recognisable to all parties in the nego-tiation process.[5] Who, then, were the the previous chapters' poor writers and vestry attendees, whose appeals started the process of poor relief? How did they understand their purpose and selfhood, and how in turn were they understood and constructed? Was there an ideal or represen-tative self, as much historiography would have us believe?

Answering these questions is significantly tied up with the wider sense that the later eighteenth century witnessed a change in the nature, under-standing, and construction of selfhood. This shift was consequent on ris-ing literacy and publication, an expanding linguistic register,[6] a changed understanding of the emotional landscape and its expression, a fracturing of older frameworks for containing and shaping individuality,[7] and the rise of autobiography and other life writing as simultaneously a discovery and codification of self, a means for its expression, and a testament to its dynamism.[8] Similarly, Dror Wahrman suggests that war and socio-economic change in the last decades of the eighteenth century saw a crisis of identity, the solution to which "privileged interiority over exteriority, and assumed a stable core of selfhood as an innate and essential compo-nent of every individual."[9] The learned process of creating a credible iden-tity that fitted a particular cultural or historical setting faded, as did the resort to role-playing and effective disguise in the case of all those navi-gating a relationship in which power was unevenly distributed.[10] These changes were to influence the thinking of the middling and governing or-ders first and most keenly, such that for these groups the process of self-creation was replaced by a sense of selfhood in which individuals became the source of their own self-generated and self-expressive meaning. In this situational position, rehearsing and constructing stories and histories was an important navigation point that crystallised an emotional framework, exemplified and justified self-determination, encoded the journey by which individuals had become as they were, and projected individualised values such as improvement, agency, and resistance.[11]

It is unclear how much of this changing dynamic of selfhood trickled down to ordinary people and, more problematically, to those who were or might become dependent on the parish.[12] The increasing density and depth of sources on this group from the 1750s onward – and even more so from the early 1800s – might simply afford a better window on the sense of self rather than embodying and signifying any real change in the way that selfhood was constructed and understood. Perceptions of continuity or change might in this sense be simply an illusion patterned onto the deeply coloured letters and vestry minutes employed here. Nonetheless, it is possible to read the very existence (rather than simply survival) of an increasingly large corpus of correspondence in the tripartite epistolary world of the parish as itself evidence of the changing ways that the dependent and almost dependent poor understood their place in the world. Certainly, many contemporary commentators felt that the poor of England and Wales in the late eighteenth and early nineteenth centuries had become more vocal and insistent and that officials had in turn connived to turn a blind eye to this more assertive sense of self. If, as Peter King suggests for the late 1790s, an imbalanced socio-structural architecture continued to have a central role in how ordinary people defined themselves and their place in society, the existence of shared linguistic registers and understandings of the fictive nature of claimants' cases points forcefully to the passing of this older referential system.[13] Martyn Lyons argues that by the 1860s ordinary writers had "acquired a sense of self and defined themselves as individual personalities, with their own histories, their own memories and their own struggles." Poor people were, he suggests, "the dramatic personae of a new history from below."[14] In effect, then, the last decades of the Old Poor Law constitute a significant gap in our understanding of the development of selfhood among ordinary people. We cannot be certain that the poor gained a *new* interiority in this period as opposed to a forum – letters and vestry encounters – in which models of self were recorded and tweaked, but it seems likely that they did.

Understanding the nature of this new selfhood is not easy. A broad survey of the words of the writers and vestry attendees treated in this study confirms that poor writers infused their approaches to parish officers with individual personality. We have encountered the arrogant and swaggering, the respectful and submissive, the determined, the colourful, and everything in between. Most letters in the corpus had both a material and emotional purpose; they were written by people who had migrated and who had thus lost the continuity of story and self-identity that (theoretically) went with stable residence. For this reason, writers went to great lengths to make themselves known and knowable, elaborating where they could a shared history, or what David Gerber calls a "plot line."[15] These observations suggest that the dependent and potentially dependent poor had indeed participated in the reinvention of selfhood. Yet there are also counter-indications and numerous underlying ambiguities of evidence. Thus we have seen that within the limits of the tolerance of fiction, some writers and vestry attendees had to create an acceptable, not simply knowable, persona and history, a clear nod to older eighteenth-century mechanisms for constructing identity. And although many letters drip with the emotion, anger, pain, and shame that might suggest their writers were fully aware of new models for thinking of the self, they were also constrained by firm structures of epistolary ethics.[16] Some letters focused on the individuality of a case or experience and on the uniqueness of the author, a clear hint that their writers were drawing on interior resources. And they were all centrally concerned with exercising, evidencing, and executing the personal and individual agency that we might associate with new nineteenth-century constructs of selfhood; the very act of writing and corresponding challenged the place of the writer in the socio-cultural order of the two parishes that it connected and was an assertion of the singularity of the case represented.[17] Nor should we forget that the letters of the poor were infused with silences, de facto evidence that their writers had taken control of the referential process. Máire Cross and Caroline Bland warn us that what "goes as unrecorded must not go unnoticed,"[18] and a careful reading between the lines in sequences of letters by or about the same person reveals striking evidence that poor writers and vestry attendees edited out their contentious selves by deliberately creating silences of the sort already outlined in chapter 4.[19] Nonetheless, some silences were unacceptable and might be exposed over a series of letters as the poor, officials, and subsequent historians endeavoured "to reassemble the scattered elements of [an] individual life and to regroup them in a comprehensive sketch."[20] In this sense, some of the written versions of selfhood and identity constructed from what Roy Porter labels "an unstable heap of impressions" might not be permissible or remain intelligible.[21] Even where they were allowed and could be comprehended, we have also seen persistent and substantial evidence that poor writers could not always retain their position as individual selves with individualised stories. Nor was it always desirable to do so. For the aged and other groups, sustained relief depended upon an ability to extend the rhetoric of deservingness by universalising the individual story to the wider and inevitable condition and position of all the poor of the same age or group.

The selfhood of the poor in the late eighteenth and early nineteenth centuries, in other words, is a particularly complex aspect of the redefinition of selfhood over the same period. The rest of this chapter thus focuses on how both the in- and out-parish poor constructed and owned their identity. Some sense of this emerges from previous chapters, and I consciously revisit and reread earlier material for this discussion. The rhetorics of honesty, character, struggle, and dignity were all elements central to the formation of a self and to its projection in public arenas. In this chapter, however, it is necessary to go further. I look first at the ways that poor writers and in-parish vestry attendees orchestrated their identity when threatened by imposed images that other parties in the epistolary world of the parish created or by those that emerged in wider commentary about the poor on the national stage. Second, and centrally, it is important to understand through an analysis of rhetorical variables such as belonging, sanguinity, shame and pain, and ordinariness how the poor in effect tried to create an identity and selfhood that focused on their indivisibility from the rest of the population. I will argue that poor writers aimed to give a sense, within and between their letters and engagements with the parish, that their interior worlds were just like those of people who had not (yet) applied for poor relief. Indeed, they were not so very different from those of the officials and advocates who formed the other nodes of the epistolary world of the parish. Nor were these worlds so very different from those of the ratepayers who funded the end results of the process of poor relief and who, as we saw in chapter 1, have been constructed as withdrawing their recognition of and support for the poor during the crisis period of poor law spending between the 1790s and 1830s.[22] Particular characterisations of self were not patterned onto the nature and scale of the "ask" for either the in- or out-parish poor precisely because the poor and their advocates assumed that a universal selfhood spoke for itself. Finally, the chapter turns to the question of how the process of poor relief and the nature and reach of structures of inclusion and exclusion were fostered by an ability on the part of poor people to elaborate both an autonomous and representative self.

## IMPOSED IDENTITIES[23]

As suggested by the experiences of the unnamed father from Clewer outlined above, *both* the in- and out-parish poor were peculiarly susceptible to rumour and impression. Their relationships with parishes and their officers involved vigilance on both sides.[24] Letters had public afterlives that the writer could not control, and parochial responses were also public responses that could generate controversy. It was thus important for poor writers, vestry attendees, and those approaching overseers in person to avoid the unwitting and unwanted imposition of particular identities by others and the generalised images of the poor as a group emerging out of some national commentary.[25] In particular, the poor were keen to correct the record when an inspection, accusatory letter, or rumour cast them as liars, scroungers, or people of ill-repute. Negative identities were hard to change once they gained traction, enmeshing individuals within the moral and administrative structures and languages of relief and fundamentally curtailing the potential for agency.[26] John Gibson of Great Baddow in Essex recognised this much in his renewing letter of 18 June 1828, when he sought assistance not for himself but for his children. Noting (and repeating) that he had not approached his parish for fully three years, he ended with the assertion that "i hope Jentelmen it Will Be 3 years More Be fore i Shall ask you for Eany thing More i Will Not in Less I an forst."[27] More widely, five types of negative identity can be discerned in the corpus. Individuals might be variously labelled and thus imagined as bad managers, particularly of parish resources; bad mothers and fathers or brothers and sisters; unreliable witnesses to their own stories and those of others, or at least conveyors of testimony that transcended the boundaries of accepted fiction; bad characters; and persons showing disregard for the parish or its officers. Over a one year period, the letter book for Lancaster in Lancashire, for instance, constructed John Becket as "but a loose character"; John Cole as a spendthrift, and "we dare not trust him with Money"; Mary Pennington as "not a character that deserves encouragement"; and Thomas Little as "both idle and saucy."[28] In turn, we might regard the ability to confront and contest these third-party characterisations in order to control one's own image and its projection as a major yardstick for discerning a poor self.

Against this backdrop, established and putative claimants went to considerable lengths, sometimes in a single letter but more often through a series of correspondence, to refute or chip away at the foundations of the character thus painted. Thomas Ifold, clearly seeking to overturn a sense of him as workshy, wrote from Herne in Kent on 18 May 1810 to say that he had been turned out by his latest master but that "I have Got a job now but being out of work some Time that I am very much Distress and Not being able to do as a nother man can My Wages are very low and I should be very Thinkfull if you Could ave the goodness to send me a trifel to my [r]elief." Ifold, then, sought to establish himself as inventive in the face of adversity given that he had found a new job, beset with accumulated misfortune since he had been out of work for some time, and in some way impaired through no fault of his own and thus unable to work like other men.[29] James Smith, starting his series of narratives in the middle of a story, wrote from Woolwich in Kent on 5 September 1831 to tell the overseer that he had "*at last*" got "A good Situation in Canterbury." The implication that he had a "history" with his settlement parish of Aveley in Essex and that it was not a good one is unmistakeable. Now, in this letter and several other later examples, he sought to rehabilitate his image by noting variously that he hoped to take his family "off the parish," that he would approach the parish only if sickness prevailed, that several of his children had died, and that he had done and would do everything he could as a man and father to support his dependants.[30]

Writers like Smith used the rhetorics of character, contribution, and struggle to contradict what they feared or knew were ingrained negative images of them. In other cases, appropriating the words, personae, and implicit support of others was important. The majority of letter series relating to a single person contain interspersing letters from different sorts of advocate, as we have seen.[31] Even more voluminous were attestations of, or insertions to, letters written by the poor themselves – and their equivalent in the form of reported inspections for the in-parish poor – that originated with advocates or interested parties such as doctors, churchmen, landlords, creditors, and employers. Some of this testimony was clearly anticipatory, as for instance where those capable of at least some work but now incapacitated through unemployment, underemployment, or sickness sought and gained the words of employers. Such attestations generally constructed the claimants as good, honest hard workers who would find employment again once the current situation had passed. Thus Thomas Venerd had in January 1804 been unable to work for six months and had four small children and a wife to support. His former employer Samuel Croggon constructed him as a "very good workman and none more willing to work than he is when able, we have found him strictly honest."[32]

Other testimony of this sort was rather more corrective in nature, clearly enlisted to offset an articulated negative perception of the poor person concerned in either the host or settlement parish.[33] Thus Hannah Billingshurst, the mother of an illegitimate child named Alfred, enlisted the voice of Arthur Onslow, the rector of Merrow in Surrey, in response to a rumour that she had continued to claim allowance for the boy after his decamping to a relative elsewhere. Certifying that the child was still resident, Onslow noted that Billinghurst hoped her parish would "continue the allowance as heretofore without compelling her to appear with the child at the committee, which would occasion her a great deal of expence & inconvenience."[34] In similar fashion, the overseer of Egham in Surrey wrote a testamentary letter on behalf of (aptly named) Widow Wants on 10 March 1819. Noting that she had managed to pull herself back from the brink of ruin, Michael Duck observed that "the Woman tryes hard to live but if she is ill and cannot Earn aney thing all stands still but the 5 small Children Must be fed. <u>I do Recommend her this time as a deserving object of Charity.</u>"[35]

These colourful examples are important. They speak to the widening reach of networks of information, confirm the essential contestability of poor law "knowledge" and decisions, and show forcefully that correspondence was about attracting attention and sending signals as much as it was about gaining relief. Moreover, although we need to move away from crude notions of the success or failure of letters, it is striking how often poor writers and vestry attendees did manage to shift or roll back negative images of themselves, a process that suggests both the powerful traction of poor selfhood and the fluidity of acceptable identity. But the poor did not *just* create reactive selves. Rather, their stories and the histories they embodied were also carefully remembered, augmented, preserved, and told in a way that points to a much more positive, consistent, and conscious process of creating the self. The remainder of the chapter considers this process.[36]

## BELONGING

Our understanding of the poor as people who were not physically and conceptually marginalised but who instead belonged, often in *both* host and settlement communities, is indebted to the work of Keith Snell.[37] Belonging was multilayered and fluid, it could be negotiated, and it lasted for much longer in the popular memory than we could ever have thought. In this context, the poor, even the migrant poor, were not automatically seen as outsiders, nor were they inevitably pushed to the social, cultural, physical, and conceptual margins of the communities in which they resided. Indeed, the core lesson of table 1.1 is that such marginalisation of "others" must have been extremely problematic given the deep currents of migratory experience to be found in most communities and the difficulties inherent in proving someone's nominal identity before the twentieth century.[38] It is unsurprising, then, that we have seen evidence throughout this study and across the spatial, chronological, and typological dimensions of the corpus that the in- *and* out-parish poor had a keen sense of their legal belonging and kept or gave their stories to evidence it.[39] The overseer of Oundle in Northampton-shire, for instance, retained a copy of his letter to an unnamed counter-part in Orton Conquest in Bedfordshire dated 19 January 1834. Asking how he should act in the case of the sick pauper John Slater, the Oundle overseer noted,

> He [i.e., Slater] informs me his father lived in your Parish and that he never gained any other settlement by hiring or service that last winter he was relieved by Mr Martin George the overseer twice and the year before by the overseer of the time that he is known to the Reverend William Barker the clergyman and that his brother is Lord Bedford's keeper.[40]

This sort of detailed rendering, involving story, history, and current indi-cators of belonging – for instance, his having recently been relieved by a previous overseer and thus been recognised – is duplicated in thou-sands of other cases made by advocates, poor writers, or the settled poor engaging directly with vestries and overseers. Although the rhetoric of settlement and belonging appears unrelated in form or depth to the nature of the "ask," it was particularly important for those whose set-tlements were either derived – as for instance with married women and bastard children – or chronologically distant and thus outside of recent memory. John Nurse's undated letter from Thorney in Cambridgeshire to Oundle occasioned correspondence between officials in both parishes, with the Oundle official noting that Nurse "is entirely unknown to me but *no doubt* some person at the vestry will know something of him."[41] Authorising Thorney to provide interim relief, he returned to the theme in a letter of 27 July 1833 when he said that "no one there [at the vestry] knowing anything of him I am desired by the Vestry to inform you that they do not consider him to belong to us and I was therefore desired to write to you to request you do not give him one farthing more on Acct of this parish ... as *at present* we know nothing of him."[42] The sense that belonging was mutable, provable, and claimable is given form by the words "at present," and in this case Nurse was indeed able to elab-orate upon his story. Other writers sought to establish a deep legal history of belonging in their instigatory and other letters, as for instance did John Salisbury, writing from Preston on 27 April 1824. Telling the overseer that "you need not dispute me," he entered into a six-line rendering of his time since he had left his father's parish.[43]

Yet, although poor writers like Salisbury did concentrate on legal forms of belonging – particularly in extremis and thus in ending or extending letters or in desperate notes – most of those who wrote for themselves, wrote for the poor, or argued their case in person sought to create a softer sense of self, one anchored in place and place-based community identity and visibility. Aside from the threat or willingness to "come home" that we find in almost all letters, the poor employed in sequence or parallel a complex variety of rhetorical devices, many of them familiar from earlier chapters but rethought here. For those outside their parish, particularly when they had been absent for a time, it was normal to try to construct or evidence belonging to a host community. Thus writers talked about their ability to get credit and work in host communities. In such places, they were "known," and writers consistently pointed out the hidden costs of repatriating them to settlement communities given that being known was in these two senses an economic resource. Such claims might be regarded as rhetorical flourishes and as adjuncts of attempts to create a wider sense that the writer aspired to be independent, but we have enough testimony from epistolary advocates, many of whom referred to the utility of being known in a place, to be convinced that the rhetorical claims were in fact based on reality. In turn, the most sophisticated letters were those that talked about having belonged to a locale in terms of access to work and credit but, through exogenous circumstance, having lost this status. Here, support with a trifle or a small allowance could lead to a restoration of belonging and a rebuilding of the writer's self.

Other signals of belonging to host parishes were also important. Advocates and officials echoed the words of the poor themselves in evidencing small acts of charity of the sort that one might advance to someone who belonged: the giving of temporary relief by the overseer of a host parish when there was no legal reason to do so, support from neighbours and friends that had kept individuals from dependence for longer than might otherwise have been the case, or the act of advocating itself.[44] Both the poor and (less often) their advocates also deployed other subtle rhetorics and examples of belonging to a community: attendance at church or the inability to do so because of poverty and a lack of clothing, belonging to a friendly society, and petty work opportunities. Thus, although the striking lack of removal activity under the settlement laws in most places and at most times has conventionally been explained in terms of legal complexity, cost, and the time limitations of officials, an alternative reading might identify the ability of the absent poor to project a self with belonging at its core as an alternative constraint on parochial action. Certainly, the construction of belonging to a host community is done in this corpus with more confidence, certainty, and hope than are allowed by the assertion of Sydney Webb and Beatrice Webb that the average poor labourer was "harassed by the uncertainty and intimidated by the risk" of removal.[45]

For the out-parish poor, a second (and simultaneous) rhetoric and sense of belonging, derived from their roots in the settlement parish, was also important. As we saw in chapter 1, parishes had an obligation to receive the claims of those who had a provable settlement, but there was no obligation to meet such claims. Simply establishing a legal settlement was not, in the majority of cases, enough. The absent poor thus referenced continued contacts in their settlement communities whenever they could, claiming association, kinship, or connection to remaining family, parish officers, former neighbours and employers, former landlords or (for apprentices) masters, and friends. They sought to be remembered.[46] As a rhetorical model, this might take the form of John Terry's letter from Horsham in Sussex on 28 May 1810, which suggested that "Mr Wood knowd" both his father and family.[47] Many writers, however, sought to reinforce such rhetorical vehicles by asking officials to actively extend their greetings and news to the people named, as did James Best, writing to Arundel in Sussex to say that his boy remained sick and to request that the overseer "Remember me to my mother and tell her We are all Well Except the Boy."[48] This active engagement of officials or other parish co-respondents did not happen by accident but reflected a determined attempt to keep a currency of presence in the settlement parish and to construct a self that both belonged to and remained concerned about the people inside that parish. We should remember, in turn, that the language of settlement and belonging was also part of the case made by the in-parish poor, notwithstanding that they could be inspected and that there was current community knowledge of them. This situation was particularly true in larger or dispersed parishes, where the extent of the knowledge possessed by officers, who changed annually or regularly, was likely to be very much confined.

Two other vehicles for belonging are also notable. Some 15 per cent of letters – and almost all letter series about a single individual – record physical visits to the settlement parish by the writer or a close relative. Although often related to the continuity of relief or to the renewing of allowances, such physical visits also emphasised a sense of the rootedness of the individual in a distinct place-based history. In the sense that physically returning to a place involved sacrifices – of time, income, travel costs, and so on – it was in itself a powerful indicator that individuals had respect for the parish and its efforts on their behalf. Unsurprisingly, those who could not attend settlement parishes with any regularity, or who simply could not afford to make these sacrifices, often went to great lengths to explain why. The in-parish poor who could not attend vestries because of illness or cost used exactly the same rhetorical infrastructure. And the fact that epistolary advocates also offered such explanation points to a shared sense that physical contact with a home parish helped to define both deservingness and the perceived identity of the writer. In the absence of such visits, and sometimes in support of them, as we have seen in earlier chapters, people wrote letters that were clearly *meant* to be circulated. Just like letters home from emigrants, these narratives were meant to maintain connections, and their circulation or multiple circulations spoke of duty to family and parish as well as concern and consideration on the part of someone who might otherwise simply be constructed as a drain on ratepayer resources. Ann Emery, for instance, in an undated letter from Hillen in Somerset, wrote that "i wish you [i.e., her co-respondent Mr Woolger] whould give this letter to whoever it is to know about it" because she was desperate for relief and was concerned that people would "laugh at me and make game of me."[49]

As we saw in chapter 3, such letters increasingly arrived by post, but for much of the eighteenth and early nineteenth centuries, and in a strong core of cases thereafter, they were also carried by people. At the most impersonal level, they might arrive by the carrier or tradesman who conducted parish business. In other cases, however, letters circulated with people who were known by or related to the individual writer: children who moved between related families, often with support from the poor law; brothers and sisters visiting relatives; nephews, nieces, and grandchildren becoming apprentices to distant family members; and wives or husbands returning home to visit relatives. This connectivity of both the letter and the person offered powerful evidence of continued belonging and underpinned a construction of poor claimants in which their history and their present intermelded to create an identity outside of the dependence that might be the lot of the poor for only the smallest part of their life. Through a complex rhetoric of belonging and knowability, we come to understand these writers as people with a history that had transcended and would transcend relief. For similar reasons, in-parish claimants seem to have felt themselves obligated to explain notable recent absences from the parish where these were public knowledge.

To belong to a place (or more than one place) can identify someone as having not only a story but also a history and a present. Belonging speaks to rootedness, to being respected by and having respect for others, and to a latent responsibility for individuals on the part of those with power. In a situation where the dependent poor were, even by the 1830s, likely to spend almost all of their lives outside the ambit of the poor law, belonging and its history created socio-cultural, not just economic, capital. Claims to belonging, then, were *not* mere words and rhetoric, whether expressed by out-parish claimants in their letters or by in-parish attendees of the vestry. Rather, the feelings and structures that were embodied by elaborations of belonging signified a shared sense of the poor self as someone who, although officially without right, demanded consideration by dint of having a story and a history. These stories and histories simultaneously nourished and replenished the rhetoric that underpinned agency and the negotiated process of poor relief. Their writers felt that history mattered, and we see this even more keenly played out when that history was flattering, a matter to which I now turn.

## SANGUINITY IN THE FACE OF SUFFERING

In chapter 8 we saw that suffering because of exogenous circumstance and the response to it was a key rhetorical marker of character for both the in- and out-parish poor. Sanguinity in the face of that suffering,[50] however, denotes a step from character to selfhood in which interiorised emotions like despair, depression, and hopelessness are juxtaposed against rational belief – most sickness could not be cured, for instance – and against the irrational "hope" associated with the fact that the decisions of parish officers could either reduce suffering or accelerate the trajectory of decline.[51] Of course, poor writers and their in-parish equivalents never used the word "sanguine" in reflecting upon their response to suffering. Nor did they reserve the meaning for particular types of claim. But they had many placeholders for the sentiment and experience. Mary Hughes of Torrington in Devon had "quite impoverish'd" herself "by so many years keeping her Father and Mother from the Parish to near one hundred" years old.[52] Susannah Halls of Ipswich in Suffolk pointed to the fact that she had got herself into debt and required relief but said that since she was eighty-eight years of age, "I Shall not Trouble you much longer." As an indicator of her essential sanguinity in the face of such suffering, she reminded the overseer that "Gods will be done I Must wate my apointed time let It be Long or Short."[53]

Those seeking to extend allowances or to convert irregular payments to regular pensions were particularly likely to employ a rhetorical sense that the trials of age or infirmity and sickness were severe and just had to be contended with prior to inevitable and terminal decline. Widow Jacobs wrote from Crieff in Perthshire, Scotland, on 19 March 1825 to "Certify that we [her and a daughter] are both alive at present but I am in a Bad state of health with a Gasping and want of breath all last winter and has little apearance of getting better as yet and I hope you will not neglect to send my allowanse as soon as this comes to hand."[54] She renewed her correspondence a year later, on 25 March 1826, noting in the most sanguine of ways that "these few lines" would certify that "I am still in life and my Daughter Jamima, but as for myself I am very poorly and Extreamly ill of Dercline and Jamima has been this last half years very poorly Too." The veracity of both letters was testified by the appended signatures of two "Elders" of this remote Scottish village.[55]

It is possible, of course, that sanguinity may have been a rhetorical invention designed to speak to the expectations of the recipients of letters. Indeed, such a sentiment had deep roots in the petitioning culture of earlier periods when those approaching charities, magistrates, or courts were expected to emphasise their powerlessness.[56] This perspective must be balanced by cases such as that of Margaret Nelson, writing on 15 May 1830 "at the Advanced Age of 84 or 5," who was "as may be Expected unable to Rise out of Bed or do the least Thing" for herself. It would be reasonable, she reminded the overseer, to do something for someone who suffered the inevitable consequences of aging and who had for many years been a person of independence.[57] Moreover, sanguinity as an emotional and practical response to suffering was not confined to the out-parish poor. Those who attended vestries also constructed themselves as sanguine, even though they could easily be inspected and rhetorical figments exploded by local officials. Thus Elizabeth Frey applied to the vestry of Halliwell in Lancashire on 26 June 1790 through the intermediaries Lawrence Fletcher and John Haslam. Her children "were very near naked," and Frey had suffered previously because her husband "had formerly been a drunken fellow but was now reformed, for which reason and to prevent them being sold up," the vestry granted help with rent. Suffering, sanguinity, and reform, then, went hand in hand, and reform and the return to a stable family life were combined in a journey of selfhood.[58] The in- and out-parish poor reminded those in power that they and their histories were comprised of more than the relief they received or requested.

Nor perhaps should we forget that sanguinity was a referential yardstick for the construction of the pauper self by others. Advocates of all stripes and in all periods did not confine themselves to factual statements, as we have consistently seen in earlier chapters. Rather, they evidenced individual and familial suffering. Thomas Darwen, the overseer of Lancaster, is a typical example. Writing to the master of the Leeds workhouse on 12 May 1817, he commented on the suffering, sanguinity, and honesty of Mary Talor, to whom he "would willingly have granted more than three shillings per week if we could have afforded it, for my part I know not how the year will be got over."[59] More than providing this context, however, advocates pointed (approvingly) to poor people who had variously suffered in silence, coped admirably until the current crisis, faced their fate with resignation, embraced God's will, or been philosophically accepting of loss, decline, and pain. Thus William Pearce wrote from Newbury in Berkshire to Marlborough in Wiltshire on 21 September 1830 to say that Stephen Brown was very ill and had been for some time. He noted approvingly that Brown and his wife "have done as long as they could." Pearce "need not recommend them to you" given that the severe illness and the way it had been borne should lead Marlborough to treat them in the same was as "our own Parishoners in the same circumstances."[60] There is less evidence of the way that suffering was constructed by third parties for the in-parish poor, largely because of the constrained and structured reporting formats required in parochial accounts. Even in this context, however, vestrymen or their agents sent to explore and confirm the conditions of poor applicants to the vestry occasionally did more than report facts. George Lacey's report of 20 June 1832 on paupers in Hull, for instance, contained embellishments on individual people and families, such as "a very bad state of health and I think quite unable to work," "very put hard to it for bread for his family," "a very pitiable state," and "I think she should be look'd after."[61] These were all positive statements that both confirmed the poor were telling the truth in their accounts to the vestry and drew attention to the sanguinity of those who were just about making do on parish allowances despite terrible circumstances.

Third-party rhetorics of suffering and sanguinity are important. They acted as confirmation of the honesty of the poor, could be used as a rhetorical tool in further correspondence, and went some way to establishing or re-establishing the characters of poor writers and claimants. Yet, in the sense that such rhetoric embodied, drew upon, and embellished stories told by the writer, they also fulfilled a rather deeper purpose. As William Reddy argues, the speaking of a story – and in this study also its writing, given that writing was broadly oral – can crystallise and bring out the story's lived emotional content.[62] The letters of doctors on behalf of sick poor who might or might not be their patients are a good example. Some of these letters consisted of the mere reporting of facts, whereas others contained opinion, embellishment, and the telling of wider stories seen first-hand or gleaned from the sick person. In both cases, the letters of medical men – which, we should remember, were also sent on behalf of the in-parish poor – had a powerful hold on parochial officers. They located the stories that might be told by the poor themselves as broadly true, such that their sourcing by claimants constitutes an important element of agency. Yet they also filled another function. When such letters melded together the stories of the poor and the medical opinion of doctors to create a rhetorical situation where there was little hope of life or where there was little chance of a return to anything like full health, these letters could be and were used by poor writers and vestry attendees themselves to construct a self as defined by the prospect of impending death or the life of a chronic invalid.

Similarly, when employers wrote on behalf of sick and injured younger employees or on behalf of aged people for whom they no longer had use, their letters served in part to locate and fix the emotional state of these individuals and their status as claimants who could no longer follow a learned or customary trade or who had become beyond work. In the society of the eighteenth and early nineteenth centuries, where work was both the core part of the makeshift economy and an anchor for the colour and flavour of selfhood, the inability to labour had a profound emotional cost that was fixed clearly in advocate letters. For both the in- and out parish poor and irrespective of the "ask," being workless and constructed as workless in the eyes of others meant a rewriting of one's place in society as one moved from an active to a passive and dependent persona. Thus James Sykes in a series of letters to Tilehurst in Berkshire persistently dwelt on his worklessness, partly as a rhetorical tool but also with real feeling. His renewing letter of 17 March 1830, for instance, apologised for his worklessness and said that he was "very sorry it is not in my power to send you any better news." He assured the parish that to be without work was "sorely against my will" and also inconsistent with his history. Other letters continued the theme even when the time that had elapsed since the last correspondence was slim, such that Sykes might have expected officials to remember his apologies. On 21 April 1830, for instance, he expressed his "deepest sense of regret" at a continuing lack of work and said that he would "trust in god I shall be able to attend my daily occupation" as soon as possible. For Sykes and his in-parish counterparts, worklessness was not simply rhetoric but also reached to the heart of his everyday, or "daily," identity.[63]

## SHAME AND PAIN

The opposite side of sanguinity was, of course, feelings and elaborations of pain and shame. Alannah Tomkins has argued persuasively that male and female claimants were increasingly capable of rhetoricising a sense of melancholy when faced with declining health and compromised gender and societal roles.[64] Moreover, welfare historians have come to understand that the so-called "shame-faced" poor – those falling down the social scale into dependence upon charity or (worse) poor relief – were not confined to the Scandinavian countries where the term was originally coined.[64] In this broad context, poor writers *and* vestry attendees frequently elaborated upon their shame and sometimes pain. Thomas Lomax, for instance, wrote a renewing letter to Middleton in Lancashire on 18 April 1822 to tell the overseer that "my misfortune is a daily source of grief."[65] It is easy, as chapter 7 noted, to see this statement as an instance of artfully constructed rhetoric that fitted the conventions of writing, on the one hand, and the expectations of the official recipients, on the other. Yet some of the in- and out-parish poor in our corpus went further, linking the emotional turmoil of shame and pain to a compromised sense of self. Thus, when John Stafford wrote from Macclesfield in Cheshire on 8 January 1829, he did so with "painful anxiety." He and his family were shoeless, workless, creditless, and hopeless – as the parish well knew, he asserted, from previous letters. Stafford was "reduced to the lowest extremity." If assisted, he would "maintain my ground if horrible in this town."[66] We can never be sure in such examples whether words became fixed onto *real* emotions or whether they were a shared fiction of the sort that we saw earlier in the study. Occasionally, however, the corpus contains material that speaks to how a new (and usually unexpected) emotional balance could lead to a restored sense of selfhood. Thus Bathsheba Bennett wrote on behalf of her mother to West Grinstead in Sussex on an unknown date (but probably in the early 1800s) to say that the mother was

> very much oblig'd to the gentlemen of Westgrinsted for the Money she has received from them for her relief wich She returns them maney thinks for and I have now to Inform you that by the melancholy Death of her Brother who has left her enough to live on during her life with out troubling the gentlemen for any further assistance wich is a great Comfort to her in her old age.

To simultaneously emphasise her mother's return to respectability and reinforce a sense of belonging to West Grinstead, the daughter asked that "if it is not taken to great a liberty and giving you to much trouble my Mother will think you to make our kind respects to Mr Wickerson that is Mrs. Woodwards Cook."[67] A restored sense of self, then, enabled an old woman to hold up her head in public – and in the context of public knowledge of her – and emphasised that the dependent self characterised but a moment in her history.

Relatively few writers or vestry applicants had the rhetorical confidence of Bathsheba Bennett. Rather, in the letter series and texts associated with extended individual contact with vestries, we often see a much more gradual and layered accretion of indicators of shame, loss, and pain. The very elaboration of these feelings slowly but surely influenced the emotional state of the writer and – usually at the end of a series of correspondence – created a self rather different from the one who had made the initial claims. Advocate letters provide a particularly compelling rendering of this situation. That from William Roberts on the subject of James Tregoning ended a series in which gradual decay was the watchword. We first encountered Roberts in chapter 9 when Tregoning's wage at the mine had been cut, prices were high, and his co-resident daughter was underemployed. Roberts argued,

> were you to go into his house & see the picture that presents itself, you would say he had a poor advocate in me, – I can feel for his Distress, but I cannot paint it out, – In fact the poor Old Mans face tells you he wants, – This is [to] desire you will speak to the Gentl[n] of your parish for him to have a little relief, – I know the Parishes are particularly burthened – but very very many that are receiving relief from the parishes are not in so much need of it as this poor Old Man [I've] known the Old Man very many years – & from the spirit he possesses – I'm sure he would not have given occasion to my writing this, if he had not in very [illegible] wanted.[69]

Read as a whole rather than perceived through the parts used for chapter 9, this letter signals a proud and independent man who had been driven to the very verge of despair. His sense of self, even his voice in this case, had been gradually whittled away. Of course, this was a powerful rhetorical vision calculated to put maximum pressure on the settlement parish and to justify the continued attention and resources of the parish officers. But this broad patterning of experience leading to compromised identity and self-identity is duplicated too often in the corpus and in advocate representations made directly to vestries for this to be mere rhetoric. When, in effect, Roberts asked the overseers to feel for and with Tregoning, he constructed and captured a sense of the universal emotional canvas.

Others expressed it even more forcefully, as for instance did Mary Dewhurst, who wrote from Blackburn in Lancashire because "I am in great distress having no bed to lie on but obliged to lie on the bare ground this gentlemen is a bad case." Asking the overseer of Billington in Lancashire for help with debts and new tools, she expressed her shame at the application – "I do not like coming to crave your assistance" – but in this "heart rending case" she had no choice. Dewhurst ended with an appeal to the universal condition:

Do Gentlemen let humanity have a place in your hearts consider if you were placed in similar circumstances reason this way and let things come home to your hearts how unpleasant it would appear to you and no person is certain but it may be his case if he has riches – riches sometimes make themselves wings and fly away.[70]

Shame, then, was tempered by a sense that the parish would judge her and her situation soundly, with reference to her very humanity, and in light of a self that was never meant to be dependent. Here, then, was a reflective, individual self, able to assert her place in the world and within a network of parochial power to which the casual observer of end-of-process overseers' accounts might simply have assumed her to be subject.

### BEING ORDINARY

When Mary Dewhurst asked the officials to imagine sharing her circumstances, she was constructing her condition and situation as universal. She was also constructing herself as essentially ordinary, or in some way "normal." In turn, this ordinariness is a powerful theme. It runs across the claims of the in- and out-parish poor, is present in all of my sources, and is not tied to any particular type or size of claim. Disability in life and inability in old age were such common variables that the dependent poor citing and living these conditions were different only by a small degree from those who remained independent. Sickness could befall anyone, and its effects on the family economy would be devastating no matter where one initially stood on the social ladder. Widow Lake noted this when she was forced to make application for relief because sickness meant she could not pay her rent as she had done for sixteen straight years. Not "being able to pay as formerly [she] grieves and frets herself at the thought of breaking up her house."[71] Even for the healthy, exogenous factors such as unemployment could, as we saw in chapter 4, rapidly evaporate the resources of the most prudent family. John Hammond of Leeds moved fluidly between sickness and unemployment (and sometimes both) as a cause for writing to his settlement parish of West

Tanfield in North Yorkshire in a series of undated letters. Falling behind with his rent, having to sell his bed and clothes, and struggling on the very edge of honesty, Hammond claimed in one letter that "I ham willing to work for my family if I can get plenty of work but I ham very slack and has been for this 3 weeks." Yet he also sought to generalise his position, reminding officials that "no man can fight against [missing word] and this will be 11 weeks that I have been laid up from work I had saved near 4 pounds and it is hall gon now." Hammond, then, was distinguished by his very ordinariness, by being no man and any man.[72] More widely, both the corpus and those sources that reflect on the experiences of the settled poor, such as vestry minutes, are littered with examples of ordinary people doing their best to cope with the unforeseen and sudden circumstance: a wife whose husband joined the militia; grandparents taking in bastard children; relatives adopting orphans; wives and husbands beset with recurrent illness, horrible accident, or mental disturbance; families assailed by greedy landlords; mothers and fathers mentally laid low by an inability to fulfil their roles; and old people aplenty struggling with unanticipated decline.

For these people, being ordinary was the core of a sense of self, and with it came a desire to fit closely into the different communities that defined and limited their everyday lives. But this was a sense of self that was fragile and susceptible to disruption and forced reinvention, which could be both traumatic and life-long. The further example of Anthony Harris, his wife, and their three children can help us to develop this sense. On 12 February 1812, Rotherfield Greys in Oxfordshire received a letter from John Mitchel, the vicar of Isleworth in Hertfordshire, concerning Harris. The rector outlined the activities of a man who had supported the family through diligent labour for many years but who "became deranged in his Intellect some months ago, & it is now no longer safe to himself & others." Having begun to wander off,

On Thursday morning he left his Home again, & has not since been heard of – His poor Wife is half distracted, & after walking yesterday 30 Miles, & making every Inquiry where there was a chance of any Intelligence, is very ill from Anxiety, Fatigue & Distress – It has occurred to her that he has probably gone down to his own Parish, & it is for the purpose of ascertaining whether you have seen or heard any thing of him that I am induced to trouble you with this Letter.[73]

On 2 March 1812, Mitchel wrote again, noting that Harris had been found and committed "to St Luke's [private] lunatic asylum by the good offices of his friend."[74] He was not to get better, despite the fact that "no human Means have been left unattempted to restore his Reason," and Harris died in the asylum on 31 May 1833.[75] In the meantime, a series of letters from the rector traced the decline of a formerly respectable and independent family into complete destitution because of the loss of a breadwinner and a proximate downturn in the local economy:

They have now no work; & you may know, by reference to your own Neighbourhood, that when so many men are out of employ, there is little chance of procuring any for women & children. The summer too, as you must well know, has been so bad for all agricultural Purposes, that the poor creature has not been able, as she has usually done, to lay by any of the summer's produce for the winter's use. The children are nearly naked, & she herself is reduced by hard labour & illness to great distress.[76]

Child sickness and disability compounded the familial problems. In this way, an ordinary family was laid low by quite extraordinary suffering not of their making. For John Mitchel, the universalising experiences of Anthony Harris demanded action. Indeed, recuperative action was the only logical stance in such a case.

Harris and his wife were essentially voiceless. We hear much more about them than from them. Other writers and vestry attendees were, as we saw in chapter 5, actually or strategically speechless or breathless. For most in- and out-parish claimants, however, having a voice despite their ordinariness and being able to exercise it through correspondence or

vestry appearances was as integral to their sense of self as it was for middling women deeply enmeshed in closed epistolary circles.[77] They could
thus construct and understand themselves as retaining a right to be heard
and to receive consideration, on the one hand, and to be involved in a relationship of co-respondence, on the other. Above all, a voice allowed
them to think of themselves as more than passive actors dependent upon
the will of others. The evidence for this understanding is substantial. Thus
Jane Broadbridge wrote from Hastings on 17 August 1834 to remind the
overseer of Broadwater in Sussex that her allowance was due:

> the Quarter Being up the Twentyfourth of July for Mee to Receive
> My Money and I have Not Received it & Wish To Now Weather
> you Intend To Send My Money or Not *A Cording to your agree-
> ment* as I have No Means of Matinenences for My self and The
> Child *your Agreement was* for Mee to have Two Shillings P Week
> For The Child and To Bee Payed To Mee Quartely.[78]

Broadbridge went on to note that she was incapable of maintaining her
bastard child without parochial support, recording for a third time the
agreement she believed that she had with the officer. She was one of 849
writers who referred to such agreements in their letters. Other writers
and vestry attendees asserted a powerful sense of natural justice, as for
instance did John Brooks, writing from Brighton in Sussex on 12 September 1825. Stating his intention to be brought home, he asserted that "To
suffer in the manner I have done since last Tuesday, sick in bed neither
[fire] or food several times – I am determin'd not to endure it any longer
~~unless the parish will grant some allowance~~ the poor house will be
preferable to my present condition."[79] The crossing-out of the remedy
in this letter – an allowance – and the potentially confrontational reference to the poorhouse can be read as a deliberate attempt to construct a
self, one drawn to the very edge of disintegration. Instances like these
point to the existence and exercise of agency and to a self-confident persona secure in the ability to engage with officials. To be ordinary was,
in other words, empowering.

## CONCLUSION

A late-eighteenth- and nineteenth-century explosion of life writing, which might be seen as tangentially including the letters of the poor writers in the corpus, testifies to and provides a mechanism for a changing sense of self. Middling and educated writers disentangled themselves from the traditional constraints and restraints on understanding and constructing their place in the world. They assembled the fragments of their lives and those of others, viewed them through the lens of interiorised reference models, and created histories that could feed into and nourish multiple autonomous personae.[80] Neither the in- or out-parish poor were immune from this process of self-accounting and self-construction. Rather, like early modern women writers, by the early nineteenth century at least they had come to devise and determine "the versions of themselves that they might bring to life on the written page."[81] But this was a complicated selfhood and associated identity. Whereas autobiographies and other life writing, at least in the early nineteenth century, drew on a sense that the individual was extraordinary and that one's life was thus worth recounting, the poor writers and vestry attendees in the corpus actively and powerfully constructed themselves and their situations as ordinary. This rhetoric did not constitute "an erasing of the self into ordinariness"[82] but rather indicated that "the identity of one [poor person was] intermingled with or even superimposed upon the identity of others" in a conscious process of elaboration that "becomes a critical means of understanding the self."[83] The resulting narratives share with other life writing and ego documents a suite of veiling techniques, a structure of performance meant to help project a version of self to a distant public forum, partial representations, and silences. Yet the striking thing about the writing of the poor (and the recording of their voices in vestry minutes) is the frequency with which we get the unvarnished story or at least most of it. These stories were, as I have observed, fictive and confected. But they were not fictional or invented, and they always embodied the writer's or vestry attendee's sense of a self that was not by nature a claimant. The resulting poor selves are complex and dynamic, not least because the letters or vestry appearances from which we can read such selves embodied acts of self-preservation and self-construction as well as self-representation.[84]

Here, however, were men and women who suffered under the twists and turns of cruel fate and exogenous influences, who belonged, who were respectful of their parishes, and who had dignity, pride, and shame. Despite their apparently fragile place in the relief process, they had agency, and believed that they had it, and they shared with officials an understanding of the proper place of the poor in the world. We cannot definitively assume that this vision of selfhood was "new" by the early 1800s, as opposed to a reflection of the emergence of new sources at this time, but the act of writing is itself a function and embodiment of selfhood, and it seems inherently unlikely that the poor were excluded from the refiguring of the language and mechanism of self as experienced by the middling sorts in this period. Writers were not always honest, and over a series of letters or vestry appearances by or about the same person, their identity and sense of selfhood shifted. Like gypsies, immigrants, and other marginal groups, however, these multiple selves, played out as they were in a poor relief system in which discretion was heavily fettered for all of the reasons we saw in previous chapters, can be read as a weapon of the weak.[85]

These multiple selves were not simply constructs to be patterned onto perceived models of deservingness. We have seen that some writers and vestry attendees were angry, that others were supplicatory, and that many were annoyingly persistent. Where we can construct their histories through a series of correspondence or appearances, then, it becomes clear that the poor deployed numerous interlocking, complementary, and sometimes conflicting versions of self across their engagements with parochial officials. They were variously deserving and (sometimes) supplicatory, they were striving to return to a past history of proud independence, they were fathers and mothers unable to fill their roles, they were people with natural rights to have their dignity protected, they were members of a community or multiple communities, and they were sullen, sanguine, bitter, ordinary, extraordinary, accepting, and despairing. Poor writers, advocates, and vestry attendees did not confect these yardsticks of self based on the nature and scale of the "ask," the distance over which they wrote, or the length of time that they had either lived or been away from the parish. Rather, the selves they created were simultaneously tailored and universal. The lack of patterning is itself a signal of the existence and development of an ingrained selfhood.

In turn, this selfhood met with a willing reception on the other side of the parochial relief process. Poor writers and vestry attendees largely avoided the imposition of negative identities in and by the epistolary world of the parish. Indeed, there is little evidence of a desire to make, or at least maintain, such impositions or to classify and demand permissible and acceptable selves. As I have observed throughout this study, the unworthy got poor relief even when parishes understood writers and vestry attendees as essentially dishonest and despite the notional power of officials to sweep away groups with dubious reputations. In this sense, the claim of some commentators that the poor were being conceived in national debates and literature as a number, problem, or "lump," and were thus losing their legitimacy, is only one version of reality.[86] In (real) practice, the process of poor relief was contested by people who, in the construction of their ordinariness, claimed unprecedented agency even at a time when the poor law is seen to have moved into crisis mode.

# 13

## *Process and Agency Reconsidered*

In this study, I have pulled apart the letters of poor writers to analyse how they claimed and maintained entitlement in the spaces of negotiation that a discretionary Old Poor Law afforded. Putting them back together again is instructive. We have seen that rhetoric and strategy might be situational and differ according to life-cycle stage, gender, or age. There was even a seasonal element to the way that letters were framed. Correspondence was inflected with regional dialect, but there was little difference in the way that the poor and their advocates used and constellated rhetoric according to region, distance from the settlement parish, or the nature and scale of the claim made. Requests for the tiniest additions to a pension or for a "trifle" could occasion more complex and sustained rhetorics of dignity, deservingness, and suffering than claims for large lump sums to pay debts or meet doctoring bills. What is true for letter writers was also true for the settled and proximate poor appearing before the vestry or at the home or office of the overseer. Although their words are mediated and summarised in minutes, some of the material used in this study has suggested that those who could be seen and might engage with officials on a daily basis used the same linguistic registers and rhetorical ecologies as those who were out of their settlement community when they fell into need.

My study has focused particularly on these rhetorical and strategic regularities in the claims making of the poor. These regularities often appeared, and were meant to appear, across a series of letters by or about the same person, but the corpus also contains examples of writers combining the whole canvas of such regularities in a single narrative. Richard Reed, writing an extending letter from Kidderminster in Worcestershire to Tetbury in Gloucestershire on an unspecified date (but around 1804), is a good but not unrepresentative example. He wanted to take

> the Opportunity of Informing you of my present situation Acording to your Requets I have the promise of Employment providing I can Get some money to Satisfie the man at the shop & a Trifle To start with myself For I Can well Asure you sir that I ham in A Distressing Circumstance at thiss time & As Sir my wife it is not in her power to Do anything for me it is as much As her can do to maintain herself Depend upon it Sir If you stand my friend thiss one time I Trust with the help of God it will Be the Last time I Shal Trouble you It as been my Study this Long time To Lighten the Burden of A paresh [damage to document] you know your self perfectly well I have Dome my Utmost Endeavour & this present period my Case Requires a Speedy Assistance for I ham in A lingering Situation Neither Living nor Dieing Dear Sir I have To Inform you the mens Request is twenty Shillings I thought it would Be more if that favour Can Be Granted with A Trifle for me to start with you will most Sincerely Oblige your humble Servant Richard Reed.[1]

Making an implicit assumption that relief would be forthcoming, Reed added a directional postscript: "Bfor The Conveyance of the favour I shall entirely Leave it to your own Judgment you will Be So Kind as To Deirrect for me at Henry Bells Bromsgrove Street Kidderminster."[2] Reed, like so many of the poor writers who have peopled these pages, was suffering acute distress in both a material and mental sense. Like so many of the settled poor who turned up at the vestry or the office of the overseer, he needed help with a lump sum and a "trifle" to help him on his way. Only the friendship of the parish and its officers, an implicit assertion of paternalist duty, could relieve his material wants *and* his emotional turmoil. Reed constructed himself as honest, just as vestry attendees did. He aspired to regain the dignity that came with independence and had strained every sinew to achieve this state and – a mark of ingrained good character – to lighten the potential burden on his settlement parish. The letter drips with a sense of belonging. Reed was known to his parish – "you know your self perfectly well" – and with this letter and its further detail of his situation, he made himself knowable.[3] Perhaps counter-intuitively, in-parish claimants appearing before the vestry also used this sort of approach, reflecting the ease with which one could become invisible or the subject of rumour in all but the smallest and most concentrated of parishes. Having dealt honestly with his community and suffered for some time before approaching Tetbury, Reed felt himself to be in decline, and in this context he subtly melded together an assertion of a universal parochial duty to someone in his position and a triple acknowledgment – trifle, favour, judgment – of the absolute discretion of the overseer in the process of poor relief. With such strategy and sentiment went at least a veneer of deference and submission and a determined effort to marshal and maintain his story in case it should be needed again. Those who attended vestries paid exactly the same attention to their stories. Yet surprisingly few people rested their case solely on such veneers or sublimated their reference model to what might have been expected. Ultimately, Reed and his peers showed the self-reflection and self-knowledge that allowed him to construct a self that had become, through prolonged suffering, liminal. Only the favour of his parish and its officers could at last bring him back to a proper standing in the community.

These rhetorical themes will be familiar from earlier chapters. How poor writers constellated them and with what emphasis depends in part on the type of letter written. I suggested a new model for the categorisation of letter types and associated rhetorical infrastructure in chapter 7. Such categorisation is an important way to bridge a corpus that in effect has two very different kinds of claimant: those who wrote single or small multiples of letters and those who entered into sustained co-respondence with officials. Mirroring other studies, those in the latter group – and their equivalent in terms of those appearing multiple times before the vestry – have been the mainstay of my own discussions. This is more than a matter of convenience or colour. Letter series from individuals contained, and were meant to contain, interspersing material from advocates and officials. A sequence of vestry attendance might also contain such material. Indeed, sometimes these voices numerically dominate the material by or about an individual or family.[4] This tripartite epistolary world of the parish must be considered in the round, rather than individually or sequentially, if we are ever to understand the nature of the poor law process and the agency of the poor. As I have shown, because those involved in this tripartite epistolary world shared modes of reference, linguistic models, and rhetorical ecologies, as well as a certain tolerance for fiction, the depth and limits of pauper agency can be understood only holistically. These people spoke and wrote (largely) the same language and used the same currencies. This was also the case for those who might appear in person before the vestry or in the office of the overseer.

Starting at this point has fundamental consequences for a range of issues explored directly and indirectly through previous chapters. One is the accepted chronology for the emergence of mass literacy. Richard Reed's letter is around the mid-point in a spectrum of epistolary literacy that runs from the highly oral, almost transient, abilities of Frances Soundy through to the controlled hand and logos of Samuel Parker.[5] Although there is evidence that some writers found scribes, even pointing to their compromised literacy in the letters they dictated, this experience was not representative. The vast majority of letters were written by those who signed them, and that these are "ordinary writings" is as clear as for the autobiographies and diaries that underpin analysis of the "coming" of literacy by David Vincent.[6] To be sure, such letters are evidence of the overlapping of oral and literate culture in the early nineteenth century. I regard this aspect of the letters as self-evident. The nuances of this overlap and its consequences for the way that rhetoric was found and constellated require a study in their own right. Nonetheless, it is clear that by the later eighteenth and early nineteenth centuries, writing had a determined pulse among the most marginal – and theoretically least literate – section of the population. The considerable archives of places such as Kirkby Lonsdale, Thrapston, Tetbury, and Sandal Magna survive by accident of preservation. They certainly reflect what the parish chests of other places could and would have looked like in the 1820s. The logic of this argument is compelling, as implied by table 1.1's depiction of the composition of an ideal-typical village or town population. At any point, the communities considered here were comprised of a churning group of people of varying degrees of settlement and belonging, which necessitated multilayered contacts with host and settlement parishes when poverty struck. The extensive archives that do survive capture this experience and point inexorably to the scale and complexity of the overseer's job, on the one hand, and to the deeply ingrained notion of negotiation, on the other. Above all, the corpus suggests that the very poorest and most marginal had a determined grasp of postal and conveyance systems, that letters were not a vanishingly rare occurrence in the everyday lives of ordinary people, and that the timing of mass literacy – the democratisation of writing – must be reined back firmly into the 1820s at the latest. The act of writing was in itself a tool for and record of the creation of a selfhood for the poor that by the 1800s had become striking.

That the poor used letters – a tool of the powerful and a vector for administrators and officials – in such numbers has important consequences for the way that we ought to understand the process of poor relief and the nature and scope of agency. I have argued in this study that end-of-process spending is an inadequate guide either to the character and role of the poor law or to people's experience of its local policies. Two pension payments of 5 shillings recorded side by side in the end-of-year overseers' accounts approved by the vestry do *not* mean the same thing, either in terms of the process by which those payments were generated or in terms of the understanding of them by the two individuals involved. This is not a new observation. Indeed, its meaning underpinned some of the earliest historiography of the Old Poor Law, which drew on the uncertain outcomes of vestry encounters to make the same point.[7] We have, however, forgotten the lessons arising from the fact that poor relief was, and was meant to be, a negotiated process. Vestry minutes reveal hostile receptions for some of those who wrote from a distance but whose letters do not themselves survive. And plenty of poor writers sent interspersing, renewing, and testamentary letters to note that officials had simply not responded or to dispute being turned down or having allowances reduced. Yet few of those rebuffed either went away or exercised their right to appeal to local magistrates. Rather, they renewed their applications, and as we know from the epistolary world of the parish, they interspersed their personal attempts with representation by advocates, officials, and professional figures such as doctors. In turn, allowances had to be renewed, extended, defended, and retrieved, which involved constant interaction with officials in person or by letter. It is tempting to think that the settled and proximate poor had a different experience, one in which their allowances simply rolled on or were negotiated in different ways and perhaps with more certainty. This is not the case. Plenty of in-parish applicants were turned down at vestries, and vestry minutes confirm that allowances had to be negotiated and renegotiated with exactly the same risks and periodicity as for those living outside the parish. Both the settled and out-parish poor who received parish pensions applied regularly for extensions and augmentations or had their allowances revisited, and we miss this sort of dynamism where recorded allowances show no action or tiny changes. It is thus unwarranted to presume the finality and precision of a 5 shilling entry in an overseer's accounts, and I have suggested a new language of outcomes to reflect such encounters in the borderlands of entitlement. It follows, too, that the in- and out-parish poor used similar strategic and rhetorical models across all sorts of claim precisely because they were not that different from each other in terms of their standing in or experience of the process of poor relief.

The poor thus had agency as well as voice. Welfare historians have certainly overstated the degree to which the applications for support that started the process of poor relief had to be wrapped up in the rhetoric and actuality of deference, submission, gratitude, powerlessness, and supplication. It is clear that most letters from the out-parish poor apologised for writing and offered greetings and gratitude from humble servants of the parish to its officers. Angry confrontation and bitterness can be found but generally only after patience had been lost on all sides of the relief equation. It is also clear that almost all writers recognised that the Old Poor Law was part of a discretionary world in which officials had to balance their own interests and those of ratepayers, claimants, and advocates. The settled and proximate poor did not have different experiences, and it is no surprise that the majority of in- and out-parish applicants requested trifles or simply support, an explicit confirmation of their knowledge of this discretionary world. In turn, poor writers *and* vestry applicants could be subject to repeated surveillance, time-limited support, the offer of less than was asked for or than was needed, slow replies and even slower action, and an elongated decision-making process of the sort outlined in chapter 4. An entry in the overseers' accounts tells us nothing about this process. Nor can such an entry tell us about the limits of theoretically unlimited power. Yet there were limits, and we see them clearly in the almost universal failure of parishes to terminate the relief careers of those whom officials themselves constructed as unworthy, whether they lived proximately or remotely. The lies and deceptions of people like Jacob Curchin of Wisbech in Cambridgeshire were dressed up in gratitude and supplication, but they were lies nonetheless. His relief was delayed, less than requested, and granted with fury and condescension, but it was provided and he kept applying. Curchin's appearances in the end-of-year accounts for Thrapston in Northamptonshire did not mean, and were not meant to mean, the same thing as the appearance of George May, the aged and respected claimant who cost the parish just as much. Both of these poor writers, however, negotiated their relief, used the rhetorical ecology outlined in earlier chapters, and exercised a compelling agency. In fact, continuing relief for the unworthy was the price of a fiction shared by officials, poor writers and vestry attendees, and their advocates. In this fictive landscape, it was possible and appropriate for officials to receive and claimants to tell partial stories and histories, for sender and recipient to understand and accept key rhetorical signals of deservingness, such as a desire to return to independence, for silences to be deliberate but to go unpunished, and for all parties to assume de facto rights to relief and analogous obligations for parishes when none in fact existed or could exist under the law.[8] That this fictive landscape was co-owned as well as co-authored by all three parties in the epistolary world of the parish – and that in effect ratepayers themselves connived through their advocate roles both to limit the discretionary power of the poor law and to foster a sense of pauper agency[9] – gave it a totemic power and perhaps explains why the Old Poor Law lasted so long.[10]

It follows, then, that the rules of the state as they manifested at the local level were, and were meant to be, malleable. This situation should perhaps be no surprise given the work of Joanna Innes and Samantha Shave on what the latter has dubbed the "policy process."[11] We also see this malleability in the language of welfare republics – the sense, in other words, that policy could and did vary as much within counties and regions as it did between them. Recent attempts to reimagine welfare law actually afford it more unity of purpose, meaning, and local purchase than in fact existed.[12] The sheer uncertainty of who was eligible, settled, and deserving introduced a degree of rule fluidity that was essential for the working of the Old Poor Law in practice. This observation applies as surely to the settled and proximate poor as it does to their out-parish peers. We might also add some of the observations of earlier chapters: that officials, in considering the claims of the poor, were and remained susceptible to backward-looking referential and rhetorical models of custom, duty, and Christian paternalism at the same time as they grappled with new models of exogeny and curative potential; that character and dignity remained two basic building blocks of entitlement; and that officials themselves understood, conveyed, and sometimes imposed – particularly through suspended removal orders after 1795 – normative standards of relief appropriate to their localities. Against this backdrop, malleability is striking but also inevitable, and the discretionary power of officials that so troubled Sydney Webb and Beatrice Webb was essentially fictional.[13]

But fluid rules also signal the need to look again at how we understand the structures of power within the parish. In the background to my sources, vestrymen fell out with each other and, surprisingly frequently, with their officers; advocates, both inside and outside the parish, came into conflict with each other; and parish officials confronted individual ratepayers. A unified face was not presented to the public of the parish, and the cases of poor people, often themselves played out in public, were not always resolved with agreement whether they lived remotely or not. In this sense, we have afforded the parish as a unit of social organisation, control, and order too much purpose. Whether national debates about poverty and the moral character of the poor gained local traction among the powerful of the parish state is key to understanding whether the final decades of the Old Poor Law really constituted a "crisis."[14] Legislation on select vestries certainly embodies this sense of crisis.[15] We see a balancing sentiment and broadly contemporaneous response in the scaffolding sources for this study, where episodic concerns over costs, and attempts to control them, can easily be traced. Hostility to the unemployed can also be evidenced in vestry minutes and the correspondence of officials.

Yet there is absolutely no evidence in the material that the process of poor relief changed or tightened in the last decades of the Old Poor Law. The rising tide of letters did not generally go unanswered, even if some overseers were notorious for delays. Intolerance was fractured rather than consistent. In the end, almost all claims from outside the parish ran to an outcome, even if not one that was desired by the writer. Officials felt that they *had* to respond, and that was because they did. Vestry minutes record a similar sentiment, even if couched in irritation, for the settled and proximate poor. Custom, parochial reputation, Christian paternalism, the deployment of absolute indicators of need and dignity such as starvation or nakedness, the existence of the tripartite epistolary world of the parish, and the requirement to balance the deference and gratitude of applicants with consideration and polite address and process all conspired to leave officials with limited room to manoeuvre.[16] It is this situation that goes some way to explaining why writers and vestry attendees did not simply aim to paint a picture of themselves that conformed to what they thought officials wanted to hear. Where officials failed to work within these frameworks, advocates and, even more frequently, other officials were on hand to point out the error of their ways. It is simply not the case that the poor saw their legitimacy in the eyes of ratepayers and the wider elite culture of the parish drain away from the later eighteenth century onward or that their ability to influence the system of which they were a part evaporated. The almost complete absence of the rhetoric of class, unrest, riot, and radicalism in the corpus, even though we might have expected to see it emerge strongly in this period, points forcibly to a balancing, rather than an execution, of power in relation to the dependent or prospectively dependent poor.[17] The poor, proximately resident or not, negotiated their relief because that was how the system was supposed to work.

Thus, although Robert Sharp of South Cave in East Yorkshire argued in June 1826 that "the chief consideration of [the vestry] was to make the pauper live on the least possible allowance" and, more widely and repeatedly, that landlords "think the poor of almost a different species," I have seen hundreds of balancing examples of officials and vestrymen – many of whom themselves acted as advocates on different occasions – taking a completely different stance when writing about the character and deservingness of the poor.[18] Almost all of the largest letter collections contain copy letters from officials to each other saying in effect that, notwithstanding the burdens on the parish, they must do their best for the poor. We have seen, for example, the overseer of Lancaster writing to a counterpart in Leeds to say that he would be inclined to give one poor writer much more than he had in fact done but could not action this sentiment until parochial cash flow improved. This official assumed implicitly that his counterpart would understand. We might, with justice, extend and deepen Pat Thane's observation that a sense of community equated to a "tangible mesh of support and exchange," with the relationship between the poor and officials at its core.[19]

The poor were alive to this complex situation, actively seeking to construct a multilayered poor self. They emphasised their individuality and the situational nature of their need, on the one hand, but constructed a picture of ordinariness, on the other hand. The latter found its greatest expression in phrases like "think what," "ask yourselves," or "think wot a mother must feel."[20] The letters of the poor and their advocates invariably called attention to character. They did so deliberately as a way of fabricating an image of self as they would want to be known, and in the past had been known, rather than as hapless petitioners for welfare. They had a history that mattered. In this sense, it was perfectly possible for authors to claim to be telling the truth – as well as for advocates and officials to confirm such truth telling – and yet for the information they conveyed to be hedged round with invention. It was this sort of rhetoric, if wrapped in the familiar structural form, that allowed overseers to act, sometimes in defiance of vestries. Exactly the same points can be made about the way that the in-parish poor approached overseers and vestries. In this sense, the poor remained fellow creatures rather than losing their individual identity and just claims on the parish and its payers. The poor of the early nineteenth century retained purchase on their communities rather than being pushed to the physical and conceptual margins denoted by the "other."

This experience was remarkably uniform. Given my work on welfare regimes and regions in Britain and Europe, I would have expected to see notable spatial differences in either the rhetorical infrastructure of appeal or the balancing responses and sentiments of officials and parishes, or both.[21] Such regional variations *can* be observed, especially differences between England and Wales and some subtle differences in rhetorical emphasis between northern and southern communities.[22] But these are not *striking* differences. Nor do other modes of spatial differentiation have much traction. It is remarkable, for instance, that letters sent from the largest urban areas were not generally more rhetorically sophisticated than those from smaller rural communities or market towns. This finding does not mean the beginning of the end for my own linguistic register of welfare spaces and welfare regimes. Quite the contrary; the corpus and the welfare process that it represents encourage us to move even further away from welfare outcomes and to focus rather more on the influences that shaped who applied for welfare, at what point in their descent into poverty, and how the initial stages of the poor relief process were negotiated.

My modelling of welfare regimes dwells specifically on these broad framework conditions. It suggests, for instance, that exclusionist regimes generally tended to relieve relatively small numbers of people with relatively small amounts of welfare. This was the case precisely because they enforced expectations that applicants would suffer and struggle for longer than they might have done under an obligatory regime, that they would request more "trifles," and that more of them would fall away during the initial stages of negotiation. Other aspects of the data also support my sense that we can and must look for spatial regularities in welfare sentiment. Thus one of the most insistent themes in the letters of poor writers – as echoed in the mediated testimony of vestry minutes – is that of prior suffering and a wider sense that writers had revealed only a share of their misfortune. Both experiences, I have argued, were honestly related, not least because they could so easily be checked. Writer after writer and vestry attendee after attendee told officials about their efforts to make do and about the spectrum of endurance, which could stretch from hours to years. Such testimony provides rich colour: wives pawning wedding rings, children eating out of the pig trough, men and women walking thirty miles in a day for work, and the ubiquitous support of friends. Underneath such situational colour, however, was an ecology of making do that has distinct spatial dynamics and feeds naturally into the search for spatial regularity. The regional and intra-regional patterning that we can map on the basis of end-of-process poor law spending owes less to the numbers relieved or the size of the rate base and rather more to the typological patterning of those who applied, to what they asked for in the first place, and to the kinds of relief – whether limited to a single point in time or granted over a relief cycle – that adhered to different forms of belonging and to different complexions and durations of "struggle."

Focusing on the economies of making do also highlights some of the other contributions of this study. Previous chapters have been peopled to a disproportionate degree by the old, yet the singular lesson of their letters is how successful they were in keeping away from the poor law and supplementing their allowances when given. The "aged," variously constructed, were among the most rhetorically rich writers. In their negotiations with officials, whether conducted in letters or recorded in vestry minutes, they fused together self-appreciation and self-construction, supplication, character, natural right, and ordinariness. This register and this range were shared with officials and advocates, who invariably used the same rhetoric. Barnard Sewell, writing an ending letter from Workington in Cumberland to Greystoke in Westmorland in 1822, is typical. He said, "my time is over for laber." At seventy-four he had "fought the world fareley," and in his decrepitude, he asked the vestry to "consider we cannot live on the air."[23] The balancing response was a regular allowance. Although Henry French has traced fundamental change in the age and gender composition of the poor relief register of Terling in Essex in the early nineteenth century, in other places it is clear that old age and decline were invariably seen at the start of the poor relief process as conferring de facto rights.[24]

Women and the sick, whether in- or out-parish poor, employed equally distinctive rhetorical approaches to their parishes, and in most places they seem to have convened an obligation on the part of parish officers to fufil the ubiquitous request for a reply by return. The Old Poor Law and the society that it represented thus retained an important and enduring infrastructure of paternalist sentiment, whether the poor lived proximately or not and whatever the nature and scale of the "ask." People were not always well treated, but for every scandal and story of parsimony, I could find a story of gratitude and generosity, even when the discretion of an overseer faced with raising a rate might have pushed in the opposite direction. Women, the old, and the sick seemingly had a powerful and influential voice. It did not in general garner them riches, but it must have given them status and a form of power and currency in their own settlement or host communities.

Voices, agency, rights, negotiation, influence, and the expectation of a process of poor relief have profound implications for the New Poor Law, for which there is as yet no history from below. With its advent in the 1830s, writing to parish officers became largely redundant except to co-opt such people as advocates.[25] Remarkably few of the prospective poor took the next step up and wrote to guardians or the relieving officers. Over a protracted period, the issue of out-parish paupers was to fade away as regulations on removability were tightened. Yet the poor *did* write in huge numbers to the central authorities in order to contest local policy. Their voices did not often result in action against union employees, except in medical neglect cases, or against guardians, but letters generally received a response, and the poor kept writing in their turn.[26] They continued to act and write as though poor relief were a negotiated process, and in the sense that almost nobody would see the inside of a workhouse for any length of time, it was. The New Poor Law inherited a body of the poor with agency and the expectation of agency, with rights and the expectation of rights, and with very considerable experience of shaping the system to which they were subject. This situation, above all, explains why its ideals were so quickly diluted in the 1840s.[27]

When those ideals were revived under the crusade against outdoor relief in the 1870s and 1880s, the deeply ingrained tradition of advocacy for the poor was also revived, and this last great experiment in poor law policy collapsed. Negotiation and malleability were, and were meant to be, the central planks of poor law policy right up to the 1920s, and we would do well to remember this basic lesson of social policy.

Like their counterparts under the Old Poor Law, the poor of the later nineteenth century who wrote to the central authorities did so in their own voices. There were few scribes, and they usually seem to have been acknowledged. The letters of both eighteenth- and nineteenth-century writers were not exactly "familiar" or personal, but nor were they the petitions and supplications of the sort that dominate the writing of ordinary Germans to public authorities. Nonetheless, they are not unique. In France, Norway, Italy, and parts of Belgium, the poor wrote to those with authority and power in the same way. They asserted agency and sought to negotiate the benefits that they thought ought to be attached to different variants and degrees of citizenship.[28] Indeed, wherever the poor were out of their place, however that was defined, informal mechanisms of appeal and approach sprang up if the local or national state failed to set up its own system. Only now are welfare historians beginning to recognise the value of those sources and to institute them in a proper comparative and linguistic framework.[29] Here, as we reach the point where we can look forward to a genuine poor law history from below for England, Wales, and Scotland in the eighteenth and nineteenth centuries, the challenge is to develop a comparative canvas for poverty and the balancing welfare mechanisms across Europe.[30] If, to paraphrase Roy Porter, the poor used words to make, unmake, and renew their lived worlds, it is important to understand whether basic questions of nationality and ethnicity influenced this exercise in drawing and stitching.[31]

Going forward - next steps

# Notes

CHAPTER ONE

1 See Innes, *Inferior Politics*, 21–47, although for Wales as a laggard, see ibid., 10. See also Slack, *From Reformation*.

2 For contrasting views on this matter, see Charlesworth, *Welfare's Forgotten Past*; Marshall, *English Poor*, 252; Green, *Pauper Capital*, 2; and S. King, "Negotiating the Law." Eastwood, *Governing Rural England*, 121, 133–4, believes that reforms to the poor law in 1795 and recourse to magistrate intervention meant that the poor came to expect relief and at commonly accepted rates, such that "Local government had overreached itself."

3 For the patchwork of local and regional variation prior to 1750, see Hindle, *On the Parish?* For after 1750, see S. King, *Poverty and Welfare*.

4 P. King, *Crime and Law*; P. King, "Rights of the Poor." See also Eastwood, *Governing Rural England*, 44, 106, 112, 133; and Marshall, "Role of the Justice." Goldie, "Unacknowledged Republic," 183, memorably notes that in 1833 the Poor Law Commission talked to "fourteen thousand republics." Fletcher, "Territorial Foundations," 104, suggests that the 1834 New Poor Law was underpinned by a sense that each parish had been "an independent nation" within a "bewildering mosaic of administrative units."

5 Broad, "Parish Economies," 989, argues for instance that there were ingrained and long-term differences between gentry and nongentry communities in the attitudes toward poor people and their relief.

6 Langton, "Geography of Poor Relief." For wider theorisation of the relationship between topography, distance, and state power, see Scott, *Domination*.

7 Innes, *Inferior Politics*, 78–105.

8  Innes, "'Mixed Economy of Welfare.'"

9  This leitmotif is most keenly expressed in Solar, "Poor Relief."

10  Innes, S. King, and Winter, "Settlement and Belonging." More widely, and for a small selection of this work, see Innes, "State, Church and Volunterism"; Jütte, "Poverty and Poor Relief"; and Scheutz, "Demand and Charitable Supply," 65, 68, 72. For a more sceptical view of overlapping English and European experiences, see Lindert, *Growing Public*, 47.

11  Pooley and Turnbull, *Migration and Mobility*; Lis and Soly, *Poverty and Capitalism*, 126, 174–83.

12  For example, see Winter and Lambrecht, "Migration, Poor Relief"; and Winter, "Caught between Law and Practice."

13  As a very recent example, see contributions to Althammer, Raphael, and Stazic-Wendt, eds, *Rescuing the Vulnerable*.

14  Nonetheless, see the discussion of unifying factors at early vestries in "Hindle, "Political Culture."

15  Farming the poor involved contracting their care and custody to a third party in a competitive tendering exercise that usually asked applicants to name a fixed price per head of pauper.

16  French, *Middle Sort of People*; Hindle, *On the Parish?*; Neuman, *Speenhamland County*, 148; Eastwood, *Government and Community*, 29. For an excellent example of such a dispute, one that resulted in persistent attempts by Richard Kay to resign from the select vestry of Tottington in Lancashire, see MCL L21/6/1/1-2, resignation letters, 24 July 1821 and 16 May 1822.

17  S. King and P. Jones, "Testifying for the Poor." For a wider rendering of advocacy, see Tabili, *Global Migrants*. Contributors to T. Harris, ed., *Politics of the Excluded*, note the significant numbers of local elites and even humbler sorts who necessarily had to be involved in different aspects of local governance and government.

18  P. King, "Social Inequality"; Dunkley, *Crisis*, 76; G. Morgan and Rushton, "Magistrate."

19  For an excellent summary of this sort of conundrum, see Fideler, *Social Welfare*; and Goldie, "Unacknowledged Republic," 172. Marshall, *English Poor*, 11, has a rather less charitable view of the sentiments of officeholders.

20  Shave, "Impact"; Hindle, "Political Culture," 128–35. For a good study of Berkshire vestries, see Neuman, *Speenhamland County*, 180–92.

21  Boulton, "Double Deterrence." Marshall, *English Poor*, 10, characterises overseers as careless and lazy. The evidence used in this volume is replete with statements from officials that refer to the length of their stay in office, which at its maximum extent might be thirty years.

22 See Innes, *Inferior Politics*, 3; and Green, *Pauper Capital*, 2.

23 Eastwood, *Governing Rural England*, 40.

24 R. Smith, "Ageing and Well-Being."

25 Hurren and S. King, "Public and Private Healthcare."

26 S. Williams, "Malthus, Marriage"; Sokoll, "Families, Wheat Prices." For a sceptical view rooted in the sense that the poor law was a tool for manipulating labour markets, see Lindert, *Growing Public*, 23.

27 On this issue, see the particularly acute analysis of Hindle, "Political Culture," 137, 144.

28 Shave, *Pauper Policies*, 5–26.

29 P. King, "Summary Courts," 136. See also, however, Costello, "'More Equitable.'"

30 French, "Irrevocable Shift"; French, "How Dependent?" These perspectives accord with the observation by Stapleton, "Inherited Poverty," 343–7, that successive cohorts of relief recipients grew ever younger.

31 For wider attempts at codification, see S. King, "Welfare Regimes."

32 Wall, "Some Implications," table 15.2; S. Williams, "Poor Relief"; Horrell and Humphries, "Old Questions," note 31; Marshall, *English Poor*, 101.

33 J.S. Taylor, "Impact of Pauper Settlement," 59–60, argues for instance that 11 per cent of all poor rates in Lancashire between 1813 and 1815 were spent on "administration."

34 Care, "Significance." On the rise of guidance manuals for overseers, see S. King, "'In These You May Trust.'" See also J.S. Taylor, "Impact of Pauper Settlement," 59, who argues that overseers' habit of talking to each other led to standardised practice.

35 Peyton, *Kettering Vestry Minutes*.

36 For a particularly good discussion of poorly done recordkeeping see Redford, *History of Local Government*, vol. 2, 95–102.

37 Even where allowances are recorded, the accounting format gives an illusory sense that the allowances were actually paid as opposed to simply allowed to accumulate as a liability. See J.S. Taylor, *Poverty, Migration*, 163.

38 On regional disparities in the presence of vestries, see Dunkley, *Crisis*, 52; and Walsh, "Poor Law Administration," 94.

39 Emerging perspectives from the Continental literature, set alongside a sense that the Old Poor Law entered a crisis of legitimacy sometime in the later eighteenth century, should perhaps cause us to expect more, rather than less, exclusion. Dunkley, *Crisis*, 54–6, 78; Hollen Lees, *Solidarities of Strangers*, 20, 82.

40 For broad summative work, see Wells, "Migration, the Law." See also Connors, "Parliament and Poverty."

41 S. King, "'It Is Impossible.'"

42 The sense that the poor understood this situation is confirmed by their persistent offer or threat to "come home" at subsequently greater cost to their settlement parishes.

43 J.S. Taylor, *Poverty, Migration*, 146, argues that such writers constituted a professional marginal class, but I have found no evidence for this in the pattern of letters described later in the chapter.

44 For the purposes of this volume, I understand agency as the "ability [of the poor] to take purposeful action and to have determinative effect in their own lives." Dierks, *In my Power*, 5. For an outstanding discussion of this definitional matter, see ibid., 3–6.

45 French and Barry, "Identity and Agency," 26, 31.

46 Hindle, "Civility, Honesty," 40, 47, 52.

47 Hallam, "Speaking to Reveal," 241.

48 Esser, "'They Obey All Magistrates,'" 75, argues that the extension of uniform structures of law and governance increased the voice of socio-political elites and made that of the poor "increasingly less audible."

49 Shepard, "Poverty, Labour," 51–2.

50 Hindle, "Destitution, Liminality." On wider referential structures, see M. Williams, "'Our Poore People.'"

51 Healey, *First Century of Welfare*.

52 See S. King, "Negotiating the Law."

53 Burt and Archer, "Introduction," 4. The London Lives project also focuses, although largely for the eighteenth century, on the way that ordinary Londoners understood and operated in the borderlands of the criminal justice and welfare systems.

54 J. Crowther and P. Crowther, eds, *Diary of Robert Sharp*, 38. For wider context on cultures of violence, see Dunkley, *Crisis*, 100.

55 Geering, *Our Sussex Parish*, 101.

56 S. Webb and B. Webb, *English Poor Law History*, 149, argue that the law determining how the Old Poor Law should be run was only casually related to local practice: "the two were separated by ... ignorance and indifference amid the assumption of unfettered local autonomy that characterises English local government." Marshall, *English Poor*, 60, likewise accuses officials of carelessness and extravagance. For a particularly acute case of neglect in which officials at Horsham allowed visitors to view a chained female lunatic who had made friends with rats, see Burstow, *Reminiscences of Horsham*, 28.

57 For an excellent discussion of these ambiguities, see Ely Jr, "Eighteenth-Century Poor Laws," who notes that significant numbers of removal orders were quashed based on procedural and evidential criteria because settlement was an administrative matter, not a legal one.

58 This spectrum is also reflected in the limited traceability of the poor in family reconstitution records. For an excellent discussion of this matter, see Barker-Read, "Treatment of the Aged Poor," 27–33.

59 Pilbeam and Nelson, eds, *Mid Sussex*, 58–9. The core message of table 1.1 adds weight to David Feldman's observation that urban migration in particular could create a "population of strangers" and that in practice the dividing line between those who belonged and those who did not was "thin and permeable." See Feldman, "Migrants, Immigrants," 83, 88.

60 Vincent, *Literacy and Popular Culture*, 95, argues that literacy may actually have *declined* by the early nineteenth century. On the overlap of oral and literate cultures, see Bushaway, "'Things Said or Sung.'"

61 See Lyons, *History of Reading*, 90–5. See also Ellis, *Educating Our Masters*. The Reverend Edward Boys Ellman, reflecting on the 1850s, found an ex-servant of his keeping a school at Lewes "though she could neither read nor write." See Boys Ellman, *Recollections of a Sussex Parson*, 263.

62 Lyons, *Writing Culture*, 8–10; Vincent, *Bread, Knowledge and Freedom*.

63 Healey, *First Century of Welfare*; Houston, *Peasant Petitions*. For comparative work on Europe, see Gestrich and Heinisch, "'They Sit for Days.'" On wider European petitioning, see contributions to Gestrich, Hurren, and S. King, eds, *Poverty and Sickness*.

64 P. Jones and S. King, "From Petition"; P. Jones and S. King, "Voices from the Far North."

65 Carter and S. King, "Keeping Track."

66 Muldrew and S. King, "Cash, Wages." See also Hutter, "Visual Credit," 28.

67 For example, see Wilde, *Medicine by Post*; and Armstrong, "Writing Women."

68 Geering, *Our Sussex Parish*, 60–1.

69 Lyons, *Writing Culture*. "Ordinary" in this sense does not include the dependent poor, whose writing is absent from this otherwise compelling analysis.

70 On the rise of nineteenth-century petitioning, see Tilly, *Popular Contention*; and Fraser, "Public Petitioning." For work on earlier periods, see Hirst, "Making Contact"; Loft, "Involving the Public"; and Knights, "Participation and Representation." The rise of petitioning was an international phenomenon with a language and style that transcended national boundaries. For contrasting examples, see Pyle, "Peasant Strategies"; and Taillon, "'All Men Are Entitled.'"

71 Later chapters return to aspects of intertextuality, but for this context, see Fumerton and Guerrini, "Introduction."

72 For instance, see Fitzpatrick, "Supplicants and Citizens"; and Gerber, *Authors of Their Lives*.

73 Sokoll, *Essex Pauper Letters.*

74 I am grateful to Peter Jones, Ben Harvey, Jane Rowling, Richard Dyson, Richard Gilbert, and Steven Taylor for their extensive work on this task. The collection is still of course incomplete. We know from record office catalogues or local knowledge that collections are still in churches, vestries, or the houses of members of the Parochial Church Council, as for instance the significant collection at Marazion in Cornwall, but we have been unable to gain access. Some letters and letter sets noted in record office catalogues are missing or lost, as for instance what promised to be a brilliant petition from a leper to Launceston parish. Across the county sample, many items were deemed by record offices to be unfit for presentation, which is testimony to the transient nature of correspondence and to the lack of subsequent care. Even some copy or bound letter books, however, are too fragile to consult, including for instance the potentially very valuable correspondence ledger for St Andrew Enfield.

75 Detailed guidance for transcription, including multilevel checking mechanisms, drew on M. Hunter, *Editing Early Modern Texts*; and Sokoll, *Essex Pauper Letters*, 1–74.

76 Green, *Pauper Capital*, 18, argues that the importance of London in terms of the national experience of the poor law – numbers of removals, proportion of relief spending, and so on – increased in the period of study.

77 For the classic statement of this position, see Landers, *Death and the Metropolis*.

78 The corpus also contains letters from across the organisational forms of the Old Poor Law, including Gilbert Unions and private incorporations. For a good discussion of this variety, see Walsh, "Poor Law Administration," 60–75.

79 It is impossible to break the sample down by "cause" of writing. Within and between letters, the poor usually outlined several reasons for their need. Only those who wrote because they were unemployed or underemployed, and some of the very old, tended to focus on a single issue. Welfare historians have lost this sense of multiple causes by focusing on end-of-process sources.

80 Englander, "From the Abyss," 76, similarly argues that London children were not "prone to put pen to paper." However, see Vincent, *Literacy and Popular Culture*, 26, who argues that by the nineteenth century parents drew heavily on their own children for support with writing.

81 Tabili, *Global Migrants*. We might note in this context the assertion of Redford, *History of Local Government*, vol. 2, 106, that in Manchester during the early nineteenth century, the Irish poor who were longer set-

tled, with twelve or more years of residence, were treated much as their English counterparts.

82 The presence of these immigrants in the collection should not surprise us given the size of their background populations. On early history, see Selwood, "'English-Born Reputed Strangers.'" On later periods, see Land, "Bread and Arsenic."

83 P. Jones and S. King, "Voices from the Far North."

84 Historians differ considerably over the timing of this waning sentiment: Valenze, "Charity, Custom," 78, argues that the poor lost their legitimacy in the later eighteenth century; Eastwood, *Governing Rural England*, 101–2, 118, sees a softening of attitudes that began in 1750 systematically reversed in the 1790s; Tomkins, "Women and Poverty," 166, suggests that favourable sentiment toward female paupers had disappeared by 1810; Land, "Bread and Arsenic," sees a hardening of attitudes to the coloured poor by the early nineteenth century; Innes, "State and the Poor," 262, argues that only post–Napoleonic War dislocation and agrarian depression led the "old confidence in the traditional relief system [to] wane to [the] vanishing point"; and Green, *Pauper Capital*, 6, also sees the post-1800 period as a time when "new, more pessimistic views about poverty prevailed."

CHAPTER TWO

1 BRO D/P 91/18/7, letter.

2 Ibid.

3 On the importance of reading aloud, see Sokoll, "Old Age in Poverty," 131. Lyons, *Writing Culture*, 14–18, argues that ordinary writing fused oral and written culture in a "deeply embedded" way and believes that such writing can be the basis for a new history from below. It is unclear how long Soundy had lived in Battersea, but the orthography in this and other letters has strong resonance with the dialect forms of Berkshire, notably the omission of *e* after or before other vowels, the inability to pronounce and thus write *ugh*, and the substitution of *a* for other letters, notably *e*. Lowsley, *Glossary of Berkshire Words*. The issue of regional linguistic traditions is taken up in chapter 4, but see Fox and D. Woolf, "Introduction," 16–17; and on the fluidity of boundaries between writing, visual imagery, and the spoken word, see Hallam, "Speaking to Reveal," 242. Whyman, *Pen and the People*, 61, 93, argues that the writers of such texts must be regarded as "unlettered" given that grammar and punctuation had been increasingly standardised by 1800.

4 The letters of the poor constitute one, albeit rarely acknowledged, strand of the growing and deepening epistolary culture of eighteenth- and nineteenth-century England and Wales. We now understand this culture to be deeply gendered, increasingly classless, and strongly interconnected to analogous literary and reading cultures. For an excellent overview of the burgeoning practice of letter writing, see Brant, *Eighteenth-Century Letters*.

5 For a discussion of signing as opposed to authorship, see ibid., 12; and Gerber, "Epistolary Masquerades," 142.

6 Vincent, *Literacy and Popular Culture*, 41–2. See also Lyons, "Ordinary Writings," 27. The Sussex vicar Edward Boys Ellman provides a quite brilliant account of the way that ordinary people used the postal system to convey information without paying for postage. See Boys Ellman, *Recollections of a Sussex Parson*, 52–3.

7 Snell, "Belonging and Community." Vincent, *Literacy and Popular Culture*, 13, 32, argues that the labouring poor systematically sought out their literate neighbours, as does Whyman, *Pen and the People*, 8. Lyons, "Ordinary Writings," 23–7, warns us that mediated literacy makes both the contemporary writer and subsequent historians vulnerable to omission and to narrowed phraseology or linguistic registers.

8 P. Jones, "Widows, Work and Wantonness."

9 These narratives also provide a clear sense of the base standards of literacy in the English and Welsh populations. For an important discussion, see M. Campbell, "Development of Literacy."

10 BRO D/P 91/18/10, letter.

11 SURO Par.29-37-10/17, letter, 14 December 1834.

12 Métayer, *Au Tombeau des secrets*; Tóth, *Literacy and Written Culture*; Engels, *Königsbilder*. The corset maker Thomas Jeffries, charged with theft at the Old Bailey on 22 February 1786, is one of the few examples. A character witness said that Jeffries "maintained himself by writing letters and petitions." See *Old Bailey Proceedings Online*, trial of Thomas Jeffries, 22 February 1786, t17860222-104, https://www.oldbaileyonline.org/browse.jsp?div=t17860222-104.

13 Lyons, *Writing Culture*, 48.

14 Gestrich and Heinisch, "'They Sit for Days.'" See also contributions to Gestrich, Hurren, and S. King, eds, *Poverty and Sickness*.

15 Poster and Mitchell, eds, *Letter-Writing Manuals*; Fergus, "Provincial Servants' Reading." In any case, most writers on the epistolary culture of this period point to other widely circulating sources for understanding the form and content of letters, including migrant letters home, newspapers, epistolary novels, printed and manuscript copies of "successful letters," and even royal proclamations. See Whyman, *Pen and the People*, 5, 28;

van Ginderachter, "'If Your Majesty,'" 80; and Hannan, *Women of Letters*, 11–13. Brant, *Eighteenth-Century Letters*, 10, 28, argues persuasively that manuals were descriptive as well as prescriptive and constituted "not examples of best practice but examples of actual practice." See also Bannet, *Empire of Letters*.

16  Sokoll, *Essex Pauper Letters*, 68. Vincent, "Decline of the Oral Tradition," 24, refers to the same sort of writing as "tenuous literacy"; and Whyman, *Pen and the People*, 10–11, develops a model of "epistolary literacy" as a "cumulative self-generated technology" that is often patchy and irregular.

17  NRO 261p/220-252a, bundle 242, letter.

18  The addressing of letters was partly dependent upon how and when they were intended to be sent. As chapter 3 will suggest, the mode of conveyance was frequently opportunistic and might thus have required addresses to be written at the last minute.

19  NRO 325p/193 and 194, overseers' correspondence; MCL M10/808-816, Hulme letter books.

20  NRO 261p/220-252a, bundle 244, letter.

21  SURO Par.29-37-10/12, letter.

22  van Ginderachter, "'If Your Majesty,'" 76. A similar point is made by Sokoll, "Negotiating a Living," 29–30. See also McShane, "'Ne sutor ultra crepidam,'" 224, who argues that the concept of the sole author is essentially a modern invention. Van Voss, "Introduction," 8–9, suggests that scribal input can easily be detected. For a wider discussion of the "scriptual power" of the poor, see Sokoll, "Old Age in Poverty," 134; and Lyons, *Writing Culture*, 48.

23  LIRO Croft Par. 13/27/15, letter. Appended to the bottom of the original, a draft reply notes that "in favour of M^rs Browns Request Concerning Half a Years Rent Due Martlemas Last for a house in Lincoln the Parish of Croft is Willing to pay, therefore you may Rest satisfied that it shall be paid, the first Opertunity by me." This sort of annotation reveals the complex materiality of the pauper letter as an object.

24  Reading aloud, along with the circulation of letters, dissolves unhelpful boundaries between the private and the public or the personal and the business-related. See Colclough, *Consuming Texts*, 1–20, who deals with the authority imbued in a version of a text that is read aloud.

25  On such strategies, see S. King and P. Jones, "Testifying for the Poor."

26  On this issue, see the strong discussion by Foyster, "Prisoners Writing Home," 959.

27  Nonetheless, Cross and Bland, "Gender Politics," 7, remind us that the boundaries of fact and fiction in any set of letters are fluid. See also

Gerber, "Epistolary Masquerades," 150–1, who discusses in the context of emigrant letters the difference between silences and active deception.

28 Letters were simultaneously disembodied claims – and thus potentially suspect – and a means to present the writer as an embodied individual. Some of the possibilities regarding how information was conveyed in letters written by the poor are also true of letters written for other purposes. See Gerber, "Acts of Deceiving," 320, 322, who argues that "narrative truth" was "more important for individuals than literal truth."

29 Hindle, "Civility, Honesty," 52.

30 S. King, Nutt, and Tomkins, eds, *Narratives of the Poor*, vol. 1, 75–125.

31 NRO 325p/193, letter.

32 Pilbeam and Nelson, eds, *Mid Sussex*, 161–2.

33 LCRO DE 1587/154, letter.

34 NRO 251p/100, letter.

35 Ibid. They also, of course, doubted stories told to them in person at the vestry, with vestry minutes often recording instructions for visits to take place or for further enquiries to be made.

36 LIRO Epworth Par. 13/28/7, letter. See also Sokoll, "Negotiating a Living," 27, on the inability of Essex overseers to rid themselves of even blatant drunks.

37 This was also the case, of course, for family letters, which usually became public documents. See Whyman, *Pen and the People*, 18, 23; Hannan, *Women of Letters*, 9; and Lyons, "Ordinary Writings," 18.

38 Sokoll, *Essex Pauper Letters*, 68. The best example in the corpus is Beverley in Yorkshire, where officials regularly asked George Lacey to inspect out-parish paupers in Hull. See in particular EYRO PE1-702, letter of inspection, 20 June 1832. For a wider sense that pauper letters embody truth, see Gray, "Experience of Old Age," 111.

39 NRO 249p/216, letter.

40 NRO 350p/166-69, vestry minutes.

41 LIRO Epworth Par. 13/28/6, letter.

42 MCL M10/814, letter. This use of the "tribunal of the public" to heap pressure on a co-respondent was a common vehicle, and its adoption by the poor in this context is interesting. See Brant, "'Tribunal of the Public,'" 17.

43 SURO Par.29-37-10/4, letter.

44 As chapter 1 suggested, other dimensions of the representativeness question also have more purchase. Parishes in the largest urban areas retained relatively few of the pauper letters that we know to have been sent, but other urban areas, rural parishes, and (particularly) communities in the urban hinterlands sometimes boast remarkable collections. See S. King,

"Friendship, Kinship." In the context of Song, "Parish Typology," 205, 208–12, there is no evidence in the corpus that open parishes systematically received more letters than closed parishes or vice versa. John Langton's remarkable county study of Oxfordshire, in any case, suggests that much more complex typographical and topographical variables might have influenced both poor law sentiments and pauper agency. Langton, "Geography of Poor Relief."

45 Cornleius Stovin authored thirty-seven letters to other parishes in Lincolnshire and beyond.

46 NRO 325p/193 and 194, Thrapston copy letter books.

47 J.M. Martin, "Rich, the Poor." Sokoll, "Negotiating a Living," 24, suggests that 15 per cent of Essex paupers were nonparishioners.

48 Hastings, *Poverty and the Poor Law*, 28. On the very extensive out-parish relief network in which Kirkby Lonsdale in Westmorland was enmeshed, see J.S. Taylor, "Different Kind"; and J.S. Taylor, "Voices in the Crowd."

49 For an example of heavy removal activity, see Hindle, "Power, Poor Relief," 87.

50 The frequency of migratory moves across the average life-cycle provides an idea of how this situation emerged. See Pooley and Turnbull, *Migration and Mobility*. See also Hampson, *Treatment of Poverty*, 148–50, who argues that by the 1790s nonresident relief was a "considerable item" in the parochial accounts of Cambridgeshire.

51 NRO 249p/164, vestry minutes.

52 Ong, "Writing as a Technology"; Bushaway, "'Things Said or Sung.'"

53 See Sokoll, "Old Age in Poverty."

54 COWAC B1350, letter. It is important to note that many of the middling sorts also produced oral writing, and this was certainly the case for many of the officials whose correspondence we have collected.

55 Hirst, "Making Contact," 45, notes that such "gestures of address" were an important currency for people wishing to establish a mutually beneficial and ongoing relationship. See also Barnes, *Epistolary Community*; and Bower, "Dear."

56 NRO 261p/220-252a, bundle 242, letters; NRO 261p/220-252a, bundle 244, letters.

57 See Fitzmaurice, *Familiar Letter*, 129–63. See also Englander, "From the Abyss," 78–9.

58 See P. Jones and S. King, "From Petition." See also, Brant, "'Tribunal of the Public,'" 15; and Zaret, *Origins of Democratic Culture*, 81, who argues that "petitions were objects of popular knowledge."

59 Brant, "'Tribunal of the Public,'" 18.

60 NRO 261p/220-252a, bundle 242, letter.

61 NRO 261p/220-252a, bundle 244, letter.
62 SURO Par.95-37-3, letter.
63 SURO Par.29-37-10/30, letter.
64 S. King and Stringer, "'I Have Once More.'"
65 Gerber, "Acts of Deceiving," 316, likewise argues that each emigrant letter "is a specific instance" impervious to "grand emplotment schemes." There is little support in this corpus for Favret, *Romantic Correspondence*, 24, who argues that writers were prone to "abandon all sense of propriety."
66 Sokoll, "Writing for Relief"; Sokoll, *Essex Pauper Letters*, 57; Gerber, "Acts of Deceiving," 320; Hannan, *Women of Letters*, 1.
67 See also Barnes, *Epistolary Community*, 1–2, who argues that familiar letters represent a "dialogue between familiars bound by strong affective ties [embodying] the understanding, sympathy and equality germane to an intimate community."
68 Hannan, *Women of Letters*, 23.
69 Brant, *Eighteenth-Century Letters*, 3.
70 Würgler, "Voices."
71 On the persistence of deep-rooted linguistic local countries, see Fox and D. Woolf, "Introduction," 16–17.
72 For a sense that large urban environments changed the authorial voice, see Brant, *Eighteenth-Century Letters*, 14.
73 SURO Par.29-37-10/6, letter.
74 SURO Par.29-37-10/35, letter.
75 On institutional memory, see Seed, "History and Narrative," 50.
76 NRO 261p/220-252a, bundle 246, letter.
77 In part, we see this equivalence reflected in the very materiality of vestry books. The one for St Tudy in Cornwall, for instance, noted on its opening page that the select vestry was to be convened for "hearing and relieving the complaints of the poor." CORO P241/8/1, vestry book, 1807-28.
78 SURO Par.29-37-10/23, letter.
79 Lyons, "Writing Upwards."
80 Gerber, "Acts of Deceiving," 320-8.
81 Dierks, *In My Power*, 6.

CHAPTER THREE

1 S. King, "'Stop This Overwhelming Torment.'"
2 On the moral rights of the unemployed, see Reiss, "Image of the Poor."
3 This situation makes the "meaning" of the allowances given to such groups problematic. See French, "How Dependent?"

4 van Ginderachter, "'If Your Majesty,'" 77. See also Fox, "Custom, Memory," 89–90, who notes that writing was seen as a standard of proof in part because it was a normative mode of elite culture.

5 Many advocate letters contend that people could not have survived without the continued support of friends and neighbours, and it seems unlikely that such groups were not involved in the initial decision to apply even if they had no involvement in shaping the letters that actioned the decision.

6 A. Crowther, "Health Care," 211–12.

7 On "maiden settlements," see Sharpe, "Parish Women."

8 On the status of copies like this one as texts embodying "unwanted disorder," see Brant, *Eighteenth-Century Letters*, 8.

9 CORO P128-19, letters.

10 The range of such authorities was considerable and included vestrymen; paid and unpaid overseers; guardians or other officials associated with Gilbert Unions or private incorporations; and, episodically, farmers of the poor responsible for dealing with in- and out-parish paupers for a contracted per capita fee.

11 MCL M10/808, letter.

12 For comprehensive overviews of the complexity of settlement stories, see Snell, *Parish and Belonging*; and Boulton, "Double Deterrence."

13 See S. King and P. Jones, "Testifying for the Poor."

14 On the limits of magistrate support, see P. King, "Rights of the Poor."

15 Although difficult to pin down for our period, the existence of knowledge pools is clearly demonstrated in oral history work on ordinary communities of the later nineteenth century. For instance, see A. Davies, "Youth, Violence"; Tebbutt, *Making Youth*; and E. Roberts, *Woman's Place*. On manuals, see P. Hunter, "Containing the Marvellous," 174–5.

16 The literature on middling correspondence is considerable, but see Hannan, *Women of Letters*; Whyman, *Pen and the People*; and Colclough, *Consuming Texts*.

17 Dierks, *In My Power*, 3, argues that the "remarkable social expansion of letter writing" led to the development of a new urban infrastructure of shops and suppliers to provide the raw materials of epistolarity, such that "a culture of documents ... saturated the Anglophone Atlantic world with paper by the end of the eighteenth century."

18 Favret, *Romantic Correspondence*, 2.

19 On how readers might interpret "signs of the author's intention" when considering the material elements of letters, such as paper quality, spacing, ink, and so on, see Hannan, *Women of Letters*, 20–1; and Gerber, "Epistolary Ethics," 7, 11–16.

20 For important perspective on the importance of understanding the context in which letters were produced, circulated, and received, see Brant, *Eighteenth-Century Letters*, 2–18.

21 Noblett, "Cheese, Stolen Paper."

22 Gerber, *Authors of Their Lives*.

23 On the relationship between the look of a text and its interpretation, see Colclough, *Consuming Texts*, 11. See also Lyons, *Writing Culture*, 57.

24 J. Harley, "Material Lives."

25 See contributions to McEwan and Sharpe, eds, *Accommodating Poverty*. A similar point for a later period is made by Lyons, *Writing Culture*, 39–44.

26 NRO 249p/216, letters.

27 See, for instance, Palk, ed., *Prisoners' Letters*.

28 Sokoll, *Essex Pauper Letters*, consciously reproduces only pauper letters from the wider epistolary record of Essex parishes.

29 NRO 251p/99, letter, 24 July 1833.

30 CCRO WPR-19-7-6, letter.

31 SURC P3-5-38, letter.

32 RPC, letter.

33 HRO 20M61 PO17, letter.

34 HRO 25M84 PO71, letter.

35 CCRO WPR-19-7-6, letter, 22 August 1811. Most of the substantial letter collections contain instructions to send letters or relief to the premises of local stationers.

36 Sokoll, *Essex Pauper Letters*, 227.

37 HRO 4M81 PO40, letter, 28 February 1808.

38 SURC P3-5-39, letter.

39 Sokoll, *Essex Pauper Letters*, 224.

40 As Hannan, *Women of Letters*, 22, 24, further reminds us, it is important to "ground mental spaces in the physical environment."

41 Sokoll, "Negotiating a Living," 30–1, also notes that some writers were themselves itinerant sellers of paper and ink.

42 RPC, letter.

43 It is notable that Younge does not say that the shop is a bookshop or stationers. BRO D/P 132/18/15, letter.

44 Whyman, *Pen and the People*.

45 GRO P316 OV 7-1, letter.

46 Whyman, *Pen and the People*, 19–23.

47 Cheney, *Shoemaker's Window*, 6–7.

48 HRO 25M84 PO71, letter.

49 HRO 88M81W PO7, letter.

50 BRO D/P 139/18/4, letter.

51 HRO 4M81 PO40, letter.
52 Lyons, *Writing Culture*, 3.
53 CCRO WPR-19-7-6, letter.
54 HRO 3M82W PO24, letter.
55 CCRO WPR-19-7-6, letter.
56 P. Hunter, "Containing the Marvellous," 181, suggests that people would have been aware that "an undisturbed record" without in-text alterations "went a long way towards establishing the honesty and credit" of the writer. Paradoxically, the correspondence of officials themselves tended to contain more emendations than the letters of poor writers.
57 Lyons, *Writing Culture*, 41–2. Note also, however, the sense that the poor did not want to waste the cost of postage by not using up the full page, as elaborated upon by contemporaries such as Boys Ellman, *Recollections of a Sussex Parson*, 52–3.
58 Lyons, *Writing Culture*, 41.
59 On the importance of having time to write letters, see Brant, *Eighteenth-Century Letters*, 18.
60 This observation stands in distinction to Vincent, *Literacy and Popular Culture*, 41. See also Lyons, *Writing Culture*, 35, 41, 55.
61 BRO D/P 91/18/4, letter.
62 HRO 25M84 PO71, letter. In parish claimants used exactly the same rhetoric of bad weather to instigate, augment, or extend their cases.
63 SURO PAR.183-37-3, letter.
64 CCRO WPR-19-7-6, letter.
65 RPC, letter.
66 Theft by postmen, carriers, and robbers was also a problem, but the use of elaborate schemes to deter and detect theft probably means that it was less common than we assume. For a discussion of some of these practical methods at the start of the study period, see Crossley and Saville, *Fuller Letter*, 277.
67 NRO 110p/138, letter.
68 LIRO Croft Par. 13/27/4, letter. On the need to regulate the timing of forms of exchange, see Lyons, *Writing Culture*, 56.
69 CORO ADD448-17, letter.
70 Brant, *Eighteenth-Century Letters*, 2, sees this practice as a "resupply" of conversation or engagement.
71 LIRO Crowland Par. 13/53/3, letter.
72 NGRO PR 11482, letter.
73 Brant, *Eighteenth-Century Letters*.
74 Ibid., 12.
75 Vincent, *Literacy and Popular Culture*, 39, for instance, notes that the

highest figures for per capita delivery of letters are to be found in London, ports, and resorts.

76 As Favret, *Romantic Correspondence*, 19, notes, "the structure of time and distance" might dictate a letter's form and contents.

77 For an extended discussion of the evolution of postal services, see Whyman, *Pen and the People*, 46–71. In particular, Whyman argues eloquently that by 1800 the mail had "become a private necessity and a public right" (71).

78 Brant, *Eighteenth-Century Letters*, 12; Whyman, *Pen and the People*, 3.

79 Vincent, *Literacy and Popular Culture*, 39–41.

80 Cheney, *Shoemaker's Window*, 82.

81 Whyman, *Pen and the People*, 12, by contrast, argues that there was a democratisation of letter writing in the eighteenth century.

82 Fletcher, "Territorial Foundations," 104–5, 112.

83 Vincent, *Literacy and Popular Culture*, 44, suggests that ordinary people had an "unfamiliarity with directions."

84 BRO D/P 91/18/4, letter.

85 The poor shared this language and strategy with overseers and advocates, who had frequent recourse to this approach when dealing with each other.

86 LIRO Horncastle Par. 13/32, letter, dated only 1799.

87 However, see Keith-Lucas, *Parish Affairs*, 105, who argues that in some parishes overseers already had their own relatives on the relief rolls.

88 NRO 251p/98, letter.

89 NRO 251p/98, letter.

90 S. King, "Residential and Familial."

91 NGRO PR 11482, letter.

92 NGRO PR 11482, letter from Thomas Parker of Sevenoaks, 24 November 1829.

93 Vincent, *Literacy and Popular Culture*, 35, argues that the poor found the cost of receiving letters to be prohibitive even in the 1820s and 1830s.

94 Cheney, *Shoemaker's Window*, 82.

95 HRO 25M84 PO71, letter.

96 Some writers, such as Thomas Oliver of Dorking, noted that they had managed to "get a frank" from a local advocate, thus covering the costs of postage. See HRO 25M60 PO35, letter, 11 August 1829. For wider context on franking, see Whyman, *Pen and the People*, 65; but also Hurley, *Longbridge Deverill Poor*, 3, who notes a letter from Parliament member James Buller on behalf of William Crofts, in which Buller states, "Should you write to me, you will *not* direct to me as a Member of Parliament" (my italics).

97 CCRO WPR-19-7-6, letter, 9 January 1811.

98  SURO Par.29-37-10/34, letter 19 December 1838.

99  CCRO WPR-19-7-6, letter.

100  SURO Par.400-37-123, letter.

101  SURO Par.400-37-123, letter.

102  LIRO Croft Par. 13/27/1, letter.

103  CCRO WPR-19-7-6, letter, 10 September 1819.

104  On trust and the makeshift economy, see contributions to S. King and Tomkins, eds, *Poor in England*.

105  RPC, letter. Whyman, *Pen and the People*, 55, argues that by 1800 many postmasters were also innkeepers.

106  BRO D/P 91/18/4, letter.

107  HRO 25M84 PO71, letter, 2 April 1827.

108  LMA DR03-F10-1, letter, 1 June 1800.

109  BRO D/P 91/18/4, letter, dated only 1827.

110  Caldecott in Rutland, for instance, had no street names or numbers until the twentieth century.

111  NRO 249p/216, letter, 1 December 1821; CCRO WPR-19-7-6, letter, 23 October 1829.

112  CCRO WPR-19-7-6, letter, 29 October 1829.

113  SURO Par.206-37-8, letter.

114  LMA P69-ALH4-B-052-MS18982, letter, 29 March 1750; RPC, letter, dated only 1785.

115  For an overview, see Wessel Hansen, "Grief, Sickness."

116  Richardson, "'Havying Nothing upon Hym,'" 211, reminds us for a different period that ordinary people had to carefully craft a "mental image which increases the plausibility of the action."

117  Gerber, "Acts of Deceiving," 315.

CHAPTER FOUR

1  On this relationship across genres, see Gerber, "Epistolary Ethics," 5, 15–16; Cross and Bland, "Gender Politics," 4; Hirst, "Making Contact," 47; P. Hunter, "Containing the Marvellous," 172; Innes, "State and the Poor," 243–4; and D. Harley, "Rhetoric and the Social," 415.

2  On the way that "fluid relations between writer, text and recipient" might shape and reshape the meaning inscribed into and onto texts, see Brant, *Eighteenth-Century Letters*, 16; and Gerber, "Epistolary Masquerades," 144.

3  This observation elides with a wider sense that those in power had an obligation to take notice of petitions and other avenues for the flow of information up the social and governance scale. See Zaret, *Origins of Democratic Culture*, 86–95.

4  S. King, *Poverty and Welfare*.

5  For an excellent discussion of reception, see Colclough, *Consuming Texts*, 5–19.

6  Future overseers would use the backs of letters for drafts of other correspondence or treat them as scrap paper for adding up. Some contained doodles and copying from other texts, clearly having been given to children to play with. Contemporary clergymen and some errant archivists also added unconnected text.

7  Gerber, "Epistolary Ethics."

8  NRO 325p/194, copy letter.

9  J.S. Taylor, *Poverty, Migration*, 105.

10  On the encoding of meaning and intent by the author, see the excellent discussion in Eckerle, *Romancing the Self*, 7–9.

11  NRO 325p/194, copy letter.

12  NRO 261p/220-252a, bundle 242, letter.

13  Brant, *Eighteenth-Century Letters*, 9. The most likely triggers prompting overseers to seek advice were extending or renewing letters rather than instigatory letters or those originated by advocates and officials.

14  For a sense of how the public discussion of the fragmentary and partial stories contained in letters might lead to the creation of a new narrative in the eyes of readers, see D. Harley, "Rhetoric and the Social," 422. On the wider concept of readership, see Eckerle, *Romancing the Self*, 8.

15  RPC, letter.

16  MCL M10/812, letter books.

17  NRO 249p/216, letter. Ogborn, *Spaces of Modernity*, 98, 237, argues that the founding and maintenance of vestries created an active state body that "reconfigured" the relationship between parish and public. In this construct, vestries witnessed "the uneasy intersection of the demotic and the official."

18  Colclough, *Consuming Texts*, 20. See also Whyman, *Pen and the People*, 23.

19  Colclough, *Consuming Texts*, 9.

20  BRO D/P 139/18/4, letter. Lloyd ended with a postscript confirming that the letters of poor writers were not always or even perhaps usually meant to be private documents: "You may shew this letter to Mr Leach if you Please I think it will be Proper to do so."

21  SURO Par.100-37-3, letter.

22  LIRO Horncastle Par. 13/32, letter.

23  CORO ADD448-17, letter.

24  J.S. Taylor, *Poverty, Migration*, 126.

25  BRO D/P 91/18/7, letter.

26  See Hurren and S. King, "'Begging for a Burial.'"

27 NRO 249p/216, letter.
28 NRO 249p/216, letter.
29 Hollen Lees, *Solidarities of Strangers*, 7.
30 NRO 325p/194, letter, 7 November 1827.
31 S. King, *Sickness, Medical Welfare*.
32 J.S. Taylor, *Poverty, Migration*, 4, 47–51.
33 Such observations should lead us to question broad-brush arguments that the poor law "operated as a residualist system, usually coming in late and with little." Hollen Lees, *Solidarities of Strangers*, 19. My own early characterisations of allowances as generous or parsimonious also need to be reconsidered. S. King, *Poverty and Welfare*.
34 Hurley, *Longbridge Deverill Poor*, 9–10.
35 LRO PR 2391/5, letter.
36 Hitchcock, "Begging on the Streets," 498.
37 SURC P3-5-38, letter.
38 Land, "Bread and Arsenic," 90.
39 Hannan, *Women of Letters*, 1.
40 LIRO Horncastle Par. 13/32, letter.
41 For a sense of the letter as a material object "predicated on a belief in negotiation between disparate and multitudinous voices," see Favret, *Romantic Correspondence*, 33.
42 CCRO WPR-19-7-6, letter.
43 CCRO WPR-19-7-6, letter.
44 G. Taylor, *Problem of Poverty*, 3.
45 CORO ADD448-17, letter.
46 CCRO WPR-19-7-6, letter.
47 LRO PR 866, letter.
48 CCRO WPR-19-7-6, letter.
49 CCRO WPR-19-7-6, letter.
50 On the universal nature of this observation, see Pyle, "Peasant Strategies," 46.
51 Hindle, "Political Culture," 151.
52 Chalmers, "'Person I Am,'" 174.
53 RPC, letter.

CHAPTER FIVE

1 GRO P228 OV 3-5-3, letter.
2 Lyons, *Writing Culture*, 3. On the letter as an imperfect substitute in contemporary eyes for a face-to-face conversation, see contributions to van Houdt et al., eds, *Self-Presentation*.

3  On lost literacy, see Lyons, *History of Reading*, 90–5.

4  See Fox and D. Woolf, "Introduction," 28–9.

5  See Raven, Small, and Tadmor, "Introduction"; Tadmor, "'In the Even'"; and Vincent, "Decline of the Oral Tradition."

6  See Gerber, "Acts of Deceiving," 316, who argues that a shared language created "meanings among those who often had a most tenuous hold on reading and writing."

7  For wider context on how the process of writing, receiving, and replying to letters made people knowable to each other, see Gerber, "Epistolary Ethics," 7.

8  Vincent, *Bread, Knowledge and Freedom*; Hilliard, *To Exercise*; Hilliard, "Popular Reading."

9  For a rendering of practical schooling and writing implements in the 1820s, see Cheney, *Shoemaker's Window*, 7. On writing technologies, see P. Davies, "Writing Slates." French visitors to Suffolk noted the teaching of reading and writing in the Norwich workhouse in 1784. See Scarfe, ed., *Frenchman's Year*, 90–3, 95.

10  On the importance of writing abilities – and thus the emergence and circulation of autobiographical conversion narratives – for the Methodist faiths, see Mack, *Heart Religion*.

11  Walker, "'For the Last Many Years'"; Hoyler, "Small Town Development"; E. Brown, "Gender, Occupation"; Claeys, "Political Economy." Note, however, Raven, "From Promotion," 192, who argues that publishers and organisers of circulating libraries tried to "arrange limits to the reading ambitions of the poor."

12  See Humphries, *Childhood and Child Labour*; E. Griffin, "Making of the Chartists"; Hitchcock, "Rough Lives."

13  Vincent, *Literacy and Popular Culture*, 1, 3, 26, 126; Crone, "Reappraising Victorian Literacy"; Houston, "Development of Literacy."

14  On social mobility, see Clark, *Son Also Rises*; French, "'Ancient Inhabitants'"; and Miles, *Social Mobility*.

15  At Hooton Pagnell in Yorkshire, for instance, a community of 285 inhabitants was in 1842 served by two schoolmistresses and one schoolmaster. Presumably, the upper reaches of this society – the shopkeepers, publicans, clerks, and farmers who might have populated the vestry – sent their children to such people much as did the poorer sorts. See Lindley, *Early Censuses*, 20–7. These schoolmasters and especially schoolmistresses are partly the people whom Whyman, *Pen and the People*, 106–7, has in mind when she refers to a "hidden supply of schooling."

16  This tendency for weak literacy to be experienced across the lower and middling ranks of the social spectrum has also been consistently evidenced

in Europe. For example, see Kauranen, "Did Writing Lead?" 61; and Vandenbussche, "'Lower Class Language.'"

17 Fergus, "Provincial Servants' Reading," argues that domestic servants provided a conduit for the transmission of reading and writing habits, and presumably language, between the middling orders and the labouring sorts.

18 On the way that different social groups come to use the same "pool of
symbolic concepts and criteria," see French and Barry, "Identity and
Agency," 32.

19 Some forms of reference – custom, for instance – were simultaneously
linguistic and rhetorical platforms and are considered at length later in
this study.

20 For an excellent Continental example, see Damsholt, "Peasant, Soldier
and Subject." For a wider discussion of the use of patriotic language and
concepts of citizenship, see Taillon, "'All Men Are Entitled,'" 99.

21 There is evidence that the linguistic association of deservingness in terms of
parochial relief with military service had passed out of fashion between the
early modern and modern periods. See Schen, "Constructing the Poor,"
459–62; and Hudson, "Arguing Disability." The corpus does include letters
from serving soldiers or wives left behind when their husbands joined the
militia, but service to country was rarely a referential form here.

22 BRO D/P 26/18/1, letter.

23 These routes included, for instance, petitioning for national pension
schemes. See Nielsen, "Chelsea Out-Pensioners"; and Nielsen, "Continuing to Serve."

24 For a summative review, see E. Griffin, "Sex, Illegitimacy"; and contributions to Levene, Nutt, and S. Williams, eds, *Illegitimacy in Britain*. See
also Stratmann, "Nobody's Child."

25 This was also true of the in-parish poor whose encounters with the parish
are recorded in vestry minutes. See P. King, "Legal Change," 22, who
notes that relief was given to the in-parish poor according to custom, even
when those recipients were in bitter dispute with the parish.

26 For the history of this sort of language, see contributions to Richards, ed.,
*Early Modern*.

27 EYRO PE1-702, letters.

28 LMA DR03-F10-1, letter.

29 Given that Cockerill could write but asked the overseer to send the initial
appeal, this letter is also an important reminder that literacy could be
strategic and that all parties could share both an agenda to keep someone
in their host community and a language through which that agenda might
be expressed.

30 SURC SHER-28-10-2, letter.

31 GRO P52 OV 7-1, letter.

32 GRO P76 OV 3-5, letter, dated only 1817.

33 On the Quakers, for instance, see Watson, "Poverty in North-East Lancashire"; and Stanley Holton, *Quaker Women*.

34 On the waning reach of the Church of England, see Snell and Ell, *Rival Jerusalems*; and C. Brown, *Death of Christian Britain*.

35 RPC, letter. For context, see Tadmor, *Social Universe*.

36 SURC 1505-37-F1, letter. Bayley's upbringing in Hampshire is clearly seen in the dialect representation of words like "uup."

37 Hurren and S. King, "'Begging for a Burial.'"

38 RPC, letter.

39 It may of course be the case that the rise of nineteenth-century street preaching recharged this linguistic well. See Davin, "Socialist Infidels."

40 Some sense of how this sort of language might have developed in the public domain of the poor can be seen in surviving sermon and psalm books and in notes kept by clergy in the early nineteenth century. For a particularly good example, see DRO PE/D/WPC/Z3, book of anthems, hymns and psalms, undated (but probably 1810s), kept by a former vicar of Swanage.

41 LMA DR02-E4, letter.

42 S. King, *Sickness, Medical Welfare*. See also Fissell, "Disappearance of the Patient Narrative," 106, who suggests that neighbours rather than doctors were important in shaping the language of sickness.

43 CRO P36/22/46, Lymm survey, 1832.

44 For context, see Turner, *Disability*; and Dickie, "Hilarity and Pitilessness."

45 Alhough still shared, there was a distinctive language used to describe lunacy by families, advocates, and officials, and I return to this issue in chapter 8.

46 See Tomkins, "'Labouring on a Bed of Sickness.'"

47 S. King, "Constructing the Disabled Child."

48 SURC 1505-37-F1, letters.

49 BRO D/P 91/18/4, letter.

50 S. King, "Constructing the Disabled Child."

51 NRO 110p/138, letter. This wider frame of reference resonates with Clare Brant's sense that "narratives of predicament" were used to draw out "the social impact of a case beyond its implications for one individual." Brant, "'Tribunal of the Public,'" 17. Moreover, such letters conveyed a "detailed visual, tactile and social knowledge to officials." P. Hunter, "Containing the Marvellous," 172.

52 RPC, letter. For wider context, see Timmins, *Last Shift*.

53 Unemployment or underemployment and associated languages have a continuous presence in the corpus from the 1750s onward.

54 On the Speenhamland system, see Neuman, *Speenhamland County*; and Boyer, *Economic History*.

55 French, "How Dependent?"; Langton, "Geography of Poor Relief."

56 S. King, "'In These You May Trust.'"

57 SURC SHER-28-5, letter.

58 SURC 1505-37-F2, letter.

59 Snell, "Belonging and Community."

60 NRO 249p/216, letter.

61 NRO 249p/216, letter.

62 LRO PR 2391/29, letter.

63 S. King, Nutt, and Tomkins, eds, *Narratives of the Poor*, vol. 1, 280. On the way that the summation of words added value to a testimony through "accretions of association," see Porter, "Expressing Yourself Ill," 284.

64 Jackson, "Coleridge as Reader"; Jackson, *Romantic Readers*.

65 BRO D/P 91/18/1, letters.

66 BRO D/P 91/18/1, letters. The letters in this bundle are not numbered.

67 BRO D/P 91/18/1, letters. The letters in this bundle are not numbered.

68 BRO D/P 139/18/4, letter.

69 For a discussion of the mechanisms of intertextuality, see Hannan, *Women of Letters*, 12.

70 Intertextuality is clearer for other social groups. See Glaisyer and Pennell, "Introduction"; and Beebee, *Epistolary Fiction*.

71 Benoît, "Chartist Singularity?"; Englander, "From the Abyss"; Tilly, *Popular Contention*; Durbach, "'They Might as Well Brand Us'"; Tilly, "Rise of the Public Meeting"; Innes, "People and Power."

72 Hurren and S. King, "Courtship at the Coroner's·Court."

73 This finding is in contrast to McShane, "'Ne sutor ultra crepidam,'" 226, who argues that in an earlier period "ordinary people accessed ideas from a wide range of popular and classical texts." More widely on adoption of novelistic and other book-framed language, see Fissell, *Vernacular Bodies*, 6; and Berg, *Lives and Letters*, 22. Whyman, *Pen and the People*, 5, argues that "there was an epistolary moment in the eighteenth century when letters and literature were unusually intertwined."

74 S. King, Nutt and Tomkins, eds, *Narratives of the Poor*, vol. 1, 265, 269.

75 See Foreman Cody, "'Every Lane Teams'"; Pickering, "'And Your Petitioners &c'"; and Foyster, "Prisoners Writing Home," 950–2.

76 This observation contrasts with Patriquin, *Agrarian Capitalism*; and Fideler, *Social Welfare*.

77 For context, see contributions to Fumerton and Guerrini, eds, *Ballads and Broadsides*. See also Fissell, *Vernacular Bodies*, 211; and Bertelsen, "Popular Entertainment."

78 Sokoll, *Essex Pauper Letters*, 253. We might compare Rivenhall's language to, for instance, the ballad of Tom Careless, imprisoned through no fault of his own. See http://ballads.bodleian.ox.ac.uk/view/edition/2666.

79 See F. Jones, "Welsh Balladry."

80 D. Hopkin, "Storytelling, Fairytales"; D. Woolf, "Common Voice." On the just outlaw, see Knight, *Robin Hood*; and Seal, *Outlaw Legend*.

81 LRO PR 1349, letter.

82 Hitchcock, "London Vagrancy Crisis"; Eccles, *Vagrancy in Law*; Rogers, "Policing the Poor."

83 Houston, "Church Briefs"; M. Harris, "'Inky Blots'"; Andrew, "'To the Charitable and Humane.'" Hindle, "Civility, Honesty," 51, suggests that the poor may have drawn on the language of charity briefs in framing their claims.

84 Hitchcock, "Tricksters, Lords and Servants," 185-7.

85 However, we might note cases such as the grudging acknowledgment by the vestry of Kirkham in Lancashire on 30 August 1808 of the tenacity of Ralph Morris, who had "been removed twice from this town to Warrington ... at considerable expense" but who had returned on both occasions. The town now proposed to remove him under vagrancy legislation, an interesting circularity for this chapter. See LRO PR 810, Kirkham vestry minutes.

86 CCRO WPR-5-67, letters.

87 RPC, letter. For wider context, see Englander and O'Day, *Retrieved Riches*; Freeman, *Social Investigation*; and Hilliard, "Popular Reading."

88 Heyd, *Reading Newspapers*; P. King, "Making Crime News"; Pearson, *Women's Reading*, 12.

89 Hurley, *Longbridge Deverill Poor*, 9-10. This two-way traffic should not of course surprise us. As noted by Fleet, *Glimpses of Our Ancestors*, 9-10, newspaper journalists were frequent attendees of rallies and (planned) events of unrest, and there was an inevitability that their reportage would be recycled.

90 Sokoll, *Essex Pauper Letters*, 226.

91 NRO 110p/138, letter, 10 September 1829.

92 Glaisyer and Pennell, "Introduction," 3, note that advice literature was published across a range of formats, from reference works to the flimsy, that appealed to a wide range of pockets. In this way, the boundaries of ownership and control of knowledge broke down. See also Ingram and Wetherall Dickson, eds, *Depression and Melancholy*, vol. 4; Secord, "Science in the Pub"; Wigelsworth, "Bi-Partisan Politics"; Topham, "Publishing 'Popular Science'"; and Stolberg, *Experiencing Illness*.

93 G. Smith, "Prescribing the Rules," 251.

94 Porter, "Spreading Medical Enlightenment"; Fissell, "Readers, Texts and Contexts."

95 NORO PD 358/63, letter.

96 Sokoll, *Essex Pauper Letters*, 235, 243, 462, 496–7.

97 NRO 261p/220-252a, bundle 243, letter.

98 See contributions to Elliott, Gerber, and Sinke, eds, *Letters across Borders*. On the specific use of emigrant letters, see van Ginderachter, "'If Your Majesty,'" 76, 80; and Gerber, *Authors of Their Lives*. See also Kamphoefner, "Immigrant Epistolarity."

99 Foyster, "Prisoners Writing Home," 946, 959, argues that the published letters of prisoners were an important literary source. On the wider potential for adoption of the "substantial body of non-fictional epistolary writings with which many eighteenth-century readers were familiar," see Brant, *Eighteenth-Century Letters*, 9. More expansively, see Chartier, Boureau, and Dauphin, eds, *Correspondence*.

100 For an example of a set of widely circulated letters that were of sufficient value to transcribe verbatim into a diary, see Bottomley, ed., *Southwold Diary*, vol. 1, 63.

101 SURC 1505-37-F2, letter.

102 Porter, "Expressing Yourself Ill," 278.

103 On emulative writing, see Fox and D. Woolf, "Introduction," 9.

104 Gerber, "Epistolary Ethics," 15–16.

105 Hence Joyce, "People's English," 155, argues that language did not simply reflect experience but constituted it.

106 Porter, "Expressing Yourself Ill," 283.

107 Hollen Lees, *Solidarities of Strangers*, 7, 22, 36, 39.

108 N. Hopkin, "Old and the New," 500.

109 See Brant, "'Tribunal of the Public,'" 18, who argues that "plain [writing] might offend, polite might be ignored."

CHAPTER SIX

1 SURC 1505-37-F1, letter.

2 SURC 1505-37-F1, letter.

3 This appears to be the place of his original birth or familial residence, not his place of settlement, which was Farnham.

4 SURC 1505-37-F2, letter.

5 Ibid.

6 van Voss, "Introduction," 9.

7 Joyce, "People's English," 162. G. Morgan and Rushton, "Visible Bodies," 54, characterise the eighteenth century as the "age of disguise" and

suggest that "the nineteenth century became the age of official identities," such that the poor would have become increasingly well aware of the identifiers that they absolutely had to convey.

8 Gerber, "Epistolary Ethics," 15–16, argues that although "writers are always the first readers of the text," they "read not only as themselves but to some extent as they anticipate the intended recipient of the letter will read." See also D. Harley, "Rhetoric and the Social," 414.

9 Joyce, "People's English," 169.

10 Dekker, *Egodocuments and History*; Lyons, *History of Reading*; Sczesny, Kießling, and Burkhardt, eds, *Prekariat im 19. Jahrhundert*; Sczesny, *Der lange Weg*; D. Hopkin, *Voices of the People*; Gusdorf, "Conditions and Limits." On the sense that letters and novels "sit [squarely] on the fact/fiction divide" and that their readers had to "distinguish between brute fact and fantastical whimsy," see Berg, *Lives and Letters*, 13, 15. Eckerle, *Romancing the Self*, 2, suggests that life writing is characterised by "blurry" distinctions between truth and fiction.

11 Boulton, "Double Deterrence."

12 French and Barry, "Identity and Agency," 23. See also Chalmers, "'Person I Am,'" 180, who argues that the boundaries between history and fiction were indeterminate.

13 Eckerle, *Romancing the Self*, 2, reminds us that the label "history" had fluid connotations and applied to "narratives of all types, true or fictional."

14 For the wider provenance of this sort of approach to letters and letter sets, see Fissell, *Vernacular Bodies*, 232.

15 Nor should we forget that this same process of history making and telling was played out in face-to-face encounters. Those turned down by vestries usually came back with more of their stories rather than going away or appealing to magistrates.

16 Gerber, "Acts of Deceiving," 321, reminds us that letters "are not narratives, but a collaborative process of interpersonal communication."

17 See Jütte, *Poverty and Deviance*, 1.

18 The act of retelling is implicit in subsequent discussion. Recapping and revisiting were important parts of solidifying a fiction and accreting other fictions, not least because repeated tales gain traction by additional circulation. I am grateful to Professor Helen King for this observation.

19 Gerber, "Epistolary Masquerades," 143, argues that letters "are not principally about documenting the world" but are rather an attempt to protect and configure relationships "rendered vulnerable by long-distance, long-term separation."

20 However, stories also had to be believable.

21 Gerber, "Acts of Deceiving," 322, 326; Fissell, *Vernacular Bodies*, 11.

22 On the law of familial responsibility for poor relatives, see Jütte, *Poverty and Deviance*, 86–90; and Thomson, "'I Am Not.'"

23 For wider context on these residential arrangements, see contributions to Probert, ed., *Cohabitation and Non-Marital Births*.

24 Sczesny, *Der lange Weg*; contributions to Althammer, Raphael, and Stazic-Wendt, eds, *Rescuing the Vulnerable*. In the English context, many writers reminded officials that they were known to them or known in the area.

25 SURO Par.400-37-128, letters, 4 September 1820 and 20 September 1820.

26 SURO Par.400-37-122, letter.

27 Probert, ed., *Cohabitation and Non-Marital Births*.

28 More widely, Brant and Purkiss, "Introduction," 2, remind us that stories can be truly unified and codified only in acts of telling and retelling.

29 SURO Par.400-37-123, letter.

30 Pons, "Mystical and the Modern," 92.

31 On this common European experience, see contributions to Lyons, ed., *Ordinary Writings*. For a wider theoretical framework, see Charon, *Narrative Medicine*.

32 Tilly, "Rise of the Public Meeting"; Hanley, "Public's Reaction," 394–5. See also Lemmings, "Introduction," 18.

33 Andrew, "'To the Charitable and Humane'"; Lloyd, *Charity and Poverty*, 1–35.

34 Gerber, *Authors of Their Lives*.

35 Howie, "Complaints and Complaint Procedures." For a wider sense of how ordinary people might have got used to making complaints, see contributions to Reinarz and Wynter, eds, *Complaints, Controversies*.

36 Richardson, "'Havying Nothing upon Hym,'" 211, italics in original.

37 See P. King, "Rights of the Poor."

38 Gerber, "Acts of Deceiving," 317.

39 MCL M10/808-816, Hulme letter books. The Hulme letters were originally pasted or filed (in no particular order) into large volumes comprised of A3 paper, which is 297 by 420 millimetres. Subsequently, many of them have worked loose and sit between pages. These volumes are currently undergoing conservation.

40 On the importance of public reputation, see S. Woolf, *Poor in Western Europe*, 16–17.

41 MCL M10/809, letter.

42 STRO D24/A/PO/3096, letter. I am grateful to Alannah Tomkins for giving me a copy of this letter.

43 MCL M10/809, letter.

44  MCL M10/814, letters. A selection of the Hulme letters, including the entire Hudswell series, can be found in S. King, Nutt, and Tomkins, eds, *Narratives of the Poor*, vol. 1.
45  MCL M10/814, letters.
46  See, for instance, J. Taylor, "Privacy, Publicity"; Muldrew, "Class and Credit"; and Pernau, "'By Their Feelings.'"
47  SURC 1505-37-F1, letter.
48  Innes, "'Mixed Economy of Welfare'"; Shave, *Pauper Policies*.
49  STRO D24/A/PO/3081, letter. See also Rose, *English Poor Law*, 61, who notes that such burdens meant there was an incentive to do little or nothing while in office.
50  van Leeuwen, "Histories of Risk," 39, argues that the functioning of any relief system requires "cooperation between the elites and the poor. If elites did not use poor relief as a control strategy the poor could not use it as a survival strategy."
51  G. Roberts, "Troubles of a Pauper," 114.
52  S. Woolf, *Poor in Western Europe*, 32.
53  NRO 249p/216, letter.
54  Ibid.
55  French and Barry, "Identity and Agency," 23.
56  ORO PAR 207/5/A2/7, letter.
57  SURC 1505-37-F2, letter.
58  RPC, letter.
59  BRO D/P 132/18/12, letter.
60  Shepard, "Honesty, Worth and Gender," 95.
61  The wider micro-study literature highlights many cases in which the disreputable pauper nonetheless managed to get relief. For instance, see Hastings, *Poverty and the Poor Law*, 32, who argues that "townships seem to have cared for even the least-deserving of their poor." See also N. Hopkin, "Old and the New," 141.
62  MCL M10/814, letters.
63  LRO PR 866, letter.
64  Fissell, *Vernacular Bodies*, 11.
65  P. King, "Rights of the Poor."
66  CCRO WPR-19-7-6, letter.
67  Sherman, *Imagining Poverty*, 7; Green, *Pauper Capital*, 16.
68  For a good discussion of this function of letters more generally, see Lawrence, "'Begging Pardon,'" 203.
69  Burt and Archer, "Introduction," 1.
70  On orderly sociability, see Hallam, "Speaking to Reveal," 242.
71  On the early modern period, see Hindle, "Civility, Honesty," 47.

72 Richardson, "'Havying Nothing upon Hym,'" 211.
73 As Dunkley, *Crisis*, 32, suggests, officials had to maintain a local credibility for themselves and their office. On the wider fictionality of histories embodied in letters, see Favret, *Romantic Correspondence*, 33–4.
74 Hindle, "Civility, Honesty," 53.
75 Marshall, *English Poor*, 224.
76 Hindle, "Civility, Honesty," 40.

CHAPTER SEVEN

1 NDRO EP79/99/5, letter.
2 See D. Harley, "Rhetoric and the Social," 433; and Bizzell and Herzberg, *Rhetorical Tradition*.
3 See Richards and Thorne, "Introduction," 10–13; Wertheimer, "Introduction," 18; and C. Lambert, "Patient and Communication."
4 I do not consider interspersing letters separately because the diversity of their purpose and timing means that they embody many of the rhetorical themes outlined in tables 7.1 to 7.6.
5 See Poland and Pedersen, "Reading between the Lines," 298–300, 305, who argue that silences constitute a "paralanguage" and that we can see three forms of silence: that of estrangement, that of familiarity, and that which is encultured.
6 On faith as a rhetorical tool, see D. Harley, "Rhetoric and the Social," 431.
7 On "battle" narratives, see Frank, *Wounded Storyteller*, 97–136.
8 WYRO WDP20/9/3/8, letter.
9 D. Harley, "Rhetoric and the Social," 417, 434, argues that the social construction of sickness, and through sickness respectability and deservingness, required a "great deal of rhetorical work" to establish and maintain.

CHAPTER EIGHT

1 NRO 261p/220-252a, bundle 244, letter.
2 On the dynamics of settlement legislation and case law, see Snell, *Parish and Belonging*.
3 Legislation passed in 1795 allowed parishes to seek and suspend orders where paupers were not fit to be removed, charging settlement parishes for relief given in the meantime.
4 For wider commentary on the use of friendship and patronage as a rhetorical tool in ordinary narratives, see S. King and P. Jones, "Testifying for the Poor."
5 NRO 261p/220-252a, bundle 244, letter.

6 The implication, of course, is that South believed he had acted with integrity and honesty and that nonresponse was a test of both his credit and his credibility. See Shepard, "Honesty, Worth and Gender," 90, 93, for an important discussion of these issues that is also applicable to my period.

7 NRO 261p/220-252a, bundle 244, letter.

8 Ibid. On the wider importance of ordinary writers weaving personal connections into their texts in a type of "invasive commentary," see Adell-Gombert, "Total Writing," 47–8.

9 Richards and Thorne, "Introduction," 16.

10 On conceptual vocabularies, see D. Harley, "Rhetoric and the Social," 420. On the roots of the rhetoric of struggle and suffering in martyrological literature, see Lawrence, "'Beggin Pardon,'" 201.

11 Bailey, "'Think Wot a Mother Must Feel.'"

12 COWAC B1344, letter.

13 WYRO WDP20/9/3/9, letter.

14 The power of nakedness and compromised clothing as a rhetorical strategy is revisited in chapter 10. On the concept of entreaty and the related rhetorical vehicle of amicus, see Richards and Thorne, "Introduction," 15; and P. Jones and S. King, "From Petition."

15 NRO 249p/166, vestry minutes, 1832–35.

16 On this issue and broader trends in national thought on the dependent poor, see Poynter, *Society and Pauperism*; Himmelfarb, *Idea of Poverty*; and French, "Irrevocable Shift."

17 WYRO WDP20/9/3/7, letter.

18 For the Keeling correspondence, see S. King, Nutt, and Tomkins, eds, *Narratives of the Poor*, vol. 1, 219–23.

19 COWAC B1344, letter.

20 BRO D/P 139/18/4, letter.

21 COWAC B1344, letter.

22 Sokoll, *Essex Pauper Letters*, 381.

23 WYRO WDP20/9/3/13, letter.

24 WYRO WDP20/9/3/11, letter.

25 LRO PR 2391/20, letter.

26 I understand custom as a framework of broadly accepted entitlements and forms of behaviour. By contrast, precedent might be constructed as a set of backward-looking or contemporaneous reference points. Although precedent equally seeks to constrain and direct action, it is more particular to the circumstance of the individual or place. For this chapter, I consider the two as synonymous because both poor writers and others in the epistolary world of the parish also considered and used them as such. On the rela-

tionship between custom, precedent, and common law, see Charlesworth, "How Poor Law Rights," 275.

27 On the process by which implications and statements of custom could be transformed into real customary rights, see Bushaway, "'Things Said or Sung,'" 259.

28 Dunkley, *Crisis*, 100.

29 Thompson, *Customs in Common*; Innes, *Inferior Politics*; Shave, *Pauper Policies*; Thompson, *Making of the English*; C. Griffin, *Rural War*; Prothero, "Chartism and French Radicalism"; and Navickas, *Protest and the Politics*.

30 Sherman, *Imagining Poverty*, 4–5.

31 French, "How Dependent?" But see for comparison Sokoll, "Families, Wheat Prices."

32 WYRO WDP20/9/3/8, letter. This is also, of course, evidence of the shared fictions outlined in chapter 6.

33 Sokoll, *Essex Pauper Letters*, 301.

34 WYRO WDP20/9/3/8, letter.

35 Sokoll, *Essex Pauper Letters*, 226.

36 COWAC B1344, letter.

37 WYRO WDP20/9/3/13, letter.

38 Charlesworth, *Welfare's Forgotten Past*.

39 COWAC K437, letter. For what remains the best discussion of the legal basis for this claim, see Thomas, "Treatment of Poverty," 39.

40 S. King, *Sickness, Medical Welfare*.

41 WYRO WDP20/9/3/9, letter.

42 WYRO WDP20/9/3/8, letter.

43 WYRO WDP20/9/3/12, letter. On the legal duty of parishes to prevent starvation, to which this passage effectively relates, see Charlesworth, "How Poor Law Rights," 273.

44 RPC, letter.

45 On this matter, see Bushaway, "'Things Said or Sung,'" 258.

46 WYRO WDP20/9/3/11, letter.

47 WYRO WDP20/9/3/11, letter.

48 WYRO WDP139/7/8, letter.

49 COWAC B1344, letter.

50 S. King, "Regional Patterns."

51 S. King, "Negotiating the Law."

52 See also Healey, *First Century of Welfare*.

53 RPC, letter, dated only 1798.

54 P. King, "Summary Courts"; P. King, "Rights of the Poor."

55 BRO D/P 91/18/3, letter. For wider context on the propensity of marginal groups to directly address the seat of the law, see Taillon, "'All Men Are Entitled,'" 93.

56 For the law on this issue, see Thomson, "'I Am Not.'"

57 BRO D/P 91/18/5, letter.

58 WYRO WDP20/9/3/5, letter.

59 RPC, letters. For the law on removing women with young children, see Levene, "Poor Families."

60 Devereaux, "Promulgation."

61 Lemmings, "Introduction," 10.

62 See E. Griffin, *England's Revelry*.

63 Outhwaite, *Rise and Fall*, 106.

64 Lemmings, "Introduction," 1, 8. Importantly, see also Churches, "False Friends."

65 NRO 110p/138, letter.

66 Such letters spoke to a deep underlying sense of the rights of Englishmen to subsistence. See Gilbert, "Towards the Welfare State."

67 BRO D/P 132/18/15, letter.

68 See S. King, "'It Is Impossible.'"

69 NRO 249p/216, letter.

70 Ibid. Presumably, "the Act of Parliament" refers to the New Poor Law of 1834.

71 Ibid.

72 BRO D/P 91/18/7, letter.

73 See P. King, "Social Inequality"; and S. King, "'Stop This Overwhelming Torment.'" For a forceful rendering of the personal and moral lenses through which the poor filtered political knowledge and ideas, see Brodie, *Politics of the Poor*, 12–13.

74 GRO P52 OV 7-1, letter.

75 Poor writers often elided – sometimes in the same letter – the concepts of humanitarianism, humanity, and goodness, even though they plainly encompass different sentiments and philosophies.

76 On this conundrum, see Horne, *Property Rights*; Fideler, *Social Welfare*; and Patriquin, *Agrarian Capitalism*.

77 EYRO PE1-702, letter.

78 COWAC B1344, letter. Many writers also elided the concept of humanity with a lack of, or need for, sympathy for their predicament.

79 NRO 110p/135, letters.

80 BRO D/P 132/18/12, letter, 29 January 1829; BRO D/P 132/18/15, letter, 21 January 1830.

81 WYRO WDP20/9/3/17, letter.

82 WYRO WDP20/9/3/18, letter.
83 P. Jones and S. King, "From Petition."
84 BRO D/P 132/18/15, letter.
85 WYRO WDP20/9/3/9, letter.
86 WYRO WDP20/9/3/10, letter.
87 COWAC B1344, letter, undated.
88 WYRO WDP20/9/3/12, letter.
89 WYRO WDP20/9/3/18, letter.
90 S. King, Nutt, and Tomkins, eds, *Narratives of the Poor*, vol. 1, 230.
91 Ibid., 293.
92 COWAC B1344, letter.
93 SORO DD/SAS/C909/23, letter, undated but likely 1804.
94 The rhetorical category of friend is sometimes indivisible from that of neighbour or kin and also fuses together willing and unwilling connections to the writer. In terms of the latter, we can detect cases in the corpus where writers in effect begged from neighbours but did not want to say so and cases of neighbours who gave support in relation to acts of begging by their neighbours and acquaintances but did not want to acknowledge it. Both relationships might be smoothed over by the use of the fiction of friendship. See Hitchcock, "Begging on the Streets," 498.
95 COWAC K418, letter.
96 RPC, letter.
97 COWAC B1344, letter.
98 COWAC K437, letter.
99 Sokoll, *Essex Pauper Letters*, 483–4.
100 NRO 325p/194, letter.
101 WYRO WDP20/9/3/6, letter.
102 CCRO WPR-5-67, letter; CCRO WPR-60-21-13, letter, dated on 1782.
103 See contributions to Johnson and Sabean, eds, *Sibling Relations*; and contributions to R. Smith and Tadmor, eds, "Kinship in Britain."
104 S. King, "Forme et fonction"; R. Smith, "Charity, Self-Interest."
105 Shepard, "Honesty, Worth and Gender," 90–1, 97–8.
106 COWAC B1344, letter.
107 On the broad framework for this point, see Higgs, "Fingerprints and Citizenship."

### CHAPTER NINE

1 SURO Par.29-37-10/3, letter. An addendum from Dr Farmer, the surgeon at the Brighton Hospital, confirmed that "The above named expenses are not defrayed by the hospital." See also Berry, "Community Sponsorship."

2 SURO Par.29-37-10/5, letter.
3 On the way that "character" could cut through other grouping mechanisms such as rank, class, or gender and for a discussion of the way that
letters themselves afforded a forum in which individuals could reimagine
themselves and be reimagined, see Brant, *Eighteenth-Century Letters*, 24.
4 On how character was established in the wider community, see Smail,
"Credit, Risk and Honor"; contributions to Ernst, ed., *Histories of the
Normal*; Offer, "'Virtue,' 'Citizen Character'"; and S. Williams, "'Good
Character.'"
5 On how these variables might constellate to shape character in the popular imagination, see Lynch, *Economy of Character*.
6 Green, *Pauper Capital*, 11. For echoing perspectives on an earlier period,
see Hindle, "Civility, Honesty," 47–8, 52.
7 NRO 249p/216, letter.
8 DRO PE/SW/VE/1/1, Swanage vestry minutes, 1788–1818.
9 In the theatre of the epistolary world of the parish, observations that a
writer could make do with a small allowance sometimes generated balancing correspondence from officers that in effect asked, "How small?"
10 ORO PAR 16/5/A11/8, letter.
11 P. Jones and S. King, "From Petition."
12 Tomkins, "Women and Poverty," 154.
13 See contributions to Bland and Cross, eds, *Gender and Politics*; Eckerle,
*Romancing the Self*; and contributions to Brant and Purkiss, eds, *Women,
Texts and Histories*.
14 Gerber, *Authors of Their Own Lives*.
15 For instance, see Sokoll, "Old Age"; and S. King, "'Stop This Overwhelming Torment.'"
16 ORO PAR 211/5/C1/1/15, letter.
17 ORO PAR 211/5/C1/1/34, letter.
18 Lloyd, *Charity and Poverty*; Andrew, *Philanthropy and Police*; Hindle,
"'Good, Godly,'" 178, 181, 188.
19 For wider context, see S. Morgan, "Reward of Public Service."
20 HRO 25M60 PO35, letter.
21 HRO 25M60 PO35, letter. For wider context on this sort of experience,
see Navickas, *Protest and the Politics*; P. Jones, "Finding Captain Swing";
and C. Griffin, *Rural War*.
22 On societal understandings of honesty and probity, see Levene, "'Honesty,
Sobriety and Diligence'"; Levine-Clark, *Unemployment, Welfare*; and
Nünning, "From 'Honour' to 'Honest.'"
23 BRO D/P 139/18/4, letter.
24 Sokoll, *Essex Pauper Letters*, 104.

25 On attitudes toward the mothers and fathers of illegitimate children, see Nutt, "Illegitimacy"; and Evans, *Unfortunate Objects*.

26 HRO 25M60 PO35, letter.

27 BRO D/P 132/18/15, letter.

28 Ibid.

29 Ibid. See also S. King, "English Pauper Letter."

30 HRO 25M60 PO35, letter.

31 For an important discussion of suffering as a rhetorical concept, see D. Harley, "Rhetoric and the Social."

32 BRO D/P 71/13/1, letter.

33 CORO X326-60, letter.

34 BRO D/P 26/18/1, letter.

35 S. King, "Regional Patterns."

36 This duration almost certainly reflects a more dense makeshift economy in large urban areas, something that fostered longer struggle at or slightly below the margin between dependence and independence. See Tomkins, *Experience of Urban Poverty*.

37 LRO PR 1349, letter.

38 LRO PR 866, letter, 12 June 1812.

39 S. King, *Poverty and Welfare*.

40 LRO PR 866, letter.

41 S. King, "Welfare Regimes."

42 For context, see S. King and P. Jones, "Testifying for the Poor."

43 Sokoll, *Essex Pauper Letters*, 116, my italics. This use of the "tribunal of the public" to heap pressure on a co-respondent was a common vehicle, and its adoption by the poor in this context is interesting. See Brant, "'Tribunal of the Public,'" 17.

44 LRO PR 866, letters, 27 June 1816 and 1 July 1816.

45 For broad background on the socio-medical construction of disability in this period, see Borsay, *Disability and Social Policy*; and Turner, *Disability*.

46 On fakery, see Hitchcock, *Down and Out*.

47 S. King, "Constructing the Disabled Child."

48 DRO PE/SW/VE/1/1, Swanage vestry minutes, 1788–1818.

49 See Sokoll, *Essex Pauper Letters*; and Thane, *Old Age*.

50 On fragile family economies, see Sokoll, "Negotiating a Living"; Sokoll, "Families, Wheat Prices," 78–106; and Humphries, *Childhood and Child Labour*.

51 LIRO Epworth Par. 13/28/7, letter.

52 Hurley, *Longbridge Deverill Poor*, 1.

53 CORO P170-16, letter. For context, see contributions to Fisher, ed., *Studies in British Privateering*.

54  Hurley, *Longbridge Deverill Poor*, 2–3.
55  LRO PR 1349, letter.
56  CORO P170-16, letter.
57  Ibid.
58  Ibid.
59  HRO 25M60/PO35, letter.
60  CORO FS3-176, letter.
61  Hurren and S. King, "'Begging for a Burial,'" 332.
62  HRO 25M60 PO35, letter.
63  LRO PR 866, letter.
64  MCL M10/812, letter.
65  D. Harley, "Rhetoric and the Social," 411–12, 415, 417, 427–31.
66  CORO ADD448-17, letter.

## CHAPTER TEN

1  ORO PAR 211/5/C1/1/25, letter.
2  Spicksley, "Dynamic Model," 114, reminds us in a different context that language has a prescriptive rather than just a descriptive function. For wider context, see S. King and P. Jones, "Testifying for the Poor."
3  ORO PAR 211/5/C1/1/26, letter.
4  ORO PAR 211/5/C1/1/27, certificate and letter.
5  ORO PAR 211/5/C1/1/28, certificate and letter. See also Hollen Lees, *Solidarities of Strangers*.
6  Ayres, *Paupers and Pig Killers*, 272.
7  On work and dignity, see Harvey, "Craftsmen in Common"; and Begiato, "Between Poise and Power."
8  Marshall, *English Poor*.
9  Horne, *Property Rights*; Himmelfarb, *Idea of Poverty*; Wrigley, "Malthus on the Prospects."
10  French and Barry, "Identity and Agency," 26, 31; Collard, "Malthus, Population"; and Shepard, "Honesty, Worth and Gender," 94.
11  Hindle, "Civility, Honesty," 40–52.
12  See P. King, "Social Inequality"; Braddick and Walter, "Introduction"; and Patriquin, *Agrarian Capitalism*.
13  MCL L82/6, letter.
14  As French and Barry, "Identity and Agency," 10, point out in the context of a wider discussion of the ability to shape one's identity, certain avenues of claims making were closed off by custom, strategy, or self-interest.
15  Such was the case for the Buckinghamshire labourer Joseph Mayett. See P. King, "Social Inequality."

16 Brant, *Eighteenth-Century Letters*, 15, argues in a different context that letters must convey "discourse which is meaningful to particular people at particular places on particular occasions."

17 This question is particularly relevant in a context where, as we are reminded by Eckerle, *Romancing the Self*, 20, writers needed to combine a personalised and self-referential narrative with a referential framework that drew on wider textual and conceptual understandings.

18 On this issue, see the particularly acute analysis by Brant, *Eighteenth-Century Letters*, 21-4.

19 Such rhetoric constructed the problem of poverty as a shared rather than individual experience and as something more than suffering and struggle, and it constructed the alleviation of poverty as a general principle rather than a matter of individual Christian or humanitarian response.

20 NRO 325p/193, letter book.

21 NRO 325p/193, letter book.

22 NRO 110p/135, letters. See also S. King, Nutt, and Tomkins, eds, *Narratives of the Poor*, vol. 1.

23 S. King, Nutt, and Tomkins, eds, *Narratives of the Poor*, vol. 1, 266-7.

24 BRO D/P 91/18/10, letter. For wider context on the taking-in of children or other kin, see Sharpe, "Poor Children"; and S. King, "Forme et fonction."

25 I have argued, for instance, that the quality and cost of parish responses to requests for clothing were comprehensive, such that the poor on relief were better and more regularly clothed than the independent labouring poor. S. King, "Reclothing the English Poor"; S. King, "'I Fear You Will Think.'" By contrast, for the argument that parishes invested more selectively and strategically in clothing, see P. Jones, "'I Cannot Keep'"; and P. Jones, "Clothing the Poor." On second-hand clothing, see M. Lambert, "'Cast-Off Wearing Apparel.'"

26 CCRO WPR-102-116, letter.

27 On tensions around the commodification of dress, see Ogborn, *Spaces of Modernity*, 232.

28 LRO PR 866, letter, 17 August 1814.

29 On the roots of this basic element of dignity, see contributions to Richardson, ed., *Clothing Culture*; and King, "Kleidung und Würde."

30 Hurley, *Longbridge Deverill Poor*, 9.

31 LRO PR 866, letter.

32 The idea that dignity involved leading a life of self-determination can also be seen in letters written by advocates.

33 NRO 261p/220-252a, bundle 244, letter.

34 NRO 261p/220-252a, bundle 244, letter.

35 LRO PR 2391/29, letter.

36 NRO 325p/193, letter.
37 Ibid.
38 S. King, Nutt, and Tomkins, eds, *Narratives of the Poor*, vol. 1, 248.
39 Ibid., 251.
40 Ibid., 252.
41 Ibid., 253.
42 BRO D/P 91/18/5, letter.
43 See Scholl, *Hunger Movements*; Bohstedt, *Politics of Provision*; and Booth, "Food Riots."
44 BRO D/P 91/18/5, letter.
45 S. King, "Pauvreté et assistance."
46 Hurley, *Longbridge Deverill Poor*, 18.
47 GRO P328 OV 7-1 to 7-10, letter.
47 Geering, *Our Sussex Parish*, 101. The term "overseer" here clearly denotes the Old Poor Law rather than the New Poor Law.
49 Hurren and S. King, "'Begging for a Burial.'" For the definitive work on burial traditions of the later nineteenth century, see Strange, *Death, Grief.* For an unparalleled description of the decency of a pauper funeral, see Dorothy Wordsworth's description of an 1800 event in Grasmere in Cumberland, reproduced in A. Taylor, ed., *Country Diaries*, 222-3.
50 NRO 325p/193, letter.
51 NRO 325p/194, letter. There is an attached draft reply authorising burial "as you would bury a pauper in your parish" but as economically as possible.
52 NRO 325p/194, letter.
53 BRO D/P 91/18/10, letter.
54 LRO PR 2391/38, letter, 16 February 1808.
55 LMA P95-MRY-1-427, vestry book; PLSC, vestry book.
56 S. King, Nutt, and Tomkins, eds, *Narratives of the Poor*, vol. 1, 225.
57 Sharpe, "Survival Strategies and Stories," 239.
58 On the ways that people might seek to remap the essential attributes of an identity – dignity, honesty, civility, and so on – see Spicksley, "Dynamic Model," 131.
59 P. King, "Social Inequality," 82.
60 On the way that letters "dematerialise bodies" and on corresponding attempts in the wider epistolary culture to symbolise body language, see Brant, *Eighteenth-Century Letters*, 22-4. For poor writers, this sort of connectivity can be seen in terms such as "bowed down," "confined to bed" (or home), "broken," and "thin."
61 GRO P328 OV 7-1 to 7-10, letter, 7 May 1835.

62 Thane, *Old Age*; Ottaway, *Decline of Life*; R. Smith, "Ageing and Well-Being."

## CHAPTER ELEVEN

1 Sokoll, *Essex Pauper Letters*, 103.
2 Charlesworth, *Welfare's Forgotten Past*.
3 On the way that the confection and telling of stories of need associated with old age could create a "community of experience" and a narrative thread recognisable to all parties in the epistolary world of communities, see Seed, "History and Narrative," 47.
4 Even in these cases, however, there were often subsidiary claims and causes, as the discussion of the broad dynamics of the pauper letter corpus in chapter 1 noted.
5 Tomkins, "'Labouring on a Bed of Sickness.'"
6 For a broad rendering of the debate about when old age "starts," see von Kondratowitz, "Medicalisation of Old Age," 132; Ottaway, *Decline of Life*; Thane, *Old Age*; Bonfield, "Was There a 'Third Age'?" 43; and Barker-Read, "Treatment of the Aged Poor," 24–7.
7 See E. Campbell, "Introduction"; Beam, "'Should I as Yet?'" 99–104; Thane, *Old Age*, 103–14; and Hunt, "Paupers and Pensioners." For a particularly good rendering of how differences of gender and age among the sorts of people absorbed into the households of kin could influence those approaching the poor law and thus writing letters or attending vestries, see Sokoll, "Household Position."
8 FRO P/30/1/235, letter.
9 R. Smith, "Ageing and Well-Being"; French, "Irrevocable Shift."
10 Ottaway, "Introduction," 7, suggests that at best the aged poor "were undoubtedly patching together lives of independent misery," a sentiment we see in many of the letters from the aged poor and their advocates.
11 MCL M10/813, letter.
12 On the scale of the aged population at different dates, see Thane, *Old Age*, 20, 90, 114–30, 214; Hunt, "Paupers and Pensioners," 414; Ottaway, "Providing for the Elderly"; and Pearson, "'Labor and Sorrow,'" 129–39.
13 ORO Wootton P.C. IX/iv/9, letter.
14 For wider commentary on the visible struggle for independence and the limits to reinvention, see Thane, "Untiring Zest for Life," 242.
15 NDRO EP79/99, letter.
16 NDRO EP17/26/1, letter.

17 GRO P52 OV 7-1, letter.
18 GRO P328 OV 7-1 to 7-10, letter.
19 Sokoll, *Essex Pauper Letters*, 120–1.
20 Ibid., 147.
21 Ibid., 148–9.
22 Ibid., 140.
23 Ibid., 150. On mimetic capital – the accumulation of a bank of images and stories about what old age was and looked like, which could form the basis for a final claim – see E. Campbell, "Introduction," 4–5.
24 NDRO EP79/99, letter. On widely understood entitlements to claim assistance from parishes in the face of physical decline, see Ottaway, "Introduction," 6.
25 NDRO EP79/99, letter.
26 GRO P328a OV 7-1 to 7-20. Gray, "Experience of Old Age," 112, argues that the rhetoric of advanced and disabling old age created a widely understood entitlement to a favourable reading of appeals.
27 GRO P328 OV 7-1 to 7-10, letter.
28 FRO P/30/1/235, letter.
29 GRO P328 OV 7-1 to 7-10, letter.
30 ORO PAR 211/5/C1/1/45, letter.
31 GRO P154 OV 3-5-5, letter.
32 GRO P193 OV 7-1, letter.
33 On writers' difficulty discerning whether they had said "enough" when they did not have the visual clues of a face-to-face encounter, see Poland and Pedersen, "Reading between the Lines," 296.
34 In turn, written statements (and the spoken word) helped to fix the experience and crystallisation of the emotion in the minds of the poor. See Reddy, *Navigation of Feeling*; and Reddy, *Making of Romantic Love*. For a wider discussion of how depression might silence the self and shape the content, rhetoric, and tone of writing, see Jack, *Silencing the Self*.
35 LRO PR 866, letter, 9 January 1813.
36 Brant and Purkiss, "Introduction," 2.
37 Richards and Thorne, "Introduction," 7, 13.
38 Daybell, "Introduction," 6. Poland and Pedersen, "Reading between the Lines," 304, argue that even where the rhetorical structure of male and female writing was the same, its meaning to the different participants in the local epistolary world was different.
39 For wider context, although largely focusing on elite women, see contributions to J. Campbell and Larsen, eds, *Early Modern Women*.
40 Such requests in effect adopted the language of the state itself as framed in instruction books to overseers that told them to take up and punish errant

fathers. This subtle rhetorical theme has a much wider purchase in the writing of ordinary women. See Pyle, "Peasant Strategies," 50.

41 ORO MSS. D.D. c.7/i/3, letter.

42 ORO MSS. D.D. c.7/i/4, letter.

43 GRO P328a OV 7-19, letter.

44 On the art of letter writing to "restock personal credit" and for the important argument that "for women, a good name was a question of propriety, not, as for men, of property," see Brant, "'Tribunal of the Public,'" 20, 24. On the disproportionate dangers of workhouse confinement for lone women, see Mackay, "Culture of Poverty?" 217–20.

45 ORO Wootton P.C. IX/iv/3, letter.

46 On the way that, at least for the middling orders, abandonment by a wife might contravene masculine identity, see Tosh, *Manliness and Masculinities*. Men sometimes blamed other women for leading their wives astray, thus adopting a much wider cultural construction of the danger of female networks. See Piper, "'Women's Special Enemy.'"

47 BRO D/P 91/18/7, letter.

48 BRO D/P 91/18/7, letter.

49 For evidence that men needed more dependent children than did women to be pushed into destitution, see Mackay, "Culture of Poverty?" 224.

50 Sokoll, *Essex Pauper Letters*, 159–60.

51 Moring and Wall, *Widows in European Economy*; Erickson, "Property and Widowhood"; Foyster, "Marrying the Experienced Widow."

52 Schmidt, "Survival Strategies of Widows," 270.

53 GRO P78-1 OV 7-2, letter. Sharpe, "Survival Strategies and Stories," 235, argues that widows were peculiarly likely to use the rhetoric and methods of (male) officials when they engaged with parishes, notably emphasising respectability and self-help, both of which we see in this letter.

54 Sharpe, "Parish Women."

55 See Sokoll, "Household Position," 213, 216, 220; and Botelho, "'Old Woman's Wish.'"

56 GRO P328 OV 7-1 to 7-10, letter. See also Sharpe, "Survival Strategies and Stories," 221, 230–7.

57 Wertheimer, "Introduction," 11.

58 The use of the word "Charity" is important here, as it shows recognition of the discretionary nature of parochial support.

59 GRO P328 OV 7-1 to 7-10, letter.

60 On the rhetoricisation of suffering as a deliberative speech act, see Richards and Thorne, "Introduction," 16.

61 For wider context, see ibid., 13–15; Barnes, *Epistolary Community*, 9; and Pyle, "Peasant Strategies," 55.

62 However, unlike in other contexts, the occurrence of these similarities is not due to the fact that the letters were written by men. See Cross and Bland, "Gender Politics," 10. For discussion of a register shared by the genders, see Wertheimer, "Introduction," 8.

63 This self-construction accords with broad historiographical agreement that old men were less likely to be taken in by relatives. See Green, "Icons of the New System."

64 On the wider connectivity between this rhetorical infrastructure and the construction of masculinity on which it draws, see Tosh, *Manliness and Masculinities*, 130–42.

65 The letter was addressed to "The Overseers of the Parish of Brumton Co of Berks to the Care Thos Hales to be left at the Angle Inn Wilhamton England." The letter was initially misdirected, and a different hand has annotated the letter with "Try Woolhampton nr Newbury." Eventually, the letter went to three other places before it reached Brimpton, which emphasises, as we saw in chapter 3, the precariousness of postage.

66 BRO D/P 26/18/1, letter. On how "the endless struggle" to provide affected the mental health of nineteenth-century men, see Suzuki, "Lunacy and Labouring Men."

67 MORO D.365.82, letter.

68 Wall, "Families in Crisis"; S. King, "'Particular Claims.'" On the economic impact of nursing and the analogous parochial response of increasing formal nursing provision to preserve family economies, see S. King, "Nursing under the Old Poor Law."

69 Bailey, "'Think Wot a Mother Must Feel.'" On the wider concept of maternal failure and the way that it might be turned to advantage in negotiations, see Bowers, *Politics of Motherhood*, 25.

70 GRO P328 OV 7-1 to 7-10, letter.

71 DERO PD-38-1-180, letter, translation by Dr Pamela Michael. Walter, "Faces in the Crowd," 111, reminds us that this sort of rhetoric of compromised feminine roles was duplicated in the ways that women sought to justify their presence at times of mass protest. The letter also speaks to the different way that many female writers constructed the term "home." Men generally rhetoricised home in terms of settlement, whereas most women tied together residence, local credit and respectability, and having a defined local persona.

72 MORO D.365.657, letter.

73 EYRO PE1-702, Dorothy Styrin letters.

74 Walter, "Faces in the Crowd," 114, argues that this ability of women to "turn their marginal relationship to the structures of power" to good effect can also be seen on the wider canvas of social relations.

75  Walter, "Faces in the Crowd," 122.
76  BRO D/P 139/18/4, letter.
77  GRO P328a OV 7-19, letter.
78  GRO P328a OV 7-20, letter.
79  See Tosh, *Manliness and Masculinities*; contributions to Broughton and Rogers, eds, *Gender and Fatherhood*; Strange, *Fatherhood and the British*; Jenkins, *Fatherhood, Authority*; and contributions to Delap, Griffin, and Wills, eds, *Politics of Domestic Authority*.
80  GRO P328a OV 7-18, letter.
81  GRO P328 OV 7-1 to 7-10, letter.
82  NRO 325p/194, letter.
83  ORO PAR 211/5/C1/1/23, letter.
84  MCL L82/8, letter.
85  On the Speenhamland system, see Neuman, *Speenhamland County*; and Boyer, *Economic History*.
86  For a summary of this literature, see Sokoll, "Families, Wheat Prices."
87  BRO D/P 91/18/7, letter.
88  CORO P128-19, letter.
89  CORO ADD448-17, letter.
90  Tomkins, "Women and Poverty," 168–9, argues that despite the gradual emergence of rights-based claims among women, they "could not be confident" of their claims succeeding and they "lacked influence." Letters like that of Mills, and corresponding parochial decisions, suggest a very multi-layered and situational world for female claimants.
91  This shared understanding of risk is elaborated upon by S. Woolf, "Order, Class," 194.
92  Deacon, Russell, and Woollacott, "Introduction," 2. On how this messiness might play out for older parish residents, see Sokoll, "Old Age," 143–5.
93  Brant, "'Tribunal of the Public,'" 18.

CHAPTER TWELVE

1  NRO 251p/98, letter. On the cathartic purpose of letters, see Daybell, "Introduction," 8; and contributions to Benstock, ed., *Private Self*, 9.
2  Likewise, modern historians have to struggle with the "identity" of letters as simultaneously works of fiction, fact, and literature. See Boutcher, "Literature, Thought or Fact?"; and van Houdt and Papy, "Introduction."
3  ORO PAR 207/5/C1/3, letter, dated only 1754.
4  ORO PAR 207/5/C1/4, letter. This strong refutation is evidence for the assertion by Adell-Gombert, "Total Writing," 39, that ordinary lives

comprised a "continuous thread of disorder which required stabilisation through writing."

5 Joyce, "People's English," 169, argues that officials actively constructed "images of themselves and of the poor, especially the poor they most desired to see."

6 French and Barry, "Identity and Agency," 3, argue that self and self-identity are crucially dependent upon the dynamic systems of language required to give them meaning. See also Porter, "Introduction," in Burke and Porter, eds, *Language, Self and Society*, 11, who suggests that an expanding linguistic register was the "midwife of individual identity."

7 Thus French and Barry, "Identity and Agency," 29, argue that during the early modern period individual self-identity could not stray far from the shackles of "embedded social assumptions about status or gender." See also Spicksley, "Dynamic Model," 129–31; and contributions to Earle, ed., *Epistolary Selves*.

8 On the deeper histories of self, see contributions to L. Martin, Gutman, and Hutton, eds, *Technologies of the Self*.

9 Wahrman, *Making of the Modern Self*, 78.

10 On identity as masquerade, see Brant, *Eighteenth-Century Letters*, 24.

11 On storytelling as a mechanism through which those breaking out of the collective identities of religion, class, place, or occupation made sense of their lives for themselves and others, see D. Hopkin, "Storytelling, Fairy-tales," 188, 196–7. More widely, see contributions to Regard, ed., *Mapping the Self*; and Nussbaum, *Autobiographical Subject*.

12 However, for a particularly penetrating analysis of autobiography among the occasionally poor, see Tomkins, "Workhouse Medical Care."

13 P. King, "Social Inequality," 69.

14 Lyons, *Writing Culture*, 70. One of his other key tests for the existence of a whole self (223) – that we can find evidence of the elaboration and understanding of individual personality – is clearly played out in the letters analysed for earlier chapters of this study.

15 Gerber, "Ethnic Identification," 10.

16 Gerber, "Epistolary Ethics."

17 There is no evidence here to support Daybell, "Introduction," 10, who suggests that men were disproportionately likely to "write themselves." On writing and singularity, see van Houdt and Papy, "Introduction," 10–11.

18 Cross and Bland, "Gender Politics," 7.

19 On the ambiguous meaning of silences, see Poland and Pedersen, "Reading between the Lines"; and Burt and Archer, "Introduction," 6.

20 Gusdorf, "Conditions and Limits," 35.

21 Porter, "Introduction," in Porter, ed., *Rewriting the Self*, 9. Eckerle,

*Romancing the Self*, 9–17, notes that the capacity for self-examination was an important component of any constructed self. We see such self-examination across the corpus, even if at times it was superficial.

22 Favret, *Romantic Correspondence*, 4, argues that a letter reaches into the interior as well as exterior worlds of the recipient.

23 For a particularly strong discussion of imposed identities, albeit for a very different period, see Shepard, "Honesty, Worth and Gender," 90.

24 We are more used to thinking of ratepayers as needing to have vigilance. See Hindle, "Civility, Honesty," 53. On sentiment at the end of my study period, see Shave, "Impact."

25 Sherman, *Imagining Poverty*, 3, notes that readers of popular literature were encouraged to think of the poor not as individuals but as a group "configured by numbers uninflected by personal anecdote" and thus, as it were, "commodified."

26 See Porter, "Introduction," in Porter, ed., *Rewriting the Self*, 11.

27 Sokoll, *Essex Pauper Letters*, 107. On the need for the notionally powerless to avoid the "proliferation of identities" and to engage in "recuperative portrayal" if a negative identity should adhere, see Chalmers, "'Person I Am,'" 182, 185.

28 LRO PR 866, letters, 1 January 1817, 8 October 1817, 17 November 1817, and 12 December 1817.

29 SURO-Par.100-37-3, letter.

30 Sokoll, *Essex Pauper Letters*, 91–7.

31 S. King and P. Jones, "Testifying for the Poor."

32 CORO B-Lis-340, letter, 11 January 1804.

33 On mechanisms for salvaging character by appealing to the tribunal of local opinion, see Brant, "'Tribunal of the Public,'" 24.

34 SURO Par.29-37-10/17, letter, 14 December 1834.

35 Hurley, *Longbridge Deverill Poor*, 12.

36 On the importance of stories and a narrative past for creating and reshaping selfhood and identity, see Seed, "History and Narrative," 46, 48; Rich, "Storied Identities"; and Hannan, *Women of Letters*, 10.

37 Snell, *Parish and Belonging*.

38 Higgs, "Fingerprints and Citizenship." On the deep roots of problems in understanding who "belonged," see Hindle, "Destitution, Liminality."

39 On the importance of marshalled and retained stories, see Mascuch, *Origins of the Individualist Self*.

40 NRO 249p/216, letter. This letter, of course, fuses together identification and personal identity.

41 NRO 249p/216, letter.

42 NRO 249p/216, letter. On attempts on the Continent to reduce disputes

by introducing stamped identity documents, see Adell-Gombert, "Total Writing," 41–6.

43 LRO PR 1349, letter.

44 For a wider discussion of the signifiers of belonging, see Tabili, *Global Migrants*.

45 S. Webb and B. Webb, *English Poor Law History*, 335. On low levels of removal, see Innes, S. King, and Winter, "Settlement and Belonging."

46 On the important relationship between maintaining contact and maintaining memory, see Hirst, "Making Contact," 33.

47 SURO Par.100-37-3, letter.

48 SURO Par.183-37-3, letter.

49 SURO Par.183-37-3, letter.

50 In parochial correspondence, taking the time to write was itself an indicator of sanguinity. See Hannan, *Women of Letters*, 19.

51 On this complex function of letters, see Richards and Thorne, "Introduction," 16.

52 SURO Par.100-37-3, letter, 21 September 1781.

53 Sokoll, *Essex Pauper Letters*, 187.

54 SURO Par.183-37-3, letter.

55 SURO Par.183-37-3, letter.

56 P. Jones and S. King, "From Petition." On the idea of a "public poor," see Hitchcock, "Publicity of Poverty," 166.

57 NYRO EP17/26/1, letter.

58 BALS PHA 1/3, Halliwell vestry minutes. We find parallels to this sort of logic and rhetoric in sickness narratives that focus on wellness and restitution. See Frank, *Wounded Storyteller*, 97–136.

59 LRO PR 866, letter.

60 WRO 871/185, letter.

61 EYRO PE1-702, letter.

62 Reddy, *Navigation of Feeling*; Reddy, *Making of Romantic Love*.

63 BRO D/P 132/18/15, letters.

64 Tomkins, "'Labouring on a Bed of Sickness.'"

65 For a discussion, see Wessel Hansen, "Grief, Sickness." See also Suzuki, "Lunacy and Labouring Men."

66 MCL L21/3/13/2, letter.

67 CRO P183/10/18, letter.

68 SURO Par.95-37-3, letter.

69 CORO X326-60, letter, 28 August 1811.

70 LRO PR 2391/46, letter, 16 June 1823. This was decidedly an attempt to create the "authoritative and trustworthy rhetorical persona" that Richards and Thorne, "Introduction," 13, see as the aspiration of all women writers.

71  NGRO PR 11482-86, letter, undated.

72  NYRO PR-TAW-13-9, letters, undated.

73  ORO MSS. D.D. c.11/1, letter.

74  ORO MSS. D.D. c.11/2, letter.

75  ORO MSS. D.D. c.11/3, letter; ORO MSS. D.D. c.11/24, letter. The relationship between mental illness, the sense of self of the subject, and that of their family members is complex. See Suzuki, "Lunacy and Labouring Men."

76  ORO MSS. D.D. c.11/6, letter.

77  See Hannan, *Women of Letters*, 12; Eckerle, *Romancing the Self*, 14–17; Berg, *Lives and Letters*, 15–18; and Favret, *Romantic Correspondence*.

78  SURO Par.29-37-10/9, letter.

79  SURO Par.183-37-3, letter.

80  For a strong rendering of this position, see Liljewall, "'Self-Written Lives.'"

81  Eckerle, *Romancing the Self*, 9.

82  Ibid., 15.

83  Pons, "Mystical and the Modern," 98; Eckerle, *Romancing the Self*, 17. See also Porter, "Introduction," in Porter, ed., *Rewriting the Self*, 12.

84  Cross and Bland, "Gender Politics," 7.

85  Illuzzi, "Negotiating," 436; Pons, "Mystical and the Modern," 85.

86  Sherman, *Imagining Poverty*; Himmelfarb, *Idea of Poverty*; Poynter, *Society and Pauperism*; Innes, *Inferior Politics*; and Hollen Lees, *Solidarities of Strangers*.

CHAPTER THIRTEEN

1  GRO P328a OV 7-20, letter.

2  Ibid.

3  On the act of making oneself knowable, see Gerber, "Epistolary Ethics."

4  The importance of this point can be seen in the frequent footnotes about other correspondence appended to pauper letters themselves in Sokoll, *Essex Pauper Letters*.

5  On the wider character of this spectrum, see Ashplant, "Oral, the Aura."

6  Vincent, *Literacy and Popular Culture*; Vincent, *Bread, Knowledge and Freedom*; Lyons, *History of Reading*; Lyons, *Writing Culture*.

7  For the classic statement, see S. Webb and B. Webb, *English Poor Law History*.

8  On silences, see the particularly acute Collins, "Women's Voices."

9  We see this role reach its most sophisticated form in printed advocate cards. These cards contained space for advocates to write their names, the name of the poor applicant, and a suggested amount and date, but they

had the story of the deservingness and good character of the applicant as a pre-printed section. For a good set of examples, see GRO P328a OV 7-20, advocate cards.

10  J.S. Taylor, *Poverty, Migration*, 173, goes further, arguing that "only those who view British history *in vacua* can remain blinkered critics of that welfare system." However, see Sherman, *Imagining Poverty*.

11  Innes, *Inferior Politics*, 2-4; Shave, *Pauper Policies*, 10, passim.

12  Charlesworth, *Welfare's Forgotten Past*.

13  S. Webb and B. Webb, *English Poor Law History*.

14  For particularly good renderings of the crisis, see Valenze, "Charity, Custom"; and Hollen Lees, *Solidarities of Strangers*, 7, 19, 20, 40, 82, and 114. See also Innes, "State and the Poor," 253-4.

15  Shave, "Impact."

16  On the importance of reciprocating polite forms of address, see Hirst, "Making Contact," 45.

17  For context, see Thane, *Old Age*, 113, who argues that poverty was ubiquitous enough for its relief not to result in the formation of a distinct underclass. On the wider presence of a radical linguistic register, see Sanders, "From 'Technical' to 'Cultural'"; Joyce, "People's English," 154-85; and Rowe, "Writing Modern Selves."

18  J. Crowther and P. Crowther, eds, *Diary of Robert Sharp*, 38, 57.

19  Thane, *Old Age*, 107-8.

20  On the emergence of a linguistic register to map onto new constructions of emotion, see Dixon, "Patients and Passions."

21  S. King, *Poverty and Welfare*; S. King, "Welfare Regimes."

22  See earlier chapters but also S. King, "Regional Patterns."

23  CCRO WPR-5-67, letter, dated only 1822.

24  French, "How Dependent?"; French, "Irrevocable Shift."

25  However, Warwickshire parishes in particular seem to have remarkably dense archives of local New Poor Law correspondence.

26  Price, *Medical Negligence*.

27  S. King, "Rights, Duties."

28  Innes, S. King, and Winter, "Settlement and Belonging."

29  Gestrich and S. King, "Pauper Letters and Petitions."

30  Gestrich, Hurren, and S. King, eds, *Poverty and Sickness*.

31  Porter, "Introduction," in Burke and Porter, eds, *Language, Self and Society*, 2. On the importance in this context of following the story rather than the person or the material object, see contributions to Deacon, Russell, and Woollacott, eds, *Transnational Lives*; and Brant and Purkiss, "Introduction," 2.

# Bibliography

## ARCHIVE SOURCES

Berkshire Record Office (BRO).
D/P 2/16/1 and 18/7. Abingdon overseers' papers and letters.
D/P 3/18/3. Aldermarston petitions for relief.
D/P 9/12/1-6 and 9/18/1. Ashbury request for relief.
D/P 18/18/2A. Binfield inhabitant list.
D/P 23/12/9 and 23/18/8. Bray bills and vouchers.
D/P 26/18/1. Brimpton parish requests for relief.
D/P 27/12/5-7. Buckland vestry minutes.
D/P 29/8/1. Burghfield vestry minutes.
D/P 41/18/1. Great Coxwell miscellaneous overseers' papers.
D/P 45/18/4. Cumnor parochial correspondence.
D/P 71/13/1-7 and 19/5-6. Hungerford overseers' correspondence.
D/P 73/18/4. Hurst lunatic letters.
D/P 78/12/15. Kintbury overseers' correspondence.
D/P 84/28/2. Marcham letter book.
D/P 91/8/1. Pangbourne vestry minutes.
D/P 91/18/1-18. Pangbourne parochial correspondence.
D/P 96/18-19. Reading St Giles letters and papers.
D/P 98/12/216. Reading St Mary vouchers.
D/P 98/18/3. Reading St Mary petitions for relief.
D/P 102/18/1/1-18. Sandhurst correspondence.
D/P 110/8/1. Shinfield vestry minutes.
D/P 128/18/2. Sutton Courtenay papers and correspondence.
D/P 129/8/1. Swallowfield vestry minutes.

D/P 132/8/2-3. Tilehurst vestry minutes.

D/P 132/12/1-26. Tilehurst vouchers.

D/P 132/18/1-20. Tilehurst overseers' correspondence.

D/P 132/19/1-16. Tilehurst correspondence.

D/P 139/18/1-4. Wallingford parochial correspondence.

D/P 144/12/6 and 19/3. Casualty book and correspondence.

D/P 153/19/1. Little Wittenham correspondence.

D/P 162/8/1. Caversham vestry minutes.

D/P 162/18/1-10. Caversham overseers' papers, including correspondence.

Bolton Archives and Local Studies (BALS).

PHA 1/2 and 1/3. Halliwell vestry minutes.

ZZ/7/23. Thomas Bromwell correspondence.

ZZ/238/1. Bolton agreement, 1763.

ZZ/287/1. Enoch Davies letter book.

ZZ/318. Claridge family of Bolton and Stroud correspondence.

Bristol Record Office (BRIRO).

P-Abs-OP-9. Abson parochial correspondence.

P-B-OP-6h/1 and 5. Bitton St Mary parochial correspondence.

P-Dy-OP-5-1. Dyrham parochial correspondence.

P-Fc-OP-9. Frampton Cotterell parochial correspondence.

P-OV-OP-17. Ovelston St Mary parochial correspondence.

P-StJB-ChW-7-6. St John the Baptist parochial correspondence.

P-StM-OP-5. St Michael on the Mount Without parochial correspondence.

P-W-OP-14 and 22. Westerleigh parochial correspondence.

Cardiff Record Office (CARO).

P32-11. Cogan parochial correspondence.

P36-5. Llancarfan parochial correspondence.

P51-CW-20. Wenvoe parochial correspondence.

P62-29. Llantrisant parochial correspondence.

P99-71-1-3, P99-CW-47, P99-CW-49-1-11, P99 CW-72-10 and 14. Merthyr Maws parochial correspondence.

Cheshire Record Office (CRO).

P10-18. Handforth parochial correspondence.

P13/37. Middlewich overseers' papers.

P36/22/1-72. Little Budworth overseers' papers.

P68-24-12-16. Warburton parochial correspondence.

P82-22-1-12. Church Hulme parochial correspondence.

P88-2356-19. Wildboarclough parochial correspondence.

P119/24 and P128/28/77. Lymm overseers' correspondence.

P120/4525. Nantwich overseers' papers.

P143/19/9 and 22. Addeley overseers' correspondence.

P158-18. Winwick parochial correspondence.
P173/11/31-44. Baddiley overseers' papers.
P183/10/18. Macclesfield overseers' papers.
PC5/8/5. Partington vouchers.
PC16/7 and 8. Preston on the Hill vouchers and bills.
PC28/15. Sutton overseers' vouchers and correspondence.
Chorley Public Library (CPL).
Chorley vestry minutes, 1781-1823.
City of Westminster Archives Centre (COWAC).
A2250. St Anne, Soho, pauper letters.
B1344 and B1350. St Clement Danes pauper letters.
K418 and 437. Liberty of the Rolls pauper letters.
Cornwall Record Office (CORO).
AD749-1-10. Ludgvan correspondence book.
ADD448-17. Phillack overseers' correspondence.
B-Lis-340. Liskeeard overseers' correspondence.
CA-B34. Lanteglos overseers' correspondence.
FS3-176. St Breock overseers' letters.
P19-19-25. St Austell parochial correspondence.
P42-16. Crowan correspondence.
P57-16b and uncatalogued. St Erme overseers' correspondence.
P107-19. Landulph overseers' correspondence.
P111-16b. Lanlivery overseers' correspondence.
P113-16b. Lanreath overseers' correspondence.
P128-19. Loswithiel parish correspondence.
P130/13/7/6. Luxulyan letters.
P132/19/1-9. St Mabyn overseers' letters.
P170-16. Padstow parish correspondence.
P214/15/1. Saltash parish complaints.
P241/8/1. St Tudy vestry book, 1807-28.
X326-60. Trwergie overseers' correspondence.
Cumbria Record Office (Carlisle, Whitehaven, and Kendal) (CCRO).
SPUCO-12-7. Keswick overseers' papers.
WPR-5-63 and 5-67. Greystoke parish correspondence.
WPR-9-87-88. Staffield overseers' letters.
WPR-19-7-6. Kirkby Londsale parish correspondence.
WPR-60-21-13. Brampton overseers' letters.
WPR-83-7-11. Hawkshead parish correspondence.
WPR-85-39-7. Langdale parish correspondence.
WPR-102-116. Hayton overseers' correspondence.
WPR-105-71. Penrith overseers' papers.

Denbighshire Record Office (DERO).
    PD-19-153. Chirk parish overseers' correspondence.
    PD-20-1-48 to 54. Clwyd parish overseers' correspondence.
    PD-34-1-329. John Davies charity record.
    PD-38-1-176 to 191. Henllan parish correspondence.
    PD-39-1-39. Meliden parish correspondence.
    PD-78-1-159 to 1160. Llanynys parish overseers' correspondence.
    PD-89-1-136. Ruabon parish correspondence.
Devon County Record Office (Plymouth, Exeter, and Branstaple) (DCRO).
    132A-PO157-72. Cheriton Bishop overseers' papers.
    695/87. Plympton parish correspondence.
    723/303. Brixham parish correspondence.
    731/837-44. Yealmpton overseers' papers.
    854/297. Ugborough parish overseers' papers.
    1718A-PO11-31. Exeter parish correspondence.
    1843A-PO39. Northam overseers' correspondence.
    1855A-PO40. Sidmouth parish correspondence.
    2217A-PO20. Dartmouth parochial correspondence.
    2288A-PO27. Bideford overseers' correspondence.
    3137A-PO69-70. Plymouth overseers' correspondence.
    3731A-PO11. George Nympton parish correspondence.
    5579A-24. Totnes parish correspondence.
Doncaster Record Office (DORO).
    P15/6/2/4. Campsall parochial correspondence.
    P21/6/B6/1. Wadworth parish records.
    P39/10/7. Hook parish correspondence.
    P50/6/B7/1. Snaith overseers' correspondence.
    P51/6/B7/10. Adwick upon Dearne parochial correspondence.
    P59/6/B7/1-4. Swinton parish correspondence.
    P60/6/2. Rawcliffe parochial correspondence.
    P71/6/B7/1. Braithwell parochial correspondence.
    P81/6/2/41 and 42. Darfield parochial correspondence.
Dorset Record Office (DRO).
    PE/ABB/OV/1/3/1. Abbottsbury account book of extraordinary payments.
    PE/ABB/VE1/1. Abbotsbury vestry minutes, 1833-35.
    PE/BCN/3-10. Buckland Newton bills and correspondence.
    PE/BE/OV/8/1. Beaminster overseers' correspondence, 1783-1847.
    PE/BER/OV/7-9. Bere Regis bills, receipts, and correspondence.
    PE/BF/OV/13. Blandford Forum accounts and correspondence.
    PE/CAN/OV/16/1-6. Canford Magna receipts and vouchers.
    PE/CEA/OV/7/1-11. Cerne Abbas correspondence.

PE/CMO/11/2. Charmouth overseers' correspondence.
PE/COC/OV/195. Corfe Castle correspondence.
PE/D/WPC/Z3. Swanage book of anthems, hymns, and psalms.
PE/FOR/OV/8/4. Fordington overseers' correspondence.
PE/GLW/OV7/1. Glanvilles Wootton correspondence.
PE/SML/OV/1-9. Sturminster Marshall bills and letters.
PE/SW/VE/1/1. Swanage vestry minutes, 1788-1818.
PE/WM/OV7/3-6. Wimborne Minster correspondence.
East Yorkshire Record Office (EYRO).
PE1-702. Beverley overseers' correspondence.
Flintshire Record Office (FRO).
P/30/1/235. Hollywell parish correspondence.
P/45/1/1-205. Northop parish overseers' correspondence.
PD/28/1. Hawarden parish overseers' papers.
Gloucestershire Record Office (GRO).
P30 OV 7-1. Awre overseers' papers.
P47 OV 7-5. Bisley parish correspondence.
P52 OV 5-3, 7-1, and 7-4. Blockley overseers' papers.
P76 OV 3-5. Charlton Kings overseers' papers.
P77a OV 3-5-2. Chedworth parochial correspondence.
P78-1 OV 7-1 to 7-3. Cheltenham St Mary overseers' correspondence.
P81 OV 7-1. Chipping Campden parochial correspondence.
P97 OV 7-1. Coln St Dennis parochial correspondence.
P112a OV 3-5-2. Deerhurst overseers' papers.
P154 OV 3-5-2, 3-5-5, and 3-5-7, P154-15 OV 5 and 7-1, Gloucester
    St Nicholas overseers' papers.
P170 OV 7-1. Hawkesbury letters.
P193 OV 7-1. Kingswood overseers' correspondence.
P198a OV 5-2. Leckhampton overseers' papers.
P213 OV 5-1. Marshfield parochial correspondence.
P228 OV 3-5-1 to 3-5-3. Newnham overseers' correspondence.
P297 OV 8-1. Upper Slaughter parochial correspondence.
P316 OV 7-1 and 7-2. Stonehouse overseers' correspondence.
P328 OV 7-1 to 7-10, P328a OV 7-1 to 7-256. Tetbury St Mary
    overseers' correspondence.
P345 OV 3-5-1. Uley parochial correspondence.
P354 OV 3-5-2. Westbury on Severn parochial correspondence.
P362 OV 3(V) and 5. Whitminster overseers' correspondence.
Gwent Record Office (GWRO).
D.365.54-88, D.396.60 and 61. Chepstow parish correspondence.
D.Pa.6.53 and 54. Llanfihanger Crucorney parochial correspondence.

D.Pa.14.43. Bedwelty parish correspondence.

D.Pa.104.71. Usk parochial correspondence.

Hampshire Record Office (HRO).

3M82W PO24-25. St Peter Chesil overseers' correspondence.

4M81 PO40. Brockenhurst overseers' correspondence.

20M61 PO17. Stockbridge overseers' correspondence.

25M60 PO35. Fawley petitions for relief.

25M84 PO25 and 71. Lyndhurst overseers' correspondence.

25M84 PO55. Lyndhurst vestry minutes.

31M67 PO33. Milford-on-Sea overseers' correspondence.

71M81W PO78. St Michael Winchester correspondence.

88M81W PO7. St John Winchester parish correspondence.

145M49 PO79. Bishopstoke parish correspondence.

PL3-4-131. Andover Union New Poor Law correspondence.

Herefordshire Record Office (HERO).

A95/EB/40/4. Pateshall collection.

AB55/82. Lyonshall parochial correspondence.

AC16. Abbey Door parish records.

AC86/17. Moccas parochial correspondence.

AG55/55. Dorstone parochial correspondence.

AJ32/91-93. Eardisland parochial correspondence.

AJ35/66/125 and 126/157. Brampton Bryan parochial correspondence.

AT26/57/61 and 100-111. Dinedor parochial correspondence.

BF16/57. Goodrich parish overseers' accounts.

BL/91-2. All Saints Hereford parochial correspondence.

BO92/58. Ledbury parochial correspondence.

CG81/95/118 and 122. Holmer with Huntington parochial correspondence.

E38/40. Norton parochial correspondence.

E38/62-63. Winslow overseers' accounts, 1800-35.

E38/63. Winslow parochial correspondence.

E38/74. Winslow township correspondence, 1800-34.

F35/box 27 RC-IV-E-323 to 386. Dymock parochial correspondence.

F71/70-7. Amestry parish miscellaneous records.

G53/6/12, 22, and 24. Stoke Edith parochial correspondence.

G53/18. Peterstow parochial correspondence.

G65/36/1/8. Leintwardine parochial correspondence.

L51/242/261. Mathon parochial correspondence.

M61/30-43. Bodenham parochial correspondence.

N31/163. Hope under Dinmore complaints book, 1825-27.

N32/37/39. Bullingham parochial correspondence.

W43/29. Peterstow parochial correspondence.

Hertfordshire Record Office (HALS).
    D/P/4/8/1. Great Amwell vestry minutes.
    D/P/6/8/1. Ardley vestry minutes, 1707-82.
    D/P/15/12/2. Chipping Barnet overseers' accounts.
    D/P/29/18/20. Cheshunt parish correspondence.
    D/P/48/8/8-10. Hertford All Saints vestry minutes.
    D/P/87/18/2-5. Royston overseers' correspondence.
    D/P/90/18/1-7. St Albans Abbey overseers' correspondence.
    D/P/108/8/1. Thorley vestry minutes, 1714-96.
Lancashire Record Office (LRO).
    DDGa 30. Caton Incorporation correspondence.
    DDLi boxes 89-93. Warrington overseers' papers.
    DDLx 10/1. Clayton-le-Moors overseers' papers.
    DDNw 9/8 and 12. Newton-with-Scales petitions for relief.
    DDX 1/6. Bispham-with-Norbreck town book.
    DDX 28/257. Clitheroe select vestry minutes.
    DDX 386/3. Garstang vestry minutes.
    DDX 1822/1. Cliviger vestry minutes.
    MBCo 7/1. Colne ratepayers' minutes.
    MBCh 6/1. Chorley poor's book.
    PR 445. Ormskirk out-parish papers.
    PR 810. Kirkham vestry minutes.
    PR 811-12. Kirkham out-parish payments.
    PR 866-67. Lancaster letter books, 1809-19.
    PR 1349. Barnacre-with-Bonds overseers' correspondence.
    PR 2067. Kirkham vestry minutes.
    PR 2389/3. Billington bills and vouchers.
    PR 2390/1-51. Billington out-parish poor's claims.
    PR 2391/1-58. Billington overseers' correspondence.
    PR 2596/3/5. Downholland petitions for relief.
    PR 2675/1. Oswaldtwistle memorandum book.
    PR 2827/5. Blackburn overseers' correspondence.
    PR 2827/15-16. Chorley overseers' correspondence.
    PR 2995/1/29 and 31. Easington bills and vouchers.
    PR 2995/6/10. Easington overseers' correspondence.
    PR 3031/10/4. Mitton overseers' correspondence.
    PR 3053/7/18. Accrington pauper appeals, 1817-19.
    PR 3168/5/1. Tarleton select vestry book, 1822-36.
    PR 3440/7/3/1-6. Barnoldswick out-parish bills.
    UDCa 2/9. Carnforth overseers' accounts.
    UDCl 9/5 and 10/3. Clayton-le-Moors memorandum books.

UDCl 9/6 and 10. Clayton-le-Moors overseers' correspondence and payment books.

Leicestershire Record Office (LCRO).

17D64. Belgrave St Peter parish bills and letters.

23D52/7/1-5 and 16/1-21. Leicester St Nicholas pauper letters.

DE 64/32. Desford parochial correspondence.

DE 199/24. Anstey miscellaneous papers, 1706-1817.

DE 394/51-53. Shepshed vouchers and correspondence, 1733-1832.

DE 400/72. Ullesthorpe overseers' correspondence, 1815-37.

DE 432/28/1-3. Ashby-de-la-Zouch vestry orders.

DE 516/119-39. Stapleford vouchers and correspondence.

DE 1265/25. Cold Overton vouchers, 1825-31.

DE 1437/25 and 26. Stoney Stanton letters and bills, 1789-1836.

DE 1587/152-70. Market Harborough vouchers and correspondence.

DE 1728/77/3-8. Wymeswold correspondence.

DE 1998/52. Great Bowden vestry minutes, 1818-34.

DE 2559/37-69. Lutterworth accounts and bills.

DE 2575/48 and 64. Glaston correspondence books and letters.

DE 3074/2. Market Harborough select vestry minutes, 1759-86.

DE 3178/9-13. Oakham letters.

Lincolnshire Record Office (LIRO).

Caistor Par. 13/2. Caistor parish overseers' correspondence.

Croft Par. 13/27/1-32. Croft parish overseers' correspondence.

Crowland Par. 13/53/1-9. Crowland parish requests for relief.

Epworth Par. 13/28/1-43. Epworth parish overseers' letters.

Horncastle Par. 13/32. Horncastle parish overseers' correspondence.

London Metropolitan Archives (LMA).

DR02-E4. Staines parish correspondence.

DR03-F10-1. St Mary Harrow overseers' correspondence.

MSP-1734. St-Giles-in-the-Fields petitions.

P69-ALH4-B-052-MS18982. Allhallows Lombard Street correspondence.

P69-SEP-43. St Sepulchre parish letters.

P85-MRY-134. Lambeth overseers' papers.

P87-MRY-008. Paddington Green assistant overseers' report book.

P87-MRY-172. Paddington Green letter book.

P95-MRY-1-427. Putney vestry book.

Manchester Central Library (MCL).

L21/3/7/1/1-845. Tottington bills and vouchers.

L21/3/8/1-10. Tottington parochial disputes letter bundle.

L21/3/12. Tottington survey of the poor, 1817.

L21/3/13/1-28. Tottington overseers' correspondence.

L21/3/16/1-86. Tottington overseers' vouchers.

L21/6/1/1-2. Tottington letters.

L82/6 and 8. Higher Booth parochial correspondence.

M10/23/1 and 2. Rusholme overseers' accounts and correspondence, 1776-1813.

M10/23/2/1-6. Rusholme overseers' accounts and correspondence.

M10/23/3. Rusholme vestry minutes, 1819-28.

M10/808-816. Hulme letter books.

Monmouthshire Record Office (MORO).

D.365.82. Chepstow parochial correspondence.

D.365.657. Llantrisant parochial correspondence.

Norfolk Record Office (NORO).

PD 50/69. Gissing petitions.

PD 52/210 and 218. Swaffham parish overseers' correspondence.

PD 55/46. West Tofts parish overseers' correspondence.

PD 78/62. Winfarthing parochial correspondence.

PD 108/101 and 107. Kenninghall parish overseers' correspondence.

PD 111/113. Bressingham pauper lunatic correspondence.

PD 119/117 and 125. Starston parish letters.

PD 124/52. Carbrook overseers' vouchers.

PD 144/78. Fersfield parish vouchers and papers.

PD 147/44. Skeyton parish vouchers and papers.

PD 164/38. Acle bills and vouchers.

PD 167/72, 74, and 79. Thetford St Peter vouchers and correspondence.

PD 168/52. Thetford St Cuthbert correspondence.

PD 169/84-86 and 109. Thetford St Mary bills, correspondence, and vouchers.

PD 204/85. Fakenham parochial correspondence.

PD 209/207. North Elmham overseers' correspondence.

PD 218/15. Watton parish overseers' letter book.

PD 254/98 and 100. Carleton Roade overseers' correspondence and vouchers.

PD 286/60. Elsing parish vouchers and bills.

PD 295/103-04 and 106. Redenhall order books.

PD 295/113, 122, 126-37. Redenhall parish letters, vouchers, and papers.

PD 297/82 and 83. Tasburgh parish letters.

PD 298/40. East Bradenham vouchers.

PD 307/90-112. Denver overseers' vouchers and correspondence.

PD 309/49-53. Besthorpe parish overseers' papers, 1742-1821.

PD 313/51. Methwold parish vouchers and correspondence.

PD 337/140-45. Shipdham parish vouchers.

PD 358/49-68. Shelton overseers' accounts and vouchers.

PD 382/58-65. Hilgay parish overseers' correspondence, vouchers, and papers.

PD 390/83 and 88. Wrokham parish overseers' correspondence.

PD 434/26 and 27. Blickling blls and vouchers.

PD 489/51-54. Great and Little Moulton overseers' correspondence and vouchers.

PD 492/65. Stiffkey parish papers.

PD 499/81-87. Norwich St Mary parish letters.

PD 504/31-36. Brinton parish overseers' correspondence and memoranda, 1831-50.

PD 520/47. Pulham St Mary parish overseers' correspondence.

PD 553/74-77. Wighton parish certificates, bills, and applications.

PD 553/108. Wighton Committee order book.

PD 582/96 and 98. Little Walsingham parish relief orders.

PD 603/123 and 126. Dersingham parish letters.

PD 639/141. East Winch parish select vestry records.

PD 675/65-7. Foulsham out-parish letters.

PD 691/62, 63, 66, and 67. Ingoldisthorpe parish overseers' bills and vouchers.

PD 699/72/88 and 89. Heacham parish vouchers.

PD 703/86-213. Mattishall parish overseers' papers, bills, vouchers, and accounts.

Northamptonshire Record Office (NRO).

22p/78-79. Thomas Green of Badby's book of villagers.

40p/16. Bozeat bills and receipts for.

40p/BZ/19. Bozeat vestry minute book, 1822-37.

42p/39/1-2. Brackley appeals to overseer.

42p/254. Brackley pauper letter, 1810.

58p/120-121. Castle Ashby overseers' correspondence.

79p/161-74. Corby St John parish correspondence.

96p/Md 698. Daventry select vestry for the concerns of the poor, 1819-35.

110p/135-38 and 168. Earls Barton overseers' correspondence.

113p/330-38. Easton-on-the-Hill overseers' vouchers.

121p/71-91. Eye overseers' correspondence.

122p/27. East Farndon account book of collections for briefs, 1804-25.

129p/170-74. Flore overseers' vouchers.

129p/227-30. Flore pauper letters.

132p/57, 112, and 113. Gayton pauper correspondence.

150p/88. Hardingstone letter book.

185p/105, 145, 501, and 704-15. Kettering overseers' correspondence.

240p/76. Northampton St Peter requests for relief.

241p/162. Northampton Holy Sepulchre applications for relief.

243p/237. Norton overseers' papers.

249p/164-66. Oundle vestry minutes.

249p/216. Oundle letter book.

251p/98-199. Great Oxendon overseers' correspondence.

252p/131-56. Passenham overseers' correspondence.

261p/220-252a. Peterborough overseers' correspondence.

283p/5/11. Rothersthorpe vouchers and correspondence, 1810-30.

283p/33. Rothersthorpe overseers' correspondence, 1810-30.

284p/189. Rothwell vestry minutes.

285p/ii/ii. Rushden overseers' accounts.

285p/ii/vii. Rushden overseers' correspondence.

295p/6. Spratton vestry minutes.

298p/91. Stanion requests for relief.

308p/55. Sudborough legal dispute letters.

325p/193 and 194. Thrapston copy letter books.

339p/99-107. Wappenham miscellaneous overseers' papers.

342p/253. Warmington receipts and papers.

345p/120. Weedon Lois parish correspondence.

347p/141-45. Great Weldon miscellaneous papers.

350p/166-69 and 295. Wellingborough vestry minutes.

350p/270, 524, 527, and 570-79. Wellingborough letters and letter books.

356p/28. Welton vestry minutes.

364p/43. Wicken parish papers.

377p/105-15 and 169. Yardley Hastings notes, notebooks, and letters.

Northumberland Record Office (NDRO).

EP17/26/1-6. Ancroft St Anne overseers' correspondence.

EP52/A/208. Tynemouth select vestry minutes, 1827-33.

EP79/97-101. Tweedmouth overseers' correspondence.

North Yorkshire Record Office (NYRO).

PR-CAT-8-7. Catterick overseers' correspondence.

PR-FYS-7. Fylingdale overseers' correspondence.

PR-KLB-11-7. Kilburn parochial correspondence.

PR-KLD-28-7-3. Kildwick overseers' correspondence.

PR-TAW-13-9. West Tanfield parish letters.

Nottinghamshire Record Office (NGRO).

PR 17/962/1-1. Carlton-in-Lindrick overseers' correspondence.

PR 938 and 953. Norwell parochial correspondence and vouchers.

PR 2099, 8393/1-7, and 11482-86. Mansfield overseers' correspondence.

PR 2277-78. Misson overseers' vouchers.

Oxfordshire Record Office (ORO).

MSS. D.D. b.8/9/9. Charlbury parish correspondence and letters.

MSS. D.D. b.12/10/9. Hook Norton parish correspondence and letters.

MSS. D.D. c.7/i/3-7. Souldern parish correspondence and letters.

MSS. D.D. c.11/1-24. Rotherfield Greys parish correspondence and letters.

MSS. D.D. c.25. Oxford St Clements parish correspondence and letters.

MSS. D.D. c.27/48 (no date). Oxford St Giles parish correspondence and letters.

MSS. D.D. c.44 c/4. Witney parish correspondence and letters.

PAR 16/5/A11/8. Bampton parish correspondence and letters.

PAR 199/35/L1/2. Oxford Holywell parish correspondence and letters.

PAR 207/5/A2/7-8, A7/1-9, and C1/1-48. Oxford St Martin parish correspondence and letters.

PAR 211/5/C1/1/1-60. Oxford St Michael correspondence.

PAR 236/5/A13/2/1-4. Shipton under Wychwood parish correspondence and letters.

Wootton P.C. IX/iv/1-14. Wootton Parish Council correspondence and letters.

Powys Record Office (PORO).

B-EP-59-0-X. Llangatwg parochial correspondence.

B-X-15-40. Crucadarn parochial correspondence.

M-EP-19-0-X-1. Llanefyl parochial correspondence.

M-EP-41-0-X. Meifod parochial correspondence.

M-EP-45-0-X. Pennant Melangell parochial correspondence.

M-EP-50-0-X. Trefeglwys parochial correspondence.

R-EP-41-0-BB. Llanstephan parochial correspondence.

Private Papers.

Allen family letters.

Brington overseers' papers (Stephen Mattingly Archive).

Buxton, Cheltenham, Harrogate, and Bath overseers' papers (courtesy of Michael Penrose).

Kent, Sussex, and Hampshire "strays" (courtesy of Margaret Hanly and Susan Field).

Lyddington overseers' papers (Lyddington Manor History Society).

Otley, Idle, Tong, and Cleckheaton overseers' correspondence (Irwen Thomas collection).

Pelham family letters.

Pretty family letters.

Staffordshire, Shropshire, and Cheshire "strays" (courtesy of Margaret Hanly).

Taunton overseers' papers (Richard Briggs collection).

Tottington, Bacup, Wigan, Ormskirk, Abram, Culcheth, Easington, and Newchurch correspondence (courtesy of Alan Weaver).

Varley family letters.

Whitehaven and Rydal overseers' papers (courtesy of Mary McHugh).
Yorkshire "strays" (courtesy of Margaret Hanly and William Groves).
Putney Library Special Collection (PLSC).
Putney vestry book.
Rawtenstall Library (RL).
RC 352. Newchurch overseers' correspondence, 1759-71.
RC 352 Raw. Cowpe, Lenches, Newhallhey, and Hall Carr overseers'
accounts.
RC 552. Higher Booths overseers' accounts.
Rochdale Archive Service (RAS).
Castleton select vestry minutes.
Spotland township papers and select vestry minutes, 1734-1838.
Rothersthorpe Parish Church (RPC).
Parish chest letters and overseers' correspondence.
Shropshire Record Office (SHRO).
LB-15-2-1351 to 1386. Ludlow parochial correspondence.
P6/L/3/5-9. Alderby parochial correspondence.
P33/L/2/10. Bishop's Castle parochial correspondence.
P35/L/11/1/63. Bolas Magna parochial correspondence.
P43/L/28/1/158. Bromfield parochial correspondence.
P58/L/17/8. Cheswardine parochial correspondence.
P60/L/8/1/15. Chetwynd parochial correspondence.
P67/L//28/1. Church Stretton parochial correspondence.
P68/L/5/2. Claverly parochial correspondence.
P81/L/1/18/12. Condover parochial correspondence.
P83/L/3/1/2. Cound parochial correspondence.
P109/L/3/12/13. Fitz parochial correspondence.
P114/L/5/1. Great Ness parochial correspondence.
P139/L/10/1/9. Hapton parochial correspondence.
P161/L/15. Lilleshall parochial correspondence.
P177/L/21/1/3. Lydbury parochial correspondence.
P194/L/5/6 and 15/1. Moreton Corbett parochial correspondence.
P220/L/14/5/9. Pontesbury parochial correspondence.
P241/L/6/45 and 11/1/13. Shawbury parochial correspondence.
P246/L/1/23a. Shifnal parochial correspondence.
P267/L/2/4/2/3 and 1/4/1. Stanton upon Hine Heath parochial correspondence.
P316/L/8/174. Wrockwardine parochial correspondence.
PL2/2/3/1-7. Shrewsbury Court weekly minutes.
Somerset Record Office (SORO).
D/P/b.hl/13/3/6. Bishop's Hull overseers' correspondence.
D/P/ba.ab/13/10/1. Workhouse survey, 1822.

D/P/ba.mi/9/4/6. Bath St Michael parochial correspondence.

D/P/barr/13/7/1. Barrington overseers' correspondence.

D/P/baton/13/3/4. Batheaston overseers' correspondence.

D/P/bec/13/7/1-2 and 10/1/16. Beckington overseers' correspondence.

D/P/broo/13/7/1. Broomfield overseers' correspondence.

D/P/brut/13/3/9. Bruton overseers' correspondence.

D/P/can/13/2/5 and 13/3/6. Cannington overseers' correspondence.

D/P/cha.ma/13/7/1. Charlton Mackrell overseers' correspondence.

D/P/chard/9 and 13. Chard overseers' correspondence.

D/P/che.m/13/3/13 and 13/7/1. Chew Magna overseers' correspondence.

D/P/chewt.m/13/10/1-5. Chewton Mendip overseers' correspondence.

D/P/chin.e/13/7/1. East Chinnock parochial correspondence.

D/P/clut/13/7/1. Clutton overseers' correspondence.

D/P/com.dn/13/7/2. Compton Dundon overseers' correspondence.

D/P/con/13/10/3. Congresbury overseers' correspondence.

D/P/crch/13/3/8 and 13/7/2. Creech St Michael overseers' correspondence.

D/P/crew/13/2/8. Crewkerne overseers' correspondence.

D/P/cros/13/7/1. Crowscombe overseers' correspondence.

D/P/cur.r/13/7/3. Curry Rivel parochial correspondence.

D/P/dit/13/3/8. Ditcheat parochial correspondence.

D/P/e.in.g/13/2/1, 13/7/1, and 13/10/3. Easton parochial correspondence.

D/P/eve/13/10/5. Evercreech parochial correspondence.

D/P/h.ep/13/7/1. Huish Episcopi parochial correspondence.

D/P/hut/13/1/1-2 and 13/10/4. Hutton parochial correspondence.

D/P/ilm/13/7/1. Ilminster parochial correspondence.

D/P/ilt/13/3/10/11. Ilton parochial correspondence.

D/P/kingst.m/13/7/1-2. Kingston St Mary parochial correspondence.

D/P/kew/13/7/1-3 and 13/10/3. Kewstoke overseers' correspondence.

D/P/lit.h/13/3/8. High Littleton parochial correspondence.

D/P/mar.b/13/7/1. Marston Bigot parochial correspondence.

D/P/mar.m/13/7/1. Marston Magna parochial correspondence.

D/P/mea/13/2/5 and 13/7/1. Meare parochial correspondence.

D/P/mk/13/7/1. Mark parochial correspondence.

D/P/mls/13/2/9. Mells parochial correspondence.

D/P/morl/13/7/1. Moorlinch parochial correspondence.

D/P/mudf/13/3/5. Mudford parochial correspondence.

D/P/new.s.l/13/3/3. Newton St Loe parochial correspondence.

D/P/nor.h/13/10/1. Norton-sub-Hamdon parochial correspondence.

D/P/nun/13/10/1-2. Nunney parochial correspondence.

D/P/pawl/13/10/1. Pawlett parochial correspondence.

D/P/pen/13/7/1/3. Pendomer parochial correspondence.
D/P/pet.n/13/10/1. North Petherton parochial correspondence.
D/P/pit/13/3/11. Pitminster parochial correspondence.
D/P/pitc/13/3/5. Pitcombe parochial correspondence.
D/P/she/13/7/1-9. Shepton Mallet parochial correspondence.
D/P/som/13/10/4. Somerton parochial correspondence.
D/P/stapg/13/8. Staplegrove parochial correspondence.
D/P/tau.ja/13/7/1-8. Taunton St James parochial correspondence.
D/P/tau.m/13/3/13-14. Taunton St Mary parochial correspondence.
D/P/twn/9/1/1. Twerton copy letter book, 1832-33.
D/P/w.st.c/13/10/1-7. Wells St Cuthbert parochial correspondence.
D/P/wal.sw/13/2/2. Walcot parochial correspondence.
D/P/wea/13/7/1. Weare parochial correspondence.
D/P/wor/13/5/4. Worle parochial correspondence.
DD/LW/7, 12, and 13. Frome St John parochial correspondence.
DD/SAS/C909/1-70. Chard overseers' vouchers.
DD/WY/38/29. St Decumans parochial correspondence.
Staffordshire Record Office (STRO).
D24/A/PO/2892-3106. Colwich letters.
D5343/1. Leek survey, 1816.
Surrey Record Office (SURC).
1505-37-F1 to F4. Farnham parish correspondence.
1956-1-11. St James Shere overseers' correspondence.
P3-5-38 to 40. Oxted St Mary parish correspondence.
P5-5. Wimbledon St Mary parish correspondence.
SHER-28-1 to 11. Shere parish overseers' papers.
Sussex Record Office (East and West) (SURO).
Par.19-37-5-1. South Bersted New Poor Law correspondence.
Par.29-37-10/1-73. Broadwater parish appeals and overseers' papers.
Par.95-37-3. West Grinsted overseers' correspondence.
Par.100-37-3. Henfield parochial correspondence.
Par.183-37-3. Steyning parish correspondence.
Par.206-37-8. Westbourne parish correspondence.
Par.210-37-11. Wisborough Green parish papers and correspondence.
Par.284-10-1. Burwash parochial correspondence.
Par.343-12-1 and 2. Framfield parochial correspondence.
Par.353-37-11 to 18. Hailsham parochial correspondence.
Par.372-12-1. Heathfield parochial correspondence.
Par.400-37-120 to 128. Hurstpierpoint parish correspondence and vouchers.
Par.409-37-2. Laughton parochial correspondence.

Par.411-35-1. Lewes St Anne parochial correspondence.

Par.412-35. Lewes St John parochial correspondence.

Par.414-35-1. Lewes St Michael parochial correspondence.

Par.458-37-1. Wadhurst parochial correspondence.

Par.477-12-1 and 2. Robertsbridge parochial correspondence.

Par.492-37-16 to 18. Ticehurst parochial correspondence.

Par.492-12-2-1 to 5. Ticehurst select vestry minutes.

Par.492-12-12. Ticehurst vestry minutes.

Par.496-37-3. Uckfield parochial correspondence.

Par.516-37-8. Worth parochial correspondence.

Warrington Archive Service (WAS).

MS 115, 121, and 122. Warrington parochial papers.

MS 1113, box 106. Great Sankey parochial papers.

MS 1116, boxes 1-5. Poulton with Fearnhead parochial papers.

Warwickshire Record Office (WARO).

CR III/1-4. Wootton Wawen parish vestry orders.

DR 39/10. Wyken parish overseers' accounts.

DR 75/12. Great Packington parish papers.

DR 75A/2. Great Packington parish select vestry minutes.

DR 87/95-118. Warwick St Nicholas parish vouchers and correspondence.

DR 126/5-8. Warwick St Mary parish overseers' vouchers.

DR 126/42. Warwick St Mary parish select vestry book.

DR 126/854. Warwick St Mary "odd" papers.

DR 189/240-43. Kenilworth parish correspondence.

DR 198/76-78. Bulkington overseers' papers, including complaints
  of the poor.

DR 198/126. Bulkington parish letters.

DR 198/130. Bulkington parish correspondence.

DR 225/356/1-3. Bedworth parish distraint cases.

DR 225/323/1-121. Bedworth parish papers.

DR 259/42/1-43. Astley parish bills, vouchers, and correspondence.

DR 360/100. Alcester parish bills, vouchers, and correspondence.

DR 362/33B. Halford vestry minutes.

DR 362/51/1-3. Halford parish letters.

DR 468/58/1-3. Quinton parish letters.

DR 583/82-83. Southam parish correspondence and vouchers.

DR 613/189. Berkswell parish orders.

DR 613/192/1-2. Berkswell parish distraint cases.

DR 613/195. Berkswell parish correspondence.

DR 911/Z/568. Welford-on-Avon parish vouchers.

DR 1012/19-44. Southam parish vouchers and bills.

DR(B) 3/129-52. Kingsbury parish parochial correspondence.

DR(B) 19/91, 93, 101, and 112. Tanworth parish letters, vouchers, and orders.

DR(B) 100/90. Coleshill parish memorandum book, 1797-1800.

DR(B) 100/92-93. Coleshill parish vestry orders, 1810-36.

DR(B) 100/94. Coleshill parish relief orders.

DR(B) 100/98. Coleshill parish correspondence.

NZ/136 and 184. Hartshill parish bills and vouchers.

NZ/190-93, 505, 507, and unnumbered bundles. Hartshill parish letters.

West Yorkshire Record Office (WYRO).

6D74. Idle township papers, 1737-1923.

15D74. Idle, Manningham, and Bowling overseers' papers, 1734-1837.

23D98/3/11. Guiseley poor book, 1795-96.

29D93/1. Bingley township book.

33D80. Bingley and Haworth township records.

BDP29. Guiseley township papers.

BK100/1. Guiseley workhouse book, 1789-98.

DB16/C12/17. Pudsey bills, 1815-17.

KC1023. Gomersal township records.

KC1042. Dewsbury township records, 1691-1837.

KX296-316. Dewsbury overseers' papers.

MMC/38-42. Bingley township records.

RDP17/83-88. Calverley cum Farsley overseers' papers.

RDP43. Horsforth overseers' papers.

RDP96. Spofforth overseers' and township papers.

SpSt/11/2. Horsforth town books, 1607-1767.

Sta/217-19. Sowerby overseers' papers.

Tong/1/1-687, 10/1-38, and 12/a-h. Tong bills and vouchers.

Tong/2/1-12. Tong overseers' papers.

Tong/78/6. Tong appellant brief, 1796.

WDP20/9/3/5-24. Sandal Magna overseers' correspondence.

WDP139/7/8-9. Darrington correspondence book.

Wigan Record Office (WIGRO).

Tr/Ab/1-3. Abram miscellaneous papers, 1668-1819.

Tr/Ath/C/7/3 and 5. Atherton orders for relief.

Tr/Ath/C/7/31. Atherton schedule of paupers, 1830-47.

Tr/Ath/C/7/61 and 65. Atherton correspondence, 1718-1841.

Tr/Ath/C/22/40-60. Atherton vouchers.

Tr/Pe/f18. Pennington miscellaneous papers.

Tr/Pe/p18. Pennington miscellaneous bills.

Wiltshire Record Office (WRO).

77/133, 137-38, 143, and 250-51. Bradford-on-Avon parish correspondence.

77/248-49 and 257. Bradford-on-Avon miscellaneous papers.

167/9-10. Mildenhall parish correspondence.

206/52-54 and 93. Trowbridge parish correspondence.

482/46. Horningsham miscellaneous papers.

543/22. Devizes survey of the poor, 1800-02.

543/189/22. Devizes St Mary letters and vouchers.

551/96. Wroughton parish correspondence.

673/17. Lydiard Millicent overseers' correspondence.

730/277. Ashton Steeple vouchers.

735/1814/8. Chilton Foliat parish correspondence.

811/194-95. Chippenham letters and orders.

871/62, 69, 177, and 185. Marlborough vouchers and correspondence.

1020/56, 89, 102, 108, and 115. Longbridge Deverill letters and vouchers.

1076/43, 51 and 53. Stratford-sub-Castle St Lawrence vestry minutes
and vouchers.

1089/4. Broughton Gifford vestry minutes, 1827-29.

1189/57. Cricklade pauper letters.

1242/85. Wilton parish correspondence.

1306/65-101. Downton St Lawrence vouchers and correspondence.

1312/2238/23. Calne vestry minute books, 1817-24.

1438/35 and 39. Codford St Peter parish correspondence.

1607/64. Brinkworth St Michael vestry books and letters.

1719/5-8. Box vestry minutes.

1719/32. Box overseers' correspondence.

1764/51. Berwick St John vouchers.

2441/61. Bishopstone overseers' papers.

Worcestershire Record Office (WORO).

1671/21. St John Bedwardine parish correspondence.

3572/13-16. Ombersley bills and correspondence, 1800-32.

3802/10-13. Powick overseers' records.

4462/12. St Andrews Worcester parish letter books.

4869/6/iv. Broadway overseers' papers.

5476/12-17. Droitwich St Peter vouchers, letters, and bills.

9581/20. Castlemorton select vestry books.

## PRINTED SOURCES

Adell-Gombert, Nicole. "Total Writing: The writing Practices of Compagnons on the Tour de France." In M. Lyons, ed., *Ordinary Writings, Personal Narratives: Writing Practices in 19th and Early 20th-Century Europe*, 33–49. Bern, Switzerland: Peter Lang, 2007.

Althammer, Beate, Lutz Raphael, and Tamara Stazic-Wendt, eds. *Rescuing the Vulnerable: Poverty, Welfare and Social Ties in Modern Europe*. Oxford: Berghahn, 2016.

Andrew, Donna. *Philanthropy and Police: London Charity in the Eighteenth Century*. Princeton, NJ: Princeton University Press, 1989.

– "'To the Charitable and Humane': Appeals for Assistance in the Eighteenth-Century London Press." In H. Cunningham and J. Innes, eds, *Charity, Philanthropy and Reform: From the 1690s to 1850*, 87–107. Basingstoke: Macmillan, 1998.

Armstrong, Nancy. "Writing Women and the Making of the Modern Middle Class." In A. Gilroy and W. Verhoeven, eds, *Epistolary Histories: Letters, Fiction, Culture*, 29–50. Charlottesville: University of Virginia Press, 2000.

Ashplant, Timothy. "The Oral, the Aural and the Written: Genre and Discourse in a British Working-Class Life Narrative." In A.-C. Edlund, T. Ashplant, and A. Kuismin, eds, *Reading and Writing from Below: Exploring the Margins of Modernity*, 61–76. Umeå, Sweden: Umeå University and the Royal Skyttean Society, 2016.

Ayres, Jack, ed. *Paupers and Pig Killers: The Diary of William Holland, a Somerset Parson, 1799–1818*. Stroud: Sutton, 1984.

Bailey, Joanne. "'Think Wot a Mother Must Feel': Parenting in English Pauper Letters, c. 1760–1834." *Family and Community History* 13, no. 1 (2010): 5–19.

Bannet, Emma. *Empire of Letters: Letter Manuals and Transatlantic Correspondence, 1680–1820*. Oxford: Oxford University Press, 2005.

Barker-Read, Mary. "The Treatment of the Aged Poor in Five Selected West Kent Parishes from Settlement to Speenhamland, 1662–1797." PhD diss., Open University, 1988.

Barnes, Diane. *Epistolary Community in Print, 1580–1664*. Aldershot: Ashgate, 2013.

Beam, Aki. "'Should I as Yet Call You Old?': Testing the Boundaries of Female Old Age in Early Modern England." In E. Campbell, ed., *Growing Old in Early Modern Europe: Cultural Representations*, 95–116. Aldershot: Ashgate, 2006.

Beebee, Tomas. *Epistolary Fiction in Europe, 1500–1850*. Cambridge, UK: Cambridge University Press, 1999.

Begiato, Joanne. "Between Poise and Power: Embodied Manliness in Eighteenth- and Nineteenth-Century British Culture." *Transactions of the Royal Historical Society* 26 (2016): 125–47.

Benoît, Agnes. "A Chartist Singularity? Mobilizing to Promote Democratic Petitions in Britain and France, 1838–1848." *Labour History Review* 78, no. 1 (2013): 51–66.

Benstock, Shari, ed. *The Private Self: Theory and Practice of Women's Autobiographical Writings.* Chapel Hill: University of North Carolina Press, 1988.

Berg, Temma. *The Lives and Letters of an Eighteenth-Century Circle of Acquaintance.* Aldershot: Ashgate, 2006.

Berry, Amanda. "Community Sponsorship and the Hospital Patient in Late Eighteenth-Century England." In P. Horden and R. Smith, eds, *The Locus of Care: Families, Communities, Institutions, and the Provision of Welfare since Antiquity,* 126–52. London: Routledge, 1988.

Bertelsen, Lance. "Popular Entertainment and Instruction, Literary and Dramatic: Chapbooks, Advice Books, Almanacs, Ballads, Farces, Pantomimes, Prints and Shows." In J. Richetti, ed., *The Cambridge History of English Literature, 1660–1780,* 61–86. Cambridge, UK: Cambridge University Press, 2005.

Bizzell, Patricia, and Bruce Herzberg. *The Rhetorical Tradition: Readings from Classical Times to the Present.* Boston: Bedford Books, 1990.

Bland, Caroline, and Máire Cross, eds. *Gender and Politics in the Age of Letter-Writing, 1750–2000.* Aldershot: Ashgate, 2004.

Bohstedt, John. *The Politics of Provision: Food Riots, Moral Economy, and Market Transition in England, c. 1550–1850.* Aldershot: Ashgate, 2010.

Bonfield, Lloyd. "Was There a 'Third Age' in the Pre-Industrial English Past? Some Evidence from the Law." In J. Eekelaar and D. Pearl, eds, *An Aging World: Dilemmas and Challenges for Law and Social Policy,* 37–53. Oxford: Clarendon, 1989.

Booth, Alan. "Food Riots in the North-West of England, 1790–1801." *Past and Present* 77, no. 1 (1977): 84–107.

Borsay, Anne. *Disability and Social Policy in Britain since 1750: A History of Exclusion.* Basingstoke: Palgrave Macmillan, 2005.

Botelho, Lynn. "'The Old Woman's Wish': Widows by the Family Fire? Widows' Old Age Provisions in Rural England, 1500–1700." *History of the Family* 7, no. 1 (2002): 59–78.

Bottomley, Alan, ed. *The Southwold Diary of James Maggs, 1818–1876.* Vol. 1, *1818–1848.* Woodbridge: Boydell, 1983.

Boulton, Jeremy. "Double Deterrence: Settlement and Practice in London's West End, 1725–1824." In S. King and A. Winter, eds, *Migration, Settlement and Belonging in Europe, 1500–1930s: Comparative Perspectives,* 54–80. Oxford: Berghahn, 2013.

Boutcher, Warren. "Literature, Thought or Fact? Past and Present Directions in the Study of the Early Modern Letter." In T. van Houdt, J. Papy, G. Tournoy, and C. Mattheeussen, eds, *Self-Presentation and Social Identification: The Rhetoric and Pragmatics of Letter Writing in Early Modern Times,* 137–64. Leuwen, Belgium: Leuwen University Press, 2002.

Bower, Anne. "Dear —: In Search of New (Old) Forms of Critical Address."

In A. Gilroy and W. Verhoeven, eds, *Epistolary Histories: Letters, Fiction, Culture*, 155–75. Charlottesville: University of Virginia Press, 2000.

Bowers, Toni. *The Politics of Motherhood: British Writing and Culture, 1680–1760*. Cambridge, UK: Cambridge University Press, 1996.

Boyer, George. *An Economic History of the English Poor Law, 1750–1850*. Cambridge, UK: Cambridge University Press, 2008.

Boys Ellman, Edward. *Recollections of a Sussex Parson*. London: Skeffington and Son, 1912.

Braddick, Michael, and John Walter. "Introduction: Grids of Power: Order, Hierarchy and Subordination in Early Modern Society." In M. Braddick and J. Walter, eds, *Negotiating Power in Early Modern Society: Order, Hierarchy and Subordination in Britain and Ireland*, 1–38. Cambridge, UK: Cambridge University Press, 2001.

Brant, Clare. *Eighteenth-Century Letters and British Culture*. Basingstoke: Palgrave Macmillan, 2006.

– "'The Tribunal of the Public': Eighteenth-Century Letters and the Politics of Vindication." In C. Bland and M. Cross, eds, *Gender and Politics in the Age of Letter-Writing, 1750–2000*, 15–28. Aldershot: Ashgate, 2004.

Brant, Clare, and Diane Purkiss. "Introduction: Minding the Story." In C. Brant and D. Purkiss, eds, *Women, Texts and Histories, 1575–1760*, 2–12. London: Routledge, 1992.

– eds. *Women, Texts and Histories, 1575–1760*. London: Routledge, 1992.

Broad, John. "Parish Economies of Welfare, 1650–1834." *Historical Journal* 42, 4 (1999): 985–1006.

Brodie, Marc. *The Politics of the Poor: The East End of London, 1885–1914*. Oxford: Oxford University Press, 2004.

Broughton, Trevor, and Helen Rogers, eds. *Gender and Fatherhood in the Nineteenth Century*. Basingstoke: Palgrave Macmillan, 2007.

Brown, Callum. *The Death of Christian Britain: Understanding Secularisation, 1800–2000*. London: Routledge, 2000.

Brown, Elaine. "Gender, Occupation, Illiteracy and the Urban Economic Environment: Leicester, 1760–1890." *Urban History* 31, no. 2 (2004): 191–209.

Burstow, Henry. *Reminiscences of Horsham*. Horsham: Free Christian Church Book Society, 1911.

Burt, Roger, and John Archer. "Introduction." In R. Burt and J. Archer, eds, *Enclosure Acts: Sexuality, Property and Culture in Early Modern England*, 1–13. Ithaca, NY: Cornell University Press, 1994.

Bushaway, Bob. "'Things Said or Sung a Thousand Times': Customary Society and Oral Culture in Rural England, 1700–1900." In A. Fox and D. Woolf, eds, *The Spoken Word: Oral Culture in Britain, 1500–1850*, 256–83. Manchester: Manchester University Press, 2002.

Campbell, Erin. "Introduction." In E. Campbell, ed., *Growing Old in Early Modern Europe: Cultural Representations*, 1–8. Aldershot: Ashgate, 2006.

Campbell, Julie, and Anne Larsen, eds. *Early Modern Women and Transnational Communities of Letters*. Aldershot: Ashgate, 2009.

Campbell, Michael. "The Development of Literacy in Bristol and Gloucestershire, 1755–1870." PhD diss., University of Bath, 1980.

Care, Verna. "The Significance of a 'Correct and Uniform System of Accounts' to the Administration of the Poor Law Amendment Act, 1834." *Accounting History Review* 21, no. 1 (2011): 121–42.

Carter, Paul, and Steven King. "Keeping Track: Modern Methods, Administration and the Victorian Poor Law, 1834–1871." *Archives* 60, nos 128–9 (2014): 31–52.

Chalmers, Hero. "'The Person I Am, or What They Made Me to Be': The Construction of the Feminine Subject in the Autobiography of Mary Carleton." In C. Brant and D. Purkiss, eds, *Women, Texts and Histories, 1575–1760*, 164–94. London: Routledge, 1992.

Charlesworth, Lori. "How Poor Law Rights Were Lost but Victorian Values Survived: A Reconsideration of Some of the Hidden Values of Welfare Provision." In A. Hudson, ed., *New Perspectives on Property Law, Human Rights and the Home*, 271–93. London: Cavendish, 2005.

– *Welfare's Forgotten Past: A Socio-Legal History of the Poor Law*. London: Routledge, 2009.

Charon, Rita. *Narrative Medicine: Honoring the Stories of Illness*. Oxford: Oxford University Press, 2006.

Chartier, Roger, Alain Boureau, and Céline Dauphin, eds. *Correspondence: Models of Letter Writing from the Middle Ages to the Nineteenth Century*. Cambridge, UK: Polity, 1997.

Cheney, Christopher, ed. *Shoemaker's Window: Recollections of Banbury before the Railway Age by George Herbert, 1814–1902*. Banbury: Phillimore, 1971.

Churches, Christine. "False Friends, Spiteful Enemies: A Community at Law in Early Modern England." *Historical Research* 71, no. 1 (1998): 52–74.

Claeys, Gregory. "Political Economy and Popular Education: Thomas Hodgkin and the London Mechanics' Institute, 1823–8." In M. Davis ed., *Radicalism and Revolution in Britain, 1775–1848*, 157–75. Basingstoke: Macmillan, 2000.

Clark, Gill. *Correspondence of the Foundling Hospital Inspectors in Berkshire, 1757–68*. Reading: Berkshire Family History Society, 1994.

Clark, Greg. *The Son Also Rises: Surnames and the History of Social Mobility*. Princeton, NJ: Princeton University Press, 2015.

Colclough, Stephen. *Consuming Texts: Readers and Reading Communities, 1695–1870*. Basingstoke: Palgrave Macmillan, 2007.

Collard, David. "Malthus, Population and the Generational Bargain." *History of Political Economy* 33, no. 4 (2001): 697–716.

Collins, Andrew. *Finchley Vestry Minutes, 1768–1840.* London: Finchley Library, 1968.

Collins, Vicki. "Women's Voices and Women's Silence in the Tradition of Early Methodism." In M.-M. Wertheimer, ed., *Listening to Their Voices: The Rhetorical Activities of Historical Women,* 233–54. Columbia: University of South Carolina Press, 1997.

Connors, Richard. "Parliament and Poverty in Mid-Eighteenth Century England." *Parliamentary History* 21, no. 1 (2002): 207–31.

Costello, Kevin. "'More Equitable Than the Judgment of the Justices of the Peace': The King's Bench and the Poor Law, 1630–1800." *Journal of Legal History* 35, no. 1 (2014): 3–26.

Cowe, Frederic, ed. *Wimbledon Vestry Minutes, 1736, 1743–1788: A Calendar.* Guildford: Surrey Record Society, 1964.

Crone, Rosalind. "Reappraising Victorian Literacy through Prison Records." *Journal of Victorian Culture* 15, no. 1 (2010): 3–37.

Cross, Máire, and Caroline Bland. "Gender Politics: Breathing New Life into Old Letters." In C. Bland and M. Cross, eds, *Gender and Politics in the Age of Letter-Writing, 1750–2000,* 3–14. Aldershot: Ashgate, 2004.

Crossley, David, and Richard Saville, eds. *The Fuller Letters: Guns, Slaves and Finance, 1728–1755.* Lewes: Sussex Record Society, 1991.

Crowther, Anne. "Health Care and Poor Relief in Provincial England." In O. Grell, A. Cunningham, and R. Jütte, eds, *Health Care and Poor Relief in 18th and 19th Century Northern Europe,* 203–19. Aldershot: Ashgate, 2002.

Crowther, Janice, and Peter Crowther, eds. *The Diary of Robert Sharp of South Cave: Life in a Yorkshire Village, 1812–1837.* Oxford: Oxford University Press, 1997.

Damsholt, Tine. "Peasant, Soldier and Subject: Military Service and Patriotic Discourse in Danish Peasant Writing." In K.-J. Lorenzen-Schmidt and B. Poulson, eds, *Writing Peasants: Studies on Peasant Literacy in Early Modern Northern Europe,* 98–115. Gylling, Denmark: Landbohistorisk Selskab, 2002.

Davies, Andrew. "Youth, Violence, and Courtship in Late-Victorian Birmingham: The Case of James Harper and Emily Pimm." *History of the Family* 11, no. 1 (2006): 107–20.

Davies, Peter. "Writing Slates and Schooling." *Australian Historical Archaeology* 23, no. 1 (2005): 63–9.

Davin, Anna. "Socialist Infidels and Messengers of Light: Street Preaching and Debate in Mid-Nineteenth-Century London." In T. Hitchcock and H. Shore, eds, *The Streets of London: From the Great Fire to the Great Stink,* 165–82. London: Rivers Oram, 2003.

Daybell, James. "Introduction." In J. Daybell, ed., *Early Modern Women's Letter Writing, 1450–1700*, 1–15. Basingstoke: Palgrave Macmillan, 2001.

Deacon, Delsey, Penny Russell, and Angela Woollacott. "Introduction." In D. Deacon, P. Russell, and A. Woollacott, eds, *Transnational Lives: Biographies of Global Modernity, 1700-Present*, 1–11. Basingstoke: Palgrave Macmillan, 2010.

– eds. *Transnational Lives: Biographies of Global Modernity, 1700-Present*. Basingstoke: Palgrave Macmillan, 2010.

Dekker, Rudolf, ed. *Egodocuments and History: Autobiographical Writing in Its Social Context since the Middle Ages*. Hilversum: Verloren, 2002.

Delap, Lucy, Ben Griffin, and Abigail Wills, eds. *The Politics of Domestic Authority in Britain since 1800*. Basingstoke: Palgrave Macmillan, 2009.

Devereaux, Simon. "The Promulgation of the Statutes in Late Hanoverian Britain." In D. Lemmings, ed., *The British and Their Laws in the Eighteenth Century*, 80–101. Woodbridge: Boydell, 2005.

Dickie, Simon. "Hilarity and Pitilessness in the Mid-Eighteenth Century: English Jestbook Humour." *Eighteenth Century Studies* 37, no. 1 (2003): 1–22.

Dierks, Konstantine. *In My Power: Letter Writing and Communications in Early America*. Philadelphia: University of Pennsylvania Press, 2011.

Dixon, Thomas. "Patients and Passions: Languages of Medicine and Emotion, 1789–1850." In F. Bound Alberti, ed., *Medicine, Emotion and Disease, 1700–1950*, 22–43. Basingstoke: Palgrave Macmillan, 2006.

Dunkley, Peter. *The Crisis of the Old Poor Law in England, 1795–1834: An Interpretive Essay*. New York: Garland, 1982.

Durbach, Nadia. "'They Might as Well Brand Us': Working-Class Resistance to Compulsory Vaccination in Victorian England." *Social History of Medicine* 13, 1 (2000): 45–62.

Earle, Rebecca, ed. *Epistolary Selves: Letters and Letter Writers, 1600–1945*. Aldershot: Ashgate, 1999.

Eastwood, David. *Government and Community in the English Provinces, 1700–1870*. Basingstoke: Macmillan, 1997.

– *Governing Rural England: Tradition and Transformation in Local Government, 1780–1840*. Oxford: Clarendon, 1994.

Eccles, Audrey. *Vagrancy in Law and Practice under the Old Poor Law*. Farnham: Ashgate, 2012.

Eckerle, Julie. *Romancing the Self in Early Modern Englishwomen's Life Writing*. Aldershot: Ashgate, 2013.

Elliott, Bruce, David Gerber, and Suzanne Sinke, eds. *Letters across Borders: The Epistolary Practices of International Migrants*. Basingstoke: Palgrave Macmillan, 2006.

Ellis, Alec. *Educating Our Masters: Influences on the Growth of Literacy in Victorian Working Class Children.* Aldershot: Gower, 1985.

Ely, James, Jr. "The Eighteenth-Century Poor Laws in the West Riding of Yorkshire." *American Journal of Legal History* 30, 1 (1986): 1–24.

Engels, Jens. *Königsbilder: Sprechen, Singen und Schrieben über den französischen König in der ersten Hälfte des achtzehnten Jahrhunderts.* Bonn, Germany: Bouvier, 2000.

Englander, David. "From the Abyss: Pauper Petitions and Correspondence in Victorian London." *London Journal* 25, no. 1 (2000): 71–83.

Englander, David, and Rosemary O'Day. *Retrieved Riches: Social Investigation in Britain, 1840–1914.* Aldershot: Scolar, 1995.

Erickson, Amy. "Property and Widowhood in England, 1660–1840." In S. Cavallo and L. Warner, eds, *Widowhood in Medieval and Early Modern Europe*, 145–63. London: Longman, 1999.

Ernst, Waltraud, ed. *Histories of the Normal and Abnormal: Social and Cultural Histories of Norms and Normativity.* London: Routledge, 2006.

Esser, Raingard. "'They Obey All Magistrates and All Good Lawes ... and We Think Our Cittie Happie to Enjoye Them': Migrants and Urban Stability in Early Modern English Towns." *Urban History* 34, no. 1 (2007): 64–75.

Evans, Tanya. *Unfortunate Objects: Lone Mothers in Eighteenth-Century London.* Basingstoke: Palgrave Macmillan, 2005.

Favret, Marie. *Romantic Correspondence: Women, Politics and the Fiction of Letters.* Cambridge, UK: Cambridge University Press, 1993.

Feldman, David. "Migrants, Immigrants and Welfare from the Old Poor Law to the Welfare State." *Transactions of the Royal Historical Society* 13 (2003): 79–104.

Fergus, Jan. "Provincial Servants' Reading in the Late Eighteenth Century." In J. Raven, H. Small, and N. Tadmor, eds, *The Practice and Representation of Reading in England*, 202–25. Cambridge, UK: Cambridge University Press, 1996.

Fideler, Paul. *Social Welfare in Pre-Industrial England: The Old Poor Law Tradition.* Basingstoke: Palgrave Macmillan, 2006.

Fisher, Simon, ed. *Studies in British Privateering, Trading Enterprise and Seamen's Welfare, 1775–1900.* Exeter: Exeter University Press, 1987.

Fissell, Mary. "The Disappearance of the Patient Narrative and the Invention of Hospital Medicine." In R. French and A. Wear, eds, *British Medicine in an Age of Reform*, 92–109. London: Routledge, 1991.

– "Readers, Texts and Contexts: Vernacular Medical Works in Early Modern England." In R. Porter, ed., *The Popularization of Medicine 1650–1850*, 72–96. London: Routledge, 1992.

– *Vernacular Bodies: The Politics of Reproduction in Early Modern England*. Oxford: Oxford University Press, 2004.

Fitzmaurice, Susan. *The Familiar Letter in Early Modern English: A Pragmatic Approach*. Amsterdam, Netherlands: John Benjamins, 2002.

Fitzpatrick, Sheila. "Supplicants and Citizens: Public Letter Writing in Soviet Russia in the 1930s." *Slavic Review* 55, no. 1 (1996): 78–105.

Fleet, Charles. *Glimpses of Our Ancestors in Sussex*. Lewes: Farncombe and Co., 1882.

Fletcher, Andrew. "The Territorial Foundations of the Early Nineteenth-Century Census in England." *Historical Research* 81, 211 (2008): 100–22.

Foreman Cody, Lisa. "'Every Lane Teams with Instruction, and Every Alley Is Big with Erudition': Graffiti in Eighteenth-Century London." In T. Hitchcock and H. Shore, eds, *The Streets of London: From the Great Fire to the Great Stink*, 82–100. London: Rivers Oram, 2003.

Fox, Adam. "Custom, Memory and the Authority of Writing." In P. Griffiths, A. Fox, and S. Hindle, eds, *The Experience of Authority in Early Modern England*, 89–116. Basingstoke: Macmillan, 1996.

Fox, Adam, and Daniel Woolf. "Introduction." In A. Fox and D. Woolf, eds, *The Spoken Word: Oral Culture in Britain, 1500–1850*, 1–51. Manchester: Manchester University Press, 2002.

Foyster, Elizabeth. "Marrying the Experienced Widow in Early Modern England: The Male Perspective." In S. Cavallo and L. Warner, eds, *Widowhood in Medieval and Early Modern Europe*, 108–24. London: Longman, 1999.

– "Prisoners Writing Home: The Functions of the Letter, 1680–1800." *Journal of Social History* 47, no. 4 (2014): 943–67.

Frank, Arthur. *The Wounded Storyteller: Body, Illness, and Ethics*. Chicago: University of Chicago Press, 1995.

Fraser, Peter. "Public Petitioning and Parliament before 1832." *History* 11 (1961): 195–211.

Freeman, Mark. *Social Investigation and Rural England, 1870–1914*. Woodbridge: Boydell, 2003.

French, Henry. "'Ancient Inhabitants': Mobility, Lineage and Identity in English Rural Communities, 1600–1750." In C. Dyer, ed., *The Self-Contained Village? The Social History of Rural Communities, 1250–1900*, 72–95. Hatfield: University of Hertfordshire Press, 2006.

– "How Dependent Were the Dependent Poor? Poor Relief and the Life-Course in Terling, Essex, 1762–1834." *Continuity and Change* 30, no. 2 (2015): 193–222.

– "An Irrevocable Shift: Detailing the Dynamics of Rural Poverty in Southern England, 1762–1834: A Case Study." *Economic History Review* 68 no. 3 (2015): 769–805.

– *The Middle Sort of People in Provincial England, 1600–1750.* Oxford: Oxford University Press, 2007.

French, Henry, and Jonathan Barry. "Identity and Agency in English Society, 1500–1800: Introduction." In H. French and J. Barry, eds, *Identity and Agency in England, 1500–1800,* 1–37. Basingstoke: Palgrave Macmillan, 2004.

Fumerton, Patricia, and Andrea Guerrini. "Introduction: Straws in the Wind." In P. Fumerton and A. Guerrini, eds, *Ballads and Broadsides in Britain, 1500–1800,* 1–9. Farnham: Ashgate, 2010.

– eds. *Ballads and Broadsides in Britain, 1500–1800.* Farnham: Ashgate, 2010.

Geering, Thomas. *Our Sussex Parish.* London: Methuen, 1884.

Gerber, David. "Acts of Deceiving and Withholding in Immigrant Letters: Personal Identity and Self-Presentation in Personal Correspondence." *Journal of Social History* 39, no. 2 (2005): 315–30.

– *Authors of Their Lives: The Correspondence of British Immigrants to North America in the Nineteenth Century.* New York: New York University Press, 2008.

– "Epistolary Ethics: Personal Correspondence and the Culture of Emigration in the Nineteenth Century." *Journal of American Ethnic History* 19, no. 1 (2000): 3–23.

– "Epistolary Masquerades: Acts of Deceiving and Withholding in Immigrant Letters." In B. Elliott, D. Gerber, and S. Sinke, eds, *Letters across Borders: The Epistolary Practices of International Migrants,* 141–57. Basingstoke: Palgrave Macmillan, 2006.

– "Ethnic Identification and the Project of Individual Identity: The Life of Mary Ann Woodrow Archbold (1768–1840) of Little Cumbrae Island, Scotland, and Auriesville, New York." *Immigrants and Minorities* 17, no. 1 (1998): 1–22.

Gestrich, Andreas, and Daniella Heinisch. "'They Sit for Days and Have Only Their Sorrows to Eat': Old Age Poverty in German and British Pauper Narratives." In B. Althammer, L. Raphael, and T. Stazic-Wendt, eds, *Rescuing the Vulnerable: Poverty, Welfare and Social Ties in Modern Europe,* 356–81. Oxford: Berghahn, 2016.

Gestrich, Andreas, Elizabeth Hurren, and Steven King, eds. *Poverty and Sickness in Modern Europe: Narratives of the Sick Poor, 1780–1938.* London: Continuum, 2012.

Gestrich, Andreas, and Steven King. "Pauper Letters and Petitions for Poor Relief in Germany and Great Britain, 1770–1914." *Bulletin of the German Historical Institute* 35 (2013): 12–25.

Gilbert, Geoffrey. "Towards the Welfare State: Some British Views on the Right to Subsistence, 1768–1834." *Review of Political Economy* 46, no. 1 (1988): 144–63.

Glaisyer, Natasha, and Sarah Pennell. "Introduction." In N. Glaisyer and S. Pennell, eds, *Didactic Literature in England, 1500–1800: Expertise Constituted*, 1–18. Aldershot: Ashgate, 2003.

Goldie, Mark. "The Unacknowledged Republic: Officeholding in Early Modern England." In T. Harris, ed., *The Politics of the Excluded, 1500–1850*, 153–94. Basingstoke: Palgrave Macmillan, 2001.

Gray, Louise. "The Experience of Old Age in the Narratives of the Rural Poor in Early Modern Germany." In S. Ottaway, L. Botelho, and K. Kitteridge, eds, *Power and Poverty: Old Age in the Pre-Industrial Past*, 107–23. Westport, CT: Greenwood, 2002.

Green, David. "Icons of the New System: Workhouse Construction and Relief Practices in London under the Old and New Poor Law." *London Journal* 34, no. 3 (2009): 264–84.

– *Pauper Capital: London and the Poor Law, 1790–1870*. Aldershot: Ashgate, 2010.

Griffin, Carl. *The Rural War: Captain Swing and the Politics of Protest*. Manchester: Manchester University Press 2012.

Griffin, Emma. *England's Revelry: A History of Popular Sports and Pastimes, 1660–1830*. Oxford: Oxford University Press, 2005.

– "The Making of the Chartists: Popular Politics and Working-Class Autobiography in Early Victorian Britain." *English Historical Review* 129, no. 538 (2014): 578–605.

– "Sex, Illegitimacy and Social Change in Industrializing Britain." *Social History* 38, no. 1 (2013): 139–61.

Gusdorf, Georges. "Conditions and Limits of Autobiography." In J. Olney, ed., *Autobiographical Essays Theoretical and Critical*, 28–48. Princeton, NJ: Princeton University Press, 1980.

Hales, Janet. *"On the Parish": Recorded Lives of the Poor of Holt and District, 1780–1835*. Dereham: Larks, 1994.

Hallam, Elizabeth. "Speaking to Reveal: The Body and Acts of Exposure in Early Modern Popular Discourse." In C. Richardson, ed., *Clothing Culture, 1350–1650*, 239–62. Aldershot: Ashgate, 2002.

Hampson, Elaine. *The Treatment of Poverty in Cambridgeshire, 1597–1834*. Cambridge, UK: Cambridge University Press, 1934.

Hanley, James. "The Public's Reaction to Public Health: Petitions Submitted to Parliament, 1847–1848." *Social History of Medicine* 15, no. 3 (2002): 393–411.

Hannan, Leonie. *Women of Letters: Gender, Writing and the Life of the Mind in Early Modern England*. Manchester: Manchester University Press, 2016.

Harley, David. "Rhetoric and the Social Construction of Sickness and Healing." *Social History of Medicine* 12, no. 3 (1999): 407–35.

Harley, Joe. "Material Lives of the Poor and Their Strategic Use of the Work-house during the Final Decades of the English Old Poor Law." *Continuity and Change* 30, no. 1 (2015): 71–103.

Harris, Mark. "'Inky Blots and Rotten Parchment Bonds': London, Charity Briefs and the Guildhall Library." *Historical Research* 66, no. 1 (1993): 93–110.

Harris, Tim, ed. *The Politics of the Excluded, 1500–1850.* Basingstoke: Palgrave Macmillan, 2001.

Harvey, Karen. "Craftsmen in Common: Objects, Skills and Masculinity in the Eighteenth and Nineteenth Centuries." In H. Greig, J. Hamlett, and L. Hannan, eds, *Gender and Material Culture in Britain since 1600*, 68–89. Basingstoke: Palgrave Macmillan, 2015.

Hastings, Robert. *Poverty and the Poor Law in the North Riding of Yorkshire, 1780–1837.* York: Borthwick Institute, 1982.

Healey, Jonathan. *The First Century of Welfare: Poverty and Poor Relief in Lancashire, 1620–1730.* Woodbridge: Boydell, 2014.

Heyd, Utte. *Reading Newspapers: Press and Public in Eighteenth-Century Britain and America.* Oxford: Voltaire Foundation, 2012.

Higgs, Edward. "Fingerprints and Citizenship: The British State and the Identi-fication of Pensioners in the Interwar Period." *History Workshop Journal* 69, no. 1 (2010): 52–67.

Hilliard, Christopher. "Popular Reading and Social Investigation in Britain, 1850–1940." *Historical Journal* 57, no. 1 (2014): 247–71.

– *To Exercise Our Talents: The Democratisation of Writing in Britain.* Cambridge, MA: Harvard University Press, 2006.

Himmelfarb, Gertrude. *The Idea of Poverty: England in the Early Industrial Age.* London: Knopf, 1983.

Hindle, Steve. "Civility, Honesty and the Identification of the Deserving Poor in Seventeenth-Century England." In H. French and J. Barry, eds, *Identity and Agency in England, 1500–1800*, 38–59. Basingstoke: Palgrave Macmillan, 2004.

– "Destitution, Liminality and Belonging: The Church Porch and the Politics of Settlement in English Rural Communities, c. 1590–1660." In C. Dyer, ed., *The Self-Contained Village: The Social History of Rural Communities, 1250–1900*, 46–71. Hatfield: University of Hertfordshire Press, 2006.

– "'Good, Godly and Charitable Uses': Endowed Charity and the Relief of Poverty in Rural England, c. 1555–1750." In A. Goldgar and R. Frost, eds, *Institutional Culture in Early Modern Society*, 164–88. Leiden: Brill, 2004.

– *On the Parish? The Micro-Politics of Poor Relief in Rural England, 1550–1750.* Oxford: Clarendon, 2004.

– "The Political Culture of the Middling Sorts in English Rural Communities,

1550–1700." In T. Harris, ed., *The Politics of the Excluded, c. 1500–1800*, 125–52. Basingstoke: Macmillan, 2001.

– "Power, Poor Relief and Social Relations in Holland Fen, c. 1600–1800." *Historical Journal* 41, no. 1 (1998): 67–96.

Hirst, Derek. "Making Contact: Petitions and the English Republic." *Journal of British Studies* 45, no. 1 (2006): 26–50.

Hitchcock, Tim. "Begging on the Streets of Eighteenth-Century London." *Journal of British Studies* 44, no. 3 (2005): 478–98.

– *Down and Out in Eighteenth-Century London*. London: Hambledon, 2004.

– "The London Vagrancy Crisis of the 1780s." *Rural History* 24, no. 1 (2013): 59–72.

– "The Publicity of Poverty in Early Eighteenth-Century London." In J. Merritt, ed., *Imagining Early Modern London: Perceptions and Portrayals of the City from Stowe to Strype, 1598–1720*, 166–84. Cambridge, UK: Cambridge University Press, 2001.

– "Rough Lives: Autobiography and Migration in Eighteenth-Century England." In B. De Munck and A. Winter, eds, *Gated Communities: Regulating Migration in Early Modern Cities*, 97–126. Farnham: Ashgate, 2012.

– "Tricksters, Lords and Servants: Begging Friendship and Masculinity in Eighteenth-Century England." In L. Gowing, M. Hunter, and M. Rubin, eds, *Love, Friendship and Faith in Europe, 1300–1800*, 177–96. Basingstoke: Palgrave Macmillan, 2005.

Hollen Lees, Lynn. *The Solidarities of Strangers: The English Poor Laws and the People, 1700–1948*. Cambridge, UK: Cambridge University Press, 1998.

Hopkin, David. "Storytelling, Fairytales and Autobiography: Some Observations on Eighteenth- and Nineteenth-Century French Soldiers' and Sailors' Memoirs." *Social History* 29, 2 (2004): 186–98.

– *Voices of the People in Nineteenth-Century France*. Cambridge, UK: Cambridge University Press, 2012.

Hopkin, Neil. "The Old and the New Poor Law in East Yorkshire, 1760–1850." MPhil thesis, University of Leeds, 1968.

Horne, Thomas. *Property Rights and Poverty: Political Arguments in Britain, 1605–1834*. London: University of North Carolina Press, 1990.

Horrell, Sara, and Jane Humphries. "Old Questions, New Data and Alternative Perspectives: Families' Living Standards in the Industrial Revolution." *Journal of Economic History* 52, no. 4 (1992): 849–80.

Houston, Rab. "Church Briefs in England and Wales from Elizabethan Times to 1828." *Huntington Library Quarterly* 78, no. 3 (2015): 493–520.

– "The Development of Literacy: Northern England, 1640–1750." *Economic History Review* 35, no. 2 (1982): 199–216.

– *Peasant Petitions: Social Relations and Economic Life on Landed Estates, 1600–1850*. Basingstoke: Palgrave Macmillan, 2014.

Howie, William. "Complaints and Complaint Procedures in the Eighteenth- and Early Nineteenth-Century Provincial Hospitals in England." *Medical History* 25, 4 (1981): 345–62.

Hoyler, Michelle. "Small Town Development and Urban Illiteracy: Comparative Evidence from Leicestershire Marriage Registers, 1754–1890." *Historical Social Research* 23, no. 1 (1998): 202–30.

Hudson, Geoffrey. "Arguing Disability: Ex-Servicemen's Own Stories in Early Modern England, 1590–1790." In R. Bivins and J. Pickstone, eds, *Medicine, Madness and Social History: Essays in Honour of Roy Porter*, 105–17. Basingstoke: Palgrave Macmillan, 2007.

Humphries, Jane. *Childhood and Child Labour in the British Industrial Revolution*. Cambridge, UK: Cambridge University Press, 2010.

Hunt, Edward. "Paupers and Pensioners Past and Present." *Ageing and Society* 9, 4 (1990): 407–30.

Hunter, Michael. *Editing Early Modern Texts: An Introduction to Principles and Practice*. Basingstoke: Palgrave Macmillan, 2009.

Hunter, Pamela. "Containing the Marvellous: Instructions to Buyers and Sellers." In N. Glaisyer and S. Pennell, eds, *Didactic Literature in England, 1500–1800: Expertise Constituted*, 169–81. Aldershot: Ashgate, 2003.

Hurley, Beryl. *Bradford on Avon Applications for Relief from Out of Town Strays*. Devizes: Wiltshire Family History Society, 2004.

– *Cricklade Absent Poor and Warrants for Reputed Fathers, 1787–1837*. Devizes: Wiltshire Family History Society, 2005.

– *Longbridge Deverill Poor in and out of the Parish, 1816–1821, 1826–1835*. Devizes: Wiltshire Family History Society, 2004.

Hurren, Elizabeth, and Steven King. "'Begging for a Burial': Form, Function and Conflict in Nineteenth-Century Pauper Burial." *Social History* 30, 3 (2005): 321–41.

– "Courtship at the Coroner's Court." *Social History* 40, 2 (2015): 185–207.

– "Public and Private Healthcare for the Poor, 1650s to 1960s." In P. Weindling, ed., *Healthcare in Private and Public from the Early Modern Period to 2000*, 15–35. London: Routledge, 2015.

Hutter, Michael. "Visual Credit: The Britannia Vignette on the Notes of the Bank of England." In F. Cox and H.-W. Schmidt-Hannisa, eds, *Money and Culture*, 15–36. Bern, Switzerland: Peter Lang, 2007.

Illuzzi, Jennifer. "Negotiating the 'State of Exception': Gypsies' Encounter with the Judiciary in Germany and Italy, 1860–1914." *Social History* 35, 4 (2010): 418–38.

Ingram, Allan, and Leigh Wetherall Dickson, eds. *Depression and Melancholy, 1660–1800*. Vol. 4, *Popular Culture*. London: Pickering and Chatto, 2012.

Innes, Joanna. *Inferior Politics: Social Problems and Social Policies in Eighteenth-Century Britain*. Oxford: Oxford University Press, 2009.

– "The 'Mixed Economy of Welfare' in Early Modern England: Assessments of the Options from Hale to Malthus (*c.* 1683–1803)." In M. Daunton, ed., *Charity, Self-Interest and Welfare in the English Past*, 139–80. London: UCL Press, 1996.

– "People and Power in British Politics to 1850." In J. Innes and M. Philp, eds, *Reimagining Democracy in the Age of Revolutions: America, France, Britain, Ireland, 1750–1850*, 129–46. Oxford: Oxford University Press, 2013.

– "The State and the Poor: Eighteenth-Century England in European Perspective." In J. Brewer and E. Hellmuth, eds, *Rethinking Leviathan: The Eighteenth-Century State in Britain and Germany*, 225–80. Oxford: Oxford University Press, 1999.

– "State, Church and Volunterism in European Welfare, 1690–1850." In H. Cunningham and J. Innes, eds, *Charity, Philanthropy and Reform from the 1690s to 1850*, 15–65. Basingstoke: Palgrave Macmillan, 1998.

Innes, Joanna, Steven King, and Anne Winter. "Settlement and Belonging in Europe, 1500–1930s: Structures, Negotiations and Experiences." In S. King and A. Winter, eds, *Migration, Settlement and Belonging in Europe, 1500–1930s: Comparative Perspectives*, 1–28. Oxford: Berghahn, 2013.

"An Insolent Pauper." *Annual Register*, 16 July 1828, 169.

Jack, Dana. *Silencing the Self: Women and Depression*. Cambridge, MA: Harvard University Press, 1991.

Jackson, Heather. "Coleridge as Reader: Marginalia." In F. Burwick, ed., *The Oxford Handbook of Samuel Taylor Coleridge*, 271–87. Oxford: Oxford University Press, 2009.

– *Romantic Readers: The Evidence of Marginalia*. New Haven, CT: Yale University Press, 2005.

Jenkins, Melissa. *Fatherhood, Authority, and British Reading Culture, 1831–1907*. Aldershot: Ashgate, 2014.

Johnson, Christopher, and David Sabean, eds. *Sibling Relations and the Transformation of European Kinship, 1300–1900*. Oxford: Berghahn, 2011.

Jones, Ffion. "Welsh Balladry and Literacy." In D. Atkinson and S. Roud, eds, *Street Ballads in Nineteenth-Century Britain, Ireland and North America: The Interface between Print and Oral Traditions*, 105–26. Farnham: Ashgate, 2014.

Jones, Peter. "Clothing the Poor in Early-Nineteenth-Century England." *Textile History* 37, no. 1 (2006): 17–37.

– "Finding Captain Swing: Protest, Parish Relations, and the State of the Public

Mind in 1830." *International Review of Social History* 54, no. 3 (2009): 429–58.

– "'I Cannot Keep My Place without Being Deascent': Pauper Letters, Parish Clothing and Pragmatism in the South of England, 1750–1830." *Rural History* 20, no. 1 (2009): 31–49.

– "Widows, Work and Wantonness: Pauper Letters and the Boundaries of Entitlement under the English Old Poor Law." In P. Jones and S. King, eds, *Obligation, Entitlement and Dispute under the English Poor Laws*, 139–67. Newcastle upon Tyne: Cambridge Scholars, 2015.

Jones, Peter, and Steven King. "From Petition to Pauper Letter: The Development of an Epistolary Form." In P. Jones and S. King, eds, *Obligation, Entitlement and Dispute under the English Poor Laws*, 53–77. Newcastle upon Tyne: Cambridge Scholars, 2015.

– "Voices from the Far North: Pauper Letters and the Provision of Welfare in Sutherland, 1845–1900." *Journal of British Studies* 55, no. 1 (2016): 76–98.

Joyce, Patrick. "The People's English: Language and Class in England, 1840–1920." In P. Burke and R. Porter, eds, *Language, Self and Society: A Social History of Language*, 154–90. Cambridge, UK: Polity, 1991.

Jütte, Robert. *Poverty and Deviance in Early Modern Europe*. Cambridge, UK: Cambridge University Press, 1994.

– "Poverty and Poor Relief." In S. Ogilvie, ed., *Germany: A New Social and Economic History, 1630–1800*, 377–404. London: Edward Arnold, 1996.

Kamphoefner, Walter. "Immigrant Epistolary and Epistemology: On the Motivators and Mentality of Nineteenth-Century German Immigrants." *Journal of American Ethnic History* 28, no. 3 (2009): 34–54.

Kauranen, Kari. "Did Writing Lead to Social Mobility? Case Studies of Ordinary Writers in Nineteenth-Century Finland." In M. Lyons, ed., *Ordinary Writings, Personal Narratives: Writing Practices in 19th and Early 20th-Century Europe*, 51–68. Bern, Switzerland: Peter Lang, 2007.

Keith-Lucas, Bryan. *Parish Affairs: The Government of Kent under George III*. Canterbury: Kent County Library, 1986.

King, Peter. *Crime and Law in England, 1750–1840: Remaking Justice from the Margins*. Cambridge, UK: Cambridge University Press, 2006.

– "Legal Change, Customary Right and Social Conflict in Late Eighteenth-Century England: The Origins of the Great Gleaning Case of 1788." *Law and History Review* 10, no. 1 (1992): 1–31.

– "Making Crime News: Newspapers, Violent Crime and the Selective Reporting of Old Bailey Trials in the Late Eighteenth Century." *Crime, History and Society* 13, no. 1 (2009): 91–116.

– "The Rights of the Poor and the Role of the Law: The Impact of Pauper Appeals to the Summary Courts, 1750–1834." In P. Jones and S. King, eds,

*Obligation, Entitlement and Dispute under the English Poor Laws*, 235–62. Newcastle upon Tyne: Cambridge Scholars, 2015.

– "Social Inequality, Identity and the Labouring Poor in Eighteenth-Century England." In H. French and J. Barry, eds, *Identity and Agency in England, 1500–1800*, 60–87. Basingstoke: Palgrave Macmillan, 2004.

– "The Summary Courts and Social Relations in Eighteenth-Century England." *Past and Present*, no. 183 (2004): 125–72.

King, Steven. "Constructing the Disabled Child in England, 1800–1860." *Family and Community History* 18, no. 1 (2015): 56–89.

– "The English Pauper Letter, 1790–1830." *Groniek* 204–205 (2016): 305–16.

– "Forme et fonction de la parenté chez les populations pauvres d'Angleterre, 1800–1840." *Annales* 65, no. 5 (2010): 1147–74.

– "Friendship, Kinship and Belonging in the Letters of Urban Paupers, 1800–1840." *Historical Social Research* 33, no. 1 (2008): 249–77.

– "'I Fear You Will Think Me Too Presumtuous in My Demands but Necessity Has No Law': Clothing in English Pauper Letters, 1800–1834." *International Review of Social History* 54, no. 2 (2009): 207–36.

– "'In These You May Trust': Numerical Information, Accounting Practices and the Poor Law, c. 1790 to 1840." In T. Crook and G. O'Hara, eds, *Statistics and the Public Sphere: Numbers and the People in Modern Britain, c. 1800–2000*, 51–66. London: Routledge, 2011.

– "'It Is Impossible for Our Vestry to Judge His Case into Perfection from Here': Managing the Distance Dimensions of Poor Relief, 1800–40." *Rural History* 16, no. 2 (2005): 161–89.

– "Kleidung und Würde: Über die Aushandlung der Armenunterstutzung in England, 1800–40." In S. Hahn, N. Lobner, and C. Sedmak, eds, *Armut in Europa, 1500–2000*, 82–99. Innsbruck, Austria: Studien-Verlag, 2010.

– "Negotiating the Law of Poor Relief in England, 1800–1840." *History* 96, no. 324 (2011): 410–35.

– "Nursing under the Old Poor Law in Midland and Eastern England, 1780–1834." *Journal of the History of Medicine and Allied Sciences* 69, no. 1 (2014): 1–35.

– "'The Particular Claims of a Woman and a Mother': Gender, Belonging and Rights to Medical Relief in England, 1800–1840s." In A. Andresen, T. Grønlie, W. Hubbard, T. Ryymin, and S. Skålevåg, eds, *Citizens, Courtrooms, Crossings*, 21–38. Bergen, Norway: Stein Rokkan Centre for Social Studies, 2008.

– "Pauvreté et assistance: La politique locale de la mortalité dans l'Angleterre des XVIIIe et XIXe siècles." *Annales* 61, no. 1 (2006): 31–62.

– *Poverty and Welfare in England, 1700–1850: A Regional Perspective.* Manchester: Manchester University Press, 2000.

- "Reclothing the English Poor, 1750–1840." *Textile History* 33, no. 1 (2002): 37–47.
- "Regional Patterns in the Experiences and Treatment of the Sick Poor, 1800–40: Rights, Obligations and Duties in the Rhetoric of Paupers." *Family and Community History* 10, no. 1 (2007): 61–75.
- "The Residential and Familial Arrangements of English Pauper Letter Writers, 1800–1840s." In J. McEwan and P. Sharpe, eds, *Accommodating Poverty: The Housing and Living Arrangements of the English Poor, c. 1600–1850*, 145–68. Basingstoke: Palgrave Macmillan, 2011.
- "Rights, Duties and Practice in the Transition between the Old and New Poor Laws, 1820–1860s." In P. Jones and S. King, eds, *Obligation, Entitlement and Dispute under the English Poor Laws*, 263–91. Newcastle upon Tyne: Cambridge Scholars, 2015.
- *Sickness, Medical Welfare and the English Poor, 1750–1834.* Manchester: Manchester University Press, 2018.
- "'Stop This Overwhelming Torment of Destiny': Negotiating Financial Aid at Times of Sickness under the English Old Poor Law, 1800–1840." *Bulletin of the History of Medicine* 79, no. 2 (2005): 228–60.
- "Welfare Regimes and Welfare Regions in Britain and Europe, c. 1750–1860." *Journal of Modern European History* 9, no. 1 (2011): 42–66.
King, Steven, and Peter Jones. "Testifying for the Poor: Epistolary Advocates and the Negotiation of Parochial Relief in England, 1800–1834." *Journal of Social History* 49, no. 4 (2016): 784–807.
King, Steven, Thomas Nutt, and Alannah Tomkins, eds. *Narratives of the Poor in Eighteenth-Century Britain.* Vol. 1, *Voices of the Poor: Poor Law Depositions and Letters.* London: Pickering and Chatto, 2006.
King, Steven, and Alison Stringer. "'I Have Once More Taken the Leberty to Say as You Well Know': The Development of Rhetoric in the Letters of the English, Welsh and Scottish Sick and Poor, 1780s-1830s." In A. Gestrich, E. Hurren, and S. King, eds, *Poverty and Sickness in Modern Europe: Narratives of the Sick Poor, 1780–1938*, 69–92. London: Continuum, 2012.
King, Steven, and Alannah Tomkins, eds. *The Poor in England, 1700–1850: An Economy of Makeshifts.* Manchester: Manchester University Press, 2003.
Knight, Stephen. *Robin Hood in Greenwood Stood: Alterity and Context in the English Outlaw Tradition.* Turnhout: Brepols, 2011.
Knights, Mark. "Participation and Representation before Democracy: Petitions and Addresses in Pre-Modern Britain." In I. Shapiro, S. Stokes, E. Wood, and A. Kirshner, eds, *Political Representation*, 35–60. Cambridge, UK: Cambridge University Press, 2009.
Lambert, Christine. "The Patient and Communication: Logos, Pathos and

Ethos." In A. Bartoszko and M. Vaccarella, eds, *The Patient: Probing Inter-disciplinary Boundaries*, 143–57. Oxford: Inter-Disciplinary Press, 2009.

Lambert, Miles. "'Cast-Off Wearing Apparel': The Consumption and Distribution of Second-Hand Clothing in Northern England during the Long Eighteenth Century." *Textile History* 35, no. 1 (2004): 1–26.

Land, Isaac. "Bread and Arsenic: Citizenship from the Bottom up in Georgian London." *Journal of Social History* 45, no. 1 (2005): 89–110.

Landers, John. *Death and the Metropolis: Studies in the Demographic History of London, 1670–1830.* Cambridge, UK: Cambridge University Press, 2006.

Langton, John. "The Geography of Poor Relief in Rural Oxfordshire, 1775–1832." In P. Jones and S. King, eds, *Obligation, Entitlement and Dispute under the English Poor Laws*, 193–234. Newcastle upon Tyne: Cambridge Scholars, 2015.

Lawrence, Anne. "'Begging Pardon for All Mistakes or Errors in the Writeing I Being a Woman & Doing Itt Myself': Family Narratives in Some Early Eighteenth-Century Letters." In J. Daybell, ed., *Early Modern Women's Letter Writing, 1450–1700*, 194–206. Basingstoke: Palgrave Macmillan, 2001.

Lemmings, David. "Introduction." In D. Lemmings, ed., *The British and Their Laws in the Eighteenth Century*, 1–21. Woodbridge: Boydell, 2005.

Levene, Alysa. "'Honesty, Sobriety and Diligence': Master-Apprentice Relations in Eighteenth- and Nineteenth-Century England." *Social History* 33, no. 2 (2008): 183–200.

– "Poor Families, Removals and 'Nurture' in Late Old Poor Law London." *Continuity and Change* 25, no. 1 (2010): 233–62.

Levene, Alysa, Thomas Nutt, and Samantha Williams, eds. *Illegitimacy in Britain, 1700–1920.* Basingstoke: Palgrave Macmillan, 2005.

Levine-Clark, Marjorie. *Unemployment, Welfare, and Masculine Citizenship: "So Much Honest Poverty" in Britain, 1870–1930.* Basingstoke: Palgrave Macmillan, 2015.

Liljewall, Britt. "'Self-Written Lives,' or Why Did Peasants Write Autobiographies?" In K.-J. Lorenzen-Schmidt and B. Poulson, eds, *Writing Peasants: Studies on Peasant Literacy in Early Modern Northern Europe*, 210–38. Gylling, Denmark: Landbohistorisk Selskab, 2002.

Lindert, Peter. *Growing Public: Social Spending and Economic Growth since the Eighteenth Century.* Cambridge, UK: Cambridge University Press, 2004.

Lindley, Pamela. *Early Censuses: Hooton Pagnell and Moorhouse.* Doncaster: Doncaster and District Family History Society, 2002.

Lis, Catherina, and Hugo Soly. *Poverty and Capitalism in Pre-Industrial Europe.* Brighton: Harvester, 1979.

Lloyd, Sarah. *Charity and Poverty in England, c. 1680–1820: Wild and Visionary Schemes.* Manchester: Manchester University Press, 2009.

Loft, Phillipa. "Involving the Public: Parliament, Petitioning and the Language of Interest, 1688–1720." *Journal of British Studies* 55, no. 1 (2016): 1–23.

Lowsley, Barzillai. *A Glossary of Berkshire Words and Phrases*. London: Trubner and Co., 1888.

Lynch, Diedre. *The Economy of Character: Novels, Market Culture and the Business of Inter-Meaning*. Chicago: University of Chicago Press, 1998.

Lyons, Martyn. *A History of Reading and Writing in the Western World*. Basingstoke: Palgrave Macmillan, 2010.

– "Ordinary Writings, or How the Illiterate Speak to Historians." In M. Lyons, ed., *Ordinary Writings, Personal Narratives: Writing Practices in 19th and Early 20th-Century Europe*, 13–32. Bern, Switzerland: Peter Lang, 2007.

– *The Writing Culture of Ordinary People in Europe, c. 1860–1920*. Cambridge, UK: Cambridge University Press, 2013.

– "Writing Upwards: How the Weak Wrote to the Powerful." *Journal of Social History* 48, no. 2 (2015): 311–36.

– ed. *Ordinary Writings, Personal Narratives: Writing Practices in 19th and Early 20th-Century Europe*. Bern, Switzerland: Peter Lang, 2007.

Mack, Phyllis. *Heart Religion in the British Enlightenment: Gender and Emotion in Early Methodism*. Cambridge, UK: Cambridge University Press, 2011.

Mackay, Lyn. "A Culture of Poverty? The St Martin's in the Fields Workhouse, 1817." *Journal of Interdisciplinary History* 26, no. 2 (1995): 209–31.

Marshall, Dorothy. *The English Poor in the Eighteenth Century*. New York: Augustus Kelley, 1969.

– "The Role of the Justice of the Peace in Social Administration." In H. Hearder and H. Lyon, eds, *British Government and Administration: Studies Presented to S.B. Chrimes*, 155–68. Cardiff: University of Wales Press, 1974.

Martin, J.M. "The Rich, the Poor and the Migrant in Eighteenth Century Stratford-on-Avon." *Local Population Studies* 20 (1978): 38–48.

Martin, Luther, Huck Gutman, and Patrick Hutton, eds. *Technologies of the Self: A Seminar with Michel Foucault*. Amherst: University of Massachusetts Press, 1988.

Mascuch, Michael. *Origins of the Individualist Self: Autobiography and Self-Identity in England, 1591–1791*. Cambridge, UK: Polity, 1997.

McEwan, Joanne, and Pamela Sharpe, eds. *Accommodating Poverty: The Housing and Living Arrangements of the English Poor, c. 1600–1850*. Basingstoke: Palgrave Macmillan, 2011.

McShane, Angela. "'Ne sutor ultra crepidam': Political Cobblers and Broadside Ballads in Late Seventeenth-Century England." In P. Fumerton and A. Guerrini, eds, *Ballads and Broadsides in Britain, 1500–1800*, 207–28. Aldershot: Ashgate, 2010.

Métayer, Christine. *Au tombeau des secrets: Les écrivains publics du Paris populaire, Cimetière des Saints-Innocents XVIe–XVIIIe siècle.* Paris: Albin Michel, 2000.

Miles, Andrew. *Social Mobility in Nineteenth- and Early Twentieth-Century England.* Basingstoke: Palgrave Macmillan, 1999.

Morgan, Gwenda, and Peter Rushton. "The Magistrate, the Community and the Maintenance of an Orderly Society in Eighteenth-Century England." *Historical Research* 76, no. 191 (2003): 54–77.

– "Visible Bodies: Power, Subordination and Identity in the Eighteenth-Century Atlantic World." *Journal of Social History* 39, no. 1 (2005): 39–64.

Morgan, Simon. "The Reward of Public Service: Nineteenth-Century Testimonials in Context." *Historical Research* 80, no. 208 (2007): 261–85.

Moring, Beatrice, and Richard Wall. *Widows in European Economy and Society, 1600–1920.* Woodbridge: Boydell, 2017.

Muldrew, Craig. "Class and Credit: Social Identity, Wealth and the Life Course in Early Modern England." In H. French and J. Barry, eds, *Identity and Agency in England, 1500–1800*, 147–77. Basingstoke: Palgrave Macmillan, 2004.

Muldrew, Craig, and Steven King. "Cash, Wages and the Economy of Makeshifts in England, 1650–1800." In P. Scholliers and L. Schwarz, eds, *Experiencing Wages: Social and Cultural Aspects of Wage Forms in Europe since 1500*, 155–82. Oxford: Berghahn, 2003.

Navickas, Katrina. *Protest and the Politics of Space and Place, 1789–1848.* Manchester: Manchester University Press, 2016.

Nielsen, Caroline. "The Chelsea Out-Pensioners: Image and Reality in Eighteenth-Century and Early Nineteenth-Century Social Care." PhD diss., Newcastle University, 2014.

– "Continuing to Serve: Representations of the Elderly Veteran Soldier in the Late Eighteenth and Early Nineteenth Centuries." In S. McVeigh and N. Cooper, eds, *Men after War*, 18–35. London: Routledge, 2013.

Neuman, Mark. *The Speenhamland County: Poverty and the Poor Law in Berkshire, 1782–1834.* New York: Garland, 1982.

Noblett, William. "Cheese, Stolen Paper and the London Book Trade, 1750–99." *Eighteenth-Century Life* 38, no. 3 (2014): 100–10.

Nünning, Vera. "From 'Honour' to 'Honest': The Invention of the (Superiority of the) Middling Ranks in Eighteenth-Century England." *Journal for the Study of British Cultures* 2, no. 1 (1995): 19–41.

Nussbaum, Felicity. *The Autobiographical Subject: Gender and Ideology in Eighteenth-Century England.* Baltimore, MD: Johns Hopkins University Press, 1989.

Nutt, Thomas. "Illegitimacy, Paternal Financial Responsibility, and the 1834

Poor Law Commission Report: The Myth of the Old Poor Law and the Making of the New." *Economic History Review* 63, no. 2 (2010): 336–61.

Offer, John. "'Virtue,' 'Citizen Character' and 'Social Environment': Social Theory and Agency in Social Policy since 1830." *Journal of Social Policy* 35, no. 2 (2006): 283–302.

Ogborn, Miles. *Spaces of Modernity: London Geographies, 1680–1780.* London: Guildford, 1998.

Ong, Walter. "Writing as a Technology That Restructures Thought." In G. Baumann, ed., *The Written Word: Literacy in Transition,* 23–50. Oxford: Clarendon, 1986.

Ottaway, Susannah. *The Decline of Life: Old Age in Eighteenth-Century England.* Cambridge, UK: Cambridge University Press, 2004.

– "Introduction: Authority, Autonomy and Responsibility among the Aged in the Pre-Industrial Past." In S. Ottaway, L. Botelho, and K. Kitteridge, eds, *Power and Poverty: Old Age in the Pre-Industrial Past,* 1–12. Westport, CT: Greenwood, 2002.

– "Providing for the Elderly in Eighteenth-Century England." *Continuity and Change* 13, no. 3 (1998): 391–418.

Outhwaite, Brian. *The Rise and Fall of the English Ecclesiastical Courts, 1500–1860.* Cambridge, UK: Cambridge University Press, 2006.

Palk, Deirdre, ed. *Prisoners' Letters to the Bank of England, 1781–1827.* London: London Record Society, 2007.

Patriquin, Larry. *Agrarian Capitalism and Poor Relief in England, 1500–1860: Rethinking the Origins of the Welfare State.* Basingstoke: Palgrave Macmillan, 2007.

Pearson, Jane. "'Labor and Sorrow': The Living Conditions of the Elderly Residents of Bocking, Essex, 1793–1807." In S. Ottaway, L. Botelho, and K. Kitteridge, eds, *Power and Poverty: Old Age in the Pre-Industrial Past,* 125–42. Westport, CT: Greenwood, 2002.

– *Women's Reading in Britain, 1750–1835: A Dangerous Recreation.* Cambridge, UK: Cambridge University Press, 1999.

Pernau, Margrit. "'By Their Feelings You Shall Know Them': An Entangled History of the British Discourse on Civility (c. 1750–1860)." *Geschichte und Gesellschaft* 35, no. 2 (2009): 249–81.

Peyton, Sarah. *Kettering Vestry Minutes, A.D. 1797–1853.* Northampton: Northamptonshire Record Society, 1933.

Pickering, Paul. "'And Your Petitioners &c': Chartists Petitioning in Popular Politics, 1838–48." *English Historical Review* 116, no. 466 (2001): 368–88.

Pilbeam, Norma, and Ian Nelson, eds. *Mid Sussex Poor Law Records, 1601–1835.* Lewes: Sussex Records Society, 2001.

Piper, Alana. "'Women's Special Enemy': Female Enmity in Criminal Discourse during the Long Nineteenth Century." *Journal of Social History* 49, no. 3 (2016): 671–92.

Poland, Blake, and Anne Pedersen. "Reading between the Lines: Interpreting Silences in Qualitative Research." *Qualitative Inquiry* 4, no. 2 (1998): 293–312.

Pons, Christopher. "The Mystical and the Modern: The Uses of Ordinary Writings in Identity Construction by Icelandic Spiritual Mediums." In M. Lyons, ed., *Ordinary Writings, Personal Narratives: Writing Practice in 19th and Early 20th-Century Europe*, 85–100. Bern, Switzerland: Peter Lang, 2007.

Pooley, Colin, and Jean Turnbull. *Migration and Mobility in Britain since the Eighteenth Century*. London: UCL Press, 1998.

Porter, Roy. "Expressing Yourself Ill: The Language of Sickness in Georgian England." In P. Burke and R. Porter, eds, *Language, Self and Society: A Social History of Language*, 276–99. Cambridge, UK: Polity, 1991.

– "Introduction." In P. Burke and R. Porter, eds, *Language, Self and Society: A Social History of Language*, 1–20. Cambridge, UK: Polity, 1991.

– "Introduction." In R. Porter, ed., *Rewriting the Self: Histories from the Renaissance to the Present*, 1–14. London: Routledge, 1997.

– "Spreading Medical Enlightenment: The Popularization of Medicine in Georgian England and Its Paradoxes." In R. Porter, ed., *The Popularization of Medicine, 1650–1850*, 215–31. London: Routledge, 1992.

Poster, Carol, and Linda Mitchell, eds. *Letter-Writing Manuals and Instruction from Antiquity to the Present: Historical and Bibliographic Studies*. Charlotte: University of South Carolina Press, 2007.

Poynter, John. *Society and Pauperism: English Ideas on Poor Relief, 1795–1834*. Toronto: University of Toronto Press, 1969.

Price, Kim. *Medical Negligence in Victorian Britain: The Crisis of Care under the English Poor Law, 1834–1900*. Basingstoke: Palgrave Macmillan, 2015.

Probert, Rebecca, ed. *Cohabitation and Non-Marital Births in England and Wales, 1600–2012*. Basingstoke: Palgrave Macmillan, 2014.

Prothero, Iowerth. "Chartism and French Radicalism in the 1830s and 1840s: A Comparison." *Labour History Review* 78, no. 1 (2013): 33–49.

Pyle, Emily. "Peasant Strategies for Obtaining State Aid: A Study of Petitions during World War I." *Russian History* 24, no. 1 (1997): 41–64.

Raven, James. "From Promotion to Prescription: Arrangements for Reading and Eighteenth-Century Libraries." In J. Raven, H. Small, and N. Tadmor, eds, *The Practice and Representation of Reading in England*, 175–201. Cambridge, UK: Cambridge University Press, 1996.

Raven, James, Helen Small, and Naomi Tadmor. "Introduction: The Practice and Representation of Reading in England." In J. Raven, H. Small, and N.

Tadmor, eds, *The Practice and Representation of Reading in England*, 1–21. Cambridge, UK: Cambridge University Press, 1996.

Reddy, William. *The Making of Romantic Love: Longing and Sexuality in Europe, South Asia and Japan, 900–1200 CE*. Chicago: University of Chicago Press, 2012.

– *The Navigation of Feeling: A Framework for the History of Emotions*. Cambridge, UK: Cambridge University Press, 2001.

Redford, Arthur. *The History of Local Government in Manchester*. Vol. 2, *Borough and City*. London: Longmans, 1940.

Regard, Frédéric, ed. *Mapping the Self: Space, Identity, Discourse in British Auto/Biography*. Saint-Étienne, France: Publications de l'Université de Saint-Étienne, 2003.

Reinarz, Jonathan, and Rebecca Wynter, eds. *Complaints, Controversies and Grievances in Medicine: Historical and Social Science Perspectives*. London: Rochester University Press, 2014.

Reiss, Matthias. "The Image of the Poor and the Unemployed: The Example of Punch, 1841–1939." In A. Gestrich, S. King, and L. Raphael, eds, *Being Poor in Modern Europe: Historical Perspectives, 1800–1940*, 389–416. Bern, Switzerland: Peter Lang, 2006.

Rich, Rosemary. "Storied Identities: Identity Formation and the Life Story." *Journal of Contemporary History* 15, no. 1 (2014): 1–16.

Richards, Jennifer, ed. *Early Modern Civil Discourses*. Basingstoke: Palgrave Macmillan, 2003.

Richards, Jennifer, and Alison Thorne. "Introduction." In J. Richards and A. Thorne, eds, *Rhetoric, Women and Politics in Early Modern England*, 1–24. London: Routledge, 2006.

Richardson, Catherine. "'Havying Nothing upon Hym Saving Onely His Sherte': Event, Narrative and Material Culture in Early Modern England." In C. Richardson, ed., *Clothing Culture, 1350–1650*, 209–21. Aldershot: Ashgate, 2004.

– ed. *Clothing Culture, 1350–1650*. Aldershot: Ashgate, 2004.

Roberts, Elizabeth. *A Woman's Place: An Oral History of Working-Class Women, 1890–1940*. Oxford: Wiley-Blackwell, 1995.

Roberts, Gwyn. "The Troubles of a Pauper." *Caernarvonshire Historical Society Transactions* 10, no. 2 (1949): 109–14.

Rogers, Nicholas. "Policing the Poor in Eighteenth-Century London: The Vagrancy Laws and Their Administration." *Social History* 24, no. 2 (1991): 127–47.

Rose, Michael. *The English Poor Law, 1780–1930*. Newton Abbot: David and Charles, 1971.

Rowe, Steven. "Writing Modern Selves: Literacy and the French Working Class in the Early Nineteenth Century." *Journal of Social History* 38, no. 1 (2006): 55–83.

Sanders, Michael. "From 'Technical' to 'Cultural' Literacy: Reading and Writing within the British Chartist Movement." In A.-C. Edlund, T. Ashplant, and A. Kuismin, eds, *Reading and Writing from Below: Exploring the Margins of Modernity*, 285–300. Umeå, Sweden: Umeå University and the Royal Skyttean Society, 2016.

Scarfe, Norman, ed. *A Frenchman's Year in Suffolk*. Boydell: Suffolk Record Society, 1989.

Schen, Clare. "Constructing the Poor in Early Seventeenth-Century London." *Albion* 32, no. 3 (2000): 450–63.

Scheutz, Martin. "Demand and Charitable Supply: Poverty and Poor Relief in Austria in the 18th and 19th Centuries." In O. Grell, A. Cunningham, and B. Roeck, eds, *Health Care and Poor Relief in 18th and 19th Century Southern Europe*, 52–95. Aldershot: Ashgate, 2005.

Schmidt, Ariadne. "Survival Strategies of Widows and Their Families in Early Modern Holland, c. 1580–1750." *History of the Family* 12, no. 4 (2007): 268–81.

Scholl, Lesa. *Hunger Movements in Early Victorian Literature: Want, Riots, Migration*. London: Routledge, 2016.

Scott, James. *Domination and the Arts of Resistance: Hidden Transcripts*. New Haven, CT: Yale University Press, 1990.

Sczesny, Anke. *Der lange Weg in die Fuggerei: Augsburger Armenbriefe des 19. Jahrhunderts*. Augsburg, Germany: Wißner-Verlag, 2012.

Sczesny, Anke, Rolf Kießling, and Johannes Burkhardt, eds. *Prekariat im 19. Jahrhundert: Armenfürsorge und Alltagsbewältigung in Stadt und Land*. Augsburg, Germany: Wißner-Verlag, 2014.

Seal, Graham. *The Outlaw Legend: A Cultural Tradition in Britain, America and Australia*. Cambridge, UK: Cambridge University Press, 1996.

Secord, Jim. "Science in the Pub: Artisan Botanists in Early Nineteenth-Century Lancashire." *History of Science* 32, no. 3 (1994): 269–315.

Seed, John. "History and Narrative Identity: Religious Dissent and the Politics of Memory in Eighteenth-Century England." *Journal of British Studies* 44, no. 1 (2005): 46–63.

Selwood, Jacob. "'English-Born Reputed Strangers': Birth and Descent in Seventeenth-Century London." *Journal of British Studies* 44, no. 4 (2005): 728–53.

Sharpe, Pamela. "Parish Women: Maternity and the Limitations of Maiden Settlement in England, 1162–1834." In P. Jones and S. King, eds, *Obligation, Entitlement and Dispute under the English Poor Laws*, 168–92. Newcastle upon Tyne: Cambridge Scholars, 2015.

– "Poor Children as Apprentices in Colyton, 1598–1830." *Continuity and Change* 6, no. 2 (1991): 253–70.
– "Survival Strategies and Stories: Poor Widows and Widowers in Early Industrial England." In S. Cavallo and L. Warner, eds, *Widowhood in Medieval and Early Modern Europe*, 220–39. London: Longman, 1999.
Shave, Samantha. "The Impact of Sturges Bourne's Poor Law Reforms in Rural England." *Historical Journal* 56, no. 2 (2013): 399–429.
– *Pauper Policies: Poor Law Practice in England, 1780–1850.* Manchester: Manchester University Press, 2017.
Shepard, Alexandra. "Honesty, Worth and Gender in Early Modern England, 1560–1640." In H. French and J. Barry, eds, *Identity and Agency in England, 1500–1800*, 87–105. Basingstoke: Palgrave Macmillan, 2004.
– "Poverty, Labour and the Language of Social Description in Early Modern England." *Past and Present* 201, no. 1 (2008): 51–95.
Sherman, Sandra. *Imagining Poverty: Quantification and the Decline of Paternalism.* Columbus: Ohio State University Press, 2001.
Slack, Paul. *From Reformation to Improvement: Public Welfare in Early Modern England.* Oxford: Clarendon, 1997.
Smail, John. "Credit, Risk and Honor in Eighteenth-Century Commerce." *Journal of British Studies* 44, no. 3 (2005): 439–56.
Smith, Ginnie. "Prescribing the Rules of Health: Self-Help and Advice in the Late Eighteenth Century." In R. Porter, ed., *Patients and Practitioners: Lay Perceptions of Medicine in Pre-Industrial Society*, 249–82. Cambridge, UK: Cambridge University Press, 1985.
Smith, Richard. "Ageing and Well-Being in Early Modern England: Pension Trends and Gender Preference under the English Old Poor Law, 1650–1800." In P. Johnson and P. Thane, eds, *Old Age from Antiquity to Postmodernity*, 64–95. London: Routledge, 1998.
– "Charity, Self-Interest and Welfare: Reflections from Demographic and Family History." In M. Daunton, ed., *Charity, Self-Interest and Welfare in the English Past*, 36–41. London: UCL Press, 1996.
Smith, Richard, and Naomi Tadmor, eds. "Kinship in Britain and beyond from the Early Modern to the Present." Special issue of *Continuity and Change* 25, no. 1 (2010).
Snell, Keith. "Belonging and Community: Understandings of 'Home' and 'Friends' among the English Poor, 1750–1850." *Economic History Review* 65, no. 1 (2011): 1–25.
– *Parish and Belonging: Community, Identity and Welfare in England and Wales, 1700–1950.* Cambridge, UK: Cambridge University Press, 2006.
Snell, Keith, and Paul Ell. *Rival Jerusalems: The Geography of Victorian Religion.* Cambridge, UK: Cambridge University Press, 2000.

---

Sokoll, Thomas. *Essex Pauper Letters, 1731–1837.* Oxford: Oxford University Press, 2001.

– "Families, Wheat Prices and the Allowance Cycle: Poverty and Poor Relief in the Agricultural Community of Ardleigh, 1794–1801." In P. Jones and S. King, eds, *Obligation, Entitlement and Dispute under the English Poor Laws,* 78–106. Newcastle upon Tyne: Cambridge Scholars, 2015.

– "The Household Position of Elderly Widows in Poverty: Evidence from Two English Communities in the Late Eighteenth and Early Nineteenth Centuries." In J. Henderson and R. Wall, eds, *Poor Women and Children in the European Past,* 207–24. London: Routledge, 1994.

– "Negotiating a Living: Essex Pauper Letters from London, 1800–1834." *International Review of Social History* 45, no. 1 (2000): 19–46.

– "Old Age in Poverty: The Record of Essex Pauper Letters, 1780–1834." In T. Hitchcock, P. King, and P. Sharpe, eds, *Chronicling Poverty: The Voices and Strategies of the English Poor, 1640–1840,* 127–54. Basingstoke: Palgrave Macmillan, 1997.

– "Writing for Relief: Rhetoric in English Pauper Letters, 1800–1834." In A. Gestrich, S. King, and L. Raphael, eds, *Being Poor in Modern Europe: Historical Perspectives, 1800–1940,* 91–112. Bern, Switzerland: Peter Lang, 2006.

Solar, Peter. "Poor Relief and English Economic Development before the Industrial Revolution." *Economic History Review* 48, no. 1 (1995): 1–22.

Song, Byung. "Parish Typology and the Operation of the Poor Laws in Early Nineteenth-Century Oxfordshire." *Agricultural History Review* 50, no. 2 (2002): 203–24.

Spicksley, Judith. "A Dynamic Model of Social Relations: Celibacy, Credit and the Identity of the 'Spinster' in Seventeenth-Century England." In H. French and J. Barry, eds, *Identity and Agency in England, 1500–1800,* 106–46. Basingstoke: Palgrave Macmillan, 2004.

Stanley Holton, Sandra. *Quaker Women: Personal Life, Memory and Radicalism in the Lives of Women Friends, 1780–1930.* London: Routledge, 2007.

Stapleton, Barry. "Inherited Poverty and Life-Cycle Poverty: Odiham, Hampshire, 1650–1850." *Social History* 18, no. 1 (1996): 339–55.

Stolberg, Michael. *Experiencing Illness and the Sick Body in Early Modern Europe.* Basingstoke: Palgrave Macmillan, 2011.

Strange, Julie-Marie. *Death, Grief and Poverty in Britain, 1870–1914.* Cambridge, UK: Cambridge University Press, 2005.

– *Fatherhood and the British Working Class, 1865–1914.* Cambridge, UK: Cambridge University Press, 2015.

Stratmann, Gerd. "Nobody's Child, Everybody's Child: Discourses of Illegitimacy in Eighteenth-Century England." *Journal for the Study of British Cultures* 18, no. 2 (2011): 109–20.

Suzuki, Akihito. "Lunacy and Labouring Men: Narratives of Male Vulnerability in Mid-Victorian London." In R. Bivins and J. Pickstone, eds, *Medicine, Madness and Social History: Essays in Honour of Roy Porter*, 118–28. Basingstoke: Palgrave Macmillan, 2007.

Tabili, Laura. *Global Migrants, Local Culture: Natives and Newcomers in Provincial England, 1841–1939*. Basingstoke: Palgrave Macmillan, 2011.

Tadmor, Naomi. "'In the Even My Wife Read to Me': Women, Reading and Household Life in the Eighteenth Century." In J. Raven, H. Small, and N. Tadmor, eds, *The Practice and Representation of Reading in England*, 162–74. Cambridge, UK: Cambridge University Press, 1996.

– *The Social Universe of the English Bible: Scripture, Society and Culture in Early Modern England*. Cambridge, UK: Cambridge University Press, 2010.

Taillon, Paul. "'All Men Are Entitled to Justice by the Government': Black Workers, Citizenship, Letter Writing and the World War I State." *Journal of Social History* 48, no. 1 (2014): 88–111.

Taylor, Alan, ed. *The Country Diaries: A Year in the British Countryside*. London: Canongate, 2009.

Taylor, Geoffrey. *The Problem of Poverty, 1660–1834*. London: Longman, 1969.

Taylor, James. "Privacy, Publicity, and Reputation: How the Press Regulated the Market in Nineteenth-Century England." *Business History* 87, no. 4 (2013): 679–701.

Taylor, James Stephen. "A Different Kind of Speenhamland: Non-Resident Relief in the Industrial Revolution." *Journal of British Studies* 30, no. 2 (1991): 183–208.

– "The Impact of Pauper Settlement, 1691–1834." *Past and Present* 73, no. 1 (1976): 42–73.

– *Poverty, Migration and Settlement in the Industrial Revolution: Sojourners' Narratives*. Palo Alto, CA: Society for the Promotion of Science and Scholarship, 1989.

– "Voices in the Crowd: The Kirkby Lonsdale Township Letters, 1809–36." In T. Hitchcock, P. King, and P. Sharpe, eds, *Chronicling Poverty: The Voices and Strategies of the English Poor, 1640–1840*, 109–26. Basingstoke: Palgrave Macmillan, 1997.

Tebbutt, Melanie. *Making Youth: A History of Youth in Modern Britain*. Basingstoke: Palgrave Macmillan, 2016.

Thane, Pat. *Old Age in English History: Past Experiences, Present Issues*. Oxford: Oxford University Press, 2000.

– "An Untiring Zest for Life: Images and Self-Images of Old Women in England." *Journal of Family History* 25, no. 2 (2000): 235–47.

Thomas, Eric. "The Treatment of Poverty in Berkshire, Essex and Oxfordshire, 1723–1840." PhD diss., University of London, 1971.

Thompson, Edward. *Customs in Common: Studies in Traditional Popular Culture*. London: Merlin, 1991.
- *The Making of the English Working Class*. London: Gollancz, 1963.
Thomson, David. "'I Am Not My Father's Keeper': Families and the Elderly in Nineteenth Century England." *Law and History Review* 2, no. 2 (1984): 265–86.
Tilly, Charles. *Popular Contention in Great Britain, 1758–1834*. Cambridge, MA: Harvard University Press, 1995.
- "The Rise of the Public Meeting in Great Britain, 1758–1834." *Social Science History* 34, no. 3 (2010): 291–9.
Timmins, Geoffrey. *The Last Shift: Decline of Handloom Weaving in Nineteenth-Century Lancashire*. Manchester: Manchester University Press, 1993.
Tomkins, Alannah. *The Experience of Urban Poverty, 1723–82: Parish, Charity and Credit*. Manchester: Manchester University Press, 2006.
- "'Labouring on a Bed of Sickness': The Material and Rhetorical Deployment of Ill-Health in Male Pauper Letters." In A. Gestrich, E. Hurren, and S. King, eds, *Poverty and Sickness in Modern Europe: Narratives of the Sick Poor, 1780–1938*, 51–68. London: Continuum, 2012.
- "Women and Poverty." In H. Barker and E. Chalus, eds, *Women's History: Britain, 1700–1850*, 152–73. London: Routledge, 2005.
- "Workhouse Medical Care from Working-Class Autobiographies, 1750–1834." In J. Reinarz and L. Schwarz, eds, *Medicine and the Workhouse*, 86–102. London: University of Rochester Press, 2013.
Tomlinson, Victor. *Letters of a Lancashire Luddite Transported to Australia, 1812–1816*. Manchester: Richard Bates, 1974.
Topham, Julie. "Publishing 'Popular Science' in Early Nineteenth-Century Britain." In A. Fyfe and B. Lightman, eds, *Science in the Marketplace*, 135–68. Chicago: University of Chicago Press, 2007.
Tosh, John. *Manliness and Masculinities in Nineteenth-Century Britain*. London: Longman, 2005.
Tóth, István György. *Literacy and Written Culture in Early Modern Central Europe*. Budapest, Hungary: Central European University Press, 2000.
Turner, David. *Disability in Eighteenth-Century England: Imagining Physical Impairment*. New York: Routledge, 2012.
Valenze, Deborah. "Charity, Custom and Humanity: Changing Attitudes towards the Poor in Eighteenth-Century England." In J. Garnett and C. Matthew, eds, *Revival and Religion since 1700: Essays for John Walsh*, 59–78. London: Hambledon, 1993.
Vandenbussche, Wim. "'Lower Class Language' in 19th Century Flanders." *Multilingua* 26, nos 2–3 (2007): 279–90.
van Ginderachter, Maarten. "'If Your Majesty Would Only Send Me a Little

Money to Help Buy an Elephant': Letters to the Belgian Royal Family (1880–1940)." In M. Lyons, ed., *Ordinary Writings, Personal Narratives: Writing Practices in 19th and 20th-Century Europe*, 69–84. Bern, Switzerland: Peter Lang, 2007.

van Houdt, Toon, and Jan Papy. "Introduction." In T. van Houdt, J. Papy, G. Tournoy, and C. Mattheeussen, eds, *Self-Presentation and Social Identification: The Rhetoric and Pragmatics of Letter Writing in Early Modern Times*, 1–13. Leuwen, Belgium: Leuwen University Press, 2002.

van Houdt, Toon, Jan Papy, Gilbert Tournoy, and Constant Mattheeussen, eds. *Self-Presentation and Social Identification: The Rhetoric and Pragmatics of Letter Writing in Early Modern Times.* Leuwen, Belgium: Leuwen University Press, 2002.

van Leeuwen, Marco. "Histories of Risk and Welfare in Europe during the 18th and 19th Centuries." In O. Grell, A. Cunningham, and R. Jütte, eds, *Health Care and Poor Relief in 18th and 19th Century Northern Europe*, 32–68. Aldershot: Ashgate, 2002.

van Voss, Lex Heerma. "Introduction." In L.-H. van Voss, ed., *Petitions in Social History*, 1–10. Cambridge, UK: Cambridge University Press, 2001.

Vincent, David. *Bread, Knowledge and Freedom: A Study of Nineteenth-Century Working Class Autobiography.* London: Europa, 1981.

– "The Decline of the Oral Tradition in Popular Culture." In R. Storch, ed., *Popular Culture and Custom in Nineteenth-Century England*, 20–47. London: Croom Helm, 1982.

– *Literacy and Popular Culture: England, 1750–1914.* Cambridge, UK: Cambridge University Press, 1989.

von Kondratowitz, Hans-Joachim. "The Medicalisation of Old Age: Continuity and Change in Germany from the Late Eighteenth to the Early Twentieth Century." In M. Pelling and R. Smith, eds, *Life, Death and the Elderly: Historical Perspectives*, 134–64. London: Routledge, 1991.

Wahrman, Dror. *The Making of the Modern Self: Identity and Culture in Eighteenth-Century England.* New Haven, CT: Yale University Press, 2004.

Walker, Martyn. "'For the Last Many Years in England Everybody Has Been Educating the People, but They Have Forgotten to Find Them Any Books': The Mechanics' Institutes Library Movement and Its Contribution to Working-Class Adult Education during the Nineteenth Century." *Library and Information History* 29, no. 4 (2013): 272–86.

Wall, Richard. "Families in Crisis and the English Poor Law as Exemplified by the Relief Programme in the Essex Parish of Ardleigh, 1795–7." In E. Ochiai, ed., *The Logic of Female Succession: Rethinking Patriarchy and Patrilineality in Global and Historical Perspective*, 101–27. Kyoto: International Research Centre for Japanese Studies, 2002.

– "Some Implications of the Earnings, Income and Expenditure Patterns of Married Women in Populations in the Past." In J. Henderson and R. Wall, eds, *Poor Women and Children in the European Past*, 312–35. London: Routledge, 1994.

Walsh, Victor. "Poor Law Administration in Shropshire, 1820–1835." PhD diss., University of Pennsylvania, 1970.

Walter, John. "Faces in the Crowd: Gender and Age in the Early Modern English Crowd." In H. Berry and E. Foyster, eds, *The Family in Early Modern England*, 96–125. Cambridge, UK: Cambridge University Press, 2007.

Watson, Rex. "Poverty in North-East Lancashire in 1843: Evidence from Quaker Charity Records." *Local Population Studies* 55, no. 1 (1995): 28–44.

Webb, Sydney, and Beatrice Webb. *English Poor Law History*. Part 1, *The Old Poor Law*. 1927. Reprint, London: Cass, 1963.

Wells, Roger. "Migration, the Law and Parochial Policy in Eighteenth- and Early Nineteenth-Century Southern England." *Southern History* 15, no. 1 (1993): 86–139.

Wertheimer, Molly-Meijer. "Introduction: Roses in the Snow." In M.-M. Wertheimer, ed., *Listening to Their Voices: The Rhetorical Activities of Historical Women*, 1–18. Columbia: University of South Carolina Press, 1997.

Wessel Hansen, Peter. "Grief, Sickness and Emotions in the Narratives of the Shamefaced Poor in Late Eighteenth-Century Copenhagen." In A. Gestrich, E. Hurren, and S. King, eds, *Poverty and Sickness in Modern Europe: Narratives of the Sick Poor, 1780–1938*, 35–50. London: Continuum, 2012.

Whyman, Susan. *The Pen and the People: English Letter Writers, 1660–1800.* Oxford: Oxford University Press, 2009.

Wigelsworth, Jeffrey. "Bi-Partisan Politics and Practical Knowledge: Advertising Public Science in Two London Newspapers, 1695–1720." *British Journal for the History of Science* 41, no. 4 (2008): 517–40.

Wilde, Wayne. *Medicine by Post: The Changing Voice of Illness in Eighteenth-Century Consultation Letters and Literature.* Amsterdam, Netherlands: Rodopi, 2006.

Williams, Michelle. "'Our Poore People in Tumults Arose': Living in Poverty in Earls Colne, Essex, 1560–1640." *Rural History* 13, no. 2 (2002): 123–43.

Williams, Samantha. "'A Good Character for Virtue, Sobriety, and Honesty': Unmarried Mothers' Petitions to the London Foundling Hospital and the Rhetoric of Need in the Early Nineteenth Century." In A. Levene, T. Nutt, and S. Williams, eds, *Illegitimacy in Britain, 1700–1920*, 86–101. Basingstoke: Palgrave Macmillan, 2005.

– "Malthus, Marriage and Poor Law Allowances Revisited: A Bedfordshire Case Study, 1770–1834." *Agricultural History Review* 52, no. 1 (2004): 56–82.

– "Poor Relief, Labourers' Households and Living Standards in Rural England, c. 1770–1834: A Bedfordshire Case Study." *Economic History Review* 58, no. 3 (2005): 485–519.

Winter, Anne. "Caught between Law and Practice: Migrants and Settlement Legislation in the Southern Low Countries in a Comparative Perspective, c. 1700–1900." *Rural History* 19, no. 2 (2008): 137–62.

Winter, Anne, and Thijs Lambrecht. "Migration, Poor Relief and Local Autonomy: Settlement Policies in England and the Southern Low Countries in the Eighteenth Century." *Past and Present* 218, no. 1 (2013): 91–126

Woolf, Daniel. "The Common Voice: History, Folklore and the Oral Tradition in Early Modern England." *Past and Present* 120, no. 1 (1988): 26–52.

Woolf, Stuart. "Order, Class and the Urban Poor." In M. Bush, ed., *Social Orders and Social Classes in Europe since 1500*, 185–98. London: Longman, 1993.

– *The Poor in Western Europe in the Eighteenth and Nineteenth Centuries.* London: Methuen, 1986.

Wrigley, Anthony. "Malthus on the Prospects for the Labouring Poor." *Historical Journal* 31, no. 4 (1988): 813–29.

Würgler, Andreas. "Voices from amongst the 'Silent Masses': Humble Petitions and Social Conflicts in Early Modern Central Europe." In L.-H. van Voss, ed., *Petitions in Social History*, 11–34. Cambridge, UK: Cambridge University Press, 2001.

Zaret, David. *Origins of Democratic Culture: Printing, Petitions and the Public Sphere in Early Modern England.* Princeton, NJ: Princeton University Press, 2000.

# Index

*The town of Forton is on the border between Westmorland and Cumberland. It was part of each county at various times. In the index, it appears under "Westmorland" only.*

*Several people appear in the book in more than one capacity, such as Reverend Charles Atkinson, who acted as an advocate as well as being a clergyman. To prevent the reader from having to look up a single person multiple times, these people appear with the full range of page numbers under all the headings that apply to them, and thus Reverend Atkinson appears under both "clergymen" and "epistolary advocates."*

*The George Herbert referred to here is a shoemaker, who happens to share a name with the more famous poet George Herbert.*